Award-winning television producer/director Vanya Kewley was educated in France, Switzerland and India, and qualified as a nurse in London. In 1965 she joined Granada Television in Manchester and trained as a producer/director. During the past twenty years she has worked on most major current affairs and documentary series on BBC, ITV and Channel 4. She has covered major wars and remote conflicts including those in Biafra, the South Sudan, Bangladesh, Belfast, Vietnam, Oman, Chad and the Lebanon. She has pursued human rights stories to Chile, Nicaragua and South Korea. She has also been the first journalist to profile many controversial leaders, such as Libya's Colonel Gaddafi. She writes for many papers, including the *Sunday Times* and the *Observer*, and various magazines.

In 1988 she clandestinely made the first film to come out of Tibet since the Chinese invasion forty years ago. Investigating allegations of the systematic genocide of the Tibetan people, she travelled with five Tibetans, without permission and at great risk, over 4,000 miles inside Tibet to collect and film the evidence. This book is the story of that extraordinary journey and of the courageous people who talked to her.

VANYA KEWLEY

Tibet:
Behind the Ice Curtain

GRAFTON BOOKS

A Division of the Collins Publishing Group

LONDON GLASGOW
TORONTO SYDNEY AUCKLAND

Grafton Books
A Division of the Collins Publishing Group
8 Grafton Street, London WIX 3LA

Published simultaneously in hardcover and paperback
by Grafton Books 1990

British Library Cataloguing in Publication Data

Kewley, Vanya
    Tibet: behind the ice curtain
    1. Tibet–Description and travel
    I. Title
    915.150458

ISBN 0-246-13594-8
ISBN 0-586-20866-6 (paper covers)

Printed and bound in Great Britain by
Collins, Glasgow

Set in Galliard

Contents

Acknowledgements

I am grateful to so many people for their dedication, support and help; without their assistance neither the film nor this book would have been possible. I would particularly like to thank Frederick Hyde-Chambers, who over many years has very generously given advice, invaluable research and time; Audrey, his wife, who patiently took my calls from outlandish places at unmentionable hours; and Anthony Grey for his support and advice, especially in my first hesitant days when starting the book.

The Department of Information and Foreign Affairs of His Holiness the Dalai Lama in Dharamsala has been enormously painstaking and meticulous in providing me with detailed research about one of the least known areas on earth, Tibet, and also in translating the testimony of the witnesses I spoke to. I would like to express my gratitude to Tendar La, Sonam Topgyal, and the researchers in the department, and my especial thanks to Tenzing Atisha for his cheerful patience, research and diligence in checking the manuscript.

My thanks also to Don Kerr and the Institute of Strategic Studies in London; The Institute of Defence Studies in New Delhi; Dr Gerald Segal at the Royal Institute of International Affairs in London; The Royal Geographical Society; Phuntsog Wangyal of the Tibet Foundation in London; Rinchin Khandoo and the Tibetan Women's Association in Dharamsala; and Lhasang Tsering, President of the Tibetan Youth Congress-in-exile for their help in providing valuable suggestions. Also to James Cooper, Robert Barnett and Nicholas Howen, of the Tibet Support Group, and Mrs Mary Dines of Rights and Justice.

Without Channel 4 there would have been no film, no book, and less public awareness of the plight of Tibet. I would like to thank a small band of dedicated people at the Channel for their faith in me, and their steadfast support which, in the darker moments inside Tibet, were comforting beyond words – David

Lloyd, Karen Brown, Don Christopher, Madelaine Sheahan, Anthony Rose and Liz Forgan, and particularly David and Karen for their courage in taking on what many said was a mission impossible.

Judith Kendra, my commissioning editor at Grafton, was instrumental in shaping the book and I am enormously grateful to her for her nurturing care – chapter by chapter – and her sensitive concern. My thanks also to Muriel Gascoin, who grappled with the vagaries of my atrocious spelling and the impossible Tibetan names with such fortitude; to Jane Turnbull, for her unfailing cheerful support in my uncertain moments; to Seán Bobbitt, whose dry laconic humour was comforting balm in the early fraught days when we were trying to get into Tibet and when the film was falling about our ears; to Chris Lysaght, for his unflappable support in the preparation of the film and his meticulous editing; to Vivienne Griffiths who, in the nerve-racking months of preparation, was a rock.

My overwhelming admiration and gratitude goes to Tenzin and the Boys for their courage and the risk they took with their lives in guiding, driving and sheltering me for those fraught weeks inside Tibet. And to the Tibetan researchers, contacts and guides of the Tibetan underground, both inside Tibet and in several other countries, whose help and courage in planning the whole operation cannot be quantified, my inadequate thanks.

How can I ever thank Thondup Tsering, my interpreter and life-support system inside Tibet, for his care and dedication in making the trip with me? It is impossible to do justice to his concern for me, his loyalty in the face of the enormous difficulties that we faced on the trip, and his patience with his strange English *mola*. I remember this extraordinary man with particular affection for his unfailing cheerfulness, especially when the trip got rough and dangerous and I became increasingly anxious with the intensifying danger and the incessant pain from a slipped disc. Without Thondup I would not have been able to survive in Tibet and there would have been no film.

Thondup, thuchena!

I cannot mention the numerous Tibetans, inside Tibet, who showed amazing courage, risking jail and worse by sheltering and speaking to me, both on and off camera. Nor can I adequately ever thank them, not just for their courage but also for allowing me the privilege of sharing their often painful lives for a brief while. To protect them, I have changed their identities and often the locations where we met. Throughout the book I have used Tibetan, as opposed to Chinese, transliterations for the names of both people and places.

THE DALAI LAMA

Foreword

Although restrictions on tourists visiting Tibet have been somewhat relaxed in recent years, few foreigners have been able to
assess accurately the depth of devastation wrought in Tibet over
the past three decades. This involves not only cultural destruction,
but also the disruption of traditional population patterns; in
particular massive Chinese immigration threatens to make Tibetans a minority in their own land.

Ms Vanya Kewley is one of the few outsiders to have visited
almost all the major towns and cities in Tibet and actively to have
investigated these issues. Her findings, presented in this book,
illustrate the various forms of exploitation that China's coloniz-
ation has meant for Tibet, and the suffering and discrimination
inflicted on the Tibetan people in the name of liberation.

In recent times awareness of the plight of Tibet has been
growing throughout the world and this book will further deepen
that understanding. This is important, for I believe that public
support for our cause can make a significant contribution towards
its eventual fulfilment.

For my father who, when I first
started in television, said to me:

'Look behind the headlines. Investigate injustice silenced by
oppression. Speak for people without a voice.'

And

for over 1.2 million Tibetans killed under Chinese occupation, and
for those who today are still struggling for independence inside
Tibet.

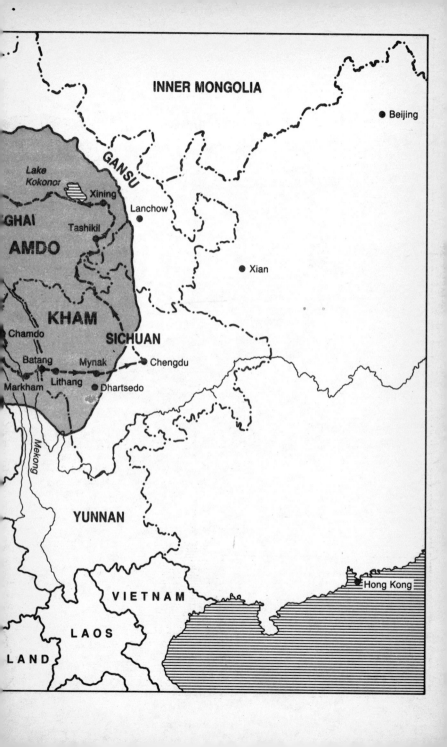

1
Yila

'*Hei! Hei!* . . . Stop!' Tenzin shrieked.

The van slithered round the corner and the back wheels swung perilously over the precipice. The front bumper impacted into the landslide and a wall of mud rose a sheer fifteen feet in front of us. We were stuck, literally and illegally, 18,000 feet up the Yila mountain in the middle of Tibet.

We had run out of road. We couldn't turn back as the monsoons had transformed the minuscule track behind us into a glutinous quagmire that had threatened to spew us over the edge at every hairpin bend for the past four hours. And somehow we still had to negotiate the Yila pass, which was another 1,000 feet above us on the other side of the impassable mud wall.

I was clandestinely in Tibet, trying to make what was to be the first film of the Tibetan massacres ever to have been shot deep inside the country since the Chinese had invaded it in 1949. I was stranded, with five Tibetans, in the middle of a maelstrom of mountains with the Chinese army all around us . . . Thousands of feet below, I could see the neat white tents of a Chinese military camp. Behind the last bend two Chinese army lorries were stuck axle-deep in the mud, waiting to be dug out. Above and beyond the mud wall Chinese voices floated down in the thin mountain air.

Jigme and Tsering, two of the group of Tibetans who had bravely volunteered to guide, hide and protect me throughout the hazardous journey, gingerly opened the van's doors and, careful not to disturb the vehicle's precarious balance, squelched knee-deep into the wet mud and went to look for stones to immobilize the wheels. Tenzin, who was the leader for the Lhasa–Batang sector of the country, was already climbing the mud wall trying to work out how to drag us all over the landslide.

Inside the van, Sumpa, our wiry young driver, lit a cigarette. I shivered. It was cold and the biting wind penetrated every crack in the battered van. I was too petrified to move, afraid that the slightest tremor would tip us over the edge. I cradled my video camera nervously on my lap, but its cold contours did nothing to comfort me, nor quell my rising anxiety. Around us was a cauldron of bare mountains ravaged and scarred by landslides. Despite the savage beauty of the jagged peaks – a palette of browns streaked with slivers of green, where lichens, defiant of the elements, clung to the harsh contours of the raw mountainsides – I felt desperately alone and afraid.

The Boys, as Thondup, my interpreter, and I had affectionately come to call our Tibetan friends, were literally risking their lives by being involved with me, since Tibetans are prohibited, under pain of imprisonment, from sheltering or transporting foreigners anywhere in Tibet. The hardships and fears we had so far endured together had forged a deep unspoken bond between us and in a way I regarded them as brothers – my Tibetan family – who I knew, should it ever come to the test, would die protecting me and getting the film to safety. They climbed and disappeared over the landslide and I heard their voices grow fainter on the other side of the mud wall. There was not a single living creature in sight, not even a bird. Just Sumpa and me, sitting in a rickety little van perched on a precipice on the roof of the world, and within touching distance of the fluffy white clouds in a brilliant cerulean blue sky.

A chilling thought struck me when I remembered that there had been no mention of this mountain, much less of the impassable tracks on our carefully detailed plans. I had no idea where precisely I was, or how on earth I was going to get out of Tibet in one piece with my film. Nor, more immediately, how we were going to get over the landslide and off the mountain by nightfall. Already the sun was moving towards the western mountains. I reckoned that we had only three hours of daylight left.

What was becoming increasingly worrying was the fact that I had on me the video tape of a highly inflammatory interview with two Tibetans talking about Chinese nuclear missiles. I had recorded it a few days previously outside a Chinese nuclear base deep inside Tibet. If I was caught with the tapes on me, I would certainly be arrested and imprisoned as a spy.

I had already violated Chinese law which strictly prohibits foreigners from travelling into the interior of Tibet. Foreigners are permitted to enter the country only with a supervised Chinese-conducted tour and are allowed to visit only Lhasa and one or two other specified towns. As for journalists and film makers, no one then had succeeded in penetrating the Tibetan hinterland to film evidence of what Tibetans in exile claim is the genocide of the Tibetan nation at the hands of the Chinese. I had no illusions about what would happen to me if I was discovered.

I wanted to investigate Tibetans' claims that the Chinese, since they invaded Tibet more than forty years ago, had systematically been exterminating the Tibetan people. I was checking and filming eye-witness accounts of survivors who had seen their countrymen gruesomely tortured or brutally killed for resisting the Chinese invasion. I wanted to examine allegations that hundreds of thousands of ordinary Tibetans, all over the country, had died of starvation when the Chinese imposed their own system of agriculture on a people who had never in their recorded history known famine. I was investigating the destruction of the last ancient civilization in the world to have survived intact into the twentieth century.

I wanted to document on film first-hand accounts of how Tibetan monasteries, repositories of Tibetan culture, had been destroyed all over the country and how a priceless, irreplaceable artistic heritage, which was a loss not only to Tibet, but to the world, had been either vandalized or removed and sold by the Chinese on the international art market for the hard currency so badly needed by China.

I was looking for evidence of Tibetan claims that their oppressors were systematically looting Tibet's natural resources. The Chinese name for Tibet is Xizang, which means western treasure house, and the country, because of its rare geological structure, at the junction of the Indian and Asian tectonic plates, is indeed a treasure trove of minerals.

It was apparently the same story with timber. The rich forests of Tibet were being exported to China with the result that the fragile top soil had been eroded, so making the land increasingly infertile. The flora and fauna had to a large extent been destroyed, and there were alarming signs that the weather patterns of the country were changing.

I also wanted to document what Tibetans claimed was their continuing suppression by the Chinese: were they indeed second-class citizens in their own land, disadvantaged by lack of education and the subtle, but effective, prohibition on the teaching of the Tibetan language, culture and religion? Were Tibetans discriminated against so that they received inferior, inadequate medical care and was, as some claimed, experimental medicine being administered to them by the Chinese? Did they live in constant fear, without those basic freedoms now claimed as a birthright by most of the world? Did they feel their long years of suffering and struggle had gone unnoticed by an unheeding world?

'But,' as a Tibetan monk said to me in Sikkim, 'our story is almost impossible to film. Unlike Auschwitz and Belsen, we have had no Allied troops to come in and film our walking dead. Our dead are buried. Our physical wounds have healed. No foreigner has been allowed free access to the interior of Tibet for forty years. There are no films, no reports, no international campaigns. How are you going to make an uncaring world believe you?' But I did believe that, despite the odds, I could investigate the allegations and, if they were true, find the survivors of what many call The Tibetan Holocaust.

The sound of squelching mud outside the van's window jerked me out of my reverie. Sumpa blew a thin stream of smoke out of the front window and casually greeted the Chinese soldier with the customary Chinese greeting, 'Ni hao' (hallo). I slipped my hat forward over my face, sank lower in the back seat, pretending to be asleep, and prayed that Sumpa would have the wit to intercept any conversation directed towards me and my non-existent Chinese.

From under my hat I looked at the young soldier. He was barely out of his teens. He smiled nervously and, as Sumpa later explained, asked for some tea. Apparently he was one of the drivers of the two army lorries stuck behind us and had been waiting three days on that mountain to be pulled out. He was out of food and his unit had not bothered to send up supplies or blankets. ('Quite normal,' Tenzin told me later. 'The Chinese treat their conscripts like animals.') Sumpa gave him some tea from his flask, offered him a cigarette and in rapid Chinese bargained hard for a barrel of petrol from the back of the soldier's truck, because we were running low on fuel.

As they talked, I looked at the soldier's pinched cold face, his thin green uniform and threadbare plimsolls caked with mud. With 60 Rmb (£15) a month, poor food, inadequate clothing and based thousands of miles from their own towns and villages in a hostile climate, among alien people and granted home leave only once every three years – if they were lucky – life was not a load of laughs for the ordinary trooper of the glorious People's Liberation Army.

The van coughed into life. Sumpa slammed it into low gear with grinding difficulty. My limbs ached from having been cramped in the same position for six hours. Ahead I saw that the Boys had dug a six-foot-wide furrow through the landslide and lined the wet mud with stones to stop – with luck – the van sliding off the mountain and give the tyres enough purchase to get across the mud-slide. It looked impossible.

More Chinese soldiers from the immobilized three-tonne trucks were standing on the side within a foot of the van but did nothing to help, so there was obviously no way I could get out. Tenzin stood at the top of the landslide, and Jigme and Tsering hovered behind the rear wheels ready to prop large stones behind the tyres should the van start sliding backwards. Sumpa slammed his foot on the accelerator, the wheels spun, the van rocked and, maybe it was an optical illusion, the precipice appeared to come nearer. He tried again and I shut my eyes hoping that some Sikorsky helicopter would suddenly winch us up to safety, as I had seen them do in Vietnam, and seen since in countless war movies!

During the third attempt, convinced that this time one of my nine lives was about to run out, in desperation I picked up the camera, switched it on, put it to my right shoulder, angled the eye-piece, pressed the record button and with my left hand holding the back of Sumpa's seat I began to film. Somehow, looking through the camera eye-piece at the daunting mud-slide, which charged at us and then receded, smugly unconquered like a menacing mirage, it seemed to lose some of its terrifying reality. Only by concentrating on the framing of the shot, and deciding whether to start it on the back of Sumpa's head and pan across to the mud-slide, or vice versa, was I able to dilute, somewhat, my sheer terror at the thought of sliding off the precipice and crashing thousands of feet down to the valley below.

The Boys, by now covered with mud, watched the wheels like hawks while Tenzin tried to cajole the obdurate van to the top of the slide. After the fourth attempt, Tenzin slithered down, opened the van's door and delved in the outside pocket of the camera-bag where I kept the special emergency incense sticks. He took one out, lit it and, murmuring a prayer, gracefully wafted the smoke round my head, round Sumpa's and then, with the solemnity of the Patriarch of the Orthodox Church anointing the congregation at St Basil's Cathedral in Moscow, he walked round the van with the incense; then, still praying, he climbed up the mud-slide trailing curling smoke and for a moment stood in silent prayer at the top, silhouetted against the jagged peaks and brilliant blue sky. I caught my breath. Looking at the man communing with his God, surrounded by primordial elements of earth and sky, there was something very powerful in his act of prayer. For a brief moment, Tenzin showed, and shared with me, his special strength and a tranquillity that emanated from the bed-rock of an unshakeable conviction. A faith that nineteen barbarous years in Chinese prisons had not been able to quench.

Sumpa allowed the van to slip to within a hair's breadth of the precipice and, with only his knuckles gripping the steering wheel showing any sign of tension, gave the engine full throttle. The van lurched forward, like a wounded bull at a matador. Even though I was still filming, I could no longer bear to look. However, when the motor cut out and I felt a sickening swaying motion, I forced my eyes open to find that we had indeed got to the top of the mud-slide, but the undercarriage had stuck on the top, the wheels were dangling in the air on either side, and the van was balanced like a see-saw in a playground. But we weren't playing games, for on each side was a sheer, 3,000-foot drop . . .

2

Myths and Misconceptions

My fascination with Tibet began as a child. My father studied comparative religions as well as Sanskrit, had a profound understanding of Buddhism, and an encyclopaedic knowledge of Tibet and its people. He shared his enthusiasm with me, his only child, and I remember captivating hours looking at pictures of Lhasa and the fabled Potala Palace. In fact, when I was six, I knew more about Lhasa than I did about London! My father was a deeply compassionate man, and although at the time I did not fully understand the enormity of what he was saying, I still recall the anguish in his voice when he told me about the Chinese invasion of Tibet. I remember my juvenile anger that no one was rushing in to save the gentle Tibetans. The burning injustice of their plight and the apparent indifference of the rest of the world has remained with me all my life.

To many people Tibet had for centuries been a mysterious and mystical place. Surrounded by the most impenetrable mountains on earth and almost physically inaccessible, it had become virtually totally isolated. It was peopled by a fiercely independent race of peace-loving Buddhists who wanted nothing more than to be left alone and to practise their religion and their unique way of life.

The very name Tibet seems to conjure magic and exotica. A Forbidden Kingdom, a Shangri-La, that has drawn explorers and adventurers from Kublai Khan and Marco Polo to the British Younghusband Expedition in 1904. But few successfully penetrated 'The Land of the Snows': the lucky handful that did returned with tales of a peaceful 'Land of Lamas' ruled by their benevolent Lama King, and fired the imagination of the outside world.

After the Younghusband Expedition, Tibet tentatively emerged into the twentieth century. It was a slow and laborious passage for a country still slumbering in the Middle Ages, but from that period onwards, the 13th Dalai Lama (the predecessor of the present one, His Holiness Tenzing Gyatso, the 14th Dalai Lama), overcoming opposition from the landowners, formulated and began to implement plans to reform the government, the country and bring twentieth-century technology to his 'backward', yet generally contented, people.

Many myths and misconceptions exist about Tibet. Few realize, for example, that (at least as claimed by the Tibetan Government-in-exile) it is nearly the size of Western Europe, seven times the size of France, an enormous 2.5 million square kilometres stretching 2,500 km from India, Afghanistan and the Pakistan border in the west to Dhartsedo and Xining on the Chinese border in the east, and over 1,600 km from Xinjiang (Eastern Turkestan) and Inner Mongolia in the north to India, Nepal, Bhutan and Burma in the south. On three sides it is surrounded by some of the most formidable mountains on earth: the almost impenetrable Himalayas in the south, the massive Karakoram Mountains to the west and the Kunlun and Tangla ranges to the north. To the east the mountains and plateaux tumble, through a series of spectacular gorges, into the plains of China in Gansu, Sichuan and Yunnan.

Tibet is an ancient land that three hundred million years ago was under the Tethys Sea that once covered much of Asia and India. Then forty million years ago the immense pressure of the Indian tectonic plate crashing north against the Asian one forced up the Himalayas and created the mineral-rich Tibetan plateau, which today averages about 14,000 feet above sea-level. Peopled by fiercely independent tribes linked to the Tibeto-Burman group, Tibet has an ancient civilization going back thousands of years.

It is not, as most people believe, only a land of awesome barren mountains, but also an unexpectedly exciting land of visually stunning contrasts where the temperature, crops and vegetation differ enormously depending on the altitude. Although there are vast areas of high cold desert in the north-west, there is an abundance of forests and fertile river valleys – becoming nearly tropical with the warmth of lower altitudes – particularly in the south-east of Tibet near the border with Yunnan, Burma, Bhutan, Nepal and India.

Although much of Tibet is criss-crossed by numerous mountain ranges and hundreds of rivers, the high tablelands and fertile river valleys support a variety of differing crops and animals: from semi-tropical trees and crops, such as maize and bamboo, and the rare panda in the low valleys, through graceful Tibetan water-meadows studded with willows and apple, peach, apricot and walnut trees in the higher valleys, to alpine vegetation in the high plateaux with vast herds of sheep and that unique animal, the yak, which is indigenous to the Tibetan plateau.

Although 40 per cent of the population were *drogpa* or nomad until 1949, the fertile valleys, particularly in the central province of Ü-Tsang, nurtured a highly evolved and sophisticated society in which literature, philosophy, theology and the arts were more important pursuits than the military prowess of the fierce warring clans that jealously guarded their own territory and the Tibetans' acutely ingrained sense of independence.

The Yalung Kings, who ruled in Tibet's Tsangpo (Brahmaputra) Valley, are, some Tibetan historians claim, the first recorded dynasty of Tibet going back to c.400 B.C. In fact the oldest building in Tibet, the Yumbulagang, in the Yalung Valley (a Tibetan version of Egypt's Valley of the Kings), south of Lhasa on the road to Nepal, where the Tibetan kings are buried, and which was wantonly destroyed by the Chinese Red Guards, dated to the time of Podekungyal, 9th King of the Yalung dynasty in 137 B.C. (although this date is disputed by some historians).

Fiercely militaristic, the Tibetan Empire at its height, under King Songtsen Gampo (617–49 A.D.), the 33rd King of the Yalung dynasty, and King Trisong Detsen (755–97 A.D.), stretched from the plains of northern India and Upper Burma in the south, to Mongolia in the north, and to Ch'ang-an (Xian) in the China of the Tang Emperors in the east. From 785–805 A.D., the Tibetan armies advanced through the Pamirs to Samarkand and pushed the borders of the Tibetan Empire to the periphery of the Ottoman Empire in the west.

King Songtsen Gampo, who was converted to Buddhism by his Nepalese and Chinese wives, promoted the faith, and slowly over the next hundred years, the whole country converted to Buddhism from its indigenous Shamanistic religion, which we now call Bön. Indian holy men were invited to Tibet, and both Songtsen Gampo and Trisong Detsen slowly convinced the fierce tribal chieftains to lay down their arms, abandon their militaristic expansionism, and adopt Buddhism and the path of peace.

Thus for the first time in history, Tibetan historians claim, a country began to adopt pacifism as state policy, and the world's first zone of peace came into being. Monasteries were set up all over the country, one-quarter of the male population eventually became monks, and religion, culture and national identity became intertwined in a unique and inseparable whole. Until the Chinese Communist invasion forty years ago, Tibetans were widely regarded as the most religious race on earth.

In 842 A.D. the assignation of King Lang Dharma led to bitter feuding in the Tibetan Royal Family, the beginning of the decentralization of authority, the eventual decline of the Tibetan Empire and the transfer of power into the hands of powerful nobles and chieftains. Over the next 500 years, the power of the Tibetan kings was slowly superseded by the rising power of spiritual leaders like the Sakya Pandita.

In 1227, after the death of the great Mongol, Genghis Khan, the Tibetans stopped paying tribute to the Mongol court and relations between Mongols and Tibetans became strained. In 1240 the grandson of Genghis Khan, Godan Khan, invaded Tibet and in the eighth month of the Dragon year (1244) invited Tibet's most holy lama (the nearest Christian analogy is a bishop) to come to his court and instruct him and his people how to 'conduct themselves morally and spiritually'.

The top Tibetan religious leader, Kunga Gyaltsen (1182–1251), who was also known as Sakya Pandita, greatly influenced the Mongol Khan with the peaceful tenets of Buddhism and established a strong personal relationship with him. In 1247 Sakya Pandita was invested as the spiritual and temporal ruler of Tibet by the Mongol ruler.

In 1251 Sakya Pandita died, followed shortly by Godan Khan. The new Khan's son, Kublai, invited Sakya Pandita's spiritual successor, Phagpa, to his court and asked for instruction in the Buddhist faith. Phagpa thus became Kublai's spiritual mentor, and also advised, but did not interfere, in the Khan's domains of China and Mongolia, thus establishing the unique priest–patron relationship between the Mongol ruler and the Tibetan 'Pontiff'.

In 1254, Kublai Khan gave Phagpa a letter of investiture granting him supreme authority over Tibet. In 1260, when Kublai became Khan, Phagpa performed the enthronement ceremonies for the Khan, who then re-confirmed Phagpa as the spiritual and temporal head of the three regions of the independent kingdom of Tibet – Ü-Tsang (central Tibet), Dotod (Kham), Domed (Amdo) – and bestowed on him the title of 'Tishri', meaning 'Imperial Preceptor'. Just as the Renaissance popes were both spiritual and temporal rulers, in a similar way spiritual and temporal power was consolidated in the Tibetan lamas as sovereign rulers of an independent Tibet. That power has been handed down in an unbroken chain through the centuries to the present Dalai Lama.

Phagpa not only consecrated the new Khan in 1260, but was often summoned to the Mongol court to advise and guide Kublai Khan. There he met the renowned dignitaries of the time who had come to pay tribute to the powerful Mongol ruler, including, it is said by some historians, the Venetian adventurer, Marco Polo. In 1268 Phagpa took with him on one of his frequent journeys to the Mongol court a script that he had devised for the Mongol language and this became the basis of the written script. He presented it to Kublai Khan who in turn further honoured the Sakya 'Pontiff' with the titles of 'Prince of Indian Deities, Miraculous Divine Lord Under the Sky and Above the Earth, Creator of the Spirit, Messenger of Peace Throughout the World, Possessor of Five Higher Sciences, Phagpa, the Imperial Preceptor'. The close and cordial relationship between the Mongol Khan and the Tibetan ruler is reflected in many aspects of Tibetan life and in fact the Dalai Lama's title originates from the Mongols, *Dalai* being a Mongolian word and title meaning 'Ocean of Wisdom'. Today there are still many Mongol influences to be found in Tibetan life and ritual. For example, in the Mahakala Prayers during the Tibetan *Losar* (New Year) ceremonies, the Dalai Lama offers a blue *kata* – an offertory scarf – (the normal Tibetan ones are white). Blue is a colour inherited from the Mongols. In many parts of northern Tibet the prayer-flags still have a distinct Mongol shape and configuration.

The unique relationship between the Mongol rulers and the Tibetan lamas cannot really be defined in Western political terms. The politico-religious relationship between the Mongol Khan and the Tibetan 'Pontiff' was maintained by mutual respect and co-operation and prevented Tibet from being invaded and devastated when the Mongol hordes swept into and conquered China in the thirteenth century.

In 1280 when the Mongols overthrew the existing Chinese Sung Emperor and established their own Yuan dynasty in China, the special relationship continued, with the Tibetan 'Pontiff' acting as spiritual guide to the Chinese Emperor. In 1720 the Manchu Emperor, and successive Chinese Emperors, sent an Imperial Amban (Ambassador) to Tibet to help and advise the Tibetan 'Pontiff', if and when necessary. And it is largely due to this institution of the Amban that the Chinese today claim Tibet. They also base their claim on the marriage of the Chinese princess Wen-ch'eng Kung-chu to King Songtsen Gampo in 641 A.D. But what the Chinese forget to include is the fact that the princess was given by her father the Chinese Emperor, T'ai-tsung, along with a considerable dowry, to the Tibetan King to appease his military designs on the Chinese Empire whose armies he had just defeated.

The present-day Chinese, in seeking historical justification for their claims to Tibet, also forget to include the fact that Songtsen Gampo, in keeping with the customs of the time that permitted polygamy, also married the Nepalese princess Bhrikuti Devi, and two Tibetan princesses at the same time! And it is significant that Nepal does not, and has never, claimed ownership of Tibet as a result of that marriage all those years ago.

Although in 1720 the Manchu dynasty claimed to have established suzerainty over Tibet, Tibetan historians insist that this was never a reality, but only an extension of the priest–patron relationship begun five hundred years before.

With various border squabbles and treaties and minor incursions by fractious local war-lords, the Chinese–Tibetan relationship continued in equilibrium until 1910 when the Chinese tried by force to exert control over eastern Tibet. It was a confused and turbulent period in the dying days of the Ch'ing (Manchu) dynasty in Beijing, and an ambitious Chinese general, Chao Erh-feng, intervened in a Tibetan monastic dispute after the murder of a Chinese official in eastern Tibet; he sacked the area and proceeded to draw up an ambitious scheme to conquer and annex all Tibetan territory from Tachienlu (Dhartsedo), on the traditional China–Tibet border in the east of Tibet, to Kongpo Gyamda 120 miles from Lhasa in the west. Despite the border squabbles over the years, the plan had no validity in history or law beyond the ambitions of the Chinese general.

The Tibetans played for time with counter-demands for territory over which they had claimed jurisdiction for over a thousand years as well as insisting that the Chinese evacuate all personnel from Chamdo. The British, who had invaded southern Tibet in 1904 and had predatory designs on the area to counter the growing influence of Russian ambitions in Central Asia, tried to placate both sides with patient diplomacy. Despite continuing negotiations, Chinese forces proceeded stealthily towards the Tibetan capital and on the third day of the first Tibetan month in the Iron-dog year, a small detachment, but well-equipped with modern weapons, of the Chinese army reached Lhasa. The Dalai Lama fled to India where he met the Viceroy, Lord Minto, on 14 March 1910, and appealed to the British, with whom he had good relations, to help Tibet.

But what was perhaps of more significance was the fact that for the first time since the thirteenth century when the priest–patron relationship had been established between the Tibetan 'Pontiff' and the Mongol Khan, the line between them was broken off by the Tibetans because China had invaded Lhasa. The Tibetan Government rightly deemed that aggression had abrogated the priest–patron relationship. A Tibetan uprising against the Chinese invasion followed. Meanwhile in China, in October 1911, Sun Yat-sen led a successful rebellion and overthrew the Manchu dynasty in Beijing; in Lhasa Tibetans attacked the Amban's residence and took him hostage while units of the Chinese garrison mutinied. In 1913 the Dalai Lama returned to Lhasa from asylum in India. Because the Manchu Emperor had now been deposed, the special priest–patron relationship between the heads of the two countries came to an end, and the Chinese Amban and a supporting garrison force in Lhasa were expelled from Tibet in 1912. No Chinese was permitted to enter the country in an official capacity until 1934 when a Chinese delegation was allowed to travel to Lhasa to pay their respects to the 13th Dalai Lama on his death.

From 1911, therefore, the Tibetans resumed self-government under the 13th, then the 14th Dalai Lama. Tibet lived in peace, slowly emerging into the twentieth century from its political isolation and maintaining diplomatic links with Bhutan, Nepal and the British Raj in India. Border squabbles between China and

Tibet continued in eastern Tibet and the British tried to mediate at the Simla Convention in India in 1913.

The new Nationalist Government of China was no less sensitive about its western borders and no less expansionist than the Manchu dynasty and claimed Tibet as a province of China. Tibet, of course, denied the validity of any such claim. The British, ever-mindful of the trade opportunities in both countries, balanced on a fragile diplomatic tight-rope between the intricate claims and counter-claims of both countries. The Chinese claims were to Tibetan eyes preposterous, with little or no documentation or proof to substantiate their allegations. The Tibetans, however, went into the Simla Conference well prepared with reams of documents – details of taxes levied and paid to Lhasa and the Dalai Lama's Government by monasteries and even households in Tibetan areas that China had claimed for itself – which proved beyond doubt the validity and legality of Tibet's territorial claims.

China's refusal to sign and ratify the Simla Convention left the labyrinthine complications of Tibet's eastern border with China up in the air. Under the treaty, the British gained considerable trade advantages in Tibet, including the right to send their representative on occasional visits to Lhasa (until then completely closed to any foreigner). Tibet's southern border was established as the watershed along the crest of the Himalayas as defined by Sir Henry McMahon, the British Plenipotentiary to the China–Tibet Conference. Tibet gained Britain's recognition of its autonomy and the assurance that Britain would not acknowledge China's suzerainty (which in the political language of the day was not synonymous with sovereignty) over Tibet unless China signed the treaty, which contained many safeguards of Tibetan autonomy guaranteed by Britain. The only restriction on Tibetan sovereignty was the obligation to refrain from negotiating with any other foreign power without Britain's prior consent.

On the eastern border the interminable squabbling with China continued sporadically, but Tibet under the 13th Dalai Lama took some tentative steps towards modernizing the country. In 1922 the British built a truck-route into Tibet right up to Gyantse, where they had established a trade outpost, school and hospital. Tibet even sent a small contingent of its minuscule army to be trained by the British in the art of modern weapons and warfare in Gyantse and a few selected Tibetan boys were sent to be educated in England and in British boarding schools in India. But with World War I devastating Europe, Britain had more urgent preoccupations than its economic concerns in Tibet.

Tibet remained neutral in the Chinese Civil War between the Nationalists and Communists and during both World Wars. During World War II, it refused all pleas from the Allies to allow Tibet to be used as a transit and staging post for troops and supplies to China and the Far East – even letters from Attlee and Roosevelt produced polite but firm refusal.

In 1931-2 the armed peace between China and Tibet on their mutual border was broken when fighting once more erupted between them, east of the Yangtse river. But on 15 June 1933, a peace treaty was effected under which it was agreed that the boundaries between China and Tibet that had existed before the fighting would be respected. The 13th Dalai Lama, aware of China's unquenched territorial ambitions and Tibet's need to modernize and the threat that it posed to the vested interests of some powerful members of the aristocracy and clergy, warned his ministers of the dangers he foresaw. It was his last testament to his people, for he died suddenly on 17 December 1933. A shrewd, broadminded man of high intelligence and ability, the 13th Dalai Lama was also a man of forceful character, with considerable insight and diplomatic skills which he deployed with significant agility playing India and China against one another and thereby ensuring Tibetan independence. There was peace from the time of his death till the Chinese invaded Tibet sixteen years later in 1949.

Tibet continued its attempts to modernize. Electricity and the motor car arrived in Lhasa, and Tibet sent its first trade missions abroad to India, Britain and the United States. The delegations travelled with Tibetan passports which were accepted by the various countries, thereby unequivocally confirming Tibet's independence as a sovereign nation.

In 1938 the child reincarnation of the 13th Dalai Lama was found and enthroned in Lhasa on 22 February 1940 with a Regent and council of ministers to supervise the affairs of state until the five-year-old boy reached manhood.

In 1949 in China the Communists seized power from the
Nationalist Kuomintang Government. In October Beijing radio
relayed an announcement from Mao Tse-tung that Tibet was a
part of China and that the PLA (People's Liberation Army) would
march into Tibet to liberate it from 'foreign imperialists'. So China
even under a Communist regime was still covetous of the vast
empty spaces of Tibet and, historically deeply paranoid about
securing its western borders, invaded from the east at Xining in
the same year.

In January 1950 India, apprehensive of China's potential for
aggression, found it expedient to recognize the new Communist
regime. Although India had always had diplomatic and trade
relations with the Tibetan Government, Prime Minister Nehru
began making pronouncements about 'Chinese suzerainty over
Tibet'.

The PLA over-ran Tibet in a series of well-planned attacks all
along Tibet's eastern front, from Xining in the north to Dhartsedo
in the south; a small force also invaded from the west. They met with
fierce resistance, but the Tibetans, who often had little more than
swords and their bare hands, were no match for the modern fire-
power of the PLA. All opposition was brutally suppressed and Tibet
was hermetically sealed off from the scrutiny of the outside world.

For years rumours of Chinese atrocities trickled out of Tibet
with the few refugees who managed to escape. But there was no
concrete proof – as no foreigners, and especially no investigative
journalists, were allowed access to the country. When I went into
journalism and television over twenty years ago, I too heard the
rumours, but at the time there was little I, or any other journalist,
could do.

In 1975, while working for the BBC, I made the first full-length
profile of HH the 14th Dalai Lama of Tibet – 'The Lama King'.
It was filmed in his home in exile, in Dharamsala, a remote
hill-station 7,000 feet up in the Himalayas of north-west India.
For the first time, I came into direct contact with recently escaped
Tibetan refugees. After years of Chinese oppression, Tibet was
still suffering the terrors of the Cultural Revolution, and the stories
brought out by the refugees were as horrific as the atrocities of
the Nazis in Europe and the Japanese in Asia during World War
II.

Then for ten years, while filming violations of human rights, mainly in the Third World, I asked my Tibetan friends to try and find a way into Tibet so that we could check the allegations and make a television film. In 1985, I finally found new reliable sources with contacts inside Tibet. I pursued the story, piecing together from harrowing refugee accounts what had happened in the country since the Chinese had invaded. With the help of the Tibetan Resistance, I worked out a way of getting into Tibet to document the evidence.

Although I had no reason to doubt the accounts of the refugees, I still had painstakingly to cross-check their testimony with evidence obtained *inside* Tibet from Tibetans – their first-hand witness of what had happened. In speaking before a foreign television camera, they would be violating Chinese laws that prohibited, under pain of harsh imprisonment, the divulging of 'treasonous libel' to foreign media. No Tibetans would run such risks unless their stories were accurate.

For two years I tried to interest every major television company in Britain in funding an investigative film on Tibet. But they all felt that it was too difficult and too dangerous and that the likelihood of my returning in one piece with a film – and therefore ensuring their investment – was more than somewhat remote.

Under considerable pressures to maintain their own teams of in-house reporters and producers, the commissioning editors in British television have to be concerned first and foremost with budgets and the return on their money. Newsworthiness weighs heavier in the balance than the plight of an obscure and unfashionable nation in danger of disappearing. I was more than once reminded, 'Tibet is not exactly screaming off the headlines! Nothing concrete has come out of that country for nearly forty years.'

Six million Jews were massacred in the Holocaust, and the world, quite rightly, has never been allowed to forget. But 1.2 million Tibetans – one-sixth of the population – have been wiped off the face of the earth and no nation has done anything to stop it: just three resolutions passed by the UN in 1960, 1961 and 1965 condemning China for violations of human rights and suppression of the right to self-determination in Tibet. No nation has taken any significant measures such as sanctions or the breaking off of diplomatic relations with China, for the simple reason, as one

Tibetan pointed out: 'China is now the world's largest market for goods and technology from the West. No one is going to rock the boat and protest. It would only adversely affect the current multi-million-pound trade deals. When trade is involved, all that the West is concerned with is balance sheets. As Napoleon said of you British, you are a "nation of shopkeepers". You and the rest are more concerned with profits and only pay lip-service to human rights when it suits you. Why else do you think Tibet is not plastered all over your screens and newspapers?' I burned at the injustice of it and went to Beirut to keep my bank manager off my back.

It was in October 1987, during a furious artillery barrage by the Shia Amal militia on the Palestinian camp of Chatilla where I was trapped doing a story on the charismatic Canadian doctor Chris Giannou, who had been incarcerated in Chatilla for two and a half years, that I heard on the BBC World Service that Lhasa had erupted into riots. The details were faint through the noise of the explosions of incoming shells, but I knew that the time was right to try again. I had to get out of Beirut and back to London to try once more to persuade a commissioning editor in British television to do something about the worsening situation in Tibet.

After a week's blockade in the camp, I returned to London to find a message waiting on my answering machine from David Lloyd, senior commissioning editor of Channel 4's News and Current Affairs. David is a quiet man with a formidable track record. An ex-BBC staffer, he has run practically every current affairs programme on BBC Television; he has an eye for a good story.

After intense questioning in Channel 4's Charlotte Street headquarters in London's West End by David Lloyd and Karen Brown, his tough assistant editor, David agreed to take the Tibet project on board. There followed months of furtive meetings with Tibetan contacts in London and various countries in the Far East. I had endless discussions and long briefings with the two 'messengers' I was sending clandestinely into Tibet to check the million and one things that would ensure our safety. It was also of paramount importance that they check whether the 'story' (the allegations of Tibetan genocide) stood up.

I remember David Plowright, my first editor on Granada Television's *World in Action*, where I trained, telling me, when I was a new and very junior researcher: 'If the story doesn't stand up, you don't make it stand up. End of story. No matter how much it has cost.' It was a principle I have stuck to all my career. David Lloyd was of the same school, and sanctioned the laborious and very expensive preparation.

It was not easy to find Tibetan researchers who were educated, impartial and who could not be manipulated; who were able to investigate thoroughly the story inside Tibet and if there were any queries on any of the witnesses to tell me, knowing that if the story did not check out, I would abandon the project. They also knew that I would recheck every allegation myself inside Tibet, and that if, even at that late stage, I had even the slightest doubt, I would not use the evidence. After intensive grilling of the proposed candidates, I selected Pedor and Nedong, who seemed reliable, educated, competent and with the requisite honesty and courage, if necessary, to abort the project.

I impressed on the researchers the need for accuracy and for cross-checking the allegations of the witnesses with other people. I told them: 'Don't tell me that 10,000 died in a particular prison. People just don't die in convenient round numbers.' The lack of verifiable statistics from inside Tibet, taken by an independent source, made their task more difficult. Until recently, the only statistics were those issued by the Chinese. But the Tibetan Government-in-exile, aware of the problem and of the need to counter Chinese propaganda, also impressed on their own researchers and Tibetan refugees the need to cross-check every fact and allegation. In fact they refused me access to the latest figures of Tibetans killed as a direct result of the Chinese occupation of Tibet. They told me that so far they had only cross-checked the names of 1,207,487 Tibetans who had died. And that figure was only up to the end of 1983.

The Chinese, of course, adamantly refute Tibetan statistics, and I knew that it was important to get evidence not only from inside Tibet, but corroboration from all parts of the country. Otherwise the Chinese would say, as they had in the past, that the findings were non-representative, the machinations of a few dissident 'splittists' from the 'Dalai Lama's clique' in Lhasa, who wanted to sow sedition and split Tibet from the 'motherland' of China, and therefore that it was non-admissible evidence.

The Chinese, despite three reports in 1959, 1961 and 1965 from the International Commission of Jurists that condemned China for perpetrating genocide in Tibet, have always denied the allegations and refused to allow any independent fact-finding mission or investigative journalists free access to the whole area of Tibet.

I spent days explaining to Tibetans, untutored in the ways of the media, how to recce a location. It was vital as our safety was dependent on my invisibility – especially with a camera – and the more information they could give me before we got to a location, the quicker and safer we could film and get out. But the most important element was to find people willing to give evidence to camera.

Having made many programmes about the violation of human rights and torture all over the world without the knowledge and permission of the relevant government, I am quite used to officials branding me as a Communist or Fascist – depending on whom my programme has offended – but one thing no one can dispute is the evidence I put on the screen.

When people contravene the laws of their countries by speaking publicly and undisguised to foreign media about human rights violations, knowing that they will go to jail – or worse – for their courage, there is an undeniable veracity in their testimony.

It is an agonizing decision to ask another human being to put their life where their mouth is. Especially when you know you will – with luck – be safely out of the country, but that the interviewee will be picked up once the programme is transmitted and taped by the particular government's embassy in London and sent back to the country in question. It has always been very painful for me to ask anyone to make such a sacrifice and I have been scrupulous about telling them the dangers. I always emphasize that I personally cannot protect them, and that I doubt that even the admirable efforts of Amnesty International will be able to do much for them, once the programme, and their evidence, has been transmitted. Some understandably balk at the prospect and that is the end of it. But many wonderfully brave people, from

Paraguay to the Philippines, have had the courage to speak to the cameras and so, perhaps, have had a part to play in their country's destiny.

I also made endless lists for the researchers, asking them to check on every detail, from where the Chinese army checkpoints were and what time the guards changed, to the locations of petrol stores in various places and the availability of spare tyres, fan-belts, cooking pots, kerosene, Tilly (pressure) lamps for filming in dark interiors, as I assumed there would be no electricity; a primus stove, candles, matches and even loo paper were included. We would be living off the land – and there was not a surplus of forage available in a poor country at 14,000 feet.

Since it was obviously impossible to get official Chinese permission as a foreigner, let alone as a journalist, to go into the hinterland of Tibet, I decided that I would enter China legally on a three-month tourist visa, and while on my closely chaperoned, Chinese-conducted tour of Tibet, I would disappear and go 'walk-about'. I planned to go in alone, as a tourist, through Hong Kong, then travel by train to Guangzhou (Canton), to Chengdu via Xian and reach the rendezvous point in Lanchow on the Sino-Tibetan border where I would be met by the Boys – my Tibetan researchers and colleagues.

We planned to go in via Xining, the site of the Chinese invasion in 1949, then south to Dhartsedo, the site of the second wave of the invasion, then west through the wild mountains of Kham, where a tragic rebellion of Khampa guerrillas took place in the mid-fifties and early sixties, then through Lithang, Batang and Markham to the alleged Chinese nuclear base at Nagchukha, and turn due south to the capital. The route had been very carefully selected to include not only places where specific witnesses could give evidence of different abuses by the Chinese but also to include examples of the same violations in all three provinces of Tibet as well as in the capital, Lhasa.

We would also be passing through towns, villages and remote areas to check whether there were the facilities, such as health care and education, that the Chinese insisted they had brought to even the remotest areas, but which Tibetans denied were available to Tibetans. And we hoped also to be able to check Tibetan allegations that China had turned Tibet into a vast arsenal and stationed significant nuclear missiles deep in the Tibetan country-side.

Then, as we were likely to have all the incriminating filmed evidence on us, it would be too dangerous to fly legally out of Lhasa; for at the airport we would be sitting ducks for the Chinese authorities, should rumours of our 'travels' have aroused their suspicions. So it was decided that we would drive to the southern Tibetan border and then walk through the illegal Black Route, over the Himalayas, into whichever neighbouring country it was easiest to enter.

It was not something I was looking forward to, for on the windward side of the Himalayas we would meet the full force of the south-west monsoon. Trying to walk for more than a week through dense, leech-infested jungle (I have a pathological fear of snakes, leeches and any reptilian creature) in a tropical downpour, with its attendant landslides avalanching down the mountainside without any warning, and with most of the journey having to be undertaken in the dark, was not my idea of an amusing hike!

By mid-May 1988, the plans were laid, the researchers sent off and D-day for my departure was set for 29 June. I met my interpreter, a young Tibetan whose parents had been killed by the Chinese. Chuma, an only child, had managed to escape from Tibet and had been smuggled by friends of his parents into Nepal. Educated in India, his English was perfect. Slim and wiry, he had a quick smile and exuded confidence; he told me not to worry and that he would look after us. He, too, was to climb into Tibet clandestinely and meet me at 8 P.M. in the lobby of the Jincheng Hotel in Lanchow on 11 July. On the way there he would double-check the arrangements that the researchers had made. We had agreed with all the contacts that they would wait three weeks from the scheduled date of meeting, which was calculated with considerable precision from our starting date of 11 July. That should, Chuma argued, give us enough time to get there should we be delayed by the notoriously impassable Tibetan roads. By early July, Tibet should be over the worst of the monsoon – but I was still apprehensive of the roads and tracks that were infamous for washing down the mountainside without a murmur of warning!

Finding a crew – cameraman and sound recordist – to go in

with me was not easy. In the 1970s there was a regular band of amazingly brave film people who were to be found in every trouble spot in the world, from Biafra, Bangladesh and Belfast, to Vietnam, Lebanon and El Salvador. But now those amazing dare-devils who had suffered so much muck and misery with me – and other colleagues – had 'grown up'. They had moved on to drama, or were themselves directing. People like the legendary Butch Calderwell, Tony Pierce-Roberts, Eric Derschmeed, Ernie Vince, Mike Dodds, Bill Braine and Chris Wangler. Filming in the Third World is becoming increasingly hazardous, with the use of more sophisticated arms and methods of detection as well as chemical warfare, not to mention the risk of being kidnapped or imprisoned. These are potent deterrents to investigative television teams, and many technicians now no longer want to risk life and limb, especially in uncharted territory like Tibet. Nor did I want to take an inexperienced, young crew with me, because when a crisis erupts, experience will out, and their lives and mine could depend on ice-cold reactions to whatever was sprung on us.

But I did find a cameraman and sound recordist who agreed to forgo all creature comforts (we were to live and sleep in the van or at best in some draughty safe house without even the basic amenities like running water, toilets and electricity). We were going off the beaten track into uncharted territory, where not even the odd foreign backpacker had ventured, to talk to relevant witnesses in remote hamlets.

Instructed to get their Chinese tourist visas, the crew then went abroad on other assignments; we agreed that they would fly from London, with two-thirds of the equipment and their own personal gear, to Hong Kong on 12 July, change planes and fly direct to Lanchow (all the flights had been booked and confirmed – and were therefore unchangeable because of the inflexible Chinese booking system) where I would meet them at 6.30 P.M. on 15 July at Lanchow airport.

Ten days before I was due to fly to Hong Kong, and in the midst of arranging last-minute shopping for Arctic-rated sleeping bags, ground sheets and thermal underwear that would protect us from the bitter cold of sleeping rough in Tibet, and for a pharmacy of drugs for practically any eventuality, I received devastating news. One of the crew had left getting his documentation and visa to the last moment and had run into problems with his Chinese visa; the other crewman refused to go without his mate.

I had nine days before my departure to find a replacement. I was sick with anxiety. I could not postpone the trip. I was locked into complex travel arrangements; the Tibetan researchers and the interpreter would already be on their way to our rendezvous points and there was absolutely no way to contact – or stop – them. If I postponed now, I knew the project would never be resuscitated. There simply was no budget for such a contingency. As it was, Channel 4 had impressed on me that it was the highest budget allocated to any documentary they had ever undertaken.

The need for total confidentiality was another major problem. I could hardly ring up a cameraman I did not know and out of the blue just explain the whole project over the phone . . . Finally, five days to my departure, I met Seán Bobbitt, a young, tall, very laid-back Texan with a mane of shaggy hair, a thick beard, a rakish ear-ring and alligator cowboy boots! Seán looked like anything but a cameraman. Jesuit-educated in Britain and in California, he surprised me with his intimate knowledge of Kierkegaard and Schopenhauer. Very un-media, I thought. If he agreed to come, I knew it would not be a boring trip. Seán had an interesting track record in many trouble spots, from Lebanon to the Philippines. After much discussion, he finally agreed. Seán suggested that as we were using amateurish-looking Sony CCD200 (Video 8) cameras, we did not really need to take a sound recordist with us. 'Waste of money,' he said, picking up the Sony Walkman Pro recorder we planned to use as back-up to the camera sound. 'I can operate both. Or teach you to. They really are so simple that a child could operate one!'

We finally divided up the equipment between us and packed it as unobtrusively as possible into anonymous-looking, black, reinforced, nylon bags. We had decided to use Video 8 equipment rather than a film camera: film stock is bulky whereas Video 8 tape is as small as an audio cassette, is more easily concealed and is transportable. Also the new Sony Video 8 camera is a minor miracle in miniaturization. Light and sturdy, its inbuilt computer provides complete auto-focus. 'Idiot-proof,' Seán had laughed, looking at me.

The camera also put the date and slate number directly onto the tape without having the tell-tale clapper-board to mark each shot and identify it for editing months later when you have forgotten the minutiae of the shooting schedule. I knew that it was capable of remarkable results, for I had seen footage of films of several Everest Expeditions that had used Video 8. The only disadvantage was that should anything go seriously wrong the camera would have to be taken into a workshop and stripped. Hardly an option inside Tibet, but we had a spare one for back-up. It was somewhat unreal to look at two small boxes of tape and know that was the equivalent of thirty hours of film-time. Normal film in 400-foot loadings (ten minutes' film-time) would have taken up three large boxes and been impossibly heavy to carry. We had also sent into Tibet with the researchers another thirty one-hour tapes and arranged for them to be left in various locations throughout the country so that, if we were rumbled by the Chinese and our film confiscated, we would have a reserve supply there and could continue working.

As we would be operating most of the time without electricity, the camera's battery-charger would be useless. Since the camera's own batteries ran for only 15–20 minutes, Seán arranged for a lithium battery, which should give an operational life of six weeks, roughly the equivalent of running 120 film rolls through a normal camera, to be adapted for the Sony. We also took a maze of different leads to meet any available adaptor possible: leads that would charge batteries off a lorry cigarette-lighter, if Chinese lorries had such refinements, and adaptors for taking a feed off even a domestic light-bulb socket.

The jumble of wires and connections snaked over my drawing-room floor in a totally incomprehensible jumble. As unfortunately I am totally untechnical and can barely change a fuse without blowing up the house, I was happy to leave Seán to test and sort it all out and hide the more suspicious items that did not look very 'touristy' – such as the heavy lithium batteries – in sweaters and underwear, hoping that the Chinese customs would not do too thorough a search.

I left one camera and recorder with Seán (you are allowed only one video/film camera and a specified amount of film/tape stock per person when entering China). After a frantic few days arranging contracts and finalizing complicated insurance details, Seán drove me to the airport, gave me a bear-hug and protectively told me to look after myself. I felt that, despite the hassle with the previous crew, I was in good hands.

On the way to Hong Kong one of my main contacts told me that Chuma, the interpreter, had not left for Tibet as arranged, and had been seen only a week ago on the border. He should have been nearing Lanchow according to the schedule. Worried, I asked why.

'We don't know. We thought of all possibilities, even sabotage,' he said casually. It was an alarming suggestion, for the Chinese were known to have infiltrators within the Tibetan 'movement'. I prayed to God that it was just a case of my febrile imagination working overtime. But there was at this late stage nothing to be done. Chuma had been dispatched, again, with a severe reprimand from the Controller and I was locked into an unbreakable schedule.

Hong Kong was hot and steamy the first weekend in July. And discussing the latest developments with my Hong Kong contact, on a seemingly innocent beach at Lantow island, did little to assuage my doubts as to whether Chuma was working for the Chinese. If not, would he, in the now incredibly short period of time, manage to climb into Tibet and travel nearly 2,000 miles to keep the rendezvous at Lanchow?

The weekend was hectic with last-minute briefings and frantic shopping to buy dried food for Tibet. I spent a small fortune in downtown Kowloon buying cartons of dried noodles in every flavour from shrimp to sweet-and-sour chicken, soups, powdered milk, coffee, packets of dried fruit, mangoes, apricots – anything that would be nutritious and appetizing. And for Seán, who had a sweet tooth, I bought dozens of bars of Cadbury's Fruit and Nut chocolate!

As we were unlikely to be eating properly, I stocked up on vitamins and last-minute things like eye lotion and throat syrup, as apparently the dust and the dryness at high altitudes give rise, for those unused to the climate, to sore and sometimes infected eyes and throats. On the advice of mountaineers who had suffered painful, and often serious, burns due to the intense sunlight at high altitudes, I also bought several tubes of ultra-violet-light barrier cream. To be as inconspicuous as possible, we had decided to buy Chinese clothes inside China in Lanchow and travelled light with only a couple of pairs of jeans, T-shirts, night things (track suits for inside Tibet), flip-flops and a sturdy pair of track shoes for walking out of Tibet. We kept everything to a minimum, not only to avoid arousing suspicion, but also to cut down on the weight, as should an emergency arise, we would have somehow to carry everything ourselves.

On 30 June, there was a spectacular sunset visible from my hotel window which looked across the bay to Kowloon, but I was oblivious to the beauty, and was racing against time to reread and try to memorize all the detail that I had amassed in three years' research. I could not take any documentation into Tibet with me and I was petrified that I would forget all those impossible Tibetan names, and whom I was supposed to interview and where. I slept very little. On the night before I left for mainland China, I was up half the night shredding documents and flushing them down the hotel loo.

3
False Starts

At 7.30 A.M. on Monday, 4 July 1988, I waved goodbye to my contact at Hong Kong's Kowloon Hung Hon railway terminus and dragged my innumerable heavy bags to the train. Beside the numbered carriages, Chinese attendants in prim blue skirts, white blouses and immaculate white gloves stood to rigid attention. They did not answer passengers' questions, blink or give any sign of animation. The air-conditioning inside the carriage was restoratively cold. Soon the train left the teeming high-rise tenements of Hong Kong for the green of the New Territories and I promptly fell asleep.

Within an hour, a well-meaning overseas Chinese, returning to Guangzhou on holiday, woke me: 'This is China now.'

There were no dragons belching fire, in welcome or warning. Only quite a few rabbit-warren high-rises, in peeling whitewash and smothered with a density of washing strung from every window. They were not as tightly packed as Hong Kong, where sometimes in downtown Kowloon or on the Island you can scarcely see the sky. Nor were they as tall and glossy. And there seemed to be no trees.

Outside the speeding train's windows the buildings were thinning; now there were neat fields of ripening green rice tended by peasants in dull blue Mao suits rolled up to mid-calf. Everywhere, on the roads, in the streets of the towns and waiting at the barrier for the train to pass, were swarms of Chinese pushing or pedalling bicycles. All the signs in the passing roads were painted with red Chinese characters. Everything looked normal – just as I had expected it to be – only I seemed to be abnormal, sitting in the train with my stomach churning with anxiety. For the start of any clandestine assignment – meeting officials at the point of entry into a country – is always fraught with tension, since one never knows if one's plans have been betrayed. By the time I reached the immigration barrier in Guangzhou I could smell the acrid stench of my own fear.

It was at Guangzhou railway station that my Chinese nightmare really began. It was hot and steamy: 115°F in the shade, with the humidity a sweltering 95 per cent. The heat, harsh sunlight and noise swamped me as I emerged from the gloom of the customs hall, and immediately I was overwhelmed by swarms of unsmiling Chinese milling everywhere. It was in those first few minutes, almost swamped by the human tidal wave, that I finally appreciated the phrase 'China's bursting population problem'. Tibetans told me that only by personally experiencing the overcrowded Chinese mainland could I possibly understand China's land-hunger, and why it so coveted the vast empty spaces of Tibet as one solution to its exploding population crisis.

I struggled with my voluminous bags, desperately looking for a porter and trying to avoid being mown down by the crushing mass of people. I had never ever seen such a density of human beings – not even in overcrowded megalopolises such as Calcutta or São Paulo. It was as though I was immersed in a Hieronymus Bosch inferno of crawling humanity!

Petrified that some marauding hand would grab one of the bags, I carefully loaded all my deliberately anonymous but bulky black bags onto a trolley that was mercifully nearby. Worried about catching my connecting train to Chengdu, I was anxiously looking for the CITS (the official Chinese travel service) representative who was supposed to meet me holding up a placard with my name on it. Suddenly a gnarled brown hand yanked the trolley away from me. Then began what at another time and place would have been an amusing farce. The hand was attached to a leathery man in a blue Mao suit who screeched harshly at me in Chinese. I had no idea what he was so agitated about, but one word came through so often that I soon learnt my first word in Chinese: '*Mei you*' (No).

It was the most frequent word, I later discovered, to be used by Chinese to a foreigner, no matter what the foreigner asked. And often even before the question was even finished. As the man seemed hell-bent on throwing my cases off the trolley – including my precious camera-case with its fragile and vital equipment, I struggled to avoid it being crashed onto the floor.

The crowd closed in on us and made the air suffocatingly hot. I was beginning to wonder how on earth I was going to get out of there, let alone get into Tibet, when a tall blond Swedish backpacker elbowed his way through the crowd to me. I explained my predicament and after a guttural stream of Chinese to the crowd, he told me that trolleys were not allowed out of the station, and helped me unload my bags.

While he explained that in China there were no porters – apparently the Chinese regarded porters as too capitalistically exploitative – the aggressive Chinese pushed himself up to me, stuck his hand under my nose, and hissed 'FEC!' In China, foreigners have officially to use Foreign Exchange Certificates, which they have bought with hard currency, to pay for goods and services, such as hotel accommodation, meals, guides, etc. Since many goods can be brought only with FECs, they are much sought after by the Chinese themselves. And the foreigner, for his part, is happy to exchange FECs for Rmb (*Renminbi* – the 'People's Money') because the exchange rate is so attractive – at least double the official rate. Corruption being what it is, the foreigner has no difficulties in using the local currency to buy goods and services at less than half the official rate.

Sven, the young Swede, was an anthropologist and had been in China for eighteen months. He told me to ignore the demand and helped me to drag my bags across the sweltering station square to the CITS office. He explained what was to become my first survival lesson in China.

'Remember two things about China and you won't go wrong,' he said. 'One: what the Chinese are essentially about, despite all the Communist claptrap, is money. The bureaucracy is riddled with corruption. Every day in the papers you read about some official being arrested for corruption.

'And the other thing you should know,' Sven went on, as we finally neared the CITS on the far side of the square, 'is that the Chinese are racists!' I laughed in disbelief, wiping the sweat out of my eyes.

'You don't believe me? Just you wait until you have been here as long as I have. For instance,' he said, easing my heaviest bag off his shoulder, 'the Chinese have an innate sense of superiority. Look at their symbol for China' – he drew on his sweaty palm a rectangle with a line through the middle – 'the rectangle is the globe, the line slashing it through the middle is China, the Middle

Kingdom, the centre of the earth. The Chinese regard themselves as the centre of the world, the most superior beings on earth. And the rest, all the minorities under their rule – the Manchus, the Mongols, the Tibetans – are all barbarians. And that applies to all foreigners too. We're barbarians to them as well!'

It was certainly the most unusual introduction to any country I had ever had.

I thanked him as we dragged the bags into the cool shade of the building. As he waved goodbye from the sunlit entrance, I wondered whether perhaps he was being a bit harsh in his assessment.

It was nearly three when I returned to the CITS office after changing some money and got my ticket. A young man, Mr Li, helped me to drag the bags back across the square, left me inside the crowded railway concourse, and said that the information desk would help me. He then disappeared into the sea of people. The noise was deafening, with the roof of the building amplifying the din of the dense throng of Chinese hurrying in all directions at once. All the signs were in Chinese. I looked at my ticket. That too was written in Chinese. I tried to attract the attention of the girl at the information counter, but I couldn't even hear myself speak. With the station clock showing ten to four, I did not have much time to find the platform and, somehow, drag all the bags onto the train, wherever that might be, so in desperation I tugged her arm and asked her for the train to Chengdu. She rudely shouted '*Mei you*' at me and, with a gesture that I was to become familiar with when dealing with any 'official' in China, dismissed me with a staccato wave of her hand. I looked at the departure board. At least I supposed it was one, as it had recognizable figures and the place names in Roman script. I saw the word Chengdu and 16.00 alongside, but could not read the Chinese characters. I tried the girl again. Same dismissive hand. I tried people around me. There was not another European face in the sea of Chinese faces. No one spoke English. I tried French, Spanish, Italian, even Hindi. Nothing but blank stares.

It was five to four. Panic started to rise in my throat. The crowds seemed to be moving more quickly. I just could not believe that it was happening to me. It was as though I was in a waking nightmare with the clock's hand creeping to four. In desperation, leaving my bags on the floor and hoisting my camera-bag on my shoulder, I ran to a policeman in a white uniform, shouted 'Chengdu', showed him my ticket and made train-like gestures. He shook his head and said, '*Mei you*.' I was frantic. The train was about to leave and I was not even on the platform. I was embarking on the most hazardous journey of my life and I could not even get on the first train! Suddenly the policeman grabbed a man in a blue Mao suit who looked at my ticket and said in faltering English, 'Ticket wrong day. Tomorrow.' I could have wept. CITS had put the wrong date on the ticket. It was two minutes past four.

Apoplectic, I returned to CITS who went into a torrent of agitated Chinese, then smiled, and said that there was a train the next day! The next day the girl from CITS was helping me drag the bags once more into the station when she paused to listen to a loudspeaker blaring across the station square. She frowned and bit her lip. Then she turned to me. The train to Chengdu had been cancelled as another train was stuck somewhere up-country. In disbelief I returned with her to the office and then went to try and get an air ticket. If she had not been there, it would have been hopeless, for the queue at the booking office ran half-way round the building. And, of course, again no one spoke English.

Having got a ticket, we hurried to the airport where she helped me with my bags and left me inside the terminal, apologizing that she had to go as the driver was waiting. Once again I was left alone, effectively incommunicado in the middle of yet another throng of Chinese. The blue TV screens which showed flight departures spread total confusion by flashing different departure times for the same flight. Then the screens went blank.

People were moving off, swallowed up by the departure gate. I tried the girl at the information desk. It was a rerun of the station's information desk. '*Mei you, Mei you, Mei you!*' Finally after refusing to go away, I was told that the Chengdu flight had been cancelled. I felt as though I was going slowly and excruciatingly mad! I then recalled that Sven had told me that foreigners called the national airline CAAC, 'Cancel At Any Cost!'

Eight days later I was still not in Lanchow. I had endured purgatory at the hands of CITS, who had booked me on wrong or non-existent trains and planes and dumped me alone in deserted railway stations all across China. Now I was stuck in Xian, the ancient capital of Chang'an, the heart of countless Chinese dynasties and civilizations. I was even too tired to bother to find out where the victory pillar was that the Tibetan King Songtsen Gampo had erected 1,200 years earlier when his armies had marched victoriously into the Chinese capital. All I knew was that I had just over twenty-four hours to get to my rendezvous in Lanchow and all the planes had been cancelled.

At 14.30, after wading through a solid crowd of passengers, we got to the train with two minutes to spare and I was bundled into a carriage crawling with people. I had paid for a 'soft sleeper' but had been put into a 'hard seat' which is the way most Chinese travel. Worried about the safety of my camera equipment, I tried to explain to the CITS man and showed him the reservations, but he shrugged. As a backpacker said cynically, 'He's probably pocketed the difference!' The train attendants flicked their hands in dismissal, locked the doors to the inter-connecting carriages, marched stiffly down the corridor to their own compartment and slammed the door. I was stuck with over a hundred Chinese, no translator, no food or water and another fifteen hours to Lanchow.

The carriage was overflowing with Chinese. They were sitting on the hard seats, on the floors, in the corridors and even in the entrance to the loo doors . . . There was not one unoccupied inch of carriage. It was utterly claustrophobic. They were in all stages of undress. The men, with trousers rolled to the knee, discarded their shirts and sat smoking in grubby singlets. The women in shapeless frocks fanned themselves listlessly with cheap paper fans. Curiously there were very few children, but one was puking quietly in the corner.

The floor was littered with debris: squashed tomatoes, cigarette butts, discarded polystyrene food boxes, sweet wrappers, orange and banana peel, spilled beer. There was spittle everywhere. The thin wooden partitions were greasy with dirt. And the poles slung under the luggage racks were festooned with socks and shirts, towels and face-cloths.

Some chatted at the tops of their voices to try and make themselves heard above the blaring music and propaganda from the loudspeaker. Others stared out of the window, consumed endless cups of tea drunk from squat glass bottles with screw-tops and a sediment of tea leaves in the bottom. And almost to a person, everyone chain-smoked cigarettes. Yet, despite the language barrier, these ordinary Chinese seemed infinitely friendlier than the unsmiling officials I had so far encountered. They smiled, offered me the odd sweet, and through sign language made me feel welcome. But it was impossible to get even remotely comfortable, let alone doze in the hard seat. The overpowering density of people and the incessant noise made this undoubtedly the most uncomfortable train journey I had ever undertaken.

Outside, the countryside was changing as we travelled northwest. The timeless image of peasants working in the fields contrasted starkly with the electricity pylons that climbed and disappeared over even the steepest hills, supplying even the most remote rudimentary mud dwelling. The landscape was becoming more barren. By 7 P.M. the leaves on the trees were getting smaller and the branches more sparse. We were approaching the arid, amoeba-shaped western province of Gansu that bordered on Inner Mongolia, with the Gobi desert somewhere beyond. The hills became steeper and the drop deeper into the brown silt-laden rivers that swirled in ferocious eddies at the bottoms of the stark ravines. Near nightfall we were going through a tunnel every few minutes. The thought of the years of hard labour put into blasting and building the rail network to link the outposts of the Chinese Empire was staggering.

As the light faded, the maize flowers glowed golden in the warm evening sunlight. In the fields neat stacks of cut wheat awaited collection. Peasants in white singlets and rolled-up trousers carried heavy panniers balanced on poles swaying rhythmically across their shoulders. The low mountains were a patchwork of green and brown. Near dusk a few willow trees began to appear and it reminded me of the pictures I had seen of willow trees bordering the Kyichu river near Lhasa. At last I felt I was getting somewhere near Tibet!

An attendant pushed a heavy metal trolley down the carriage. For the princely sum of 2 Rmb (20p) I bought a polystyrene-container dinner – piping hot, sticky boiled rice, some undecipherable bits of meat in a salty, but tasty, brown sauce, and a pair of wooden chopsticks. The Chinese filled up their vacuum flasks with hot water from the trolley, took out little tin food-boxes and set their chopsticks clicking overtime.

Occasionally the train would stop for ten minutes at a station and the passengers would descend to buy beer and anaemic-looking pastries from a station vendor. It was all very orderly with none of the colour, smells and cries of an Indian station, where the vendors with baskets on their heads shout their wares in an irresistibly melodious sing-song.

At 5.30 in the morning, exhausted after a sleepless and un-comfortable night, I found myself on another empty station: Lanchow. It was D-day. Thirteen hours to my rendezvous with my Tibetan interpreter whom I had arranged to meet in the lobby of the Jincheng Hotel at 8 P.M.

I whiled away the day sightseeing. Lanchow is not a town to tarry in. I did my statutory tourist trek round the town which took all of two hours. Although it is a modern industrial city of two million Chinese strung along the valley floor of the Yellow River between high bare sandy loess hills, Lanchow has a curiously inanimate quality. With the intense harsh light of a town at the edge of the desert, it has none of the almost romantic expectancy one usually feels when confronted with the awesome uncertainties of enormous empty spaces. Nor does it have any of the bustle or vitality of a frontier town. Just boring blocks of featureless build-ings laid out in a neat grid punctuated with industrial chimney stacks spewing pollution into what was once the pristine air of the open desert.

As I looked along the valley from the top of the White Pagoda Mountain I tried, perhaps rather foolishly, to look for the uranium-enriching nuclear facility through the pollution haze hanging over the city. My Tibetan contacts had told me that Tibet's uranium is processed in Lanchow for China's nuclear industry. But I could decipher nothing and hardly dared show an interest to my guide.

At 7.45 that evening I sat down casually in a sagging armchair in the hotel lobby near the door. In my fluorescent pink T-shirt Chuma could hardly miss me. At 7.56 my feet were numb with anxiety. Would Chuma turn up? Had he been caught? If so, how would I know and what could I do? If he did materialize, would he be in disguise, trying to look Chinese? The questions ricocheted round my brain, exacerbating an already throbbing headache.

Most people think that the life of a foreign correspondent is enormously glamorous. Exotic-sounding locations, meeting fascinating people, seeing history in the making, are some of the clichés people invariably trot out at drinks parties when they ask you what you do. But few have any inkling of the loneliness involved. I was afflicted with 'foreign correspondent syndrome', as it is called in the media, when, isolated in some God-forsaken spot trying to get a difficult story, with no one to talk to and share your fears and doubts, you try and phone home – only to be confronted with foreign telephone operators who understand not one word you say! It is a little talked of, but emotionally disorientating, aspect of the job.

Outside the glass doors the tourist coaches were neatly lined up for the night. In the avenue of trees outside the gates a few cyclists hurried home. There is no night life in Lanchow, and Chinese go to bed early. In the lobby the few tourists were drinking beer before being shepherded into the dining room for their evening meal. In a far corner of the lobby two plastic water-wheels were splashing noisily into a pool as muddy as the Yellow River. In front of the entrance door a policeman in an immaculate white uniform with red and gold epaulettes and peaked cap strutted up and down. At two minutes to eight a Chinese guide shuffled up amiably and sat down beside me. I could have screamed with tension. How on earth was I to extricate myself when Chuma appeared through the door four feet from where we were sitting?

As the minutes dragged towards nine I was in a torment of anxiety, looking at the door and trying to hold a banal conversation with the Chinese guide. At five minutes past nine I got up to go into dinner, as there was no point in waiting any longer. Both Chuma and I had agreed that we would wait only for an hour after the appointed time and try again the next day at the same time. Waiting around too long might arouse suspicion, and that for Chuma, who was in China illegally, might prove dangerous should some busybody come up to him and speak in Chinese. Or worse still, ask for his travel papers! At least I was safe, for the moment, as I had a valid visa for China and so far had done nothing illegal.

Sleep was elusive that night. Amid the frantic last few days in

London I had forgotten to pack my sleeping pills. As a qualified nurse, I have an almost pathological aversion to taking addictive medication, but I always travel with mild, short-acting sedatives to overcome bad jet lag and for occasions just like this when the night conjures up every permutation of problem that could scupper the making of a film.

The next day, tired and restless under a tightly controlled nonchalant exterior, I again sat for most of the day in the faded grey armchairs in the lobby. As tourists are usually out sightseeing and then off to the next town, the same Chinese guide asked what I was doing. I concocted a story about my cousin arriving that day from Guangzhou, but that I didn't know what time he was arriving. What made the waiting infinitely more difficult was that I had run out of reading material. And there were no Western books, newspapers or magazines to be bought anywhere in Lanchow.

About 6 P.M. I was on my way to my room to get a paracetamol for a headache when a large dark man with a straggly moustache came up behind me and hissed '*Tashi Delek*' – the usual Tibetan greeting – and furtively shoved a tiny rolled-up piece of paper into my hand. Before I could put it into my pocket, he had disappeared round the corner.

4

Defection in Chengdu

I walked into the privacy of the ladies' loo, locked the door and unfurled the crumpled note. Scrawled in pencil, it said: 'Meet me tomorrow at 3 in Jantan Park. I will come by boat.' It was signed Chuma. I was ecstatic with relief. Not only was he alive, and safe, but in the same town! I looked at the map and found the park and decided to reconnoitre it for tomorrow's meeting. I bought an ice-cream from the vendor at the park gates and stood admiring the scenery, trying to figure out the boat reference. I presumed it had something to do with the lake in the centre of the park.

Returning to the hotel, I found a telex from Hong Kong telling me that Seán had missed his connection to Hong Kong and was stuck in Delhi. My stomach churned with frustration, for that meant that Seán would miss the connecting flights to Xian and Lanchow. The hotel receptionist told me it was impossible to try and rearrange bookings from Lanchow as they were not on the computer link-up, so the rest of the night was spent on the phone. By now I was getting accustomed to the ritual pantomime of trying to get a long-distance call.

The Chinese telephone system and the giggling non-English of the hotel operators were an experience guaranteed to reduce even the most catatonic creature into a quivering mass of hysteria. I am quite used to the lack of English in the more outlandish Third World locations that I have often found myself in, from Ouagadougou to Machu Picchu. It is part of the job, and I can perfectly accept and accommodate their lack of English and my lack of the local dialect: with a joke, we make the best of it and get through, eventually.

But curiously in China, outside Beijing and Shanghai, telephone operators would say 'Hello', and when you, assuming that they spoke English, went on to place the call, they would then hang up. After the fourth attempt to get through to them, or the supervisor, or the night manager, and having been met either with the dead click of cut-off, or a gale of giggles and 'No Eenglish', nerves tended to get somewhat frayed. Particularly at two in the morning. As fellow sufferers I later met in the bar told me, 'It gets worse the further west you travel.'

Dawn crept sluggishly into a muggy sky on Thursday, the 13th. There was not a breath of wind in the trees outside the window. It promised to be another scorching day. I was already two days behind schedule. Seán just *had* to get to Lanchow by the 15th as we were due to leave on our 'Tibetan walkabout' at seven o'clock the next morning. The bad news was that all flights to Lanchow had been cancelled until further notice! When I asked why, I was met with blank stares. No explanation.

As I had spent most of the night trying to phone Hong Kong without success, I sent several cryptic telexes to London, hoping that somehow my contact there could discover where Seán was and try to cajole or bribe a seat to the nearest airport to Lanchow.

It was blisteringly hot when I set off for the meeting at the park that afternoon. Nothing was moving in the white heat of midday. 'Mad dogs and Englishmen . . .', I thought, as I walked out of the hotel in the opposite direction from the park. In case anyone was following me, I made an elaborate detour through the back streets, and nearly got lost. At ten to three I got to the park, casually wandering like any other tourist and looking at the dramatic loess escarpment on the northern horizon. I wondered whether I would ever cross it and get to Tibet, which lay a six-hour drive beyond.

I headed for the small lake in the centre and walked round admiring the scenery. With an almost permanent smile stretched nervously on my face, I said '*Ni hao*' (hello) to every passing Chinese until I felt like a braying donkey. There was no sign of Chuma. At 3.30 I was sitting under a willow tree at the edge of the lake pretending to read my guide book when I heard a splash of paddles.

A small pleasure boat was moving slowly towards me. I saw that the big man who had delivered the message was rowing, but I scarcely recognized Chuma, who, though I had seen him looking well only a few weeks before, now looked haggard and darkly sunburnt. With just a flicker of an eyebrow they motioned me into the boat and paddled off to the more secluded end of the lake.

Chuma looked a mess. His clothes were torn and dirty; his legs and arms were covered with infected insect- and leech-bites. Some were oozing a vile-smelling suppuration. He had lost a lot of weight – and his eyes, bright and dry with an obvious fever, had the tense, haunted look of someone badly frightened.

The paddles' lazy splash did nothing to soften Chuma's disturbing news. He told me that he had crossed the south Tibetan border illegally with two other companions at night. Then, in the small hours of the morning, they had run into a Chinese army patrol and in the confusion of darkness he had managed to run away. But Dorje, who was our link man for the interviews and filming in the Amdo sector from Xining south to Dhartsedo, had disappeared and the other had been arrested and jailed by the Chinese. I asked him whether the Tibetan would talk under interrogation.

'Don't worry,' Chuma said flatly. 'He is an old Khampa fighter. Those people would die rather than talk.' Khampa bravery and resilience were legendary, but how long could anyone resist modern Chinese interrogation where drugs and the whole battery of sophisticated technology were known to be employed? We would have no way of knowing whether he had cracked under torture and told the Chinese all our plans and contacts.

Were we therefore walking into a trap? I reckoned that if I was head of the Public Security Bureau – the Chinese secret police – I would do absolutely nothing to stop us filming and let my Tibetan collaborators and me continue right to the end of the trip as planned, as we would then unwittingly lead the Chinese to the Tibetan underground network. All the PSB then had to do was to arrest us just as we were about to leave with all our incriminating film.

It was an insoluble dilemma and one which I could do nothing about. To abort now, on the possibility of betrayal, was obviously prudent, but I also knew that the Tibet project would die if I returned to London before I had even got into the country, as I had already spent a considerable part of the budget. So I decided to take an enormous gamble and continue, hoping that the man had not divulged anything. I would also have to make doubly sure that we were even more cautious in our contacts and careful in covering our tracks. But the thought of possible capture at the end and jeopardizing the life of everyone was deeply disturbing.

It was to become a constant fear throughout the trip, and sitting in that tiny boat poised on the edge of Tibet, I felt a terrible sense of isolation in taking the decision alone.

Chuma went on to tell me that after the border incident he had made his way to Lhasa, found and co-opted the big man whom I nicknamed Giant, and who spoke fluent Chinese, and together they had made their way by bus via Golmud and Xining to Lanchow. I realized with apprehension that it meant that Chuma had not double-checked the contacts and arrangements the Tibetan researchers had made months before.

The final alarming piece of information was that he had no identification documents. Without them it is illegal to travel even from one village to the next; if you are caught travelling without papers, you are liable to be arrested for further questioning. I was appalled, because in a police state such as China, where movements are tightly controlled, people, and especially travellers, are always being asked for their papers by the authorities. Chuma was therefore a walking hazard.

I dredged my rapidly depleting reserves of determination, and suggested that he tried to find transport among the few Tibetans who were in Lanchow and who travelled to Tibet, and that we would, with Giant's help, then proceed on the original schedule to Xining and then south to Dhartsedo where the next sector leader would take over . . .

As Chuma spoke Tibetan and Giant spoke both Tibetan and Chinese, and as I knew the locations and what we wanted to film, we could go to Amdo ourselves and find the various interviewees and guides that were waiting for us to arrive. It would obviously take a bit longer, but it was feasible. There was no other option available. So I gave them some money, told Chuma that I would return the next day with antibiotics for his bites, and asked him to arrange for transport to Xining. We agreed to meet at the same time the next day.

I returned to the hotel and settled down to another long night of trying to locate Seán and cryptically to let my contacts in other parts of the Far East know what was happening and see if it was humanly possible to send other Tibetan researchers, who knew the Amdo sector, into Tibet clandestinely. If it was feasible they could then meet us half-way through the original schedule at Dhartsedo, in

Kham, and alert all the interviewees who were waiting for us on the original route from Lhasa that we were running late. Then, if possible, we could retrace our steps from Dhartsedo north to Amdo and try and locate some of our contacts and interviewees, if they had not waited for us. Then we would have to loop back to Dhartsedo and continue the original schedule to Lhasa.

By 2.45 in the morning I felt that the djinns were throwing more than a few spanners in the works. It had been a night of telephone operators either changing shifts and losing the call or new ones giggling and doing the 'No Eenglish' routine. But eventually I did learn that Seán had missed his direct connecting flight to Lanchow. My Hong Kong contact had managed to wangle seats on the morning flight to Guangzhou and hoped to bribe seats on a connecting flight to Xian, arriving at 10.30 P.M. the same night. That would leave only nine and a half hours to the 'walkabout' departure deadline from Lanchow on the 16th. But Xian was sixteen hours away by train, there were no planes and it was impossible to find a car and drive!

Then the phone went dead . . . Then water started pouring through the bathroom ceiling. I rushed into the corridor in my nightie, woke the sleepy floor attendant, dragged him into the room as he spoke no English and an hour later two giggling workmen came in, took a look, said 'Ah', and promptly disappeared. Ten minutes later they started banging metal outside the window and in the room above it sounded as if some people were doing sumo wrestling. I thought I might just go quietly insane before the night was out.

The next day compounded the problems. At three, in the heat of the afternoon, we met again in a deserted street not far from the hotel. We huddled in a doorway, while Giant, fiddling with his bicycle with a fictitious puncture, watched the street to warn us if someone was coming. Chuma told me it was impossible to find transport and that anyway the road to Tibet was impassable. I thought that was odd, as there had been no rain in Lanchow for months, but I was in no position to argue. He was also adamant that it was 'too dangerous' to remain in Lanchow. The man was almost incoherent with fear.

He suggested we go to Chengdu where he knew contacts who could take us into Dhartsedo. At least then we would be in Tibet, and I figured we could send someone west to the waiting contacts, telling them we would be late, and then backtrack to Xining through Amdo. It would increase the time inside Tibet, but at least we would get the story. So much for schedules, I thought, remembering the months of painstaking plotting of the route and planning the interviews down to the very hour of arrival.

I invented a serious illness for my 'cousin', who urgently needed me, and I managed with an award-winning performance of tears and a wad of FECs, to get the unobtainable – a soft sleeper to Chengdu. I telexed Seán at his last known hotel in Guangzhou telling him to meet me in Chengdu, and hoped that some guardian angel would speed the message to him.

Twenty-four hours later I finally got into Chengdu and saw Seán, in a tourist Hawaiian shirt and shorts, leaning laconically against the reception desk in the lobby of the Jinjiang Hotel. I flew into a huge bear-hug, and for the first time since London felt reassured. Seán is one of those rare people who exudes calm and a sense of assurance despite whatever mayhem is erupting all round him. In the next few trying weeks he proved an absolute godsend and remained ice-cool as all our plans crumbled into uncertainty. And as crisis after crisis broke over our heads and I became increasingly wound-up, Seán would counter by descending into an almost catatonic calm. We were a perfect, if somewhat odd, couple. That evening we sat in the hotel lobby, but Chuma and Giant did not show up as planned at eight that night.

The next evening Seán and I again sat behind the potted chrysanthemums in the lobby bar, waiting for Chuma and watching the hordes of tourists pour through the room. There was quite a display of 'local talent' in the bar. The Chinese girls looked terribly young and inexperienced. Some were ravishingly pretty, waggling their slender hips in their Westernized dresses. They did not have the appearance of hard-line hookers, and even when going through the pick-up ritual of having a drink with their prospective customers, they giggled and chatted to each other. Two of them were making each other up. It reminded me of the innocent cooing of the courting couple in Ashton's ballet *Les Deux Pigeons*. But there was nothing innocent about the brash young men, the *nouveau riche* offspring of corrupt local party officials, who, I was told, threw away in one evening at the hotel's discothèque more than a peasant earned in a year. These loud-mouthed 'gilded youth of Chengdu' had the manners of the pigsty. More than somewhat inebriated, they abused the waiter, spat on the carpets – of a four-star hotel – and unceremoniously and roughly dragged the girls out of the bar.

At eight o'clock, through a throng of package-tour tourists, I saw Chuma and Giant stroll casually into the lobby. As Tibetans are not allowed into the big hotels where Europeans stay, it must have taken a considerable amount of courage to walk past the hotel guards at the gate.

I followed them round the corner and again had a message thrust into my hand. We were to meet the next day at ten in a park away from the tourist areas. It was 20 July and we were already four days behind the original schedule and no nearer, it seemed, to Tibet. It was muggy and overcast, the pollution level was suffocating and the cough I had picked up the last time I was in Chengdu was developing into bronchitis. According to the American consul, the pollution is so bad that bronchitis is endemic in Chengdu. Seán shadowed me to the park , walking 500 yards behind and on the opposite side of the road. We hoped that if I was being followed he could possibly deflect them. It was not paranoia. I had been warned about the efficiency and thoroughness of the Chinese intelligence agencies, and with the suspicion that much had so far gone wrong because someone had infiltrated the Tibetan underground security, I had to be more than cautious.

I took a tortuous route through the back streets and a market dense with people and stalls. Vendors displayed their wares in baskets or on the ground and I noticed a profusion of juicy red and green chillies, bundles of red and white radishes, and slabs of fatty pork hung from racks; and stuck into a bamboo container strapped to the back of one vendor's cycle were bunches of white tuber roses, yellow chrysanthemums and a few pink roses. But curiously, unlike other developing countries, there were no flies, rats, smell or sewage. There were also no dogs or cats or children.

The park in contrast was dank and grey. It had previously been part of some nobleman's estate and that day scores of Chinese were shuffling through. The damp depressing grey-green of the trees and shrubbery was oppressive. No bright colour, no gaiety, no children's giggles. As the only European I was somewhat conspicuous, so I sat on a stone and pretended to sketch the scenery. At 10.30 Chuma and Giant strolled through and made for an enclosure housing an ancient tablet of rock carved with Chinese characters. While Giant sat fanning himself outside and keeping guard, Chuma again told me he could not find transport in Chengdu and that it was 'too dangerous' to remain there. He suggested that we go on to Lhasa.

I was barely able to conceal my impatience. This was the second time he had failed. The second time he had used the phrase 'too dangerous'. I remembered his earlier failure to leave for Tibet on time and began seriously to consider whether he was in the pay of the Chinese. It was hardly the time or place for recriminations. So I told him that the point of the film was to find evidence all over Tibet, not just in the capital. I gave him a large wad of notes, and told him to send Giant to Dhartsedo, two hundred miles due west, to contact our waiting collaborators, get transport and return for us.

'Friendly' transport to Dhartsedo, the ancient Tibetan frontier town, was vital, as the town and the road from Chengdu was a closed area for foreigners. We agreed to meet at another park in three days. It began to rain, in a relentless monotony reminiscent of the incessant, penetrating downpours that in Vietnam turned the jungles into a veritable green hell.

Seán had in the meantime found a young Chinese student who spoke good English and offered – for 30 Rmb a day – to be our guide. So for the next few days we explored the back streets of Chengdu and I was at last able to meet ordinary Chinese. We also did some serious shopping for the trip, for things that had been too bulky to carry from Canton. We bought Chinese food and clothes, rationalizing that should we actually be seen in the closed areas inside Tibet, we were less likely to attract attention dressed as Chinese. And I knew from previous assignments that it is the odd details – like wearing the wrong kind of shoes – that give one away.

So we bought the shapeless green trousers and shirts that the Chinese wear and which are the same colour as their military uniforms. For shoes I bought the flat, black cloth ankle-strap ones with rounded toes that most Chinese wear.

The Chinese, away from the big tourist hotels and the obstructive CITS officials, were delightfully normal and responded with smiles to 'Ni hao'. I was amazed at their industry.

Everyone in the little back-street shops was busily working, copying Western models of everything from jeans to bras at a fraction of the price of Western goods. The Chinese can copy anything — even in the ballistic missile and satellite field — and vastly undersell the West. Already, not only were clothes appearing in the West with the 'Made in China' label, but many nations were now using Chinese rockets to launch their satellites into space from China.

I was finding it increasingly difficult to breathe, and finally Seán persuaded me to see a doctor. I had brought medication for most contingencies, but no ampicillin for bronchial infections and it was impossible to buy Western medicine in Chengdu . . . The foreigners' hospital was impressive and I had to smile when I saw a large notice that hit you the moment you walked in the door: 'Pay first. FEC.' The Chinese were learning about capitalism fast. The doctor told me I had a bad bout of bronchitis and bronchial asthma and my temperature was 103. He suggested hospitalization, which was obviously out of the question. When they were about to inject me, I asked for a sterile needle because of the possibility of Aids. 'Oh,' the nurse said haughtily, 'Aids only from foreigners.' I have heard the same comment in most Third World countries from Zaïre to Saudi Arabia. Always the foreigner is to blame!

We waited a week. The trip was now becoming a nightmare of non-events and I had not turned over one foot of film. The days merged in an oppressive grey gloom. The sun seemed never to shine and only the welcome mats in the hotel elevators, which read 'Welcome Monday', or whatever day it happened to be, and which were changed every day, reminded us what day it was. I lay in bed and quelled my rising impatience and anxiety by reading voraciously — Tom Wolfe's *Bonfire of the Vanities*, Keri Hulme's marvellously absorbing *The Bone People* and Bruce Chatwin's *Song Lines*. Outside the hotel window, swarms of cyclists glided silently by and the factory chimneys on the skyline continued to belch black and red fumes into the overcast sky with total disregard for the environment.

Every evening before eight Seán and I took up our positions in the lobby bar to wait for Chuma. People, including the hotel manager, had begun to ask embarrassing questions as to why we were staying so long, and we were running out of plausible excuses. I was also running out of time and budget.

On the very day that we should have been filming in Dhartsedo, we finally met Chuma and Giant. In the pouring rain in another park near the river, the four of us huddled under one umbrella while Chuma told us that Giant, who spoke no English, had returned from Dhartsedo and that our contacts, who were supposed to be waiting, were not there. As Seán and I looked at each other in disbelief, Chuma suddenly stiffened and told us that we were being watched by a man standing and acting suspiciously under the willow tree by the river.

Chuma and Giant fled in the direction of the bus station at the end of the road, while Seán and I trudged slowly back along the river, which was grey with sediment and sludge, to the bridge. Where and how could we contact Chuma again? For security reasons he had not given us his address. We walked round in circles in the rain wondering whether someone was indeed sabotaging the film, for so far all we had to show for nearly two weeks in-country was a bunch of unsubstantiated excuses.

It was dark when we crossed the bridge near the hotel. Stopping to buy some peaches, I thought I saw Chuma in a pool of street-light near an avenue of dripping oleanders. We walked down and found him. He was a jittering mess of nerves. 'Too dangerous, too dangerous,' he kept repeating mechanically. 'Why don't you go back to London and try again?' he asked desperately. I felt even Seán's remarkable equanimity begin to crack.

Holding tenuously to the last remnants of my shaky composure, I told Chuma that I had no intention of returning to London, and that so far all he had promised had not materialized, and suggested that he return tomorrow with concrete suggestions of what and whom I was going to film in Lhasa.

The next day there was a monsoon downpour. Rain sheeted off the bamboos. The park was dank and humid when we arrived at the pre-arranged time. But after hours of waiting in the rain Chuma did not appear. We hurried to the other park in case we had made a mistake. He was not there either. We sat in the lobby scrutinizing everyone who came through the door. At midnight we went to bed. On the third day, after repeating our park and lobby vigil, we were forced to come to the conclusion that Chuma had either been arrested or done a bunk.

5

Adrift in the Abode of the Gods

It was like a bad dream. Seán and I were stuck in the middle of China, our Tibetan contacts had evaporated into thin air, and with them, it seemed, all hope of the film. I was unable to contact anyone who could help, as foreign calls were monitored in Beijing, and many of the Tibetan underground outside Tibet were not on the phone. Those who were would be known to the authorities in Beijing and a call traced from me to them would completely expose us. There was nothing else to do but go to Lhasa and hope, somehow, to contact Chuma and Giant. If they were not in jail.

It is not easy to get into Lhasa. The Chinese authorities insist that you can get there only as part of a Chinese-controlled and very expensive tour group. Some backpackers had, with difficulty, got through in groups of two or three, but since the Monlam Prayer Festival riots in Lhasa in March 1988, the authorities had clamped down on all individual travel. And all groups and airline seats, at the height of the tourist season at the end of July, were booked solid for two months. To attempt the long journey overland, back to Lanchow, and then, if possible, try and join a backpack tourist group for Lhasa via Xining and Golmud was out of the question. Many backpackers had told me how they had been forced to wait for up to three weeks to collect enough foreigners to make up sufficient numbers to fill a tourist bus-load to the satisfaction of the Chinese. With our Chinese visas and the budget running out, we had no option but to try and fly from Chengdu.

After exhausting verbal contortions, I managed to get us on a flight to Lhasa as a group of two, as part of a five-day tour of Lhasa. It cost a small fortune to circumvent the rules, and for once I blessed the corruptibility of Chinese bureaucrats. We were already twelve days behind schedule and I was worried that our internal Tibetan contacts, who were supposed to wait no longer than three weeks after the appointed rendezvous day, would leave.

As many of them would have travelled for considerable distances by horseback from remote areas without roads, there would be no way to recall them. I finally got word, by telex via London, to my main outside contact to meet me in a neighbouring country and to get me another interpreter so that we could, if I did not find Chuma in Lhasa, leave Tibet, find a replacement and try to kick-start the film again.

At 5.30 A.M. in the pre-dawn darkness, Chengdu airport was a scrum. Apart from the crowds, which I had by now got used to at the departure halls, there was a heavy presence of Chinese army personnel *en route* to Lhasa. They were a scruffy mob in an assortment of unpressed baggy green trousers, their shirts were uniform only in the various stages of undress showing a variety of coloured T-shirts and vests underneath. They shuffled along somewhat reluctantly, I thought, in an assortment of shoes from grey sandals to flimsy slip-ons, all with a uniform coating of mud. To the PLA, indeed to any Han Chinese, Tibet is a hardship posting. Passengers carrying cardboard boxes and plastic netting bursting with peaches, oranges and bananas pushed and shoved their way towards the check-in counter.

By 7 A.M. in the muddy grey dawn it was uncomfortably hot in the airport departure hall. The two air-conditioners were silent. Most of the passengers, including the soldiers, had stripped to their singlets. Not a breath of fresh air stirred the long dirty white curtains. On the walls were pictures of rocky mountains and waterfalls, mass-produced pastiches of Shan-shui landscape paintings of misty mountains and water that I saw displayed everywhere.

I had never been to China before, and knowing that after the transmission of the film I probably would never get into the country again, I had eagerly looked forward to seeing China at last. The China beyond the tourist clichés, beyond the Great Wall, the Forbidden City and the Terracotta Soldiers. I was looking for the China that had been inherited from the Shu Jing, the Confucian epics written 2,700 years ago that recounted the tales of the legendary kings of ancient China. Was there anything left, I wondered, of the country celebrated by the glorious Yuan and Ming dynasty operas like *Romance of the Western Chamber* and *The Peony Pavilion*? The harmonious relationship between nature and man that the Shan-shui landscape paintings were supposed to represent was sadly missing in the China that I had so far seen: the China that had inherited the legacy of Mao's revolution.

It was impossible to get a drink. The airport shop was closed. Its display cabinets were locked and empty shelves sported only a few bars of soap, the odd packet of Huaxi cigarettes, an assortment of horrible carved elephants, some cushion-covers in garish brocade, a couple of bottles of local firewater and a jar of pickled fruit. The passengers waited listlessly and uncomplainingly until the loudspeaker crackled into life. Assuming it was a boarding call, we pushed our way, with everyone else, to the door, which was carefully unlocked by a soldier. Standing on the tarmac were two American-built Boeing 707 CAAC planes.

The flight was uneventful and instead of glimpsing the snowy peaks of the Khawa-Kharpo and the Minyak Gangkar of eastern Kham – both over 24,000 feet – we flew most of the way over dense monsoon clouds. An hour and a half later, the aircraft came down out of the clouds and flew over the wide expanse of the Tsangpo (the Bhramaputra river) valley. The sheer scale of the brown and green mountains and the enormous expanse of meandering river was staggering. I felt a wild surge of excitement at my first glimpse of Tibet.

As I walked out of the aircraft door at Gonggar airport, I was abruptly reminded that Tibet was a country under military occupation. For, waiting at the foot of the aircraft steps, was a crowd of unsmiling Chinese soldiers. At the end of the runway were Chinese MIG 21 fighter aircraft and some poorly disguised gun emplacements.

Apart from a few ragged children, there was not one Tibetan in sight. There were no airport buildings, none of the paraphernalia of an airport, just a few low buildings with shiny roofs in the distance and a wide grassy valley surrounded by brown-green hills and immeasurable space. After the claustrophobic Chinese cities, I suddenly felt as though I could breathe freely again. I luxuriated in the cool clean air, the immense silence and the nourishing feast of vast empty space.

I reminded Seán to walk slowly, for we had come from sea-level to 12,000 feet in one abrupt step without any time for our bodies to acclimatize to the altitude. I remembered when I had first arrived in Cuzco from sea-level Lima and, unheedful of the warning from my Peruvian cameraman, an old Andean hand, had hurried across the tarmac and immediately felt terribly ill with oxygen deprivation. This time I walked very slowly and tried to breathe in deep breaths of the thin, oxygen-depleted air.

The waiting soldiers rushed to board the aircraft and I turned to a nearby gaggle of ragged children who were wearing tatters and bits of shoes held on with pieces of string. They looked at me curiously; when I said '*Tashi Delek*' in greeting to them, their faces broke into radiant smiles. The children seemed to be very surprised that I not only smiled but greeted them in their native tongue. And despite their very obvious poverty, and unlike any other children in the Third World who would have immediately shoved begging hands and imploring eyes under a foreigner's nose for 'baksheesh', these children smiled shyly, just touchingly pleased not to be pushed aside, as they usually were by the Chinese. The children were of course Tibetan, that 'ungrateful breed of dirty barbarians' as I had heard Tibetans referred to by the Chinese ever since I had arrived in China.

A young Chinese from CITS held up a card with our names scrawled on it and showed us to the buses waiting outside the single-storey customs hall to drive us the two-hour journey northeast to Lhasa. I sat by the window like an excited child, hungry to absorb every detail of my long-cherished dream and remembering all those hours when, as a little girl, I had listened to my father's stories about the country. The brilliantly sunny day lit up the countryside with an intensity of colour, in the pollution-free high altitude, that is seen only in the very high lands of the Himalayas and the Altiplano in South America.

After leaving the ugly low concrete Chinese buildings and army barracks near the airport, we drove through virtually empty countryside along the wide Tsangpo valley. The road wound through small Tibetan villages with their clusters of square flat-roofed mud homesteads surrounded by clumps of fresh green willow trees. And from the corner of each house sprouted a bunch of willow twigs with fluttering *dhar chok* or prayer-flags. Unmistakeably Tibetan, the prayer-flags were filled with minutely written verses from the Buddhist scriptures. Tibetans erect them on the roofs of their houses, at the tops of high passes and sometimes in the fields so that the wind may carry the message of the Buddha far and wide. They are usually white but can also be red, yellow, green or blue. The colours represent the elements and have a religious significance: yellow (earth), blue (water), red (fire), white (air), green (space). But here in Tibet they seemed very much smaller than those I had seen in Tibetan settlements in India, Nepal and Bhutan, where they had fluttered proudly at the end of a tall bamboo pole. I was later told that they were small because of the Tibetans' poverty and their fear of Chinese reprisals. After all, it was only fourteen years since the horrors of the Cultural Revolution had officially ended. During the Cultural Revolution the practice of religion had been forbidden and any Tibetan caught observing anything remotely connected with religion had been severely punished.

We drove through hamlets where Tibetans were sifting barley, their staple diet, and spreading it across the road for passing vehicles to crush. They were dressed in long dark *chubas*, their national dress. For women this is a floor-length, sleeveless pinafore, crossed at the back and held in place by a multi-coloured striped apron (if they are married). Men wear a shorter version but with sleeves, and hitch it up round their waists with a *khera* (cord), forming a pouch in front in which they stuff all their necessities. Under the *chuba*, both men and women wear colourful *wojuk* (shirts or blouses) made of silk or cotton, depending on their social standing; in remote areas the nomads (*drogpa*) just wear *phaktsa* (sheepskin *chubas*) with the fleece lining on the inside. I was immediately struck by the dirt and poverty of the Tibetans' clothes. Their open, weather-beaten faces smiled and they waved in response to the backpackers' greetings.

On our left, the bare sandy mountains came right down to the road which snaked round the lower spurs. In a number of places where the land had slipped into the river, we laboriously bumped our way over the rubble. The river swirled in a furious current with white caps almost within touching distance, the expanse of water and sandbanks stretching to the distant mountains. With its silt-laden waters turning blue at the horizon and reflecting the bright sky with scudding wisps of white cloud, the river became a vast watery Matisse. It was as though I was looking through an infinite spectrum of reflecting mirrors distorting all sense of space and time until I did not know where water ended and sky began.

In this landscape of such huge proportions a sense of harmony between the elements was palpable. It was a sensation I was to experience very often in Tibet, and one which I had not felt anywhere before. Not even when confronted with the gigantic expanse of the Amazon where it spends itself into the Atlantic.

After an hour and three-quarters of riverine vistas unfolding, each one even more spectacular, I saw ahead in the distance, on a red rock promontory rising from the plain like a lighthouse beckoning to the wayfarer, the Potala or Celestial Palace of the Dalai Lamas and the embodiment of spiritual and temporal power in Tibet. For years, from the time I was six years old, I had dreamt that one day I would see it, and now in front of my eyes it was coming nearer as we drove to the ancient city of Lhasa, which in Tibetan means 'the abode of the gods'. I was so excited that I had difficulty breathing. It was an incredible, almost choking sensation of simultaneous disbelief and joy.

As we approached Lhasa, the fields became green with barley and vegetables. I recognized familiar plants – cabbages, cauliflowers, tomatoes, celery, radish: common vegetables that grow in all countries that somehow I had not associated with Tibet. Lorries and Chinese cyclists began to appear. We continued eastwards and on the outskirts of Lhasa drove past the shiny petrol storage-tanks that stood out harshly against the subtle shading of the rocks of the craggy mountains thrusting into a vivid blue sky.

I strained to get a closer glimpse of that ancient city which was named Ra'ssala because of the sound the wind made in the waves of the lake near which the present city was started nearly two thousand years ago. During the time of the Yalung Kings, Lhasa had always been a town of some importance, but it rose to prominence when the 33rd Yalung King, Songtsen Gampo, moved his court and capital there in 621 A.D. He built the first palace, the *Kukhar Photrang* on the *Mapori* (Red Hill), where today the Potala Palace rises majestically into the unbelievably blue sky.

We drove through the southern edge of the town, along anonymous, tree-lined and largely deserted roads. I was surprised to see miles of low, concrete, barrack-like buildings with Chinese ideograms painted in black on the gate-posts everywhere. It seemed an alien and unexpected affront in this, the most national of all

Tibetan cities, that on our arrival we saw nothing but Chinese buildings. The only thing that was Tibetan was the omnipresent Potala, a defiant reminder of Tibetan nationalism.

We were driven through tall gates into the walled compound of the Sunlight Hotel, a Chinese-run establishment where no one, apart from our guide, who soon vanished, spoke one word of English.

It was 1 P.M. and we had missed the prescribed lunch hour. So we broke into our 'rations' and mixed a cup of noodles and some soup with hot water from the room flask, and went to bed – to give the blood time to adjust to the lack of oxygen at 12,700 feet above sea-level.

After three hours it was physically impossible for me to lie still. It seemed preposterous actually to be in Lhasa and find myself lying in bed, without having seen anything of the city. Seán was feeling the altitude badly and was suffering from a splitting headache, so I decided to go into Lhasa on my own. Another tourist, hearing me making no headway with the Chinese receptionist, offered me a lift into the centre in his waiting rickshaw. He told me that the hotel was in the Chinese quarter on the outskirts of Lhasa, and as there was no public transport, nor any taxis, it was not too clever to over-exert oneself after only a few hours of arrival from sea-level. He warned me of the effects of untreated altitude sickness, which could in some cases go on to pulmonary and cerebral oedema, haemorrhage and, in rare cases, death. It was something I was already apprehensive of, and I had taken the precaution of going to Alan Herdman's exercise classes in London to get fit and build up stamina, as I did not know how my body would react to altitude.

We climbed into the cycle rickshaw, which was like any other I had been driven in in other parts of Asia. But what was most curious was that not only were rickshaws a Chinese import into Tibet, but all the rickshaw drivers were Chinese – mainly from Sichuan, 1,500 miles east, in China. It was typical, Tibetans told me later, of how even the lowly jobs were being filled with Chinese, who could earn in Tibet three times what they would in China. All of them had left wives and families behind in China and, if they were lucky, saw them maybe once a year. Yet they considered the separation well worth while as it enabled them to save for luxuries, such as a radio, bicycle, television and maybe a fridge, which would otherwise be beyond their means at home.

Sonam, a Tibetan militant, later took me round the streets, showing me Tibetans sitting in the gutter waiting for work. 'We have 30 per cent Tibetan unemployment in the Lhasa valley alone,' he said bitterly, 'because of the transfer of Chinese people to Tibet. They come here, take our jobs, our land, our houses, our resources. Everything. It's worse than a plague of locusts. At least the locusts move on. The Chinese are here to stay!'

We drove down the clean, wide Dekyi Shar Lam, the main east–west artery that bisects Lhasa. It starts at the foot of the hills in the east amid the Chinese housing estates, runs to the edge of the old Tibetan quarter which still clusters round the Jokhang, or Tsukla-khang, the central temple and the holy of holies of Tibetan Buddhism, continues past the foot of the Potala and on to the western part of Chinese Lhasa half-way to Drepung monastery. There was not much traffic: a few green army three-tonne trucks, several green army motorcycles and side-cars ridden by stiffly seated Chinese military in green uniforms, regulation caps kept on with chin straps and immaculate, formal-looking white gloves. They looked like cardboard caricatures driving around with the arrogance of the Japanese occupying forces in an archetypal World War II movie.

There seemed to be more Chinese strolling on the dirt paths or pedalling through the street than Tibetans. Everywhere you turned there were Chinese signs: on the banks, on shops and restaurants, posters, street names and even, as I was later to find, in the Tibetan quarter. Even the houses had Chinese characters painted on them. Chinese signs were hung across the street so that whenever you looked west to the Potala, it was framed in Chinese ideograms. Later I found Chinese signs hung and painted inside Tibetan temples, even inside the Jokhang. 'It's as though,' said Tsering, a young Tibetan monk in his twenties, 'the Wailing Wall in Jerusalem was daubed with Nazi slogans!'

Chinese vendors had strung out stalls displaying racks of Chinese-made clothes – cheap, dreary, shapeless, unisex Mao suits in blue, grey and green and rows of what looked like army-surplus uniforms. It was as though Lhasa was the last bastion of China's reactionary habits of dress and a good off-loading point for China's state factories' surplus production. It seemed a far cry from the fashionably short skirts and attractively made-up young girls that I saw in Guangzhou. In a curious way, it was as though the Chinese in Tibet were frozen in a time-warp and had not progressed very far out of the rigidity of the Cultural Revolution mentality. I saw more Mao-suited Chinese in Tibet and women in pudding-basin haircuts than anywhere else in China.

Tibetans, all over Tibet, later told me that the external manifestations I had noticed were symptomatic of the die-hard calibre of Communist cadre the Chinese Government sent to Tibet. 'Everything is effectively controlled by the Chinese,' said Sonam, 'from the running of Tibet to the health service, education, housing, everything. We Tibetans have no say in the running of our own country; we are second-class citizens in our own land.'

Of course I had already heard the allegations of the transfer of Chinese to Tibet, both as a solution to China's own population problem and as the 'Final Solution' to Tibetan intransigence. Already Tibetans claimed that there were seven and a half million Chinese to about six million Tibetans inside Tibet.

Sandrop, a Tibetan historian, had told me: 'It is the same thing they have done all over the Minorities territories. Look at Manchuria. At the turn of the century you had a Manchu civilization and language. Today there are 75 million Chinese to only 2–3 million Manchus: that's thirty-five Han Chinese to one Manchurian inside Manchuria. The Manchurian culture, identity and language have all but disappeared. The same thing is happening in Inner Mongolia, where there are 13 million Chinese to 2.5 million Uighur: that's eight Chinese to one Uighur [Inner Mongolian]. In Eastern Turkestan [Xinjiang] they outnumber the local people five to one.'

Certainly the Chinese housing was unmistakeable. Block after block of barrack-like cream-painted concrete buildings laid in a grid and all protected by high-walled enclosures. Lhasa, once the quintessential Tibetan city, is today 80 per cent Chinese, however much the Chinese choose to deny it. But unlike the traditional Chinese Confucian concept of respecting and obeying the head of the family and living in walled, interlocking courtyards, where up to five generations of one family could, and did, live in harmony, today's Chinese compounds serve a very different purpose.

According to Tibetans, and the few foreigners who have lived in Lhasa and China for many years, the high wall round the Chinese compounds is a protective device against the Tibetans. Though, of course, Tibetans told me, the Chinese would never admit this. Yet occasionally in the drab cream compounds you would see a block, or sometimes just a balcony, painted with the bright, colourful geometric designs that Tibetans use. '*Shamdenpa!*' (disgrace) Tibetan friends spat, when referring to Tibetan collaborators who worked for the Chinese. And who, often for their own protection – and the obvious Chinese perks, like electricity, which is not usually found in Tibetan homes – live in houses or accommodation inside the Chinese compounds. There are Tibetan quislings, the Tibetans told me, like Dorji Tsering, Chairman of the Tibetan Autonomous Region's Administration, whom the Chinese never fail to display when accused of not allowing Tibetans a say in running their own affairs.

Suddenly, after ten minutes of pedalling down the tree-lined road, the façades on the left began to change into low, two-storeyed, white-painted, stone houses with typical Tibetan windows (*natkse*) with their distinctive, black-painted surrounds narrower at the top than the base. Around the houses, in the street, whether walking or chatting, the people, in clear contrast to the impassive Chinese, were enormously animated. Their weather-beaten faces were full of vitality. And in the space of fifty yards I heard more laughter than I had in three weeks' travel in China. They were of course Tibetans and I was at the edge of the Tibetan quarter.

I thanked the tourist for the lift. He waved goodbye and reminded me to be in time for the hotel dinner at eight otherwise I would go hungry. As I turned the corner, I caught my breath. There at the western end of the road rose the Potala again. But this time it was so close and so exactly like every photograph I had ever seen of it that it looked unreal. The sheer drama of its setting was astounding. It looked more like a stage backdrop than the eighth wonder of the world! I just sat on a stone at the edge of the road, mesmerized by the astounding scale and visual extravaganza of the building.

Framed by stark mountains, the Potala sloped elegantly towards the sky from the dungeons and store-rooms in its base which, over 1,182 feet wide, was embedded in the rock. The walls sloped inwards and up and the complex was wider at the bottom than at the top to give it, in those pre-concrete days, a greater stability. The tapering, black-painted window-surrounds increased its graceful sweep and gave an illusion of even greater height. At a height equivalent to a thirteen-storeyed building, it was reputed to be the tallest building in the world when it was constructed 350 years ago.

The dramatic way in which the Potala swept one's eye from the tangled humanity with its mundane concerns near the base bed-rock, through the ascending pristine sweep of the White and Red Palaces, through the glinting golden roofs shimmering in the bright sunshine at the top and framed against the azure sky, seemed to connect the elements of sky and earth in an unending cycle of time that Tibetans call *samsara*, the wheel of life . . . Visible from all over Lhasa, and with the ever-changing play of the intense light in the Tibetan capital, the Potala has the most extraordinary presence about it.

After the collapse of the Tibetan Empire in the ninth century, the Potala ceased to have political significance but became a temple where many incarnate lamas and learned monks (*geyche*) lived and gave religious teaching; in 1642, when the 5th Dalai Lama moved his capital to Lhasa, he began renovating the ancient buildings, and designed and started building the present complex in 1645.

Looking at the neat rows of perfectly symmetrical windows, I tried to work out the various functions that took place in what was once the power-house of the Tibetan nation. It is supposed to have over 1,000 rooms as well as many chapels and accommodated the Dalai Lama, his staff, the monks and civil servants that ran Tibet. The White Palace (*Photrang Karpo*), which rises sheer out of the rock, housed the administration and monks of the Potala. (In Tibet, all senior positions had a lay administrator as well as a monk assigned to each posting.) Each section within the complex had a specific function: the monks of the Namgyal Monastery, for example, were specifically appointed to the Dalai Lama to perform the numerous religious rituals that were incumbent on a theocratic head of state. They lived in a separate western wing in the White Palace. And rising from the top storeys of the centre of the White complex which surrounded it was the Red Palace (*Photrang Marpo*), containing the Dalai Lama's own household and official chapels and shrines which were used for private and state ceremonies. And somewhere in the labyrinth of rooms I knew there were at least two chapels – the *Songtsen Lhakang* – which were supposed to date from King Songtsen Gampo's time nearly 1,300 years ago.

I was impatient to get into the building and see for myself the fabulous artistic and religious heritage of Tibet, but it was nearly 6 P.M. and tour groups were allowed inside only in the mornings.

I turned off the main road and plunged into the maze of small, unpaved streets of the Tibetan quarter centred around the Jokhang and stretching from the road to the Kyichu river, a tributary of the Tsangpo. The narrow streets were lined with two-storeyed, grubby whitewashed houses. There was no pavement and through open archways I caught a glimpse of a jumble of run-down houses set round a muddy courtyard with a stand-pipe in the middle and crowded with firewood, women and dogs. They looked more like crude farmyards in the depths of the country than houses in the middle of a capital city.

One of the most noticeable things was the presence of well-cared-for dogs everywhere in the Tibetan quarter, for every household has dogs as pets and as guard-dogs. The Apso, the Tibetan terrier, is a small fluffy creature of the Pekingese family and looks like a cross between a King Charles spaniel and a small shaggy Snow Lion. Apsos make excellent guard-dogs – especially in the countryside to warn of intruders and wolves – and despite their diminutive size have the courage of lions; but they are so playful that in Lhasa Seán had to drag me away to prevent me from picking up and cuddling the fluffy puppies that lay sunning themselves in every courtyard and street. He reminded me that we had not had time to get our rabies injections before we left London, and no matter how adorable the puppies looked, it was not worth risking one of the most horrible deaths known to man, should any of them be infected. Yet in my travels all over Tibet, I never saw a dog cowed or badly beaten or with mange, as you see elsewhere in Asia.

'*Tashi Delek*,' smiled a Tibetan woman, who was sitting in a doorway telling her prayer-beads. She, like most Tibetans, had a strong physique, with distinctive features, a ruddy complexion and an infectious smile. Her long black hair, plaited and wound round her head, was tucked into a bright pink scarf. Her dark *chuba* and striped apron were stained with dirt and mud.

Despite their very obvious poverty, Tibetans still have an extraordinary innate sense of colour. You see evidence of this in the way they decorate not only their temples, but also their homes – however modest. The protruding roof joists are gaily painted with geometric designs in bright yellow, white, red and blue – the colours representing the elements. And even inside the houses, the walls are often painted with concentric bands of blue, red or green running round the room at waist-height. In pre-invasion days, Tibetans dressed up on feast days and holidays in a rainbow of brightly coloured silks. And even today, their natural flair is seen in the way the women pick out a colour in their faded aprons to match their blouses to. Even those too poor to wear the traditional aprons – the *pangden* – wear vibrant pink or green or turquoise scarfs round their hair.

Another endearing Tibetan characteristic is their love of flowers. Apart from the joy flowers give, Tibetans believe they are one of the best offerings to the deities, and that if they plant flowers in this life, in the next life they will be born beautiful. Flowers such as roses, carnations, cornflowers, sweet-peas, pansies, dahlias, gladioli and marigold were cultivated in great exuberance in Tibetan gardens prior to the Chinese invasion. But during the Cultural Revolution all display of colour was strictly forbidden and the garden flowers disappeared from sight. As I walked on, I saw splashes of colour from flower-pots on the window-sills of even the humblest of homes.

The Tibetan love of bright colours, an anthropologist told me, is typical of desert people, who, because of the paucity of flowers in the high deserts and mountains (although they grow in great profusion in the warmer valleys), dress themselves and their hair with colourful ornaments. But very few Tibetans had the heavy turquoise (mined in Tibet), coral or amber jewellery, either as necklaces or studded through their hair, that I had seen in photographs of Tibetans taken before the Chinese invasion.

As Dolma, a Tibetan friend, explained, for so many years

under Chinese occupation, and especially during the Cultural Revolution, there had been a strict prohibition on not only speaking Tibetan (they had to speak Chinese), but also wearing Tibetan dress (they were made to wear the drab uniform Mao suits), in an effort to stamp out Tibetan national identity, that it was only now that Tibetans were cautiously returning to traditional dress. She told me how a friend of hers, who had been in prison in Nyrong, had told her how she and all Tibetan prisoners were stripped of their Tibetan clothes, had their traditionally long hair cut, and were made to wear Chinese dress. Of course, away from Chinese scrutiny in the remote mountainous areas, the nomads never stopped wearing *chubas*.

They are a handsome race, these Tibetans, I thought as I made my way towards the Jokhang. They are physically unlike the Chinese. Although Mongoloid, they have distinctive, sometimes prominent noses. Most Tibetans are also larger and much heavier built than the small, slight Chinese. One of the Chinese arguments to attempt to legitimize their occupation of Tibet is to claim that Tibetans belong to the same ethnic race as the Chinese. But Tibetans point to independent research to prove the contrary.

In fact Tibetan historians claim that the sparsely populated Tibetan plateau was peopled by non-Chinese Ch'ing nomadic tribes who migrated into the country from the north-east between two and three thousand years ago. Tibetan historians, in the *Blue Annals*, also cite evidence of an Indian savant, Shankara Pati, who chronicled the large migration to Tibet from India of the army and followers of an Indian king and military commander called Rupati, who had been waging an unsuccessful war with the Indian Panadava kings about a hundred years after the death of Buddha (400 B.C.). Modern anthropologists, such as Turner, Morant, Risley and Buxton, who have studied Tibetan crania, claim that Tibetans are a Mongoloid race of dolichocephalic people of great antiquity. They point to the Tibetan's tall, long-headed, long-boned structure, hair, eyes, and skin colour and claim that these distinguish Tibetans as a separate race from the Chinese.

Despite the years of repression under the Chinese, Tibetans still carry themselves with panache. The women have an open directness in their dealings with men, and an amused, almost flirtatious, manner that is inbred after centuries of equal status with men – which is unique in Asia. Although not a matriarchal society – polyandry and polygamy as well as monogamy are widely practised in Tibet – women are traditionally used to having an equal say in the running of their lives. They also have a reputation for considerable sensuality, and have none of the subservient inhibitions that are so common in many Asian women. And when I got to know them later during my travels inside Tibet, I also found that they had a highly developed sense of humour and fun.

The men, especially the Khampas from eastern Tibet, looked at me with an amused macho arrogance that, despite my fatigue, made me aware of being a woman! It was flattering and amusing and I never felt uncomfortable, as I often had when travelling alone in the Middle East or Africa. Khampas in their short *chubas*, their long hair wound round their head with a red *tapshuk* (silken cord) and a knife sheathed in a carved metal (traditionally it was silver) scabbard dangling from their belts, still cut a dashing figure in the streets. Mercurial, quick-tempered, fearless horsemen, the Khampas have a reputation for great bravery. They also have, as I was to find out later, a long proud tradition of *pha-lokok* – chivalry.

The tangled alleys converged on the Barkhor, a circular street surrounding the Jokhang temple on three sides. In Tibetan it means the 'intermediate circuit' which pilgrims circumambulate, clockwise, round the Jokhang. There was a longer circuit round the old city of Lhasa and the Potala right down to the river called the Lingkhor, which pilgrims trod telling their prayer-beads to gain merit, but that has been destroyed with the construction of new Chinese roads in Lhasa.

Originally the Mayfair or Fifth Avenue of Tibet, the Barkhor was once lined with the elegant, but now run-down, houses of the aristocracy. Today it is an intriguing mixture of pilgrims from all over Asia telling their prayer-beads and chanting mantras, monks reading scriptures and accepting donations in their begging bowls and ordinary *Lhasawa* (Lhasans) walking and chatting among the small shops and stalls.

Now the street bustles with merchants selling everything from safety-pins to colourful Chinese brocades, cheap crockery from China, piles of plastic slippers and colourful Tibetan ladies' aprons – now most often made with garish modern aniline dyes. And occasionally you can find beautiful old Tibetan carpets, with their elegant patterns and distinctive vegetable-dyed soft colours, hanging on a wall. But pervading this cheerful bustle is a very tangible sense of warmth and friendliness. Tibetans greeted me with a '*Tashi Delek*' and a radiant smile. A few who spoke English asked me where I came from and whether I would like a cup of tea. After the surly, unsmiling Chinese over the past few weeks, my mood lifted and I found myself smiling widely.

The Barkhor is still the religious and mercantile hub of Lhasa, but there are several jarring reminders of the Chinese occupation. Standing strategically at a corner behind the stalls laden with Tibetan tourist jewellery, prayer-wheels and Khampa knives so that they could see pedestrians coming towards them from a distance were two Chinese men in their early thirties dressed in anonymous white shirts and slacks, and wearing dark glasses. One had a small video camera, the other an expensive-looking stills camera with a long lens attached. They were plain-clothes Chinese secret police from the hated PSB – Public Security Bureau – filming and taking photographs of what seemed to me perfectly ordinary Tibetans going about their peaceful business. I turned my face away as I walked into their view as I did not want even an accidental record of my features on file. I had been warned about them, but it was still quite a shock actually to be confronted with such blatant 'Big Brotherliness' on my first day in Tibet.

I then looked closely at the people in the street and noticed, walking anti-clockwise round the Barkhor, groups of Chinese soldiers and a few curiously well-dressed trinket-sellers who, Tibetan colleagues told me, were Chinese security stooges. To walk anti-clockwise round the Barkhor or, as I later saw, in the Jokhang, is a very deliberate insult to the religious sensibilities of the Tibetans. As one Tibetan told me, 'Particularly in the Jokhang, it's as sacrilegious as urinating on the altar of a Christian church! *Tongchung!*' When I suggested that perhaps the Chinese were ignorant of Tibetan customs, he retorted coldly, 'You can understand a tourist who comes here for the first time, but the Chinese have been in Lhasa for over thirty years. That is no accident or ignorance. It is a deliberate and continuous provocation and attempt to denigrate our religion. Go into any Tibetan temple and you will see how the Chinese behave. Even in the Jokhang.'

I followed the crowd of pilgrims round to the front of the Jokhang. They had come from all over Asia, and the memory of the naked faith I saw in their faces will remain with me all my life. As a practising Catholic who has travelled to the most obscure corners of the earth exploring other people's beliefs, the depth of the faith of these simple people was something that I had never seen or experienced before.

Some pilgrims wearing heavy aprons and with protective leather on their hands were performing *kyang-chak* – prostrating their full length on the ground, then getting up, taking three steps, and prostrating themselves again, praying quietly all the time. Dusty, painfully thin, these particular pilgrims had been prostrating themselves laboriously for four and a half years from their home in Minyak, eastern Kham, over 800 miles away. By the time they got home, prostrating all the way, up hill and down, it would have taken them nine years and they would have measured their length all of the 1,600 miles. They were the first of many similar pilgrims I saw prostrating themselves in all weathers and in all terrains throughout my journey in Tibet. It was a remarkable testament to the resilience of a faith that the Chinese have not been able to exterminate even after forty years of brutal repression.

As I turned the south-west corner, I found myself in front of a wide paved un-Tibetan plaza bordered by modern two-storeyed houses which led to tall ugly Chinese buildings harshly out of keeping with the quiet dignity of the rest of the area. A Tibetan friend later explained that in 1984 the Chinese had bulldozed all the old Tibetan houses facing the Jokhang and built the wide modern plaza and buildings. 'All the better to watch the Tibetans!' he explained, pointing out a large Public Security building on the south-west corner, and another further back in the plaza which gives an unimpeded view of the Jokhang and of any movement in and out of the square. He also told me that from the tall buildings at the bottom of the square, the Public Security people filmed and photographed Tibetans, especially during the 1987 and 1988 demonstrations.

Visually, the Jokhang is not a startlingly arresting building. It has none of the imposing architecture of St Peter's in Rome or the Byzantine splendour of Santa Sophia in Istanbul or St Basil's in Moscow. Yet this deceptively modest-looking, three-storeyed, red and white building, with white curtains shielding the windows from the fierce sun, and a glint of golden roofs at the back, has an unmistakeable gravitas that draws you to it like a powerful magnet.

Rather like Tibetan Buddhism, the Jokhang has no visual pyrotechnics that intrude into your consciousness, it does not seek to proselytize, it asks nothing from the onlooker. It just offers a comforting and welcoming presence that transcends time, belief or nationality.

On the roof parapet over the main entrance is the golden symbol of Buddhism – the *ritak-choekor* – the eight-point wheel of dharma (faith) flanked by two docile fawns symbolizing submission to the faith and to remind people that the Buddha's first teaching was given in a deer park. These simple emblems, seen on all Buddhist temples and chapels, glinted in the strong sunlight, potent symbols of Tibetan nationalism. They looked down on a crowd of pilgrims lighting twigs in two enormous whitewashed incense burners in the courtyard and on others prostrating themselves in the temple forecourt. The pilgrims were of all ages and from every part of Tibet. Some women from Amdo, in north-eastern Tibet, wore their hair in 108 long, thin plaits down their back and their *chubas* had the distinctive tawny orange, brown and white edging of the region.

I went to buy a *kata* (a gauze offertory scarf – in white – to symbolize purity of heart), which Tibetans offer on entering a temple or someone's house as a mark of respect, from one of the *kata* sellers in the forecourt. I realized with a shock that the vendors selling *katas* for religious ritual in the Jokhang were actually Chinese! As were, on closer scrutiny, all the *kata* sellers sitting on their little stools outside the Jokhang in their Chinese clothes, smoking Chinese cigarettes and reading Chinese paperbacks. I then began to understand the bitterness of many Tibetans who complained that the Chinese were not only usurping all their jobs, but were infiltrating the most sacred areas of Tibetan life.

As I approached the entrance, Tibetans came up to me and pleaded, 'Picture Dalai Lama,' in broken English. Every tourist is asked over and over again for pictures or news of their beloved '*Kundun*' (The Presence, as the Dalai Lama is known to his followers). I had not brought any pictures with me, thinking it wiser not to, for if they had been found at the airport I might have been in trouble for importing subversive literature. Feeling terrible to have to deny such a simple favour, I gestured that I had nothing. They smiled and many clasped my hand and pressed it silently to their heads.

I walked past the pilgrims prostrating themselves on the fore-court, on stones polished to a warm satin finish by centuries of devotion. In the afternoon sun some tourists, disgorged from their tourist bus, were busy clicking their cameras, recording 'the quaint customs' of these 'darling' people. As a Tibetan friend remarked to me, 'This is what the Chinese are reducing our faith to – a quaint tourist curiosity that brings in the dollars for them. All that the tourists see are the externals of our faith – they know nothing – nor do the Chinese guides tell them about the complexity of Buddhism. The tourists don't know about the Chinese restrictions on our religion that still prevent us from practising our faith – despite all the talk of Chinese liberalization. This is just another way of reducing a profound religion to an empty rite. It takes twenty to thirty years of hard study for a Tibetan to even become a competent monk. Go into the countryside, go deep into Tibet, see for yourself.'

I turned the massive brass prayer-wheel, which was intricately carved with verses from the Buddhist scriptures in elegant Tibetan *U-chen* script. All Tibetans who entered and left the Jokhang turned the wheel, which also contained portions of their scriptures inside the drum, believing that by turning it, and therefore symbol-ically propagating the teachings of the Buddha, it would earn them, and all sentient beings, merit. I walked through the massive doors, past the ferocious-looking guardian Kings Yulkhorsung, Phakkyesbu, Chenmisang and Namthose that lined the walls, and came into a courtyard, open to the sky, in which Chinese workmen were mixing cement without protecting the ancient frescos lining the walls from the dirt.

I remembered how one of the Jokhang's monks, who had escaped to India, had told me of the horror Tibetans felt when the Chinese had stormed the Jokhang in 1975 and smashed the ancient statues in this seventh-century building, defaced the frescos, killed over forty monks, beaten scores of other monks and dragged them to prison from the very place in which I was then standing. That same courtyard, in which some monks in their maroon robes were now quietly conducting *choe* (prayers), the Chinese had converted, together with the chapels leading off it, into a pigsty and abattoir. 'Doesn't the United Nations Charter of Human Rights say something about the right to worship being a fundamental human right?' the monk had asked softly, with a typically Buddhist lack of bitterness.

'And when they smashed and looted our ancient statues, and at night carted away lorry-loads of our priceless *thankas* [religious paintings on cloth, depicting scenes from the lives of Buddha and the saints], our gold and silver butter-lamps that were later sold on the international art market, when they imprisoned us monks, tortured us, destroyed our ancient books, bombed our monasteries, forbade the practice of our religion upon pain of imprisonment, and turned our holy temple into an army barracks and a recreation area for them, why was it that no one raised a voice in protest?' he asked. Before he managed to escape, he had been imprisoned and tortured for many years for resisting the Chinese, as had many of his fellow monks, most of whom had since disappeared in the terror of the Cultural Revolution.

With the pilgrims I walked past chapels that were shut to the public. Through a darkened archway at the back of the courtyard we went into a vast chamber with two enormous statues in the middle. The pilgrims shuffled along the walls telling their prayer-beads, murmuring their mantras, reciting the *Om Mani Padme Hum* – Hail to the Jewel in the Lotus – and praying for the Dalai Lama and his swift return; from time to time they ducked into the various chapels to pray and offer their modest gifts of a *kata* or a flower or a biscuit or to pour a small amount of butter offering into one of the hundreds of flickering butter-lamps in front of the statues. In the midst of this activity, I sat on one of the monks' mats on the floor of the chamber. The warm light of hundreds of butter-lamps flickering in the darkness highlighted the golden gleam on the curve of the carved gold and silver of the lamps and the gilding on the richly decorated statues. In the chiaroscuro of flickering light glancing on jewel-coloured brocade adorning the statues and hanging in long, tubular shafts from the high, carved ceiling, I was conscious that I was looking at a breathtaking medieval tableau.

The two gigantic statues in the middle of the chamber were dramatically lit by a shaft of sunlight from the overhead windows, high in the dark of the carved rafters. But something, even to my untrained eye, seemed wrong. The statue on the left of Padma-sambhava, the Indian holy man who was invited by King Trisong Detsen to propagate Buddhism to Tibet in the eighth century, glared ferociously with freshly painted, bulging eyes. And even the Maitreya Buddha (the future Buddha, or the Buddha yet to come) on the right looked suspiciously new. Neither had the unmistakeable patina that develops after centuries of existence. A monk told me that all the statues in that chamber were new replacements of those smashed or looted by the Chinese. 'You see,' the old man said, 'when we make our statues, we put holy relics inside.' The only original one is of Jowo Shakyamuni, one of the two oldest and most revered statues in Tibet, which was in the innermost chamber. 'These new ones have nothing inside. It's just like an empty *momo* [a Tibetan delicacy, a dumpling filled with spicy meat]. No use. Just for tourists,' he said, as the gentle swell and eddy of the sound of the pilgrims' mantras rose and fell around us.

As I followed the queue of pilgrims clockwise round the walls, I ducked into the numerous small, dark, almost medieval chapels off the large chamber until I came to the chapel of the Jowo Shakyamuni, Tibet's most holy image. The pilgrims filed up quietly on the left, tolled the bell at the entrance of the chapel to alert the gods to their entry, offering the sound as a prayer, and climbed the steps to the chapel. The glow of the flickering butter-lamps shone on faces deeply absorbed with their devotions as they touched their heads to the feet of the Jowo, offered a *kata*, walked round the back of the chapel and down the steps on the right. The smiling golden face of the most revered image in Tibet was surrounded by a magnificently elaborate head-dress and necklace encrusted with gold, pearls, coral and turquoise.

I turned to the monk beside me and asked if he spoke English. Luckily he was a pilgrim from India, spoke fluent English, and for the rest of my stay in Lhasa proved an invaluable guide. He told me that 1,300 years ago the Jowo Shakyamuni had been a small sandalwood statue when Princess Wen-ch'eng carried it thousands of miles in a palanquin from the T'ang court in China to Lhasa. It had originally been given to her father, T'ai-tsung, the second Emperor of the T'ang dynasty to sit on the throne of China, by the King of Bengal. The Jowo's slanting blue eyes under the curved brows seemed to be smiling. There was none of the ferocious aspects that I had seen of the statues of Hindu gods in India or some of the fearsome Tibetan pantheon. The Jowo seemed more accessible. I did not understand it.

The monk told me: 'You analyse too much. Too many questions. Just feel. There are many things you won't understand here because you look through a Western prism.' He looked at me curiously for a second and went on: 'I don't know why you are here, child. But I feel you are searching for something. Rest still for a moment. Just look and feel without questioning. Just for a moment.' He smiled. How very typical of Buddhists' openness about their religion to allow me, an unbeliever, to approach and sit in front of their holiest shrine. How unlike other religions, such as Islam, which strictly prohibits unbelievers, under pain of death, even to be in their holy city of Mecca.

The monk explained how, during the Cultural Revolution when the Chinese Red Guards had been rampaging through the temple, a few brave monks managed to hide the Jowo, thus saving it from destruction. He told me that another holy statue, the Akshobhya Varja, a representation of Shakyamuni at the age of eight, and brought 1,300 years ago to Tibet by the Nepalese wife of King Songtsen Gampo, and now in the Ramoche temple, had not been so lucky. As the statue was of enormous weight, the Chinese cut it in half, removed the torso to Beijing where it remained discarded as rubbish in a junk-yard in the suburbs until its almost miraculous recovery.

He told me about Renbuk Tulku, a Tibetan monk whom I later met in Dharamsala in India. He had been in charge of the Ramoche chapel when the Chinese soldiers attacked it. Renbuk Tulku, now a very old man, had made it his life's work to track down the statue. No mean feat in a country where the practice of religion was forbidden, and anything to do with it denigrated – and punished – as counter-revolutionary. Renbuk sent a petition to the late Panchen Lama (the second highest cleric in the Tibetan hierarchy after the Dalai Lama) who lived in Beijing, to persuade the Chinese authorities to allow him to search for the Jowo. As the Panchen Lama was then temporarily in the good graces of the Chinese, he was given permission, and after years of searching, Renbuk Tulku finally found the Jowo derelict and in atrocious condition in the middle of a junk-yard in the suburbs of Beijing, without its original diadem and necklaces of gold, coral, turquoise and precious stones.

After much laborious restoration, the statue was jubilantly returned to Lhasa. It was soldered to its bottom half and today it is to be seen, behind an iron grille, at the Ramoche temple in Lhasa. The Ramoche was very badly damaged during the Cultural Revolution when it became a 'temple' to Mao Tse-tung and the ancient altars (seventh-century) were decked with enormous pictures and statues of Mao. The damage was so extensive that it was closed until 1985. There is massive restoration still to be done and only a few of the chapels are open to the public. As one monk said sadly to me: 'We can repair the buildings, plaster the cracks, even build new statues. But how do you rebuild a shattered heritage that took nearly two thousand years to create?'

The pilgrim monk took me up a back staircase to the roof of the Jokhang. It was a golden wonderland of gracefully curved and gilded roofs, decorated with lotus spires, garuda-like mythical bird-humans (*Ja-shang-shang*), wonderfully carved dragons with cheeky faces and their tails curled upwards into the still amazingly blue sky. The sheer exuberance of the sculpture was exhilarating. Standing on the roof, with the Potala shimmering in the heat haze against the western mountains and a panoramic view over the roof-tops of Lhasa to the bowl of mountains cradling the valley, thousands of images presented themselves everywhere I turned – almost begging to be photographed and filmed. I quickly scribbled notes for Seán and thought that this part of the filming at least would be enjoyable.

The monk pointed out three stone columns that were almost completely surrounded by a whitewashed wall, so that at ground-level you could not see them. In fact I had walked right past. He pointed to one in particular: 'That's the Tsuglakhang Doke, an important witness in proving Tibet's claim to independence.' It had been erected in 823 A.D. to commemorate the treaty that ended hostilities between China and Tibet in 821. It is one of three identical pillars – the second was erected outside the Chinese

Emperor's palace in Ch'ang-an (modern-day Xian) but has since been destroyed and the third was on the borders of Tibet and China at Gugu Meru in present-day Amdo – bearing an inscription in Tibetan and Chinese, to record the agreement between the Tibetan King, Tri Ralpachen, and the Chinese Emperor, Wen Wu Hsiao-ten Wang-ti. It is very obviously a treaty between equals, and not as the Chinese would have it, between sovereign and vassal.

The monk pointed to the east side of the pillar and told me that it contained the Tibetan King's summary of the relationship between Tibet and China at the time. On the north side the names of the seventeen Tibetan officials who had officiated were inscribed. And the names of the eighteen Chinese officials who had participated were carved on the south face. On the west face was engraved the text reaffirming the boundaries of Tibet and China as established by the 783 A.D. treaty of Ch'ing-shui: 'Tibet and China shall abide by the frontiers of which they are now in occupation. All to the east [from the stele in Gugu Meru in eastern Amdo] is the country of Great China; and all to the west [of Gugu Meru] is, without question, the country of Great Tibet. Henceforth on neither side shall there be waging of war nor seizing of territory. If any person incurs suspicion, he shall be arrested; his business shall be enquired into and he shall be escorted back.' The Chinese had bricked up access to the historic pillar . . .

As I looked into the plaza in front of the Jokhang, I immediately saw why the Chinese had bulldozed the old Tibetan houses that had been in front. From their observation points in the PSB buildings at the side of the Jokhang and from the tall buildings at the end of the square, the Chinese had an unobstructed view of the Jokhang. It was also a perfect avenue to deploy rapidly a phalanx of troops and position artillery against the Jokhang. And, as the monk pointed out, the tops of the high Chinese building opposite the Jokhang were perfect positions for Chinese army snipers and a regular site from which the PSB frequently set up their cameras to photograph Tibetans.

As I looked to the left of the Potala, and directly opposite the Jokhang, was one of the sacred hills of Tibet, the Chakpori, where, until the Chinese destroyed it, had stood an ancient monastery of Bedroya Drofan Tana Noe-tsar Rigje Ling as well as Tibet's historic and world-famous school of Tibetan medicine. It had been destroyed, along with all its precious records, in the terror of the Cultural Revolution. And under its truncated top the Chinese had built a military prison with a notorious reputation for torturing 'counter-revolutionary Tibetans'. On the top, a powerful Chinese radio transmitter shot into the sky. Like the Potala, it was visible from all over Lhasa – an unsubtle and effective reminder of Chinese occupation over Tibet, 'the land of the gods'.

As we walked under the carved and gaily painted lintels of the roofs, the monk pointed out the places below in the courtyard, and on the roof, where the Chinese soldiers on 5 March 1988 had chased the monks and brutally clubbed them. Tibetans claim they have proof of eighteen killed and a further 216 imprisoned by the Chinese for daring to hold a peaceful demonstration asking for the release of one of the monks who only a few months earlier had demonstrated peacefully in the square below. Of course there had been no evidence of the deaths at the hands of the Chinese army, because, Tibetans allege, the bodies were removed at night – as we saw once again in the Beijing riots in June 1989, when the Chinese army removed at night the bodies of the Chinese civilians killed in the carnage.

In fact, until last May when film secretly shot of the Chinese soldiers chasing and brutally beating the monks was shown on British television in spring 1989, the outside world refused to believe the Tibetans, let alone condemn the Chinese army for their brutal attacks on Tibetan monks and civilians. It was only when the Chinese tanks attacked Chinese civilians in Beijing last year that the world, confronted with nightly news coverage of the atrocities, finally condemned China. But for years, the monk told me, Tibetans have suffered atrociously at the hands of the Chinese military and the world has refused even to listen.

We kept walking and talking quietly so as not to be overheard because, the monk told me, although the outside world did not believe the efficiency and brutality of the Chinese security services and the army, I could only underestimate them to my peril.

It was nearly eight, and they were closing the Jokhang; so we both walked down to the entrance. Outside I could not understand why the sun was still so high in the sky. The monk told me that all China's satellite territories, however far away, had to keep the same time as Beijing, 2,570 miles and three time zones away. It was part of being one with the 'motherland'! But geographically, we were on the longitude of Katmandu and it was 5 P.M. However, it did mean that Seán would be able to film with good light until past 10 P.M. – Beijing time!

I returned to the hotel to discuss with Seán how we were going to find Chuma and Giant, and how we were to make headway with the remnants of our filming plans. As we had booked and paid for a tour of Lhasa, we decided to go along since private transport was almost non-existent. We had to film all our external visuals now, because after we went 'undercover' we would have no idea if or when we would return to Lhasa. So following the old film maxim of always taking the opportunity to film when it presents itself, Seán and I went through the motions of being bona fide tourists while our Chinese guide took us to the usual Lhasan landmarks.

But even during the tour, while being driven from one place to another, we sat on opposite sides of the bus searching the streets for a glimpse of Chuma or Giant. It was a virtually impossible task since, naturally, I was allowed to know only the minimum about the Tibetan underground and so did not know where to locate them. The only effective link with the network was the laborious procedure of trying to telephone my London contact who then phoned contacts in the Far East asking them, somehow, to arrange alternative contacts and interpreters in Lhasa. But trying to place long-distance calls from Lhasa was a worse nightmare than in China. So, although I was experiencing a dream come true in visiting some of the most fabulous sights on earth, we were *still* in the middle of Tibet without an interpreter, without any contacts and without a single foot of relevant film having been shot. We were already nearly three weeks behind schedule and I was soon approaching my fail-safe date when not even tolerant David Lloyd back in London could sanction any more time or money.

6

Sabotage in Shangri-La?

Normally before filming, the director has the opportunity to recce the location first to see what he or she wants visually out of the scene, to decide on the angles, to experiment with light, and to plan the sequences so that the cameraman can be told what is needed for the scene and also be asked for his suggestions. But obviously that was a luxury I was to be denied. Neither Seán nor I was able to see a single location in advance of shooting. It was rather like going into a fire-fight in Vietnam or Beirut, when all the flak is flying so ferociously around that you shoot wild, catching what you can when you can, as in 'once only' locations there are no retakes. It was not an ideal way to make a feature documentary, especially one with the incredibly exotic visual potential of Tibet.

Under normal circumstances, a camera assistant would have idented each 'set-up' on a slate to record different aspects of the location. This is vital when editing hours of material back at base: after weeks on location and recording scenes with similar detail, it would be impossible to decipher which bit went where. But we did not have a production assistant, nor was it prudent to use a clapper-board on which normally the slate and take numbers are recorded. That would certainly have betrayed our ostensibly 'non-professional' status. So to begin with, Seán electronically put the date, slate and take-number location onto the tape before we started the day. He tried to change the slate and take details on the way between one chapel and another, but that proved too fiddly and time-consuming, so I surreptitiously scribbled the slate and take numbers on a piece of paper and let Seán shoot it as we dodged behind a pillar out of sight of the tourists and other unseen prying eyes.

We could not appear to be in any way professional, for if the Chinese became suspicious we would have been accompanied every minute of the day by a Chinese Government supervisor who would have had total control over what we were and were not allowed to film. In any dispute or doubt, the authorities would, as they had in the past, destroy our film and if necessary our equipment.

It was also impossible for me to look through the view-finder, as every director normally does, to see the framing of the shot that Seán had lined up. So although we discussed the shot briefly while pretending to listen to the guide, I had to guess where the beginning and end of his pans were and hope that he had managed to capture the detail I had earlier explained. In the end we developed a system of actually communicating with each other without words. Just a shift of the eyes or an inclination of the head. We must have made a peculiar pair. I read the query in the guide's eyes. We had separate rooms, but seemed to be inseparable, yet without any of the tenderness that is associated with a 'couple'. The guide – and many members of our tour group – could not make us out. Were we an 'item' – or what?

The Sony camera, slung nonchalantly over Seán's shoulder, looked sufficiently amateur not to arouse suspicions. But the tripod, although one of the smallest that we could buy, proved a problem. The tripod was vital to align the horizon of each shot correctly in the view-finder, because the human eye is not always the most accurate judge, and the spirit-level on the tripod head is infallible, especially at taking long shots and pans and zooms which require steady, smooth camera-operations and could not be hand-held. If the camera was hand-held during interviews, it would be very distracting for the viewer, as the interviewee would wobble in the picture-frame every time the cameraman breathed or got cramp. Likewise it would be totally distracting if the interviewee looked seated at an angle of forty-five degrees across the screen. Since none of the other tourists sported a tripod, ours provoked a few comments, but Seán was laconically convincing: 'Well, you know,' he would say, in his soft Texan drawl, 'it's not every day that you come to Tibet. And we want to show the folks back home . . .' He would smile his most disarmingly innocent smile . . . And it worked!

We bundled into the smart new minibus and drove along the main avenue, past the Tibetan quarter to the Potala. At its base the dignified old west gate to Lhasa, set in a picturesque white chorten-type gate-house that I had seen in early pictures, was no longer there. Instead the Chinese had bulldozed the ancient monument and pushed through a modern road to the western – and totally Chinese – part of Lhasa. I looked up to Chakpori Hill where a riot of colourful prayer-flags draped over the road connecting the two hills was the only overt sign of Tibetan identity.

Gone too was the garden at the base of the Potala where Heinrich Harrer, the Austrian author of the classic *Seven Years in Tibet*, used to pick wild asparagus with the Nepalese Ambassador before the Chinese invasion. Now a rash of scruffy little shops bordered one side of the street. While on the other, under an enormous Chinese poster, with large Chinese ideograms, was a row of photographic kiosks where a variety of backcloths of badly painted scenes depicting the Potala and the Norbulingka, the Dalai Lama's summer palace, had been strung up. And in front of them, at all hours of the day, fresh-faced young Chinese soldiers posed proudly for snapshots to send home to China. They looked too young and innocent to realize the irony of the gesture.

It proved to be a very tiring day. I had slept badly, waking several times with excruciating altitude headaches. Numerous glasses of water, which old Lhasa hands had told me should help combat the dehydration of the bone-dry atmosphere that exacerbates the effect of altitude, were not much use. Seán looked almost green as he staggered into the bus. Ideally, we should have given ourselves at least two days to acclimatize, to allow the blood to adjust to the thin, oxygen-depleted air; but we were locked into a grinding sightseeing schedule which that afternoon included climbing – on foot – 2,000 feet to see Ganden monastery floating majestically in the clouds at 16,000 feet!

Mercifully that morning we went by bus up the steep new road at the back of the Potala. Later in the week, having opted out of the 'tour' itinerary, and humping the camera gear, batteries and spare parts, we climbed the gigantic steep steps up the front to the White Palace entrance from the base of the Potala. As Seán remarked several times when we paused for breath: 'These Tibetans have got to be a super-race just to cope with these steps, let alone the mountains – and the altitude!' It was only when we got to the top and we looked out over the valley that the Sinofication of Lhasa finally hit me. From the base of the Potala, strung all along the Kyichu valley's green floor, as far as the eye could see, right to the edge of the arid brown mountains bordering the wide valley, was a sea of ugly concrete Chinese buildings with glinting tin roofs. There is absolutely no way that anyone who has been to Lhasa can possibly concur with the Chinese authorities who categorically, and *ad nauseam*, insist that there is 'not much of a Chinese presence in Lhasa'. The evidence was there in front of me that despite all Chinese denials Lhasa is today unequivocally an 80 per cent Chinese city.

The Chinese housing was smeared with a pall of thin grey smoke and in the mid-distance I saw the chimney-stack of a Chinese cement factory belching thick grey smoke into what had been, until thirty years ago, pure crystalline mountain air. How long will it be before the Chinese, with their apparent disregard for the environment – as I had already seen from the pollution in China's own cities, from Guangzhou to Lanchow – finally destroy the fragile ecology of Tibet?

The guide hurried us along as we climbed into the Deyangshar – the East Inner Courtyard of the Potala where once the fabulous Black Hat dancers (*Shanak*) performed for the Dalai Lama, his tutors and officials, on special feast days. I looked up at the towering five-storeyed *Shargyu-Simchung* – the Eastern Palace building, where once under the fluttering canopies the Dalai Lama and the nobles and the Cabinet had sat in the various balconied windows in a rainbow of gorgeous brocades. That day, however, and whenever we returned to the Potala, the courtyard was drab with the blue and green uniform Mao suits of the Chinese.

We climbed the steep steps into the *Photrang Karpo* (White Palace) past dark, mysteriously shuttered doors. Although part of the Potala was saved during the Cultural Revolution by a specific order from Chou En-lai, who ordered the PLA to curb some of the worst excesses of the rampaging Red Guards inside, it was badly damaged and sacked and many of the treasures were taken to China for sale abroad. That is why today the White Palace is shut to tourists and only a fraction of the hundreds of rooms of the Potala are open for public viewing. Eventually we found ourselves in the Red Palace and were rushed through rooms and chapels of enormous antiquity, full of the most marvellous artistic treasures, but which we were given no time to digest. With the result that we saw a great deal and understood very little.

I had thought that I would be able to buy guide books and tourist literature in China, and certainly in Tibet. But there was not a single book or pamphlet on Tibet available in any of the Chinese cities I visited, and absolutely nothing actually inside Tibet. Not even the road map that most hotels put in with the stationery pack in your room to help you orientate yourself. It seems that once in Tibet the Chinese authorities want the tourist to be totally dependent on them for transport and information or, as Seán quipped, disinformation. And sadly most tourists only learned about Tibet from the grossly distorted facts provided by the Chinese guides.

Indeed, there were no English or foreign-language newspapers or periodicals available. Unlike other cities, where if you cannot find your own accustomed newspaper, in your own language, you can at least find *The International Herald Tribune*, *Time* and *Newsweek* magazines, in Tibet there was nothing available, not even the *Far East Economic Review* which you find all over the Far East.

Filming or even taking still photographs proved an expensive obstacle-course in Tibet. The Chinese insist that each time you click a camera shutter you pay an exorbitant fee. And in many rooms photography was forbidden. So Seán and I began an elaborate game of dodging the Chinese monitors. The monks were marvellously cheerful collaborators who seemed thoroughly to enjoy hoodwinking the Chinese. So while we filmed, one held the light for us, or got a ladder, while another couple kept an eye on the doors to watch for the Chinese. They did everything to help us. We returned several times, without the Chinese guide, to attempt to do justice to the unbelievable intricacies of the best of Tibetan religious art. But without proper lighting equipment (we had not dared include it, as it would certainly have belied our tourist status) — our scope, with our elementary camera lenses, was very limited. Anyway, some of the chambers were so vast that you would need a battery of generators to bring out the minute details of richly decorated statues and frescos.

That first morning we eventually gave the guide the slip and became totally immersed in the visual extravaganza of what must be one of the most extraordinary buildings in the world. We wandered through a labyrinth of dark passageways of Byzantine complexity that led us from one spectacular chamber to another. It had been the home, work-place and seat of government for centuries for the Dalai Lamas, and the chapels built by the various Dalai Lamas to their favourite deities were endless. Much of the specific detail blurred into a cosmic mosaic of exquisitely carved images, covered with gold, studded with coral, pearls and turquoise and draped in sumptuous silk brocade of every colour of the rainbow.

The rooms, often several storeys high, were of wood polished to a satin finish and hung, sometimes from floor to ceiling, with the cylindrical banners of appliquéd brocade that I had first seen in the Jokhang. Every capital of every pillar, and even the ends of the ceiling rafters, were covered with delicately executed patterns in colours that had retained their natural brilliance, not only because of the dry, preservative atmosphere, but also because of the excellent quality of natural pigments used and meticulous application by master craftsmen. What we were in fact looking at in the Potala was a show-case of the best in Tibetan art for 1,300 years.

There were chapels to all the manifestations of the Buddha, to the fierce protector-deities of Tibet, the Tantric deities, the early religious Kings of Tibet, Songtsen Gampo, the great Indian sages, Atisha and Padmasambhava, and to Tsongkhapa, the austere monk who, in 1409, reformed existing Buddhism and founded the Gelupa (the Yellow Hat) order to which the Dalai Lama belongs. And everywhere, as in the Jokhang, I saw small coloured photographs of the Dalai Lama and one or two of the Panchen Lama placed prominently in front of the statues. Often draped with a respectful white *kata*, and sometimes with butter-lamps in front of them, they were brave reminders of the faith that the Chinese have not managed to exterminate – and courageous gestures, in view of the fact that only ten years before such acts would have earned severe punishment at the hands of the Red Guards. Not that the danger was over; my Tibetan friends constantly reminded me, 'We have a saying in Tibet, "*Namshi takstu gur do-gi-ri*," which means the wind can change any day.' And the pogroms of the Cultural Revolution could once again return to decimate Tibet.

The most spectacular chamber was the chapel of the Dalai Lamas' tombs. Embalmed in salt and sitting upright, the remains were then entombed in elaborate chorten-shaped sarcophagi covered with gold and precious stones, with every inch covered with small, elaborately worked niches of gilded statues and running the whole length of the vast room. In front of the tombs was a battery of flickering butter-lamps. But unlike the Jokhang, nowhere in the Potala did I hear that evocative ebb and flow of Tibetans murmuring their mantras.

The most awesome tomb was undoubtedly that of Ngawang Lozang Gyatso, the 5th Dalai Lama (1617–82), which contained a reputed ton of gold in its decoration, and stretched from the floor through a full three storeys until its upper spire was lost in the darkness of the roof. Instead of imparting fascinating detail about the 5th Dalai Lama, who was as great a ruler and visionary as Peter the Great of Russia and as great a patron of art as Lorenzo de Medici of Florence, and instead of drawing attention to the carving on the silver butter-lamps that would not have disgraced Benvenuto Cellini's signature, all that the Chinese guide could talk about was the 'obscene' wastage of gold in the stupa!

And everywhere in the Potala, hanging from the high rafters and strung along the walls, were ancient *thankas*. In Tibet *thanka* painting is an ancient and highly developed art form of great intricate beauty; the subtle use of colours reminded me of the chiaroscuro of Rembrandt. Painted on cloth and framed in antique brocades, they glow with soft, burnished colours. Yet curiously, despite the monks, the incense and the flickering butter-lamps, I could feel no soul in all that awe-inspiring grandeur. Even in the Dalai Lama's private rooms at the top of the Potala, I felt I was in a museum. I watched Tibetan pilgrims reverentially touch the objects that had once been used by their beloved *Kundun* and for a fleeting moment draw comfort from being near the objects used by the 'centre of their veneration'.

But as I followed them and wandered through the Dalai Lama's chapel, meditation room, audience room and even his bedroom, I could not feel the essence of the man, the simple monk whom I had first met fifteen years ago in Dharamsala. I looked out of the same window as he had as a boy. I remembered him telling me that one early summer evening, in the middle of his studies, he had heard the songs and laughter of some Lhasan children, hundreds of feet below the walls of the Potala, on their way home with their sheep. The Dalai Lama recalled how that evening in Lhasa he had dearly wished that he could join them and be like other children instead of pursuing his lonely predestined path. Now I was in his rooms, looking at the same frescos and *thankas* that for years had been his companions, but still I could not feel the sense of the extraordinary man I had grown to respect as the most compassionate person I had ever met. It was only when I was actually walking round his apartments in his summer palace – the Norbulingka, or 'Jewel Park' – that I tangibly felt his presence. I could almost see him, a simple monk in his patched maroon robe, tending his garden of flowers. The Norbulingka, which is only about one mile from the Potala, and not far from the present Holiday Inn, was the summer retreat of the Dalai Lamas and was started by the 7th Dalai Lama in 1750. Unlike the intimidating splendour of the Potala, the Norbulingka is a series of low, simple pavilions, built over the years by successive Dalai Lamas, and set in gardens of trees and shrubs with a profusion of every conceivable flower. It was very badly damaged by heavy Chinese artillery barrage during the Lhasa Uprising against the Chinese on 17 and 19 March 1959.

That spring, thirty years ago, after ten years of Chinese occupation of Tibet, the Chinese were losing patience with the obdurate Tibetans who refused voluntarily to surrender their independence and who kept rebelling against the restrictions imposed by the Chinese. The Chinese garrison inside Lhasa was heavily reinforced and the Chinese realized that without total – and physical – control over the Dalai Lama, they had no hope of subjugating the Tibetan population. So they tried by a series of clumsily disguised ruses to lure the Dalai Lama, alone and without any of his customary escort or bodyguards, into the Chinese military compound. The people of Lhasa thought, with very good reason, that the Chinese were about to kidnap the Dalai Lama. After years of Chinese repression, famine and suffering, it was the spark that ignited years of Tibetan resentment, and they rioted in protest against the Chinese.

In the dead of night, in his bedroom in the Norbulingka, on 17 March 1959, the Dalai Lama for the first time in his life took off his monastic clothes, put on a layman's *chuba*, and with a few faithful followers escaped by the back garden-gate into the freezing moonless night. With a small band of followers, he travelled on horseback, pursued by Chinese patrols and spotter planes, over the high Himalayas to exile in India.

Today, a traditionally tiled and painted ornamental gateway, set in a high wall and flanked by two newly painted Snow Lions, leads to the Norbulingka through an expanse of sombre green trees and lawns where several pavilions are set within the high-walled enclosure. But today there is a lifeless quality to the park. A sort of suspended animation hangs heavily over the green oasis set like a cluster of emeralds against the bleak brown mountains, and not even the birds sing.

Down the path from the gateway, bordered by willow trees and beds of enormous dahlias, is the 14th Dalai Lama's palace. A modest two-storeyed pavilion, it is more like a large suburban bungalow than the summer residence of the spiritual and temporal ruler of Tibet. An unpretentious white villa with windows and eaves painted in yellow (in honour of the colour of the Buddha's robe) with typical Tibetan patterns, a curving gilded roof with the wheel of dharma and two fawns on the top, it is charmingly framed by an arch of pink rambling roses. We walked through the garden filled with phlox, roses, asters, hollyhock and giant dahlias and followed Tibetan pilgrims into the building, which was completed in 1956.

On the ground floor the large and airy antechambers were unspectacular, rather like the rooms in a comfortable Indian bungalow built during the time of the Raj. The Dalai Lama's small audience chamber, with none of the pomp of the Potala, had a few statues and a wonderful frieze painted in green and gold around the walls. The tiny figures gave an illustrated and detailed history of Tibet from its mythical beginnings, through 2,067 years of history to the entry of the 14th Dalai Lama into Lhasa in 1939.

But it was in the Dalai Lama's personal rooms that I again felt the simplicity of the man, one of whose great pleasures, he had told me, was growing flowers, especially tulips and delphiniums, which now in exile he cultivates in his modest Himalayan garden in northern India. His tiny bedroom in the Norbulingka is the essence of unworldliness with a small pale wood art-deco-style bed that came from India. There is only a small nondescript bedside table, a wooden chair, a fifties Philips radiogram and tape-recorder given to him by Nehru, and a simple beige rug on a wooden floor.

And against one wall is a small altar with some beautiful images of the Shakyamuni Buddha, Manjushri (the wisdom Buddha) and a few other ancient images encased in simple gold and silver filigree frames. Looking out of his window, which gives on to the gardens and the mountains beyond which were blue in the afternoon heat haze, I could well understand how, in this modest house that he partly designed, he had found an enormous peace.

He once said to me: 'I am what I have always been, a simple monk. It doesn't matter to me whether I live in a palace or in a mud hut; I don't need much.' He went on to tell me that the early hours of dawn were his favourite time of day. 'It is very special to me,' he said, and told me how in India he goes into the garden, looks at the sky and listens to the birds, as he did when he was in the Norbulingka.

Lulled by the serenity of the warm sunny gardens, Seán and I wandered round the park and came to the pavilion of a previous Dalai Lama. While Seán was trying to film the dark interior, my curiosity was aroused by a large area of the courtyard screened off with high white cotton sheeting. When no one was looking, I slipped round a corner and ripped a seam of the covering. In the enclosure, about 40-feet long by 15-feet wide, was piled a confusion of gold and silver statues and religious ornaments. All were in a terrible condition. Some of the statues had been decapitated, some had limbs missing and not one had the usual diadems, halos and necklaces heavily encrusted with gold and precious jewels that they invariably wear. They were in great disarray and had been thrown there carelessly, with no concern at all for their artistic worth. They were, Tibetans later told me, awaiting transportation to China, either to be smelted for bullion, or if any were in reasonable condition, they would be sold on the international art market via Hong Kong. 'And then the Chinese tell us that there were only a few excesses during the Cultural Revolution!' Seán retorted in outrage as he surreptitiously filmed through the hole I had cut.

It was not an isolated incident. A couple of mornings later, Seán and I were coming out of the Potala when just below the outer walls near the top left-hand tower, we saw a group of Tibetans furiously scrabbling around in a pile of rubbish. We asked the monk with us, who spoke a little English, what was going on and why they were so obviously agitated. The monk spoke to them and returned to take us to inspect the rubbish. He told me that they were workers, employed by the Chinese to clear the rubble of the destruction caused by the Cultural Revolution in the shuttered part of the Potala that was off-limits to tourists. Under the rubble the workers had found fragments of ancient and sacred scriptures where the gold *U-chen* lettering was still clearly discernible. 'My God,' Seán said. 'It's fourteen years since the carnage was officially declared finished! And they are still finding wreckage!' He picked up the camera and began to record the evidence.

Despite what I had read about the destruction wrought in Tibet by the Chinese, especially during the Cultural Revolution, it was invariably an unpleasant shock to be confronted with the evidence of their brutality. We also went to Drepung monastery, which was built in 1416 by Jamyang Choje, a disciple of Tsongkhapa. Once the largest monastic complex in the world, housing over 10,000 monks before the Chinese invasion, it was a monastic university and a famous centre of Buddhist learning to which scholars from all of Asia came to study. Together with Sera and Ganden monasteries, also near Lhasa, it was known as *Densa* – the three pillars of Wisdom. As we drove up the tarmac airport road, Drepung did indeed look like its Tibetan name, which translated means a heap of rice. The white buildings of the monastery were scattered against the stark brown mountainside that rose behind it.

We drove off the tarmac road and up a steep, dusty, winding track through neglected orchards where peach, apricot and apple trees were just discernible through the tangled growth. The impressive monastery looked superficially undamaged under the fresh coat of white paint on its imposing façade, but after we eluded our guide and went exploring on our own, we found that the whitewash was an effective cosmetic disguise.

While the few halls and chapels that were open to the public were relatively unharmed, once away from the brilliant façade, and secreted behind the seemingly functional exteriors where the tourists are not taken or are too tired to climb the steep paths to explore, we discovered another Drepung: a world of shattered cloisters, of windows that from afar look inhabited, but on close inspection were found to be bricked-up and barred with wooden stakes. We slipped into deserted cloisters where the only sign of life was the faint breeze shifting the tumble-weed desultorily from one end of an earthen yard to another. Many bricked-up doors and windows showed the charred stains of fire damage.

That sultry afternoon as we climbed along the steep, picturesque, cobbled alleys lined with whitewashed Tibetan-styled cloisters and colleges, there was an unnatural silence broken only by the shouts of the tourists calling to one another. The Chinese say that there are 350 monks in Drepung today (before the invasion there were 10,000) and that the monastery is functioning normally. But although we did see a few monks hurrying along in the familiar maroon robes, sadly there seemed to be more dogs sunning themselves lazily in the sun than human inhabitants in that beautiful, and poignant, living necropolis.

Next day I sat on the mountain high behind Sera monastery (built in 1419 by Jamchen Choeje) while Seán was filming the fabulous rock paintings of the *Vajrapani*, a fierce protector-deity of Tibet, who stood on a yellow sun-disc with a thunderbolt in his hand surrounded by a fury of blue flames. I wondered, with some melancholy, where the protector had been on the morning of 16 March 1959 when the Chinese tanks came up the road from Lhasa with their machine-guns and cannon trained on the unarmed monastery.

Later, as I sat with Lobsang, a monk from Sera, high above the monastery, not far from the hermitages carved at a perilous angle into the living rock, and as we looked down on the gilded curving roofs of Sera, Lobsang pointed out vast areas of destruction of the monastery buildings that were not visible from the tourist trail at the front of the monastery complex. Lobsang told me how a little while before the Chinese onslaught, the abbot of Sera, hearing rumours that all the monasteries were to be attacked, had called a meeting of all the 5,500 monks in the congregation and asked for volunteers to go to the Potala armoury and get some weapons. It was a heavy sacrifice because Buddhist monks are forbidden by their vows even to carry arms and to volunteer meant the renunciation of their vows and their lives as monks. Finally, only Lobsang and three others agreed.

They made their way secretly to the Potala, broke into the armoury only to find, when confronted with the weapons, that they did not know how to use the guns! While they were trying to get to grips with the firing mechanisms, the Chinese on the Chakpori hill opposite started firing on the Potala. At the same time tanks rolled up from the direction of the Barkhor with their cannon trained on the Potala, and another Chinese artillery battalion started shelling the Potala from across the Kyichu river. With shells exploding all round them and in shock at the sacrilege of their sacred places being attacked, they grabbed 'the English guns', fired wildly on the Chakpori position and ran down to try and stop the tanks. Lobsang told me how, almost demented with anxiety that the tanks would fire on the symbol of Tibet's spiritual and temporal power-house, he had run in front of the leading tank pointing a small pistol at it to stop. But I did not fully realize the incredible bravery of that heroic gesture until a year later, on 5 June 1989 when I saw, as did millions of others, the television pictures of that single brave Chinese standing and halting the tanks in Changan Avenue. Like many of the Chinese students in Beijing last year, Lobsang was arrested, tortured and imprisoned for over twenty-two years. He was later to tell me, on camera, in horrific detail, what he had suffered.

On our fourth day in Lhasa there was still no sign of Chuma and Giant. Seán and I had been deliberately unsubtle by hiring a cycle rickshaw to take us everywhere. We reasoned, in our growing desperation, that by sitting very conspicuously in the open rickshaw we might see the two – or be seen. Giving up on the hotel's cold noodle diet, we even took to having a snack at the Barkhor café overlooking the Jokhang square, and scrutinized the square below. But not with much success.

On the last day, while Seán was having a shouting match with CITS who had overcharged us by 1,500 FEC and were refusing to refund the money, I was promenading in the rickshaw, when near the prayer-flags under the Chakpori hill I saw Giant cycling past. Without waiting for the rickshaw to stop, I jumped out, nearly knocked him off his bike and excitedly started talking in English until I quickly remembered he did not speak one word of the language!

Giant was visibly nervous as I scribbled a note for Chuma telling him to meet me at the hotel at six that evening. Unfortunately, I was delayed collecting our tickets and got back late to the hotel. Seán was waiting in my room, and during our walk round the hotel flower-bed, he told me that Chuma had indeed turned up, but that he was frightened witless and had, again, used the now familiar words, 'It's too dangerous' to be in Lhasa. He had agreed to meet me the next day in a nearby monastery and had especially asked Seán to tell me to make certain that I was not followed.

The next day, our last in Lhasa, we decided that if anyone was following us it would be wiser if we split up to throw them temporarily off the scent. So while we were filming in the street, I jumped into a passing rickshaw, and went to within a mile of the monastery and climbed the rest of the way. Chuma had said that I would be recognized and I was to follow the man who would bring me to him. As I had no idea whom I was supposed to be looking for, I strolled through the gate, and sat under some trees admiring the light and wishing I was anywhere away from Tibet and the alarums and excursions of what had become a trail of mishaps and inaction.

Tibetans walked slowly up the path telling their beads and murmuring their mantras. One passed close to me and, as he passed, he held in his hand a small passport-size photograph of me that had been sent months ago to various members of the underground in Tibet. I slowly got up, dusted my jeans, and followed the man at a distance through a maze of alleys. After half an hour of meandering, during which time I lost all sense of direction, he disappeared through a dark doorway. Hesitantly I followed, and after the brilliant sunshine outside found myself in total darkness. I almost panicked. I stood still, listening to the blood pounding in my ears, straining for the smallest sound and wondering if I had walked into a Chinese trap.

After what seemed an age, when I was completely disorientated by the musky-smelling darkness, I heard a faint noise above and a trapdoor creaked open half an inch letting in a shaft of light. I looked round. I was on the ground floor of a crude, mud-and-wattle, three-storeyed building. I grabbed the smooth pole that served as a handrail and hauled myself up the rickety steps towards the light. As I neared the top, the trapdoor opened quickly, a hand hauled me into the blinding sunlight, pushed me towards a door and I heard the trapdoor slam shut as other hands pulled me into a cool room.

As my eyes got accustomed to the diffused light from the window, I saw I was in a small room with a wooden floor, containing two low bed-benches with colourful Tibetan rugs on which three thin monks and four ordinary Tibetans sat smiling at me. In another corner was a wooden cabinet containing cloth-bound, oblong Buddhist scriptures and on the top were two pictures of Tibetan deities with the customary seven offertory bowls of clear water in front. I was in a monk's cell in a monastery.

I looked round and saw Chuma. I was too relieved for recrimi-nations and we plunged into discussing the trip. He introduced me to Tenzin, a tall Khampa with a deep scar that ran from his left eye to half-way down his cheek, who was the leader for the Lhasa–Batang sector. I told Chuma that I had to leave Tibet to meet our contacts outside, to tell them to send word to the interviewees that I was behind schedule. What I did not tell him was that after his dismal performance in Lanchow and Chengdu, I was going to get another interpreter as my confidence in him was nil.

We agreed to meet that evening with Seán to replot our itinerary and work out timings and transport details. To avoid arousing suspicion on our return to China and subsequently to Lhasa, which this time would be by plane from a foreign airport, where the customs would probably be more thorough in their examin-ation of our baggage, we agreed that I would leave the majority of our equipment outside the Kirey Hotel at six sharp. Chuma told me that it would be collected and kept till our return and that we should then follow Giant to the Pelden monastery where he and the team would be waiting for us.

Seán was not feeling well, so I turned up with the luggage at the Kirey at 5.45. I left the anonymous bulky black bags with most of our equipment, food and medicine outside the main gate and sat on a stone as though waiting for someone. The street was full of Chinese but few Tibetans. After ten anxious minutes I saw Giant get off his cycle and go into a small Tibetan café across the road. Knowing that our people should have been in place by then, I carried the bags to the edge of the road. With my heart in my mouth, I turned my back on the equipment, walked into the Kirey cafeteria and ordered a coke. By the time I got back the bags had gone and I panicked briefly wondering whether 'our boys' had got them or they had been picked up by the Chinese. As I sat sipping my coke and trying to appear calm and collected, Giant walked past. He threw a small crumpled piece of paper into the dust, walked on and disappeared round the corner.

I stood up, stretched, covered the paper with my foot, dropped my coke can and bent to retrieve the paper and the can. I wandered slowly round the back of the building, nervously unscrewed the scrap of paper and read Chuma's message scrawled in pencil: 'Go away and come back in ten days. Stay in Yak Hotel and I will contact you. Too dangerous to meet now.'

7

Underground in Lhasa

A hand shook me gently. For that brief moment, between the oblivion of sleep and the watchful anxiety of incessantly scrutinizing every sound and speck on the horizon for approaching Chinese soldiers, I was totally disorientated. Thondup's open face was smiling as he handed me a cup of noodles and hot water through the window.

'You should eat something,' he said solicitously. 'It's nearly four now and you haven't had anything since we left eleven hours ago.'

I smiled, rearranged my cramped limbs in the still perilously perched van, and looked at the interpreter silhouetted against the craggy mountains. In a few agonizing days, he had become my life-support system. It seemed as though we had been together for years battling against ridiculous odds inside Tibet. In fact, it had been only three weeks since, one steamy August afternoon, Thondup had walked into my life and saved the project.

Since leaving Lhasa, Seán and I had spent nearly three weeks criss-crossing South-East Asia looking for a volunteer interpreter who would pass Chinese scrutiny and get safely into Tibet posing as a tourist. He also had to meet fairly demanding criteria of being a fluent Tibetan and English speaker. A foreigner would be too conspicuous and there were very few who spoke Tibetan with the fluency to cope with several political interviews, nor could they possibly hope to understand the very disparate dialects of the remote provinces of Tibet that we would be passing through. The ideal would be a Tibetan with a foreign passport, and who had been resident abroad for a sufficiently long time to allay Chinese suspicions so that they would believe his excuse that he wanted to visit Tibet to see a dying relative and grant him a visa.

After weeks sitting in hot, humid 'rooms' deep in the jungle, in several South Asian countries, where the bamboos sheeted with interminable rain and everything was sticky with the damp of the south-west monsoon, one of the Tibetan underground heard of a Tibetan tourist, now resident in America, who might fit the bill.

We quickly prepared to change countries for the fourth time in two weeks.

We met Thondup in the middle of a tropical storm in yet another small damp room in the home of another Tibetan underground member. He was a tall thin man, who smiled easily. Thondup told me that he had escaped as a child from Derge in Kham in eastern Tibet. The Chinese had come to his small farming village and had arrested and executed his father, solely because he could read and write, claiming that as he was literate he must belong to the 'oppressive classes' (aristocracy). His father was not, Thondup said, an aristocrat, an intellectual or even opposed to the Chinese; he was a simple farmer who was scratching a living from the thin soil, and who had for a few years, like many Tibetans, learnt the rudiments of the Tibetan language in the local monastery, which traditionally in Tibet was the only source of education for village children in remote areas.

Such 'intellectuals' were dangerous 'counter-revolutionaries' argued the Chinese and, as a threat to the State, had to be 'eliminated'. Thondup still vividly remembers the day when, as a nine-year-old, he had been forced by the Chinese to watch the soldiers march his father, who could barely walk because of the beatings he had received while the Chinese tried to extract a confession for non-existent crimes, to the centre of the village. The Chinese made his father kneel with his hands tied behind him and shot him at point-blank range in the back of the head in front of Thondup, his brother and the whole village. And then with devastating barbarity, for which the PSB and the PLA are notorious, they asked the remaining family for the price of the bullet before they would allow them to take the body of Thondup's father for burial.

As Thondup's mother had died a few years previously in childbirth, an uncle smuggled Thondup over the Himalayas and left him with a relative in Sikkim so that at least one child might survive and grow up to have a Tibetan identity. An achievement which could not be a certainty in Tibet in the 1960s under the Red Guards, where everything Tibetan – religion, history, customs and even language – was stamped on, in a brutal attempt to eliminate all traces of Tibet's separate identity.

After years of living from hand to mouth, Thondup had got a

job as a cook with an American couple who took him to America. After six years he finally left them, married another Tibetan refugee and settled in an American coastal resort where he was employed by a hotel chain as a maintenance operator. After saving hard for eleven years, he had scraped together enough money to travel to the Far East to see relatives who had recently escaped from Tibet.

As the monsoon mist crept through the bamboo feathering over the hut, we talked late into the night explaining to Thondup the full implications of what would happen to him if we were caught. An uncomplicated man, with little formal education because of the dislocation of his earlier years in Sikkim, Thondup was enormously courageous and saw the journey as an opportunity to serve Tibet. I went over the detailed plans and explained that he must not believe everything he was told. We were there to discover the truth.

As the dawn seeped through the tropical damp and the early-morning bird chorus nearly drowned our words, I was finally convinced that Thondup would interpret honestly and correctly for me. The next hurdle was actually to get Chinese visas as I had failed hopelessly to convince the PSB officer in Lhasa to renew our existing ones. But Tsering, a resourceful member of the underground who had been in jail several times, both inside and outside Tibet, for helping Tibetan refugees, found a way round the seeming impasse. I paid over a heavy bundle of dollars and had our Chinese visas stamped into our passports in less than a day. However, when I looked at them I found that they were valid for only one month – rather than the expected three – and I knew that from the moment we left Lhasa, it would take us at least five weeks to complete the journey. Still, I thought, I'll worry about that later: the main thing was that all three of us had visas and we set about replanning the trip. We decided to do the journey backwards from the original schedule.

We would start in Lhasa, go up north to Nagchukha where the nuclear base was supposed to be. It was not ideal filming that at the beginning of our journey, as it was the most dangerous of the locations and exposed us to maximum vulnerability. I would have much rather done it last, having evacuated most of the film before, in case I got caught. Then at least the programme could have been aired while the Chinese were deciding what to do with me. But we had no option. From Nagchukha we would go east through the province of Kham, visiting all the places originally planned, to Dhartsedo on the old Tibet–China border in the east. Then, as we had received reports that in the last week the road was flooded north of Dhartsedo, the Controller of the underground decided it would be quicker to go back to Chengdu – at which both Seán and I groaned at the thought of the infuriatingly inefficient telephone service and telephonists!

The Controller routed us back into Tibet through a north-western road that would take us through Amdo to the northern Tibetan frontier town of Xining, where we should have originally started the journey. We would film all the interviews that we should have filmed first if we had followed the original plan, but of course in the reverse order. Then from Xining, the Controller warned us, we would have to make a day and night dash west and south via Golmud to Lhasa; and if we were out of time, as undoubtedly we would be, walk through the Black Route to a neighbouring country – depending which passes were free – and somehow get back to London.

The Controller sent messengers clandestinely into Tibet to alert our contacts, who were still hopefully waiting, that we were late and to give them the new dates and timings.

Seán was ill with a chest infection so I went alone to meet Tempa, a tall thin monk from Lithang, who was to be our new contact inside Lhasa. I agreed to meet him in the Jokhang at a particular chapel between eight and nine in the morning starting from 21 August. We agreed, like the previous arrangements, for each of us to wait for four days – just to give us some leeway in case either of us was delayed. Tempa was instructed to get in contact with Tenzin, the leader of the Lhasa–Batang sector, who was waiting in Lhasa with Chuma, and also to rearrange all the interviews in Lhasa.

I then met Topgyal, a businessman from Amdo, who was in charge of the Dhartsedo–Xining sector. We agreed to meet at 4 P.M. in Lhasa in the front garden of the Dalai Lama's summer home in the Norbulingka on the evening of our arrival on 20 August. Both men then disappeared to return to Lhasa by the laborious overland route.

As I was sitting at a table, sticky with humidity, outside the stifling hut with the Controller, discussing the details of the new route, I nearly choked over my *tomyam* (a traditional Thai hot and sour soup). Appearing through the mist clinging to the dripping bamboos was Dorje, the guide for the Amdo sector who Chuma had told me had 'disappeared'. I thought he was either dead or rotting in a Chinese jail after being captured on the border with Chuma on his way into Tibet to meet me in Xining weeks ago.

He looked very tired, badly sunburnt from exposure at high altitude and had lost a lot of weight. As he told us what had happened inside Tibet my alarm grew. He had gone to the border with Chuma and yes, they had been surprised by a Chinese army patrol and had run off in different directions to confuse their pursuers. They had hurriedly agreed to meet at a particular cross-roads at a specific time the next day and for three consecutive days afterwards.

Dorje told me he had waited a week for Chuma, who failed to show up at the crossroads rendezvous. He had then proceeded to the contacts *en route* to Xining where they were to have stopped while Chuma, according to the original schedule, went to fetch Seán and me in Lanchow. None of the contacts along the route had seen Chuma. Dorje arrived in Xining on 4 July, waited through our appointed rendezvous time a month ago on 15 July, waited the agreed four days more, then thinking that we had, somehow, gone on, he had travelled south alone, looking for us at all the pre-arranged places in Amdo right down to Labrang Tashikil, the great fifteenth-century monastery.

Seán's usually calm face had uncharacteristically hardened. I read his unspoken thoughts: either Chuma had lied to us earlier or Dorje was doing so now. It echoed my own rising suspicions that someone was trying to sabotage the project and prevent us from filming inside Tibet. Was someone working for the Chinese and therefore privy to our plans?

The Controller interrupted my gloomy thoughts and started drawing up a new itinerary for Dorje. With the revised schedule we agreed to meet at the white chorten in the monastery complex at Tashikil at eight o'clock on the morning of 20 September. Dorje would by then have contacted all our interviewees and rearranged all the interviews to coincide with the new dates and of course have arranged transport. It was much wiser, the Controller suggested at the beginning of the planning, to use different vehicles not only for the different sectors, but to change as often as safely possible within the sector so as to throw the Chinese – or any informers – off our trail.

Then, after we had finished our filming in Xining, Dorje was instructed to arrange transport and shepherd us back to Lhasa, and hand us over to the next sector commander for the last, and probably the most dangerous leg, of the journey – for by then we would be carrying all our exposed footage on us – out of Tibet via the Black Route.

The thorny problem was of course Chuma. Seán refused point-blank to go on the trip with Chuma as a guide. He was convinced that our first interpreter would land us in jail; even if he was not working for the Chinese, his abysmal 'delivery record' to date was a total liability to the production which by some miracle we seemed – just – to have salvaged from being aborted. We decided that the safest thing to do was for me to tell Chuma that the Controller had another assignment for him and that he was to leave Tibet immediately. The Controller made it very clear to us that under no circumstances were we to tell Chuma of our revised plans, routes or timings – just in case he was indeed working for the Chinese.

I gave Dorje another bundle of notes and he prepared to set off for Tibet by the long Black Route. Seán, Thondup and I went on another shopping spree for food and finally got ourselves to the airport for the flight to Lhasa via Katmandu.

The Everest Special should be the most spectacular flight in the world. Rather like a tantalizing strip-tease dancer, the Himalayas glided in and out of the heat haze in the distance. As the aircraft soared at 33,000 feet towards the blue-white peaks dazzlingly set in a sea of fluffy white clouds clustering round their base, my excitement rose to fever pitch. I was within touching distance of the most fabled mountains in the world. I was looking at Everest, to Tibetans *Chomolungma*, Goddess Mother of the Earth, on whose icy altar the great climbers, Mallory and Irving, had laid their lives.

I was like a child demented with ecstasy. There beneath the window I made out the mountains that for so many years as a child I had listened to my father describing. Through the blazing morning sunshine I made out the notorious Ice Fall on Everest that had taken so many lives, the infamous North Col, the immaculate final summit sending a fine spume of snow into the azure canopy that shaded into the cobalt blue of space. I made out the rugged outline of Makalu, the Dhaulagiri range in the distance, and looked for, sadly without success, my father's favourite mountain, the still enigmatic Kanchengenga, which is so sacred to the Tibetans that they will not permit climbers to desecrate the actual summit.

Seán put down the camera after the last peak disappeared south and we flew into the by now familiar Tibetan landscape of high barren mountains dotted with turquoise blue lakes and swathes of green that swept into wide sandy valleys where the mighty Brahmaputra snaked in lazy wide curves, almost playfully changing its course and leaving vast fertile sandbanks waiting for cultivation.

The service was abysmal. If ever there was an excuse for a champagne service, the Everest Special was it. Drinking ice-cold champagne at 35,000 feet is, for me, one of the pleasures of life. And I had looked forward to my last indulgence, as all foreign correspondents do, before embarking on a particularly arduous assignment. To sip champagne while watching the most unforgettable scenery in the world go past the window would have been an almost extra-terrestrial experience! Sadly, only flat Chinese cider, dry biscuits and an unripe peach were available.

We had decided that it would be more prudent if we pretended not to know Thondup and sat separately from him on the aircraft. He was sitting a couple of rows in front of me and while I was absorbed in the beauty of the carpet of mountains beneath the plane, I could not help but notice the child-like excitement on Thondup's face as we flew into Tibet. He peered intently into the deep valleys, telling me afterwards that he was looking to see if he could spot his village from the air!

Because the flight was late we finally got into Lhasa at 6 P.M., two hours later than the arranged rendezvous with the businessman from Amdo in the Norbulingka. It was full moon in Lhasa as we tried to sleep in the Yak Hotel at the edge of the Tibetan quarter which Chuma had told us to check into: 'Easier for Tibetans to get in.'

The Yak was a small, Tibetan-run hotel. There were no niceties like running water in the rooms or one's own bathroom. There was a none too private loo down the corridor and recently installed hot showers which functioned for a few hours in the morning and evening. The room was small and simply furnished with a bed, table and a bare light bulb for when the electricity was functioning. But it was clean, with a warm quilt, a flask of hot water that was filled three times a day, and a candle for the frequent power cuts. The walls were so paper-thin that you could hear the guest in the next room breathe, which meant that Seán and I could not discuss anything in our rooms. However, the spartan conditions were more than compensated for by the charming Tibetan hotel staff for whom no request or query was too much trouble.

There was no room service obviously, but the Yak restaurant next door was more than adequate. One thing distressed me greatly. For the first time in my life I saw Tibetans beg. Nowhere in exile, in India, Bhutan or Nepal, had I ever seen a Tibetan, however poor – and in India and Nepal they are pitifully poor and riddled with open TB – actually beg. But here in Lhasa, their capital, I saw many Tibetans reduced to begging. They almost shamefacedly appealed to tourists. Not in the pestering way that is endemic in the Third World, especially in India, but half-heartedly and with a marked reticence.

But what was especially painful to see were the children who came into the small Tibetan-run cafés and just looked at the food on the plates. Children in distress, of whatever colour, creed or nationality, are invariably pitiful and grab the heart-strings, however hardened one is. But I have spent too much of my life in the Third World to be duped by the professional child beggar. There is a particular whine they adopt that cautions one's heart to the presence of the professional. These Tibetan children in ragged clothes and torn canvas 'footwear' held together by bits of string were different. They were certainly not professional. Their need was real, and it was not of their own making. I discovered that the vast majority of the destitute children in Lhasa were from the distant Tibetan provinces of Kham and Amdo, east of Lhasa.

I remember the first child I met who came into the Yak restaurant in Lhasa. Nygma was a grubby, undersized nine-year-old urchin from near Riwoche in the eastern province of Kham over 400 miles away. The child's small frame was painfully thin and he walked silently between the tables, with eyes devouring the large steaming platefuls. What was particularly poignant was that this child, like dozens of similar children in Lhasa, did not put his hand out to beg. He seemed too shy even to make eye contact with the tourists. He was very obviously not a professional beggar put up by a 'control' to squeal appealingly to the tourists.

Through the interpreting waiter, I motioned the child to sit by me on the bench and pushed my plate of soup in front of him. He looked at me with unbelieving eyes and, frightened that I might change my mind, quickly drank it from the plate in noisy gulps. Despite whatever the Chinese say about the 'laziness' of Tibetans who would rather beg than work, the urgency with which that little Tibetan boy wolfed down the soup – and ate the noodles I later ordered for him – totally convinced me that the child was desperately hungry. I then asked him what was perhaps a foolish question. I asked why he was not in school . . . He shyly told me that he had never been to school, that he could not read or write, and that he had hitch-hiked to Lhasa with his ten-year-old brother to look for work so that they could eat.

Through the waiter little Nygma told me that his parents had been small farmers in Kham, but that several years before, the Chinese had taken their only field and bulldozed their adobe dwelling to gain more room for the crops; finding themselves homeless and without any means of earning their living, they tried to eke out an existence from their two yaks in the infertile highlands. Their father, Kelsang, had died from an untreated 'fever' the year before, and their mother, Chozom Pema, unable to feed her children, had told her two boys to go to the big town and find food. She had remained behind in Kham with their small sister Dolma. It was the first of many similar stories that I heard in Lhasa and throughout Tibet. What particularly moved me was that the child had not begged or even asked for anything; yet after the food, when his small stomach swelled under his torn shirt, that illiterate little boy, with the in-born courtesy of Tibetans, said 'Thu chi chay' (thank you).

Sonam, whom I later interviewed on camera, told me that begging was unknown before the Chinese came to Tibet. He explained that before the Chinese invasion, although many Tibetans were poor by modern Western standards, nevertheless there was no dire poverty in Tibet. For a tenet of Buddhism – and one well-observed in Tibet – is the injunction to look after those less fortunate than oneself. Before the Chinese invasion, no Tibetan begged, except the few mendicant monks who, as part of their religious calling, depended on the alms they received from the lay population. But after the Chinese flooded into Tibet, they systematically usurped Tibetan jobs and confiscated the best of Tibetan lands for themselves. Tibetans were reduced for the first time in their history to begging, through economic necessity.

The following morning, at 7.45, Seán and I ambled casually down to the Jokhang. I especially loved the early mornings before the doors were opened. In the pale half-light of dawn before the sun had warmed the mountains with light, I used to sit in the plaza, watching the light grow stronger behind the dark outline of the Jokhang. The whole heavy mass of the building was back-lit with that indescribable intense pale light that heralds the rising sun. I would wait in exquisite anticipation for the sun to flame the edge of the wheel of dharma like a burnished aureole, while in the forecourt a few sleepy pilgrims lit their twigs and sent the wispy white smoke in offering to the new day. Inevitably their prayers included mantras for the safety and return of the Dalai Lama.

We walked past the prostrating pilgrims, met Thondup at the heavy main door and were about to go into the first courtyard when something hard hit me on the back of the head. I jumped, swung round and in the shadow of the statues of the guardian kings of the temple, I saw the dim figure of the monk, Tempa, holding the prayer-beads he had hit me with to attract my atten-tion. He motioned us ahead of him and followed us up to the second floor of the temple. Through Thondup's translation, Tempa told us that he had waited two weeks for us from eight in the morning until the temple closed. Tempa had not received the message that the Controller had assured us he had sent, telling Tempa and the Amdo contact that we would be a week later than our scheduled arrival in Lhasa because Seán had been ill. Tempa had had the courage to wait, although by the rules he should have returned to his home in Lithang in Kham. I was so grateful that he had waited for us that I gave Thondup the money to light a butter-lamp in thanksgiving!

We arranged to meet later in the day. Seán was perturbed at the news that the Controller had failed to send the messenger, so I left him in the hotel and suggested that he shoot some visuals, while I rendezvoused with Thondup, who was to lead me through the maze of alleys in the Tibetan quarter to the safe house where we were to meet some of the interviewees. We made our way through the labyrinth of muddy, unpaved alleys of the Tibetan quarter for nearly an hour, slipping and sliding in the dark ooze of mud between the houses. The rains had been unseasonably late, and the Tibetan quarter, not having any drains or sewage facilities, had become a quagmire of stinking, insanitary slush. As we ducked through low archways into muddy courtyards that in turn led through a jumble of low stone houses in bad repair to yet another courtyard, I felt that even a snake would have broken its back trying to follow us!

Finally, we were pulled quickly out of one of the courtyards into a low doorway. Other hands hurried us into a small stark room in which Tempa was waiting with a group of Tibetans who were visibly on edge. The room, like so many other Tibetan homes I was received into, was spartan, but spotlessly clean. It was furnished with a small table and several benches, covered with small thick dual-purpose Tibetan rugs. The walls were painted in yellow with two bands in contrasting red and blue which, at waist height, ran round the entire room.

Tucked neatly under the benches were blackened pots and pans and the domestic paraphernalia of everyday living, as this tiny room was the only space for a family of six to cook, eat, sleep and wash (there were no washing facilities, running water or cupboards). The small window, looking out onto the courtyard, was the only source of light other than a kerosene pressure lamp that hung from the low ceiling. In one corner there was a makeshift altar on top of a pile of packing cases covered with a bright yellow cloth. On the top, in front of holy pictures of the deities to which the family had a special devotion, were seven metal cups offering water to the deities. The family were too poor to afford even a simple butter-lamp.

After the preliminary courtesies – Tibetans have a highly developed etiquette and even their language differs according to whom they are addressing – Tempa introduced me to the waiting

Tibetans who had all agreed to be interviewed on British television. For hours I listened to their appalling stories and then had to take a very difficult decision. As I knew that I only had a grossly inadequate forty minutes of air-time in which to document the facts, I had to select the testimony and interview only a few Tibetans. It would have been totally irresponsible to have interviewed more people than I knew it was physically possible to include in the film, because, if we were caught, it would have been criminal to carry with us the evidence of people who were not even going to appear in the film.

But how to make the selection? It was not an easy decision. Nor was it easy to explain to people, who often had travelled for several days to get to Lhasa, and who were running the ever-present risk of being caught talking to a foreign journalist, that their testimony could not be included. Even as we talked quietly in the room, friendly Tibetans were keeping watch on the roof and in the street for approaching Chinese PSB men.

I decided to interview two men and a small group of young nuns. Lobsang Norbu, a smiling ex-monk from Sera monastery, had been the insanely brave Tibetan to go down and try, on his own, to stop the tanks in front of the Potala in 1959. Sonam Tsering was a teacher from Markham, hundreds of miles away in Kham; he also had been in jail for refusing to comply with the Chinese. He was subsequently banned from teaching, as the Chinese had given him a black hat (*shamo*) which meant that he was virtually an 'untouchable', a subversive. He now made a living as a casual building labourer wherever he could find work. He was a well-educated man who burned with a passion to tell the world how Tibetans' education, culture and national identity were being systematically eroded by the Chinese. The last four were young nuns, barely out of their teens who, a few months before, had been brutally tortured by the Chinese for walking peacefully round the Jokhang in a mini-demonstration (of five nuns) asking for Tibet's independence.

As they sipped their butter-tea from small, handleless cups which the lady of the house kept filling up from a large Chinese vacuum flask, I reiterated the dangers they were facing and asked them to reconsider their decision to talk on camera. The quiet dignity with which they solemnly agreed, knowing only too well that they could easily be courting jail or worse, was an unforgettable moment. Lobsang and the nuns had a long way to travel before nightfall, so we agreed to meet in a couple of days to film their testimony.

'Listen,' Sonam said quietly. 'This is the first time a reporter from the West has come to investigate what is really happening inside Tibet beyond the confines of Lhasa. You have the responsibility to take what we are saying to the outside world. Tell them what is happening in Tibet. But first you must understand properly what it is to live like a Tibetan. But don't believe me. You can – and should – check with anyone outside in the Barkhor about the veracity of what I say. Go into the countryside, talk to people, discover for yourself, compare the facts.' He went on to explain that after 1959, even before the Cultural Revolution unleashed the Red Guards on Tibet, the Chinese had organized a highly efficient system of infiltrators that even today was extremely effective.

'The Tibetan people have been herded like animals for so long by the Chinese occupation forces that there is a general fear about speaking one's mind in public. When someone like you interviews us, there is a feeling of fear in speaking out openly. The Chinese have spies everywhere, in the monasteries among the monks, among ordinary people, office workers, in all strata of life. Even in the schools among schoolchildren! In fact it is dangerous for people to speak openly at all, about even the most innocent things that can be taken by the Chinese and twisted. There is a fear that someone might report you to the Chinese authorities and you will be arrested and tortured. It is difficult for you who live in freedom in the West to understand the extent to which this fear of informers permeates the very fabric of our lives. You have to be on your guard twenty-four hours a day.

'It started during the Cultural Revolution when the Chinese divided us into work units and we had to go to political meetings every day and criticize each other. Then their Tibetan informers would single innocent people out. There was no procedure, no real crime even. Often it was the informer taking out a personal grudge. There was no appeal. In the resulting *thumzing* [a Chinese-introduced system of forced self-criticism whereby the person was screamed at and beaten – often to unconsciousness – by the bystanders] we were kicked and tortured, sent to jail, made to work even harder with practically no food. Tens of thousands of Tibetans have died and disappeared. Sometimes the very neighbour who lived in the next room informed on you. Children had to inform on their parents. Parents had to applaud when their children were being brutally beaten. It was a "reign of terror" – like, I am told, what happened in the French Revolution. Like in Stalin's Russia.' I interrupted and said that the Chinese themselves in mainland China had also gone through the same horrors of the Cultural Revolution.

'Yes, of course they did. The Chinese did that to themselves. But *they* perpetrated the horror on *us*. That is the difference. Of course the ordinary Chinese suffered in China, and of course we feel for them. But the Chinese were an occupying power who invaded our land and held us captive by force. The crime that they committed against the Tibetans was more heinous, because we were occupied by the Chinese, and they did it to us. And of course they wreaked havoc in China and destroyed many of their own monuments and art treasures. But then they desecrated and destroyed nearly every one of our monasteries. [The Tibetan Government-in-exile has documented proof that of the 6,259 monasteries, temples and shrines that existed before the Chinese invasion, only thirteen were left in some sort of functioning capacity after the Cultural Revolution. The rest were totally destroyed.]

'When the Chinese looted our art treasures, when they forbade the use of the Tibetan language and burnt all our books – that was something more. Most Tibetans believe that the deliberate eradication of our language, religion and culture is part of China's long-term plan to eradicate Tibetans as a race.' Listening to him, I wondered whether Mao and Deng had indeed formulated a secret plan, as the Nazis had done at the Wannsee Conference in Berlin in 1942 when the Nazi High Command planned the extermination of the Jews and other 'undesirable non-Aryans'.

'At the time,' Sonam continued, 'even the United Nations condemned China for genocide in Tibet. Do you realize that during the Cultural Revolution, when we were forbidden, under pain of imprisonment, to use our native language, we had to give our children Chinese names? And when we went to register the births, sometimes the Chinese would give the child the name of the street or the house number.

'Do you realize what it is to have 85 per cent of a nation's books destroyed? And many of the books were very ancient. Some came from the eighth century and were written on palm leaves. Some were not even religious. Many were the documents of simple families recording details of their personal history, their births, their deaths, their marriages. Details of their land . . . What possible use was their destruction to the Chinese? It was as though all your culture's old manuscripts written on parchment and with painted pictures in the margins, Gutenberg bibles and Domesday books were burned. That's what happened in Tibet.

'We have lost the education of two generations of young Tibetans. The Chinese apologized in the person of Hu Yaobang, for their "mistakes" and what they did to us for thirty years. They then relaxed their rules at the end of 1979. Tibetan was allowed to be taught in the schools. But like the Chinese rule of allowing religion again in the monasteries, it is largely cosmetic. Yes, some of our children in the big towns are learning Tibetan, but the quality of the teachers is so poor that the children are badly taught. Of course in the countryside, and I have been all over Kham and Ü-Tsang, in the villages and in the mountains, despite what the Chinese say, there is absolutely no schooling for the children. They are growing up illiterate. Go and see for yourself. Ask any child you meet. You will soon find the truth.

'But there is another subtlety in education that perhaps as a foreigner who does not speak our language you are not aware of. The Tibetan language books that our children learn from are poor translations of Chinese history and culture. So you see, although the Chinese can point to schools teaching Tibetan, what in fact the children are learning is Chinese culture and not our own. Then there's another thing: the Chinese will proudly show you the new university of Lhasa. And they will tell you that there is a large allocation for Tibetan students. But don't be fooled. All the examinations to qualify to enter the university – and for better jobs, too – are in Chinese.

'And very few Tibetans speak Chinese well enough to qualify. So the Chinese here get the places. The few Tibetans who do manage to scrape in are not allowed to study medicine, science, any technical subject such as engineering, or teaching or any studies programme that would be useful for them to help their countrymen into the next century. What they are allowed to study is only Tibetan language and Tibetan medicine. Both of which subjects are taught by teachers who are not really proficient in Tibetan. Very effective, no? The Chinese appear to give us concessions, but in your journey look below the surface of what appears to be progress.

'But something more sinister is happening now in Tibet that the tourist will not see. Our children are taken away from their parents and sent to China for education. Tibetan children between the ages of twelve and thirteen can be seen at the airport or at the bus stand. I will show you [and later he did], you can see for yourself. Every year thousands of our children are deported to China. So far, over 17,000 Tibetan children have been taken to institutions in nine Chinese provinces. And what do they teach these children in China? They are not taught any Tibetan language, literature, culture or customs. Nor are they taught English or any other foreign language that might really be useful. They are taught only the Chinese language, Chinese history and customs. The aim is to alienate Tibetan children from their own people and culture and make them Chinese in thought and belief. They encourage our children to adopt the Chinese way of life. They are "wasting" our children. The precious, vital, formative years of the children's lives are being subverted. The children are being lost to Tibet. It's like pouring water into the sand.

'And another thing. The Chinese are practising a policy of deliberately restricting the Tibetan birthrate. In a totally unprecedented way they are forcing our women to have abortions and sterilizations. Normally our women have up to five or six children, an average of four, but now, no more than two. Look at my own case, we have two children and want more, but my own wife was forcibly sterilized. There is a hospital here in Lhasa, the Public Hospital No. 1, on Dekyi Shar Lam Street – I will show it to you. We Tibetans call it the Butcher's Shop because that's where they take our women for forced abortions. And remember that we are Buddhists: we believe it's a terrible sin to take any life, a *dhig-pa*, and to take the life of an unborn child ... As a Westerner you can't really appreciate how devastatingly traumatic it is for a Tibetan Buddhist to commit this crime ... But go and speak to doctors, to nurses who do these abortions. Speak to the women themselves.'

'But why are the Chinese doing this?' I asked, somewhat provocatively.

'Because,' he said, 'what you in the West just don't understand is that the Chinese are still imperialists – despite all their talk about egalitarian Communism.' I looked at him quizzically. 'You question from your own ignorance,' he said. 'We live with them; our country has a long history of dealing with the Chinese. We know. But how much in the West do you know of China's expansionist ambitions?' I shook my head. 'Well,' he went on, 'it is a well-known fact that China is the world's third largest nuclear power. But what is little appreciated in the West, particularly in the West's scramble to get into China's new trade market, is that China wants to be the world's greatest superpower – just as it was thousands of years ago under the emperors. Have you ever heard of the Chinese expression "Middle Earth"?' he asked. I told him that I had.

'Well, like the Chinese-language ideogram for China, "the Middle Earth", China believes in its core that it is the centre of the world and wants to regain its supremacy. But it can't until it solves two major problems that are crippling it. One, population – which now is out of control in China and creating terrible pressures on the land. And two, its economy. The Communist system has not worked. The Chinese urban workers are almost as poor now as they were under the Manchu dynasty. So Tibet supplies part of the answer to both problems. We are very rich in minerals and forestry resources – and they are pillaging the country and carting our patrimony away to China. And then, their "final solution" to their troublesome Tibetan problem is the transfer of Chinese population to Tibet, to our enormous empty spaces and low population density. The Chinese believe Tibet can absorb some of their population explosion.' These were arguments I was to hear everywhere I went in Tibet, but not put as eloquently.

'The pressure of the influx of over 7.5 million Chinese settlers has created tremendous hardship for the Tibetans. They do all sorts of jobs that before were done by Tibetans. Like running restaurants, shops – even the market stalls in the Barkhor are mainly run by Chinese. Even the people in the small street stalls who mend shoes or stitch clothes are Chinese. The Chinese have literally filled nearly every space in the Barkhor. Go anywhere, east, north, the west, or the Kongpo region in the south – everywhere is filled with Chinese.

'It might be an exaggeration to say that all the valleys and mountains are occupied by the Chinese, but they are almost everywhere, doing business and building things, settling down in Tibet. They are doing nothing for the Tibetans but push them out of jobs, off their land, take their houses. We are being pushed out. There is very little work and few opportunities for it. Tibetans everywhere, whether they are farmers or nomads, are suffering.

'The few jobs that do exist offer such low pay that it is not sufficient to meet the needs of a family. Take my case, for example. In our family we are four. Even if three of us work, it is still difficult from a day's wage to buy enough barley [the staple food] for one meal. And there is nothing left over for rent or clothes or education or medicine. And how can a person survive and be healthy enough to work on one meagre meal a day? And it's the same all over Tibet.

'The Chinese place difficulties upon difficulties before Tibetans and make it impossible for us to lead a decent life. We are made to feel inferior. The Chinese who live in Tibet very obviously do not like it. They live in separate areas; they call us dirty barbarians. They never mix with Tibetans; they don't even learn a few words of rudimentary Tibetan. They have their own schools; they even get their own vegetables brought over from Sichuan. Go along the road past the Potala towards the Holiday Inn: on the right you will see the Chinese market vendors selling to other Chinese all sorts of vegetables that they like eating, like chillies and water melons. There is no attempt to integrate, or even understand us, let alone our culture and history.

'They even take the stones from our houses to build theirs. Look around you; look at the way the Chinese and the Tibetans live. The Chinese have proper houses with electricity, running water, bathrooms, drains, even pavements and trees. But look outside the window. It's like living in a pigsty. Most of us do not even have electricity. It's the same thing with hospitals – go and talk to the medical people. They will tell you how there is a two-tier system for Tibetan and Chinese and how we are given inferior treatment and out-of-date medicine or the wrong drugs. We are exploited like animals. The Chinese dominate us and make us thoughtless so that all we care about is being able to work to eat. We live from day to day, without the time to think about things other than survival. They make us as ignorant as the tadpoles in the wells. That's what Tibetan life is like today. But the cancer in Tibetan society is still *Yarthonpa* – the informer system.'

'But you are taking a terrible risk in talking to me. And you propose to say all this openly on British television without a face mask. Why are you doing this? Would you like to change your mind?'

'No. No,' he said emphatically. 'I have decided to speak because for forty years we have been patient and hoped the Chinese would change their ways. They have not. We hoped that the other countries of the world would listen and help us. They have not, because until now they have believed what the Chinese told them. Now it is the time to tell the world what is really happening in Tibet. How we are treated like slaves by the Chinese people here. How, in our own land, we are exploited and treated like animals. That is why I speak openly to you, in spite of whatever might happen.'

'But how representative is what you have just told me of what the majority of Tibetans feel?' I asked.

'What I have said to you is what 95 per cent of Tibetans think and feel. Of course there are a few Tibetans who for a better standard of life work for the Chinese. But you can verify what I have said anywhere. Ask Tibetans, they will tell you privately, but very few will speak out openly, for fear of reprisals. You must realize that we live with fear as we live with our shadows. It is with us day and night.

'Be careful and watchful of the Chinese and their spies in your journey,' he warned. 'I speak of what I know.' He leaned back against the window, the light emphasizing the deep lines on his face that were their own testimony to his years in prison.

I felt drained. I thanked Sonam and we agreed to meet to film what he had just told me in two days' time. I tucked my notebook into my money-belt under my blouse, thanked my host and promised I would meet Tempa in another safe house that evening to discuss with Tenzin and the rest of the team the details of our departure for Nagchukha. One of the older children went ahead, just within range, to lead me through the maze of alleys to the edge of the Tibetan quarter.

I met Seán in another small Tibetan restaurant and told him about the day's interviews. He told me that he had gone to the Norbulingka and waited at the arranged place for the Amdo contact, who had not showed up. While we were pondering the options and eating our noodles, Seán without a trace of emotion on his face quietly whispered that Chuma had just walked into the restaurant.

I looked up as he approached, and as we were sitting at the back of the restaurant, I motioned him to join us. He looked much more relaxed and had filled out a little. I told him, as I pored over a map and pretended to work out the route to Sera, that the Controller wanted him out of Tibet as he had another assignment for him. He asked how then would we manage, and what our plans were. I told him not to worry, and that we had been assigned someone else and lied that our plans were in flux. I urged him to get out of Lhasa. 'But it will take four days to get my passport ready,' he said unconvincingly. I bit my lip and refrained from reminding him that he had told us he had come to Tibet without any papers . . . I saw Seán's face cloud over at Chuma's blatant lie.

As darkness fell, I left Seán reading in the hotel and walked to the Kirey Hotel down the road. From there I followed instructions and went to the corner where I was to turn sharp right and walk past eleven houses. Thondup or one of the others would then meet me and take me to the safe house. I reached the corner, trying to walk casually. There were few people in the street and certainly no tourists. It was very quiet. In the depths of the Tibetan quarter a few dogs barked and were echoed by other dogs in the hills at the edge of town. From an open window came the tinny tinkle of Chinese pop music. A harvest moon rose yellow over the eastern mountains and the canopy of stars began to sparkle in the ink-blue sky.

At another time I would have stopped and revelled in the beauty. But that night, poised on the threshold of my own fear, I was too preoccupied with the dangers that could be lurking in the unknown shadows. I hesitated at the edge of the Tibetan quarter. There was no street lighting and the pools of light from the odd shop that remained open seemed almost like daylight illumination compared to the total darkness beyond. My pathological fear of the darkness rose in my throat. I flinched at my own cowardice, remembering the agonies of uncertainty I underwent every time I had to go alone into a dark unknown area in previous assignments all over the world. It never got any better. I never seemed able to conquer my fear of the dark. I dug my fingernails into my palms, turned the corner and groped my way into the darkness along the rough walls of the houses.

Thondup found me, but even his guiding hand did not prevent my faltering feet from finding every rut and pot-hole of foul-smelling, clinging mud. I had deliberately worn dark jeans, jacket and even my black Chinese shoes, trying to look Chinese from a distance and hoping to avert attention should I run into patrolling Chinese soldiers. I hoped that the hood of my green Helly Hansen jacket would shield my very European face from too much scrutiny. Our path was well-shepherded by friendly Tibetans who waited in even darker doorways to guide us through the labyrinth.

We finally climbed down from a courtyard full of animals to a room below ground-level. Through a grille in the ceiling we could hear the odd pedestrian passing above us in the street. It was a storage room of sorts, with bales of hay stacked to one side, a table with a candle in the middle and a few benches huddled around. There were about seven people in the room, some of whom I recognized from the previous trip to the monastery before I had left Lhasa.

As Thondup made the introductions and told me that we were waiting for Tempa, who was held up trying to arrange transport, Chuma walked into the room. I was livid that he had found us and had seen the people involved. I knew I had to get rid of him before Tempa arrived. I asked him as calmly as I could what he was doing there when he should be on a bus out of Lhasa. He told me, a shade too quickly I thought, that he had 'been requested by Tempa' to attend the meeting! I simply did not believe him. To get rid of him, I lied and told him that he was mad – didn't he know that the Chinese were on to him? Even in the dim light I saw him blanch. He caught his breath, obviously very frightened, said something in rapid Tibetan and left.

When Tempa finally arrived, he told me that he had said nothing to Chuma at all. My anxiety about a Chinese mole grew, but I continued to discuss the detailed mechanics of the trip with the group. It soon appeared that Tempa, contrary to what had been promised, could not find transport inside Lhasa to provide the cover from which we could film the exteriors of Lhasa's prisons. There were five prisons in Lhasa: Gurtsa, Wutri-tui, Sangyib, Drapchi and the military prison – Lhasa Chun Chue. Several people had told me horrific stories of torture and maltreatment of Tibetan political prisoners in these jails: stories as appalling as the accounts I had read of the horrors of the Nazi concentration camps. And the very names of these prisons had entered the Tibetan subconscious as synonymous with the terror engendered in the Jews by the mention of Dachau, Auschwitz and Belsen.

I needed to have exterior footage of these notorious prisons as background shots for the ex-prisoners' voices. I knew from having cycled innocently past them that they were not places to linger near, for Chinese military guards with AK 47s at the ready were posted outside the gates.

Tempa explained that transport, or rather the lack of it, was yet another way the Chinese controlled the movements of the Tibetan population. It then transpired that Tenzin also had not been able to secure transport for the trip to the interior. But he seemed unconcerned and said that we could go by lorry (the normal and only way to travel for Tibetans). I nearly exploded in frustration.

'But Tenzin,' I said, trying to argue with a semblance of reason, 'don't you realize that I will be picked up immediately?'

'No problem,' Tenzin said calmly, oblivious to the reality of the situation. 'You only have to show your passport for the interior. No problem.'

'What do you mean, no problem?' I exclaimed. 'And what do you mean that I have a passport for the interior? I don't. There's no such thing!' I almost shouted in desperation.

'But the Controller said that you had a passport for the interior,' he said, perplexed at my anxiety, which by now was off the sanity register.

'Tenzin,' I almost shouted, 'there is no such thing as a passport for the interior. Foreigners are just *not* allowed into the interior. They are *not* allowed out of Lhasa. If I am caught in a "closed" area – and that includes all of Tibet outside Lhasa, Shigatse, Gyantse and Xining – I go to jail. And so do you,' I emphasized as Tenzin's eyes grew wider. 'Tibetans,' I went on, 'are not allowed to transport or shelter foreigners, and to have anything to do with them in the closed areas means that you and everyone who has anything to do with us goes to jail for a very long time.'

Tenzin was obviously very shocked, as indeed were the rest of the team. My God, I thought uncharitably, what sort of morons have I found who don't seem to know the basic laws of this country! And I am entrusting my life to them? Again I had serious doubts about my sanity! It was by then nearly midnight and every fibre of my body ached with tension. Once again the film was in tatters. I tried to muster the last shreds of my composure and drag myself out of the morass of despair.

'Look,' I said, 'we are all tired. Why don't you try and find a car or a van or something and let's meet again tomorrow night, as our visas are running out and we are due in Nagchukha the day after tomorrow.' They agreed, and I arranged with Tempa to film the nuns at the first safe house the next day. Then Thondup guided me back to the edge of the main road.

The main gate of the Yak Hotel was closed and barred for the night. With any thoughts of discretion thrown to the wind in my need to clean up and to sleep, I banged at the door loudly enough to wake a whole battalion of PSB men for a full half-hour before a sleepy caretaker let me in. I saw the candle burning in Seán's room. As the backpackers next door were having a riotous party, I whispered the night's problems to Seán. His face became drawn with tension as I told him the story about Chuma reappearing and the trouble about the 'internal passports'. He just said one word that momentarily paralysed me:

'Sabotage?'

There was nothing I could say. I left him and went to take an icy cold shower to remove the mud that had caked on my legs up to my thighs when I fell into the last pot-hole on my way back to the hotel.

There was little sleep to be had that night. My own doubts made the night infernal and the revellers made an unbearably cheerful din till 4.30 in the morning when the neighbourhood dogs kept sleep at bay by howling at the moon. By 7 A.M. I began to think I must have been certifiable even to have contemplated this insane venture.

The next day, while Seán shot some more visuals, I went with Thondup to interview more Tibetans in yet another safe house. At three, Thondup and I went to find Seán at the hotel and together we went to the Norbulingka for our rendezvous with the Amdo man. We waited until five o'clock, but he did not show up. Seán was getting more withdrawn and silent as each thing that had been promised failed to materialize. And I began to wonder whether it was my responsibility to suggest that he left and went home.

We returned to the Tibetan quarter through the meat market where huge chunks of yak meat were displayed. The cheerful banter of the Tibetan traders was in sharp contrast to the rising gloom in my belly as I realized that we were once more stuck in Lhasa.

In the safe house, with look-outs again posted on the roof and in the adjacent courtyards and street, Seán and I set up the camera and prepared to interview the four young nuns. The girls, barely in their twenties, were farmers' daughters from outside Lhasa and had only recently joined their nunnery. They were simple country girls, and light-years away from being political agitators, as the Chinese brand all who oppose their rule in Tibet.

In their simple patched maroon *tsun-che* (habits) I realized that these girls who had risked death by demonstrating peacefully for the right to practise their faith and for Tibetan independence, had never actually known what freedom was. They had been born during the Cultural Revolution. They had never known the time when the Dalai Lama was in Tibet. They had never known a free Tibet. All they had known was the oppression of Chinese rule. Yet these girls, who by the Chinese rule book should have been staunch supporters of the Communist regime, had turned their backs on the indoctrination, joined a religious order and dedicated their lives to prayer and good works. They were 'useless parasites' according to the Chinese, and should be stamped out and eradicated at any cost. But what was curious was that these children of the Cultural Revolution were the most vigorous defenders of their faith and in the vanguard of the demand for an end to Chinese oppression and for the return of the Dalai Lama: a being they had never known, had never seen, but yet for whom they displayed a fervent and touching devotion, much to the fury of the Chinese. For the young monks and nuns who had demonstrated for freedom were living, undeniable proof that China's repressive policies in Tibet had not worked. All over Tibet young people, who should have been the grateful flowers of the Communist Revolution, had decidedly turned their backs on it in the most public and irrefutable way.

Filming their testimony was one of the most painful interviews I have ever recorded in my life. These simple girls told me how they were arrested while the five of them demonstrated alone and peacefully round the Jokhang for Tibetan freedom in March 1988, a few days after the main demonstration that had resulted in so much bloodshed. They told me how the Chinese soldiers had arrested them, manacled them, beaten them, thrown them into a truck, taken them to the police station, stripped them naked despite the fact that they were nuns, beaten them until they could not even stand and during the whole proceedings had prodded their naked bodies all over – up to seven soldiers to each nun – with electric cattle-prods. Several times their testimony was inaudible through their sobs. One nun was still, five months later, so ill after the maltreatment that she was unable to come to the meeting.

That night I left Seán in the hotel cleaning the equipment and went again into the dark of the Barkhor. Again, in another safe house, the same small band of Tibetans had gathered. But this time someone I hadn't seen before, a tall dignified Tibetan woman, was there. She rose to greet me, placed the *kata* of welcome round my neck and through Thondup told me, with tears in her eyes, how grateful she was that I had come to help Tibet. She told me that she had donated the money necessary for the team to buy a jeep for the journey. The others were visibly moved and I felt a prickle behind my own eyes. It is moments like this when words are so grossly inadequate. I went on discussing the route and reiterating what we needed to film at each location, referring all the time to the details on the miniaturized memo that I had secreted into a Tampax.

That night Seán's light was not on. I went straight to bed and slept fitfully, hovering on the brink of the decision of whether to let Seán return to London. Too much seemed to be going wrong. The following morning before dawn I got up and left the hotel for a last meeting with Tenzin and the team, who were to have finalized the last details of the transport during the night. After yet another slithering match in the mud, I arrived at the safe house with Thondup to find that it was locked and that there was no sign of life in the windows. We knocked at the door as gently as we could. There was no response, but every dog in the neighbourhood barked into life as lights appeared in the nearby windows. Frightened of being discovered, I asked Thondup to give me a leg up onto the wall. As I teetered at the top, worried about breaking a leg in the long fall into the courtyard below, I suddenly visualized a headline in a London paper: 'British journalist arrested while breaking into a Tibetan house in Lhasa!' With a stupid grin on my face, I fell into the courtyard.

I opened the gate and Thondup and I tried every window and door. But the house appeared lifeless. Outside the dogs were in full voice. There were too many lights at the windows for us to remain there. With every doubt in the underworld plaguing me, we walked back to the main road. It might very well be, as Seán had suggested, that we were being set up to be arrested by the Chinese and so I resolved to tell Seán to go home. I had decided to go on, on my own. How I had not fathomed at that stage, but all I knew was that something was seriously wrong and that I could take chances with my own life, but not with Seán's.

It was still dark at 7 A.M. when I got back to the hotel. A street-sweeper was beginning to make a desultory effort in the streets. The odd cyclist glided slowly past. I woke Seán, who then stumbled sleepily into my room. I gave him a cup of black coffee and told him of my decision. Seán, who normally takes a good hour to become *compos mentis*, was suddenly jerked awake.

'But you can't,' he spluttered. 'You just can't go off on your own into the wilds of Tibet! You don't even know how to change a fuse, let alone operate a camera! Don't be so ridiculous! Come home with me. You tried harder than anyone else I know. You've done your bit for Tibet. No one will blame you. The odds are just too dangerously stacked against you. Come home with me, Vanya.'

I wavered for a perilous moment. It was so tempting to leave all the problems, the cold, the uncertainty, the fear, behind. I so longed to be in the safety of my own bed in London and just sleep for days. At that moment, all I wanted to do was to be as far away from Tibet as possible. It was the loneliest decision of my life. Suddenly, I fully realized what I was doing and was absolutely terrified.

Holding onto the last shreds of my resolve, I repeated to Seán that I *was* going on, on my own. I asked him to show me how the camera worked, and to put it on automatic, as I had fifteen minutes to meet Thondup who had arranged for a lift in a tractor pick-up to take us to Sera monastery where we were due to film the Sera monk at 8.30. And already it was 7.35.

Seán briefly ran through the mechanics of the camera, packed it and the tripod into the rucksack and nearly toppled me over as he loaded it onto my back. He said he would wait for me at the Holiday Inn: now he was off the shoot, there was no need to stay at the uncomfortable Yak. I agreed to move since it was easier to phone London from a five-star hotel. He would pack us up and organize his flight to leave four days later on Saturday.

I tottered down the stairs into the street and vomited violently into the gutter. Wiping the bitter taste of bile from my mouth, I was more than tempted to run back. But I hitched the heavy backpack more comfortably on my back, cursed the fact that I was so small, and waved to Thondup approaching in the distance. From my uncomfortable perch on the metal edge of a tractor pick-up for a bone-shaking trip to Sera, I watched the new day breathtakingly warm the bowl of mountains surrounding Lhasa.

Thondup and I saw Lobsang in the distance. We followed him along a small path below the monastery to an isolated hill where we were to do the interview out of sight of the monastery. He asked where Seán was, I fluffed a reply and tried to organize how the camera sat on the tripod. I fixed it, switched on the camera, made sure the button marked automatic was on, saw the small screen in the eye-piece flicker into white life, and then focused it on Lobsang.

I had wanted to record the interview with the Potala in the background. But Lobsang's face remained black against the bright sky. What Seán had forgotten to tell me was that on automatic reading the camera was incapable of filming *contre-jour* (against daylight) as it automatically exposed for the brightest area – the sky – leaving everything else in silhouette. I just could not figure it out. Eventually I decided on another setting, but noticed that the camera kept slipping and the horizon in the view-finder was at forty-five degrees. I simply did not know what was wrong. The more I fiddled the worse it became; the more nervous I became the more I transmitted it to the Tibetans who by now, more than an hour after our arrival, were becoming terribly jumpy.

Thondup tried to help. But he too had never used a camera before. Just as I was on the point of doing it an injury, Lobsang hissed and threw himself flat on his face on the ground. As the other Tibetans followed his example, I looked in the direction of their alarm and saw a Chinese soldier walking towards us. I pushed the camera and the tripod onto the ground, where it fell with a sickening thud, and threw myself down. It was like the chase scene in John Buchan's *Thirty-Nine Steps*. There was not much cover on that bald mountain. The short scrubby grass was barely a couple of inches high. Hardly daring to breathe, I peeped up under my straw hat and saw that the Tibetans' clothes blended happily into the brown rock of the mountainside. My green Chinese army jacket and trousers that I had bought the day before were not too bad, but sticking out like Belisha beacons were my white track shoes which in the hurry I had forgotten to change for the black Chinese ones.

I prayed hard to St Jude, patron saint of hopeless causes, and to St Rita, saint of the impossible, to do something. It would be just too ridiculous for words if I was arrested on my first abortive attempt to film with not even one foot of film shot. After what seemed like an eternity, the soldier sauntered down the path and out of sight. There was real fear on the Tibetans' faces and even I realized that we had to abandon filming there. Anyway I had to get back to Seán to find out how the tripod worked, as it would be impossible to hand-hold the camera and keep it still during the interview which would run for well over an hour.

Seán was ensconced in the Holiday Inn, which after the Yak was enormous luxury, with its own bathrooms with hot and cold running water, carpets, albeit a bit moth-eaten, and comfortable beds with thick pink and white eiderdowns and soft pillows. He looked much more relaxed and showed me how to fix the camera and tripod. I then bundled everything back into the backpack, hired a bike from the Holiday Inn and wobbled down the road to the Yak Hotel where I left the bike and walked into the Tibetan quarter to continue filming the interviews.

By now I knew the way, but I still made an elaborate detour in case anyone was following me. When I got there, I found that Thondup, knowing that I was medi-vacked out of Vietnam with liver trouble and was still unable to tolerate any fat (he was by then used to making my apologies to the Tibetans for refusing their hospitality of butter-tea) had thoughtfully bought me some powdered coffee.

We set up the camera inside the house and, using the light from the window to film, I focused on Sonam, pinned one external microphone to his chest to give me better sound quality than the camera's inbuilt microphone and fixed the other end into the external feed of the camera-body. I checked to see if the needle indicating volume was oscillating, pressed the record button and prayed to all the gods that were listening that it would work.

After two minutes' recording I stopped, rewound the tape and switched on the play-back facility. No one could have been more surprised than I was to see an image recorded on the tape. I was ridiculously thrilled. For the first time in my life I had actually filmed something.

I then proceeded to interview Sonam on the lines we had discussed earlier. I stopped the camera between my questions and his answers so that Thondup could translate. There was no point in 'turning over' – filming – as I did not want to run out of tape. The thirty rolls of tape (thirty hours' worth) that I had sent clandestinely into Tibet months ago, and which I had been re-assured in Hong Kong had arrived safely in Lhasa, had not – I was not surprised to learn, in view of all that had gone wrong – arrived. So I had to conserve tape whenever I could.

Sonam was superb. He spoke with a rare passion, and the only irritating thing was that every ten minutes a battery warning would flash in the view-finder telling me that the battery was running out. We had brought six spare batteries which took an hour each to charge – assuming, of course, that there was electricity available, which in that house, like most Tibetan houses, there was not. Frightened that in the warning time the battery would run the camera slow and distort the sound, I panicked and changed it. It was not the ideal way to conduct a major interview when the interviewee was reliving the most painful event of his life.

Sonam had to go, so wordlessly we just hugged each other, forging a languageless bond. Changing tapes, I then started Lobsang's interview. It was the most devastating and sickening interview that I have ever recorded in my life.

8

Going Solo

The sun disappeared behind the parapet of the house and it was too dark to film by the light from the window. Tempa unhooked the lamp, pumped up the pressure and hitched it back on its nail. I tried to angle it to light Lobsang from the side, using it as one would use a 'key' light in a television studio to highlight one side of the face to throw interesting shadow relief onto the features. It was a crude attempt to give some texture to Lobsang's face and I remembered one current affairs editor who always berated me for trying to make more interesting images out of even the most banal interview. 'You and your bloody visuals!' he used to yell at me. 'If I asked you to film the sodding Mona Lisa you would try and make it look more pretty! Just get on and give me a "talking head". Eyes and mouth and stop f...... around with the lighting and background!'

By hanging the lamp near the ceiling I was able to diffuse its harsh white light to 'bounce' more softly off the ceiling into the room. Lobsang, dignified in his neat threadbare clothes, sat with the stillness of a man used to the enforced patience of interminable years in prison.

After his courageous gesture of standing in front of the Chinese tanks alone, trying to stop them shelling the Potala in March 1959, Lobsang was wounded by the Chinese.

'Some artillery exploded in the street near me. I was knocked down, the force was so great that my *chuba* was ripped off and also my charm box in which I kept my holy relics. I had a terrible pain in my right leg. There was blood everywhere and I could not move it.' He tried to drag himself away from the Chinese, to try and hide in Lhasa, but inevitably he was arrested and on 4 July 1959 imprisoned in the first of thirteen jails in Lhasa and other parts of Tibet where he was to be held.

After the initial interrogation and beating, he was thrown into a prison converted from the Sera Che college at the Sera monastery, then transferred to the Sera Mei college/prison, also at Sera. While he was there he saw the Chinese destroy 95 per cent of the monastery's ancient statues and scriptures. The Chinese army occupied Sera from 1959 until 1978, and apart from desecrating and stripping the monastery, the Chinese stationed their troops in Sera (as they did in the few other monasteries that were left standing throughout Tibet). And the ancient halls, once resplendent with priceless frescos over 500 years old, were used as a grain store and to quarter PLA soldiers, stable animals, or to provide accommodation for the incarceration and torture of prisoners.

During another spell in Sera jail in 1966, Lobsang also vividly remembered how the Chinese had stripped the monastery of whatever remained of its religious artefacts – the silver butter-lamps, the long horns used in religious rituals – and loaded them onto ninety-seven three-tonne army lorries. The lorries always left for China in the dead of night when there were few witnesses around to record the fact. Lobsang heard and saw and counted the lorries as they passed the window of his tiny cell looking out over the main courtyard of the monastery. In fact many monks all over Tibet confirmed this nocturnal pattern of looting and removing the priceless artistic and religious heritage from Tibet.

'Then in 1959 I was sent to another prison in Kangpo,' he told me. 'Because of the Chinese policy of exterminating the Tibetan people, there were so, so many prisoners. Most were political prisoners who would not accept the Chinese rule. They told us, "If you publicly accept Beijing and China as your ruler, we will let you out of prison. If not, we will keep you here."

'For twelve hours a day, every day, we had to do hard labour in the mines, building roads, building bridges, in all weathers, without food, without proper clothing, without sleep. If we fell down they would beat us until we regained consciousness. Even when we had broken limbs from the beatings and the torture, we still had to work. There was no medicine, no doctors for the prisoners. To the Chinese we were less than animals. We would get frostbite because we had nothing to protect our hands and our feet. Sometimes it was so cold that the flesh on our hands would tear off and stick to the shovels.

'Then, when we returned to the prison after twelve hours' back-breaking labour, the Chinese would call us to the main prison yard for their struggle sessions (*thumzing*) to expel our bad thoughts and make us think their way. They called us reactionaries. But we told them that *we* had not gone to China to bully the Chinese. We said that *we* had not taken anything from the Chinese. We told them that *they* had come to bully a small religious country. We accused them of grabbing our country by bombing it. The Chinese addressed prisoners saying that we had "hard brains" and that if we did not change they would beat us. They would send us to meet our Buddha.

'To make us change our thinking and support the Chinese rule in Tibet, they hung prisoners upside down in empty rooms and beat them with batons. Sometimes they forced other prisoners to do the beatings so that the Chinese would not have to take the blame. If the prisoners refused to beat their cell-mates and comrades, they in turn were brutally beaten and called "difficult" and marked out for special punishment. I have experienced this beating as well,' he said quietly, without a trace of emotion in his voice. 'But I survived, even though I never renounced my belief in Tibetan independence. I told them I would never submit to the Chinese claim. It simply is not the truth.

'In 1960, '61, '62, '63, the Chinese had a priority list of prisoners whom they considered difficult,' he went on. 'Following the collection of these lists, they made plans for a series of prison meetings. Just before a meeting all the prisoners were rounded up and surrounded by armed soldiers in vehicles.

'The Chinese selected the prisoners who were to be "disposed" of. The soldiers then threw the Tibetan prisoners on the ground and held them there. With their feet on a prisoner's neck, the soldiers bound all four limbs up tight, like a chicken for the soup pot, so that he could not move.

'Then all the other prisoners were lined up and told not to move at all. They then brought the trussed-up prisoners in. One by one the Chinese called the prisoners' names and asked them to denounce Tibetan independence – otherwise they would be shot. When they did not, three or four soldiers would strangle them from the front and others would pull on the rope around their necks from behind. Often they would put a wooden tablet with the prisoner's "crime" written on it round his neck to try and make him accept the Chinese policies. The Chinese warned the rest of the prisoners, "If you do not accept Chinese rule, this will be the fate of all of you. We are going to kill you. Do not count on being alive. If you insist on saying that Tibet is independent, we will send you to your independence" – and they laughed in our faces. But they did not break us.

'Then they shot the prisoners who still refused to renounce Tibet in batches of ten or fifteen. Straight after they shot one batch, the bodies were removed by three or four soldiers into waiting vehicles. And another batch was brought in to be shot straight away. But still they did not break us. The more they killed, the greater the numbers of prisoners who defied the Chinese. The numbers of Tibetans killed like this by the Chinese was massive. Countless. It was the same in all the prisons I was in. Thousands upon thousands perished. And thousands more in prisons all over Tibet.'

Over the years, whenever Tibetan refugees managed to escape to India, they took to the Dalai Lama the stories and evidence of what had happened to them and to the others who had not survived. Painstakingly, the Tibetan Government-in-exile collated the evidence and cross-checked with survivors. Since 1949, they claim that 1,207,487 Tibetans have died as a direct result of the Chinese occupation of Tibet. These figures only go up to 1983.

Lobsang continued: 'The Chinese then moved the bodies by lorries to quiet corners between hills and buried the bodies in deep holes. This happened all over Tibet. There are so many secret places with big graves with piles of Tibetan bodies. They are still there. Go and see them on your journey.'

I told Lobsang that the Chinese did admit that they had made mistakes during the Cultural Revolution, between 1965 and 1975, and that they had already apologized to the Tibetan people for that, blaming some over-zealous extremists in Lhasa.

'Lies! Lies!' Lobsang interrupted me, his face taut with anger. 'What they did to the Tibetans started long before the Cultural Revolution. The Chinese invaded Tibet in 1949. Many of our major monasteries were destroyed *before* the Cultural Revolution. Lithang and Batang monasteries and many others were bombed by Chinese planes from the air in 1956, nearly ten years *before* the Cultural Revolution. I was in jail and tortured before, during and *after* the Cultural Revolution. And so were thousands of other Tibetans. Hundreds of thousands of Tibetans died from torture, forced labour and starvation because of the Chinese. That is not just the "few excesses of the Cultural Revolution". In your language you have a word for the killing of a nation.'

'Genocide?' I suggested.

'Well, that's what the Chinese did to Tibet. And it is still happening now. The Chinese are still exterminating the Tibetan people.'

I asked him to continue telling me what it was actually like in prison.

'The agony of starvation is terrible,' he said slowly, clearly unable to forget those searing years. 'They gave us practically no food. Sometimes a few bits of vegetable, but we were always hungry. We had to eat whatever we could get. Some ate flies. Some, and I was one, had to pick bits of vegetable out of human faeces and eat it. Some ate the flesh of rats and dogs,' he said quietly. And then, barely audible, he went on: 'Sometimes we also had to eat human beings.'

'You mean that you and the other prisoners ate human flesh? Cannibalism?'

'Yes, even the corpses of human beings. By using what little strength remained in our bodies, we crushed the long bones of the dead prisoners and drank the juice as well. This offered nourishment and restored the body and was very helpful. It also stopped the terrible pains of hunger and for a few hours allowed us to sleep at night.'

'And you ate that?' I again asked.

'Yes,' he replied. 'I ate all that . . . I had to . . . There was no choice. Most people died slowly and painfully of starvation. It was the implementation of the Chinese policy to eradicate the Tibetan race. The majority of people of my generation who were in prison have been wiped out by the Chinese. Look for yourself. There are only a few young ones left. The older ones are not around any more, they died of suffering in prison.

'In 1966–7, the Chinese toughened their policy. Prisoners were not even allowed to talk to each other. If we did, we were accused of plotting against the State and knives were stuck into prisoners' testicles. Those whose testicles were knifed did not die easily. Some did not die easily after their throats were slit either . . . The years 1976 to 1978 were very difficult for me. Also 1986 and 1987. I saw so many people die. Friends like Dankar Chazo and Phutsog Pusung. Many, like Ca Chulstra, committed suicide; many drowned themselves.'

'But isn't it against the tenets of Buddhism to take life, even your own? So why did so many commit suicide?' I asked.

'You must try and understand what our lives were like day after day, year after year. Practically no food, no proper clothes, very hard work, and at night sleep was impossible because of the cramps from hunger. And the cold. Tibetans are used to the cold, but in prison with no heating, no blankets, no beds, just some straw and the warmth of other prisoners' bodies . . . And then each morning you would find that one or two of your cell-mates had died in the night near you . . .

'And every night the Chinese tortured and interrogated us till two or three in the morning. The aim of these sessions was to find out who else was still clinging to the idea of the struggle for Tibetan independence. But when the body is weak, there is a danger that one will break under torture and be forced to give the names of one's fellow prisoners. So many Tibetan prisoners preferred to commit suicide. Because if they broke under torture, their fellow prisoners would certainly have been killed by the Chinese. It was the only way to protect one's friends and hope that they would survive for a little longer.

'In the Tibetan Buddhist tradition, if one commits suicide, one of the worst sins a Buddhist can commit, there are no more rebirths, which for us is a terrible thing. But what could we do? So many people were tortured so badly and for so long, there was no other way. We were all political prisoners who would not give up our belief in Tibetan independence. We couldn't fight back. We had no weapons. We were prisoners. The suffering was so great. There seemed no other way out for some. Some drowned themselves. Some slit their throats. These were the only means available to us.

'I saw so many people die. I would think about 99 per cent of the prisoners I saw in my twenty-two years in prison are dead. Many died in front of me. Many died around me. Many died close by. I am a left-over from death,' he said almost inaudibly.

There are no words to describe what I felt as I listened to the man eviscerate himself in front of the camera. When one reads the words describing atrocities on a cold white page in a book in the comfort of one's own home, it is an aeon of experience away from the impact of having listened to a survivor relive his years of terror. Watching Lobsang telling me of his horror through the eye-piece of the camera, watching his face in close-up, seeing the beads of sweat glisten on his forehead, his eyes glaze with pain as he talked, was one of the most traumatic experiences of my career, a career well-used to documenting torture all over the world.

Somehow, I found myself back at the Holiday Inn. It was surreal to walk through the marble-floored foyer with one of the most devastating interviews I had done in my life strapped round my middle and hear the voices of the tourists getting upset over lost laundry and the lack of picture postcards.

I got up to my room, placed a long-distance call to David Lloyd at his home in London – it was too dangerous to call Channel 4, since foreign calls from Lhasa are monitored in Beijing. As it would take the hotel operator up to two hours to connect my call, and probably longer, I went down to the coffee shop with Seán for what he laughingly called my 'Last Supper'. While Chinese waitresses in Tibetan national dress served me the most expensive steak – and a completely unexceptional one – that I have ever eaten, I told Seán about the day's work. I had already given him the tapes, which were now strapped round his middle.

We returned to my room. I neatly packed all the equipment, except for Seán's camera which was entered on his passport and therefore had to be taken out of the country. Seán had run the exposed video tapes that I had shot through the camera eye-piece and reassuringly proclaimed them fine. 'They ought to be,' he grinned. 'You've been directing long enough, and someone as fussy about visuals as you can surely get a talking head straight!'

I threw a pillow at him. Although it was nearly 11.30, Seán gave me another quick lesson on the camera, which in my fatigue and panic – for it began to hit me that I was indeed going off on my own – I had enormous difficulty in retaining. I then washed my hair, had a deep bath and wondered when I would next see a tub of hot water again.

As I set the alarm for 5 A.M. the telephone rang. It was David in London. For a minute I almost panicked. How was I going to tell the Head of Channel 4's News and Current Affairs that I had decided to go solo? So, knowing the call was monitored, I gaily chattered away: I was going on my 'holiday' alone and Seán was returning. 'I have already "turned over" solo,' I said, using the film slang to tell him that I had filmed on my own. 'And it's fine,' I ran on rather flatly. There was silence at the other end. I frantically began to marshal my arguments for insisting on going on with the project. To David's eternal credit, instead of saying, 'But you've never used a video or movie camera in your life before' (true) or 'As a cameraperson you are incapable and incompetent' (true again), he simply said, very quietly, 'Good luck, and I will look forward to your return home.'

As I put the phone down I felt completely and totally isolated. I knew that from then on I had no contact with the outside world at all.

9

Destination Nagchukha

I was awake long before my alarm went off at 5 A.M. For hours I had tossed and turned in restless torment, terrified that above all else I would forget Seán's quick lesson in how to operate the camera. His laconic reassurance that all I had to do was to put it on automatic had not calmed my growing anxiety. Instead of sleeping, my mind regurgitated in the night all the mishaps with camera equipment that had occurred in the last twenty years on locations from the deserts of Chad to the jungles of Vietnam.

Then I recalled how the previous night, in our last furtive meeting in the Barkhor, a woman had taken my hand and said quietly, 'Thank you for coming here and wanting to help us.' I immediately felt ashamed of my cowardice and hurriedly dressed in my shapeless Chinese clothes. I really had no choice.

I checked the false bottoms of several cases, where I had placed my vital possessions – a second passport, with its Indian, Nepalese, Burmese, Pakistani, Afghani and Soviet visas, surplus credit cards and large amounts of Chinese Rmb currency. If I was arrested and the Chinese searched me and confiscated money and documents, then at least I had some means of getting out of the country.

I strapped on my money-belt, wrapped my passport with its precious Chinese visa in plastic in case we had to ford any rivers, and inside the belt I tucked another wad of Chinese currency, dollar bills of all denominations and a few fifty-pound notes as well. How useful would money be? Nobody in the remote areas, I was sure, had even heard of sterling, but dollars, I hoped, would buy me out of trouble, as they had in every other Third World country.

I put more clear plastic round the two Minolta stills cameras and lenses. Dust and grit are the worst enemies of film – and stills – equipment, and if anything went wrong, I had no idea how to repair it. Simple Tibetan grit, as well as Chinese security soldiers, could mean the end of the film.

I slowly zipped and locked the heavy black nylon bags to steady my nerves. I wrapped the tape-recorder in a spare pair of thermal socks and checked the small bag Seán had prepared, containing the microphones and all the paraphernalia for recording the interviews. As I finished the preparations, there was a loud knock on the door. I jumped violently and Seán appeared, looking extremely sleepy.

'All you need is a little eye-job to add a tiny slant and you'd look the part perfectly!' he said, smiling. 'Quite a fashion plate too!'

'These are all the genuine article,' I protested, ruefully tugging at my baggy green Chinese army trousers which were held together with safety-pins. I was also wearing two sweaters under the green army-surplus jacket and my hair was tucked under a straw hat that would never have been admitted to Ascot.

I had toyed with the idea of dyeing my hair black, but decided against it. If I was caught, and my passport said that I had auburn hair, even the most simple soldier on checkpoint-duty would know that something was going on.

We had agreed that I should wait in the room until Thondup came to fetch me, I hoped, with transport. Outside the temporary security of the warm hotel room, Lhasa was pitch-dark. After the cacophony of dogs near the Yak Hotel, it was unsettlingly quiet in the Chinese quarter where the Holiday Inn was located. Pre-occupied with every doubt and disaster scenario I could think of, I lay on the bed fully clothed as the eastern sky behind the Potala began to stain the day. The thought of venturing north on an uncharted and unauthorized 4,000-mile journey, with people I scarcely knew, was far from reassuring. After the mishaps of the last few weeks I no longer expected that anything that was promised would materialize without major mishap or miscalculation.

As the hours slipped relentlessly towards noon, the likelihood of meeting the rendezvous deadline with the Boys at Nagchukha at six that evening evaporated as inexorably as the mist on the Kyichu river was burned off by the new day's sun, and my anxiety was difficult to contain. Seán, never at his most scintillating in the morning, had returned to his room. Just after ten there was a soft tap on the door and Thondup came in smiling, apologized for the delay, but the promised vehicle had not arrived; so dispensing another large wad of Rmb, he had procured a land-cruiser – a Chinese version of a Landrover cum Cherokee – which was waiting downstairs, together with a Chinese driver to take us to Nagchukha to meet the Boys.

With a quick hug I left Seán, and as we pulled out of the hotel gates I wondered when I would next see him. There was a sharp chill in the air: it was the first day of September – twenty-six more days until my visa ran out. I wondered if the first snows had already fallen and how long it would be before the high passes ahead would be blocked. As we drove past Drepung monastery and approached the outskirts of Lhasa proper, Thondup told me to pretend to be asleep and pull my hat down over my face. Neither of us knew where the checkpoints were, and as we were more than likely to run into one, it would be better if the Chinese didn't see my white face staring out of the windscreen. Foreigners, as I well knew, were not allowed outside Lhasa in private transport and Thondup had performed miracles by securing the land-cruiser. He had apparently told our Chinese driver that I was his wife, pregnant with our second child and feeling off-colour.

Outside Lhasa the scenery was just too beautiful to keep my eyes shut. The road initially ran by the fast-flowing Tsangpo. The road was bumpy with pot-holes as we climbed past groves of willows arching gracefully over the small square Tibetan mud-brick homes. Nests of prayer-flags in bright blue, red, yellow and white fluttered gaily in the breeze at the corners of the roofs.

I remembered stories Tibetan friends had told me of long summer days, of family picnics by the river. I could almost see the brightly coloured blouses and gaily striped aprons of the women as they chased the children in a playful game of *thadodah* – hide-and-seek – darting in and out of the pale green willow branches that curved gracefully down to the grass. If I shut my eyes, I could almost hear their laughter. But that was in the time before the Chinese arrived.

Now the air was filled with the grinding of lorries churning up the Qinghai–Tibet highway, from landlocked Lhasa to the mainland of China over 2,500 miles to the north-east. It was also the strategic military artery between the Lhasa garrison and those of Nagchukha, Golmud and the industrial cities of north-west China, so the road was busy with three-tonne trucks, both military and civilian. I did not yet know how to decipher the licence plates into 'friendly' lorries and 'hostile' – military – trucks, but by the end of the trip I could even read which area they came from. That morning I played safe and sat directly behind the driver to minimize detection from prying Chinese eyes that could look straight into the vehicle from the passing trucks' high cabs.

We climbed above the tree-line into Alpine meadows bright with vivid blue gentians and miniature lilac Michaelmas daisies with sunny yellow faces. At noon we stopped to picnic and sat in the warm sunshine in a field of flowers with the odd dozy yak munching quietly nearby. We opened a tin of corned beef that I had bought outside Tibet and spread it on dry bread. I didn't know it then, but it was to be the last time in six weeks that I was to feel the warm sun on my face or breathe the exhilarating mountain air without a face-mask . . .

A little barefoot Tibetan boy, dressed in a ragged sweater more holes than wool, who had been minding the yaks, came up shyly and sat with us. I offered him some food, but he sheepishly refused. Thondup in his gentle way talked to the child, whose name was Lobsang Gompa. Thondup gradually persuaded him to eat and, prompted by my questions, found out that he was twelve (but looked eight). He was undersized, as were all the Tibetan children I was to meet, and had never been to school. Nor had any of his friends or family. The child told Thondup that he knew no Tibetans in the area who went to school – though only half an hour further on we drove past a Chinese settlement where I saw Chinese children, with what looked like school-satchels on their backs, pouring out of a low concrete building and chattering excitedly in what Thondup told me was certainly not Tibetan.

The afternoon passed, one frustratingly telegenic vista unfurling after another in a panorama of constantly changing colours – towering snow-capped peaks and white-caps in the river merging into the blue of the sky and an infinity of browns and greens in the valleys. As everywhere in Tibet, I was to find that no five seconds of landscape were visually the same. It was as though we were driving through a gigantic kaleidoscope. I was sorely tempted to film but, being uncertain about the driver, I had to content myself with the stills cameras.

After the crowded countryside of Europe that I had left only a few weeks ago, and the claustrophobia of the Chinese cities bursting with people, the sheer emptiness of the landscape was breathtaking. The only signs of life as far as the eye could see were a few yaks dotted on the slopes, a few Tibetan mud dwellings huddled together and the familiar low concrete Chinese housing with their shiny roofs that clashed discordantly with the harmony of the mountains. For the first time I noticed electricity pylons marching alongside the road, branching in to supply the Chinese houses, but not once in that whole trip – or subsequently – did I see the wires turn into the Tibetan homes. I made a note to film them on my return journey.

When it was almost dusk, and way past our appointed rendezvous hour for meeting the Boys, we turned a sharp corner in the road that for hours had been winding through a totally deserted, treeless plateau of scrubby grass. And there, in the middle of nowhere, was Nagchukha. The town, unremarkable and characterless, had low white single-storeyed buildings surrounded by high walls in the same 'Chinese colonial-style' as in Lhasa.

What *was* remarkable, however, was the town's location. Miles from anywhere, with no sign of agriculture, industry, or any visible sign of support, Nagchukha squatted in its dusty, unpaved streets, reverberating to the sound of heavy lorries going to an unknown destination. And what was more than somewhat disturbing was the sight and sound of masses of Chinese soldiers wandering around the town.

We drove to the crossroads in the middle of the town where we were to meet the Boys. But by now we were more than two hours late and there was no sign of them. We parked outside a rough café full of soldiers and Thondup went for a 'stroll' round town to see if he could find them.

I slid down in my seat behind the driver, tipped my hat onto my face and pretended to be asleep. All around the land-cruiser I could hear the harsh voices of Chinese soldiers. It was dark when Thondup got back into the car. The night, by then, was full of tinny Chinese music blaring full blast from the loudspeakers, and by 9 P.M. the shouts of the soldiers had become distinctly inebriated. Thondup told me that there was no sign of the Boys, so he had booked both of us into the local hotel – saying that we were on the way to Golmud the next day.

We drove up to a two-storeyed, barrack-like concrete building without a single flower or tree to alleviate the grim outline. As it was, for Tibet, reasonably lit, with dangling naked light bulbs, I raked the angle of my hat sufficiently to cover most of my face, as we approached the 'guardian' on reception duty. We got our keys and then Thondup paid off the Chinese driver. We walked down some draughty corridors and finally got to our rooms which were lit by single 40-watt bulbs. Each had two beds, bulky pink eiderdowns and a couple of vinyl-covered chairs. But the cast-iron radiator was ice-cold. In the bathroom the bath was deeply in-grained with dirt and rust stains and the loo was heavily encrusted with faeces and rust. The taps were jammed solid and not even a trickle of water could be forced out of them.

Thondup, resourceful as ever, got flasks of hot water from the attendant and a cracked bowl. He left me to wash and went off to try and locate our Tibetan friends. By the spluttering light of the candle (there was no electricity in the bathroom) I balanced in the basin to avoid touching any of the revolting surfaces and removed most of the grime and dust from the twelve-hour drive. The room had the chill of a morgue. I got into one of the beds, pulled both eiderdowns up to my chin and tried to work out questions for the interviewees for the morning.

About 10.15 P.M. Thondup brought me a cup of hot water, a packet of dried noodles and a spoon from a spare set of cutlery that Seán had left behind. He sat on the bed and told me that he had found the Boys, who had arranged transport for the next leg of the trip. He also told me that all the Tibetans that had been selected for interview had agreed to speak to me privately and in public, to our camera, and that others were apparently waiting in the various places that we had pre-arranged along our route.

While I hungrily devoured the last of the noodles, we discussed the logistics of the next day's filming and how to get out of the hotel before light at six o'clock in the morning to meet the Boys in a side street not far from the hotel. I brushed my teeth, carefully laid out my clothes and prepared all the bags for our early departure and got back into bed. It was freezing and even though I had two pairs of gloves on my fingers were glacial.

There was an eerie quiet. Not even a dog was barking. I started to study the camera's operational manual and was going over the procedures for loading the tapes into the camera and how to monitor an interview with external microphones, when, without warning, the lights suddenly went out.

10

Nuclear Allegations

In the corridor outside, Chinese voices were talking excitedly. Footsteps, sounding like army boots, clinked on the concrete flooring. I was frozen into inactivity trying to decipher the situation. Fearing that the PSB were on to me, I slipped the camera's instruction book under the mattress, pulled the eiderdowns over my head, and pretended to be asleep.

After what seemed like an age, when the voices and feet had moved noisily down the corridor, there was a soft tapping on my door. Fumbling for my torch I stumbled to the door and listened, hoping that whoever was on the other side would not hear the thumping of my heart.

'Open up,' Thondup said urgently. 'It's me.'

He followed the narrow beam of his torch quickly into the room and locked the door behind him.

'Don't worry,' he said reassuringly. 'The electricity goes out now until tomorrow afternoon when it gets dark. I know you are frightened of the dark, so I brought you another candle.' He smiled, holding one out towards me. It was another of innumerable thoughtful incidents that endeared Thondup to me over the coming weeks. He demonstrated complete selflessness, especially as the trip wore on, when my fatigue and fear blended into pure exhaustion, and irritability, I'm afraid, often got the better of me.

After he went, I read until the candle spluttered and then fell asleep while poring over the camera instruction manual by torchlight. Suddenly I was awakened by a tap on the door. It was pitch-dark and freezing. I strained my ears listening for the least sign of movement, but everywhere seemed blanketed in silence. Only the muffled snoring of the Chinese in the next room warned me to be silent. I quietly went to the door, unlocked it, and once again found a smiling Thondup with a cup of coffee and a cup of noodles. He was already dressed and packed. It was 4.55 in the morning of Friday, 2 September.

While Thondup went to get his bags, I quickly dressed and ate at the same time by the dim light of the torch which I had balanced against the flask of hot water. The faint warmth of the coffee soon seeped into my frozen limbs as I put on my thermal leggings, long socks and the rest of my clothes that I had bought in London. With two sweaters under my green jacket and another pair of socks under the Chinese shoes, I pulled on my black balaclava over my head and over my mouth, firmly tied my straw Chinese coolie hat under my chin and drew on two pairs of gloves.

And still I felt like a block of ice. Above all else I hate the cold. Every one of my mental and physical processes seems to freeze up and in the past I have found it difficult even to think straight. That morning, fumbling around in the dark, was no exception. For me the ultimate horror would be even a short spell in the 'cold cell' like Solzhenitsyn's Ivan Denisovich!

When Thondup returned, we checked that all the luggage was locked and that both our money-belts were securely fastened under our voluminous clothes. While Thondup carried the heaviest equipment, I hitched the camera-bag on one shoulder, slung the holdall with the spare batteries, equipment and sleeping bags on the other. I picked up the grip of medicines and books in one hand and with the other an enormous red, white and blue plastic bag full of tins and packets of food and a flask full of hot water from the previous night.

As we crept down the dark corridor, my new shoes squeaked at every step and in the tension of the moment it sounded loud enough to alert every Chinese soldier stationed in Nagchukha! We struggled past reception, along darkened concrete blocks of rooms and through the hotel gate, which Thondup had arranged, by bribery, to be left open, saying that we were leaving early.

As we turned right out of the hotel, the wind howled down the deserted street and penetrated all the layers of clothing I was wearing. It was six o'clock precisely. There was not a light on anywhere. There was no sign of life in the empty street, just the dust swirling in small sandstorms from one shuttered Chinese gateway to another. We scanned the street for the vehicle that the Boys had promised would pick us up. The silence was deafening with foreboding. It was insane to hover at the entrance, because either we would be picked up by a coasting Chinese patrol or the hotel would soon spring to life and awkward questions would be asked.

'Let's move,' I whispered nervously.

'Where?' Thondup asked, looking anxious.

'Anywhere, but let's get out of this bloody doorway and off this street! We're too conspicuous standing here!' I started walking down to the right, towards the crossroads that I knew were somewhere in the dark at the bottom of the street. If only, I prayed, we could make it to the edge of town, we would not look so screamingly suspicious as we waddled down the main street heavily laden with dubious-looking bags.

The bags were murderously heavy. Thondup walked on and soon the distance between us grew. I tried to remember about controlling my breathing and using my stomach muscles to give me more stamina. At another time I suppose I would have laughed at the ridiculous sight of two people in the middle of the night (for the actual geographical time was 3 A.M.) struggling down a deserted road in a God-forsaken town in the middle of the Tibetan plateau. But as the bags became heavier and there seemed to be no sign of any vehicle, it was difficult to see the amusing side of anything.

We had walked just four blocks from the hotel when suddenly I felt a sharp pain in my lower back. I must have cried out because Thondup turned round. As I automatically tried to ease my heaviest bag to the pavement, an arrow of burning pain shot down my left leg and I found I could move neither up nor down. I was stuck like a petrified frog frozen in half-flight. I had slipped a disc and was frozen in a spasm of pain – in the middle of a garrison town alleged to be a Chinese nuclear base.

Thondup pushed and pulled me into a nearby doorway where I collapsed in agony on the ground. We could not exactly call out an emergency service – even if there had been one – so while he said he would go to the crossroads to look for the Boys, I started to rummage for keys to unlock the medicine bag for some pain relief. Every movement and sound I made seemed to reverberate down that empty street. It was too dangerous to use a torch, and while I had my hands deep in the bag trying to decode all the plastic bags I had so meticulously wrapped everything in, I heard the metallic click of army boots on concrete coming towards me.

Terror paralysed every nerve in my body. Sitting on the ground surrounded by a pile of luggage, I heard the steps becoming louder as they came inexorably nearer. From under my straw hat which I tilted forward to hide my face, I saw four black army boots disappearing into green Chinese army uniform trouser legs. A torch flashed over me. I did not look up and went on rummaging. An irritated voice in Chinese barked at me. Numb with fright, I could marshal not one single thought other than 'This is it.' All through my career I had skated on thin ice on many assignments and somehow had, so far, got away with it. But at the back of my mind I was certain that one day my nine lives would run out and I would be caught – or worse. As I sat there, the perfect 'bag lady' surrounded by her paraphernalia, I felt my luck had finally run out.

There was nothing I could do. Since I spoke no Chinese, I could hardly talk myself out of being found in a highly sensitive military location with a mountain of photographic equipment on me. All the Chinese soldiers had to do was to haul me to my feet, push my hat off and . . . the rest was too awful even to contemplate. But when faced with certain catastrophe, there is a curious moment when you feel an unnatural calm. It's as though you finally cast off the tiller and leave the winds to blow you where they will. In a funny way, it was a marvellous detachment knowing that from then on I did not have to make a single decision. I would either be arrested, interrogated and imprisoned for a very long time, or after interrogation – and they had discovered what they could about the Tibetan underground network – I would be expelled as a British spy.

I had exactly the same feeling in South Sudan when I was captured alone making the first film about genocide in that part of the world for Granada Television. After beating me up, the soldiers had taken my shoes and made me walk barefoot through the jungle in the burning midday sun with a machine-gun in my back. That time, the same feeling of aloofness had saved my life. Instead of running into the jungle, which had been my first instinct and which would have resulted in a hail of bullets in my back, I remember wondering why these soldiers were swearing in English at me, and pondering the curious heritage we British had left behind as colonizers. It was as though there was a twin-track running in my head. One had all the turmoil of panic, the other was running with cool detachment observing the idiosyncratic details of the situation.

I felt the same detached sensation as I sat on that cold doorstep in Tibet. My body was petrified, seemingly welded into immobility, but my mind clinically stood aside with my reactions on automatic overdrive. I just continued rummaging in my bag and did not look up or reply. I felt I was being minutely scrutinized in the glare of the torchlight and I idly wondered what the expression on their faces would be when they found out who I was, and what the inside of a Chinese jail would be like. I was no longer aware of the pain in my back and leg.

A furious burst of Chinese washed straight over my head. I rummaged for what seemed an eternity. In reality it could only have been a few minutes. Suddenly the boots turned right and walked briskly down the road in the direction that Thondup had taken. I peeked cautiously from the shadow of the doorway and saw the two figures, who indeed were soldiers, walk down the street flashing their torches into the doorways, obviously on patrol.

Despite the cold I was perspiring profusely. Again, and for the second time on this trip, I could smell my own fear. There was no sign of Thondup, or the Boys, or a vehicle, or any way out of that doorway. By now the pain had come flooding back. I took an aspirin, which I knew would do little to alleviate the pain. What I needed was a strong prescription analgesic and an osteopath. Both of which seemed light-years away from the desolate street. I tried to get up, to attempt to move away before the soldiers returned. Again the pain locked me into immobility.

I remember desperately hoping that I should soon awake from this nightmare when I heard the soldiers returning. I quickly pulled out the Chinese-made vacuum flask and, as soon as I judged they were level with me, I made nonchalant gestures to unscrew the top and pour myself some hot water. Again they spoke harshly to me. Again, I rummaged in the bag, found a biscuit and proceeded to eat it with my hat tipped well down on my face. Again there was a torrent of Chinese and the boots came closer. I grunted, put the mug to my lips, slurped noisily in the Chinese fashion, and wondered what the statistics were of lightning striking twice. After five minutes in which I must have consumed nearly the whole flask in my anxiety, the boots walked off in the direction from which they had originally appeared.

After an aeon of anxiety, I heard the faint hum of a motor in the distance. I wondered whether it was the Chinese returning to take me in for interrogation or the Boys with a means of escape. I cautiously looked out and saw a vehicle approaching without lights. Thondup jumped softly to the ground and hurried over. I explained I was 'stuck', and he and another shadowy figure dragged me and the bags into the merciful sanctuary of the vehicle.

We drove as quickly as we dared without lights through the town towards the brightening sky in the east. The tension was high inside the vehicle and after the customary *'Tashi Delek'*, no one spoke. We each looked nervously ahead through the windscreen as the vehicle left the outskirts of Nagchukha and bumped along an uneven track up the side of a mountain.

I looked around: there were four Tibetan men and Thondup. Thondup sat up in front with the driver and was dressed in Chinese army-surplus clothes. With a green army cap on his head, he looked the perfect Chinese, straight out of central casting. I was squashed in the back seat between Tenzin, the Lhasa–Batang section leader whom I had already met, and an unknown younger man. In the back another Tibetan was uncomfortably squeezed between the luggage which was piled to the roof of the van. It was not the time for introductions and pleasantries.

At 7.30 we left the rough track and bumped our way over a rugged mountainous terrain, green with moss and lichen. The sky was paling with light and in the distance I could see the snow-capped mountains flitting in and out of playful white clouds. After another fifteen minutes' lurching over the trackless mountain-side, we saw two dark figures coming towards us on the horizon. There was a quick burst of Tibetan and Thondup translated, telling me that these were two interviewees. He repeated the Boys' request to 'please hurry up, because here we can see the base, but when the light becomes stronger, they will see us!'

I questioned the two men through Thondup and fumbled with frozen hands to set up the camera and stabilize the spirit-level on the tripod-head. With my fear and the cold, I moved the head too jerkily and it seemed to take an age to get the small black ball floating in fluid into the ring in the middle of the gauge that tells you that you have an infallibly correct horizon. The more I jerked it impatiently, the more the little blob floated out of the ring. In desperation I asked Thondup to help while I fixed the small microphones onto the men's dark *chubas*. Seán had also told me to run a tape-recorder synchronously with the camera microphone, as it would give much better quality: that meant that I had to start running the camera, then nip over to the interviewees, turn on the tape-recorder, and tap the microphones in vision (mic-taps) so that the editor assembling the rushes in London could synchronize the sound and the picture. It was a time-consuming and fiddly job, especially as we had to stop both camera and tape-recorder between each question and answer.

As usual, I asked them if they wanted their faces shown, in case they could be identified and arrested not only for talking to foreign media, but for high treason in discussing Chinese military matters. They were very adamant that by taking the risk they hoped that the outside world would believe them. They were ordinary men with completely unremarkable faces. It was only as they spoke that their passion and concern for what was happening to their country started to illuminate their faces and the gravity of what they were saying began to hit me.

There was no evidence of any base or even habitation within a thirty-mile radius that I could see. But then, as Lhasang Tsering, the President of the Tibetan Youth Congress, had said to me in Dharamsala, 'There wouldn't be any evidence for the casual observer to see, would there?' However, led by the interviewees and crouching low in the grass so that we would not be visible on the skyline to anyone in the camp below, we crawled on our stomachs to the brow of the hill. The pain in my back – then and indeed for the rest of the trip – was so severe that in the absence of any other alternative I could function only because fear over-rode physical discomfort. We then looked down to a collection of white buildings in the valley. 'That's the base,' they said. I wondered if what I was looking at was one of the two military camps I had been told of on the Nagchukha–Namtso road.

I had originally, very foolishly, thought of filming the interview with the base behind them, much in the way television news reporters speak to camera with an identifiable building, which is immediately associated with the topic or town they are reporting on, in the background.

To look more closely at the white buildings at the bottom of the mountain, I took the camera off the tripod and focused the telephoto lens on what the interviewees had told me was the nuclear base. But as the lens was of only limited magnification, all I saw were white blobs that could really have been anything, anywhere. It certainly was not worth the risk of standing the tripod on the brow of the hill to film it. I told the interviewees that I would film it later and crawled back to ask Thondup to set up the spirit-level for me, as he seemed to have a knack with it, just under the brow of the hill.

While he did this, translating all the time, I looked round for what in film terms is called the establisher: a shot that will establish or identify the location and put the interview into context. The only thing I could think of were the tops of the snow-capped mountains in the distance. Fortunately, the camera had an automatic zoom, but the smooth operation of it depended on even pressure on the zoom button. To begin with, I just couldn't remember which way the zoom went – towards the camera for zooming in, and away from the camera for zooming out, or vice versa. It was particularly irritating during interviews, when I wanted to change the size of the interviewee in the shot from close-up – for telling emotional moments – to mid-shot or to wide shot to include the whole person and part of the background to establish some sort of context.

During those first interviews in Lhasa and in Nagchukha, I so often wavered indecisively before pressing the button: being aware that once pressed, I was committed to continue that particular move, as I was recording picture and each shudder of indecision would jar on the tape. And without knowing a word of what they were saying, until the translation at the end of the answer, I could hardly ask for a retake at any particular point. As the interviewees were speaking in Tibetan, I could not interrupt to query a point or come in with a supplementary question, so I had no idea when to go in for the close-up. All I could do was watch their facial expression, and when they seemed agitated, I zoomed in. I was filming blind – not the ideal way to film such contentious interviews.

On my fifth attempt I managed to start the shot on the snow peaks in the distance behind and hold it long enough to satisfy Chris Lysaght, the editor in London; he could then perhaps use the head of the shot as part of a mountain montage in another part of the film. I then managed to zoom out and pan down to the two interviewees sitting on the ground. At the same time I asked Thondup to start the first question when the interviewees came into shot so that on the edited film they would appear to be, as they were in reality, listening to the question.

Normally, the smooth zooms and tilting motions take years of practice to perfect the timing and faultless operation. And normally cameramen have assistants who operate the focus and check the aperture as the light values change from the distant object to the near one. I had neither experience nor the luxury of time, as the Boys who were on look-out on four nearby mounds of the same mountain complex kept anxiously coming up to Thondup and asking him to tell me to hurry.

I started to interview the two men by telling them that on 14 October 1987 there had been an article in the Sydney newspaper *The Australian* reporting the presence of nuclear missiles at Nagchukha. Subsequently, the Australian Nuclear Disarmament Party, in a press release dated 28 October 1987, expressed their grave concern and stated that twenty intermediate-range ballistic missiles (IRBMs) and seventy medium-range ones (MRBMs) were stationed at Nagchukha. I asked them, as men who had lived in the Nagchukha area for many years, if they had seen any missiles or heard of a nuclear base.

Kelsang, a tall thin man with a shock of grey hair and a solemn face, replied slowly, weighing his words: 'Yes, there is a hidden place, and this is the place.'

I asked him to elaborate.

'Many people have seen and heard movements and noises. And most people here have seen missiles coming from China. And many travellers have seen movements of missiles at different places.'

There had been numerous reports that construction work had started about ten miles north of Nagchukha in 1970 and that there had been a considerable influx of Chinese military personnel, including a special battalion of Du Li Chun Chue (the Chinese equivalent of the crack British SAS or the American Green Berets), who are answerable only, and directly, to Beijing. Most Tibetans were barred from the area. Construction work was reported finished in 1979, and there have been numerous eye-witness accounts from many Tibetans of tunnels being dug into the mountainsides and of concrete structures being made that from their description seem to be silos. Although I am sure the American CIA (Central Intelligence Agency) has detailed pictures of all China's nuclear and military installations, there had been no concrete proof available to the general public of these nuclear bases. When Major-General Zhang Shaosong, the Political Commissar of the PLA in Tibet, was asked point-blank by the BBC's Mark Braine in 1988 whether there were nuclear weapons in Tibet, he replied: 'Whether there are nuclear weapons in Tibet or not, it's up to the authorities to decide.' And he smiled.

I asked Kelsang how he, who was not a military specialist, could tell a missile from any long gun. Thondup patiently translated back and forth and the man described the shape of what could only be a missile and told me that they had come on long lorries, longer than he had ever seen before. I then asked him why, here in the middle of a vast empty plateau, there should be so many soldiers.

'The main aim of this base is not only the complete subjugation of the Tibetan people, but also to create conflict with other countries and inflict destruction.' The other man, Topgyal, a sombre man wearing a dark *chuba*, nodded in agreement.

I asked again what proof he actually possessed that there was a nuclear base in the valley.

'Because of the secretiveness, because of so much army here in the middle of nothing, because no one is allowed there, and because of strange things happening to our animals and children.'

I asked him what he meant.

'As a result of the situation here, animals are getting strange diseases and dying. Some people are dying and children are being born deformed. In many places water is contaminated and undrinkable. The moment you drink it you get ill or get diseases that we never had before. People get ill and go to different hospitals. They don't get better and the doctors don't tell us what it is and then we have to keep quiet about it.'

While I was changing tapes, I puzzled at these disturbing

allegations and tried, from my very limited knowledge of nuclear warheads, to discover what actually was happening. It is most unlikely that there would be a radiation leak from nuclear warheads. Yet when I got out of Tibet and later spoke to one defence expert in a well-known national strategic defence studies think-tank, he told me that I should not necessarily jump to the conclusion that the human and animal abnormalities were due to contamination from a radiation leak from an unsuspected nuclear reactor in the area. He told me not to discount the possibility of a radiation leak from a nuclear warhead. For, although the Chinese had made enormous and rapid strides in the development of their nuclear capability, they had not, in his experience, perfected the close attention to safety details that could categorically rule out a leak from this unusual source.

There have of course been other nuclear-related contamination incidents that have resulted in an abnormally high incidence of leukaemia, especially among children, in areas like Sellafield, allegedly due to the proximity of nearby nuclear facilities. But babies being born deformed and animals dying spoke of a massive nuclear contamination. It made me think of the brilliant Peter Watkins film *The War Game* and its sobering scenes of mutants born grotesquely deformed due to nuclear contamination.

Nuclear verification is highly problematic at the best of times, as the recent negotiations between Nato and the Warsaw Pact for missile de-escalation have proved. And no nation willingly allows foreign access and scrutiny of its sensitive defence facilities. China is more secretive than most, yet the fact that China now has a considerable nuclear capability has been cited by the many specialist sources who have identified its nuclear assets.

As long ago as 6 February 1980, an article in the Hong Kong newspaper *Shin Bao* mentioned that China deployed seventy MRBMs (CSS-1) and twenty IRBMs (CSS-2) at Nagchukha, with a range of 1,100–1,300 and 2,800–3,200 kilometres respectively. (These figures are based on the range at the time of commissioning, which was 1966 (MRBM) and 1971 (IRBM).) It is strongly rumoured that the Chinese have upgraded and modified their existing missiles, which were originally based on the Soviet model, to perform to longer range and higher yield specifications. Certainly in September 1984 an improved CSS-2 IRBM was fitted with an

MIRV (multiple independently targeted re-entry-type nose cones). Others feel that because the railway from China, the Tibet–Qinghai railway, terminates in Golmud, 980 miles north of Nagchukha, that would seem the more likely site as the transport of materials would obviously be facilitated.

China's ICBMs (inter-continental ballistic missiles), which are in the same class as the Soviet SS-9 and the US Titan, came into service in 1978. The Dong Feng 4 (CSS-3) has a limited range of 7,000 km. In 1981 the full-range Dong Feng 5 (CSS-4) was deployed with a range of 15,000 km and with the yield of a five-megaton nuclear warhead. They are reported to be sited in Kongpo Nyitri near the border with India's eastern Arunachal Pradesh province, at Powo Tomo in southern Tibet and of course at other bases in China nearer the Soviet border. As Lhasang Tsering, the radical young President of the Tibetan Youth Congress, in exile in Dharamsala in northern India, told me: 'It is known, through various independent sources, that China has placed up to one-quarter of its nuclear arsenal in Tibet. These are targeted against Russia, against the major industrial and population centres of India, and they could certainly reach other South-East Asian countries; and some experts say that they have the range even to hit American bases in Guam and cities on both coasts of America. Of course, Tibet's high altitude, an average of 14,000 feet above sea-level, gives them an additional advantage. I believe that the strategic military and nuclear advantages that bases in Tibet give China simply mean that China will not willingly relinquish its hold on Tibet.'

The Chinese categorically refuse to disclose the details of their military and nuclear deployment. But what is certain is that despite the art of nuclear deception, and although China has in the past few years made cuts in the overall number of its armed forces, its funding for its nuclear programme has consistently expanded and today absorbs a reported 5 per cent of its defence budget, which Tibetan experts conservatively estimate at over $10 billion. As one defence expert, who is well-versed in China's strategic deployment, said to me: 'Do not fall into the naïve assumption that though China is at the moment economically a developing country, its militaristic, and especially its nuclear ambitions, are in any way commensurate. For China, nuclear weapons are a symbol of self-reliance and a very powerful way of rectifying the humiliation that China believes it has suffered over the last hundred years at the hands of Western colonizing powers. A Chinese propaganda film confirming, Chinese nuclear capability, stated: 'Imperialists' blackmail through nuclear monopoly is smashed. Let American imperialists and other reactionaries quake. This [China's nuclear capability and strike force] is the triumph of the thoughts of Chairman Mao, the triumph of the Chinese people.' In 1987 the BBC transmitted a film about the PLA, and reporter Mark Braine interviewed Colonel Lin Xingqui, Commander of the 112th Division of the 38th Army, who said: 'We have prepared for nuclear and chemical war. But we do not want to use our weapons first. But in any future war we have the ability to use them.' While I was in Tibet in September 1988, a Beijing newspaper reported the successful completion of a chemical warfare exercise in Tibet.

The defence expert also pointed out that China's remarkable industry and ability to absorb – and copy – Western technology has effectively meant that China, which had no nuclear capability or facility in the 1950s, has managed to use laser technology to obtain the U-235 uranium which was used in its first successful fission test, detonated on 16 October 1964. He pointed out, and various Strategic Studies Institutes around the world confirm, that more than forty-five uranium deposits have been verified in China, including the largest deposits of uranium in the world – which are in Tibet. China also has the other necessary minerals, like lithium (found in Tibet), needed to produce sophisticated nuclear explosive devices. China is known to have five uranium and plutonium processing facilities and current output of weapon-grade radioactive material was in 1987 believed to be about 1.2 metric tonnes (1,200 kg) annually – enough to produce at least seventy-five nuclear warheads. Public reports indicate that China operates at least three fission and fusion warhead manufacturing installations: at Huangyan and Haiyen in Qinghai, both of which are capable of thermo-nuclear weapon production, and a third at Harbin in Heilongjiang not far from the Soviet border.

Tibetans also claim that there are two underground complexes that manufacture nuclear warheads – one north of Lake Kokonor, between Thensong and Gangtsa, and the other near Tonyela, south of the lake and two and a half hours' drive south-west of

Xining. Both areas, Tibetans report, are strictly off-limits to local Tibetans.

Western nuclear defence experts claim that China has at least two ICBM (DF5) with nuclear warheads, six DF4s, over sixty DF3s, and twelve submarine-launched ballistic missiles, as well as up to 120 Hong 6 bombers capable of delivering two nuclear warheads each.

There have been reports that the testing base has been moved from its Lop Nor site to further south in Tibet, but to date there is no documentary proof available. What is certain is that the Stockholm International Peace Research Institute, which monitors nuclear testing, reported that on 29 September 1988 China exploded another underground nuclear device in the Lop Nor region. And many Tibetans whom I spoke to, all over Tibet and totally unconnected with each other, reported strange phenomena. For example, nomads told me that on the shores of Lake Kokonor the grass is all burnt (but not, they told me in reply to my questioning, from natural causes like drought, or the seasons, nor from the fires of other nomads) and that many of the fish in the lake are dying.

The nuclear testing has not occurred without protests from the local inhabitants, both in Tibet and in Xinjiang. Although there is total censorship of the press in China, foreign correspondents filed reports in December 1985 of an unprecedented protest march by 200–300 students of the Uighur minority people who marched through Tiananmen Square to the high-walled Zhongnanhai Compound where China's leaders live. They were protesting about nuclear testing in Xinjiang Autonomous Republic, which has a mutual border of hundreds of miles with north-western Tibet and the Soviet Union and Pakistan. A student leader then phoned a Western correspondent in Beijing and told him that the Beijing protest was a follow-up to an earlier one held in Ürümqi, the capital of Xinjiang.

Several Tibetan groups in exile, worried by China's growing nuclear arsenal in Tibet, have been monitoring alarming rumours of nuclear dumping in the country. China undoubtedly needs nuclear reactors to accommodate its burgeoning energy supply demands and patently cannot afford the technology or find sufficient foreign exchange to finance the ones under construction (at Qinshan, seventy-five miles south of Shanghai, and then the $4.1 billion plant at Daya Bay – a Franco-British GEC enterprise near Guangzhou). Tibetan groups claim that they are collecting irrefutable evidence to show that in return for foreign exchange, China is willing to allow certain industrialized countries in the West to dump their spent nuclear fuel in Tibet.

As the dumping of toxic and nuclear wastes is an enormously sensitive ecological issue, conclusive verification is difficult, but it is believed that West Germany and Switzerland have been in negotiation with China to dump their nuclear waste in Tibet.

Lhasang Tsering went on to point out to me that Tibet is far from geologically stable and cited the numerous earthquakes that have, in Lhasa alone, in the past centuries damaged, among other things, the Potala. He told me: 'China is offering to accept nuclear waste at a tremendously low price [to the dumper]. Now, this is extremely dangerous, as you know. I am not just talking about this from unconfirmed refugee sources,' he emphasized. 'I was in Switzerland earlier this year [1988] in June, and there was a debate in the Swiss parliament where they were discussing this specific issue – of buying uranium from China and giving them [China] back the waste – and they are still having discussions on the deal.

'And there was an earlier report after the visit of Chancellor Kohl to China that the West Germans were thinking of a similar idea.'

'So you mean to say that they are actually going to dump nuclear waste in Tibet?' I asked.

'Yes,' he said, 'we fear that if any one of the rivers which flow from Tibet is polluted by nuclear waste, millions of people who today depend on them for sustenance will find that tomorrow the rivers may bring death and destruction to millions of people in South-East Asia.'

Actually to find conclusive proof of nuclear contamination would necessitate scientific access to the area, which obviously the Chinese would not allow. But although I left without tangible proof, the allegations that the Tibetans raised are serious enough to warrant further investigation. And if allegations like nuclear dumping were proved, it would become vital to institute proceedings against the relevant countries to stop the practice before nuclear contamination of Asia's major rivers could unleash a catastrophe of cataclysmic proportions – as well as destroy the lives of thousands of innocent Tibetans.

The claims of the two men in Nagchukha were disturbing, but, I asked them, could it be simply a military complex, possibly for the Special Forces?

Kelsang replied: 'Why should the Chinese build any sort of [military] base there? It is miles from anywhere, with no habitation and at least two days' hard drive from any population centre. It just makes no sense; there have been no reports of Wujing [the Chinese SAS] in the area, and anyway they are trained at a base outside Beijing. There is no population here. It is too far from any border to be much use, and anyway the PLA have their listening posts and radar-tracking stations in border towns like Dingri, near the Nepalese border, and at Rudok, in the Askai Chin near the Indian and Pakistani borders – as well as at Kongpo Nyitri in the south of Kham and nearer to the Arunachal Pradesh [India] border.'

Then I asked the two Nagchukha interviewees how I could be certain that they were not lying. Their reply was simple and compelling. They suggested that I walk down to the base and check for myself – but I would certainly be arrested. They also pointed out that they were appearing on British television without being disguised, knowing full well that they would certainly be arrested when the programme was transmitted.

I asked the two men why, in view of the danger to themselves, they were taking the risk. Kelsang answered: 'We have violated the law because of the destruction of Tibet and our civilization. In Tibet there is not much we can do. We cannot speak out. So we ask you: you are the only one who can tell the world outside what is happening inside Tibet. There is no one else to appeal to, apart from you. We depend on you . . . We have no regrets. We do not fear the consequences, even if it means death.'

Tenzin interrupted the interview to say that a group of people were approaching. Without field-glasses he did not know who they were. I pulled the camera off the tripod and we all ran for the cover of the van.

I decided that it would be safer to send the tapes with a note to Seán. They were so incriminating, it would be safer if he took them out of Tibet with him. If I was caught with them on me during the trip, I would certainly be arrested as a spy and put many members of the Tibetan underground in jeopardy. Seán had a much better chance of getting away safely with them as he was going out officially with a lot of other tourists.

In my note I asked Seán to leave me a message at the Holiday Inn to await my return to tell me that he had received the tapes; I also asked him to telex me when he was out of Tibet to tell me, in cryptic language, that the tapes were safely out of the country. If for some reason they were seized, or wiped by the powerful airport X-ray machines, then I could try – heaven only knew how – to redo the interviews. Although I did not like putting the two men at greater risk than they had already placed themselves, I felt I had no choice but to ask them to take the tapes to Lhasa for me.

After we said goodbye, the two brave men left to catch the bus to Lhasa to deliver the tapes, and the Boys and I set off for our next location, a monastery twelve hours' drive east. Later, while I was enjoying the scenery and searching for some stills film in my camera-bag, I found that somehow I had forgotten to give the Nagchukha men one of the incriminating interview tapes. There was nothing to be done but continue.

11

Almost a Khampa Idyll

Friday, 2 September was visually an idyllic day.

After driving east-north-east from Nagchukha for three and a half hours, the Boys stopped by the side of a sparkling stream and found a sheltered mossy hollow near the road. From a plastic gunny sack they took a kettle, lit what looked like an acetylene torch under it, and proceeded to brew up Tibetan tea.

Tsering, who was officiating that day, broke off a chunk of tea from a long 'brick' (*cha bakchung*) that had been wrapped in a straw mesh. He crumbled it straight into the pot, cut a slab of butter off a block, and with a dash of salt mixed them vigorously in the kettle. *Boe-ja* – Tibetan tea – tastes to Westerners more like a nourishing soup than a delicate Earl Grey or Lapsang Souchong, and it is most definitely an acquired taste.

Usually, Tibetan tea is brewed in a *dhongmo*, a large cylindrical vat ten inches across, made of wood and hooped with metal. The tea-maker pumps a piston-like ladle in and out to churn it up. Now, however, in Tibetan towns and in the monasteries, the tea is more often poured from Chinese-made vacuum flasks with gaudy flowers printed on the side. I later asked a doctor whether in view of the butter Tibetans consume they suffer from cholesterol problems. He laughed and said: 'How on earth are we going to know about such sophisticated diagnoses when in most areas of Tibet, Tibetans don't even have doctors, hospitals or medicine? Before the Chinese arrived we drank much butter-tea and we were very healthy and lived to an old age. Butter helps to insulate us against the cold. We consume butter like the Eskimos eat blubber.'

While the tea brewed, the Boys relaxed in the warm sunshine, took off their sweaters and visibly unwound after the tensions of filming at Nagchukha. They started talking animatedly with Thondup whom they started to call '*gyen-la*' (teacher) and who, over the weeks ahead, revealed to them a strange world beyond the boundaries of Tibet. Thondup told them about America, about television, express highways, hamburgers and Disneyland. In return, Thondup was experiencing the journey he had always dreamed of. For the first time, he was seeing parts of Tibet that he had only heard about as a child, before he had left his village at the age of nine.

For him, it was a voyage of discovery as the others answered his queries about the landscape, the customs and the people. Thondup was like an excited wide-eyed child and he and the Boys talked non-stop. For me it was also a journey across unknown territory, but without access to the language it was infuriatingly frustrating when the hassle of translation made every single query an effort for everybody.

And so often, especially when I saw some breathtaking vista or watched a particularly beautiful sunset or dawn, it was painful not to be able to turn to someone, to touch an arm, to be able to say 'Hey, look!' Not to be able to share some of the most beautiful – and some of the most frightening – moments of the journey, and perhaps of my life, with someone: that in many ways was the hardest part of the trip, and inevitably as I grew progressively more tired, I withdrew a little. The Boys must have thought I was very odd.

When the tea was ready, Tenzin delved into a stained cloth bag and brought out a chunk of dried yak meat. He unsheathed his knife from its silver scabbard and carved me a slice. I gingerly took it and was quite surprised at its pleasant salty taste. Air-dried yak meat is quite a delicacy for Tibetans, who normally live on butter-tea, *tsampa* (roasted barley flour) and occasionally a few vegetables.

The Dalai Lama once told me that the one thing he missed about Tibetan food was dried yak meat. 'Especially the air-dried kind that comes from around Lake Yamdrok [the famous Turquoise Lake not far from Lhasa]. It is simply delicious!' The only drawback to my indulgence in Tibetan culinary delicacies was that without Western niceties, such as napkins, or the opportunity to brush my teeth, the smell of yak meat soon became rancid and permeated my ski-mask. (I wore my mask all the time and at the sight of an approaching lorry I automatically pulled it up to hide my Western nose.) At the end of the second day the smell made me retch so badly every time I hitched it over my nose that I had to stop near a stream, wash it and decline further offers of yak meat.

As the safety of all of us depended on my invisibility, Thondup, like a solicitous nanny, used to bring my food to me inside the van. Breakfast was half a cup of muesli made with milk powder and hot water from the flask which we tried to fill up the night before either from the safe house in which we were staying, or after the Boys had brewed up, we would fill the kettle from a nearby stream or river. And like all journalists, who seem unable to function without a mug of coffee, I also had a solitary cup in the morning. I offered the Boys some but I think they disliked its bitter taste – and as I could not stomach butter-tea, we decided to stay each with our own brew.

There were no fixed hours for food and the Boys drove on from early morning until three or four in the afternoon, when they would stop, brew up, and eat a little *tsampa* mixed with tea; on the rare occasion that we managed to buy some meat, they cooked it with butter and salt. But there was never any fruit or vegetables. In fact, although I was carrying several thousand pounds in my money-belt, in the depths of the countryside there simply was nothing to buy. And if we had not brought our own few provisions with us, or had not passed through several small towns where we were able to buy Chinese tins of fatty stew, packets of noodles and bottles of excellent, crisply preserved fruit, we would have been very hungry indeed.

So my gastronomic delights in Tibet were limited – noonish and night – to half a cup of noodles made with hot water. Fortunately I had bought a quantity of packets in Hong Kong and, as the trip progressed, I anticipated the little sachets with garlic and soya sauce with as much relish as I would the finest Seguva caviare! There were of course none of the formalities that one usually associates with dining, such as tables and chairs, or even plates and cutlery – just the cup and a teaspoon I had 'borrowed' from the Lhasa Holiday Inn. I had bought a few tins of fish and meat but, sharing them with the Boys, they lasted only two days.

It was curious how little food or drink came to matter. I was so totally absorbed in the changing countryside and deciding what and where I was going to film, that if it had not been for Thondup constantly bringing me a cup of noodles or whatever, I probably would quite genuinely have forgotten to eat. Throughout the trip it was important to eliminate all the inessentials of life, all the appendages and trivia that so easily accumulate as superfluous baggage and clutter up our physical and mental powers in modern urban life. I was surprised how very few necessities I needed for survival and, although I lost a lot of weight and was for most of the time in a considerable amount of pain and discomfort, I gained a great deal in other, more lasting, ways from this period, when everything had to be slashed to the bare minimum.

As the days progressed, I learnt interesting things about the lives of the Boys – but not too many, in case I was caught and interrogated. Tenzin, the tall Khampa I had met in Lhasa, was actually from Derge, further north-east in Kham. Married with five children, he had a smallholding there but supplemented his meagre income, as many Tibetans do, with petty trading. When the Chinese invaded Kham, he joined the Tibetan Resistance Movement and fought in many battles; he saw the aerial bombing of the monasteries and witnessed the killing of innocent Tibetans all over Kham. Then one morning, while fighting against impossible odds of superior Chinese artillery and ordnance, his unit was surrounded by Chinese soldiers; fighting to their last bullet, they were captured, tortured under interrogation and either killed or imprisoned. Tenzin was one of the lucky ones: he spent only nineteen years in jail, and is still alive.

Sumpa, our young driver, came from Chamdo, where he worked as a casual labourer on a building site when he could not find work as a long-distance lorry driver, because, as he told us, with the influx of Chinese settlers, all the jobs went first to them. Tsering was a petty trader from Khanse, also in eastern Kham. A quiet man, in his forties, he was superb at diagnosing what ailed the van when, usually in the middle of the night, we broke down. The fourth member of the team was Jigme, a sturdy thirty-year-old, who came from Shigatse, from a long line of farmers who worked in the fertile Tsangpo valley (the granary of Tibet). With a merry twinkle in his eye, he usually had the other Tibetans roaring with laughter from a never-ending stream of jokes, which, being in Tibetan, went straight over my head. His gaiety and sense of humour, for which Tibetans are renowned, lightened what, for the Boys, were wearisome hours of relentless and uncomfortable driving. The team had deliberately been picked from various towns in Tibet for their knowledge of local conditions in different areas.

The vans, which we changed several times on the trip, were each as uncomfortable as they were robust. The bench behind the driver's seat on which I was wedged, between Tenzin and Jigme, was a purgatory of bone-shattering metal covered with small Tibetan carpets. The constant jolting, on the worst roads I have ever travelled on in my life, was excruciatingly painful for my back until I found a way of sitting by one of the doors and twisting my left shoulder and hip in opposite directions: this somehow seemed to stretch some ligaments in my back and relieve the pressure on my slipped disc. None of the vehicles we travelled in had any luxuries such as springs to cushion the bumps or any heating at all and I spent a considerable amount of time and effort trying to prevent myself and my precious cameras from crashing to the floor.

I had to keep the video camera readily accessible in case I saw that unforgettable shot that needed to be filmed. But as a lot of dust and dirt blew up from the roads and through the floorboards as well as icy winds whistling through the cracks of the ill-fitting doors and windows, keeping the camera dust-free was extremely difficult. So I wrapped the Sony in a pillowcase that I had 'borrowed' from the Lhasa Holiday Inn, put it in a plastic laundry bag (also from the same hostelry) and rested it on an inflated neck-pillow that travellers use on long-distance flights. But that too proved far from fail-safe as, in the hurry to get out of the van to record a fleeting scene or in the rush to scramble back at the arrival of the Chinese army, I invariably dropped one or other of the covers and was incessantly worried about the dirt.

The stills cameras were also a problem. Tenzin put one into the voluminous folds of his *chuba*, while I kept the other ready in a camera-bag behind my head and resting on the luggage at the back, with the various lenses, microphones, tape for the video camera, film for the stills camera and of course the cleaning materials. That was the theory. But as we got thrown round the van, the neat compartmentalizing of the camera-bag proved impossible to maintain and I had to rummage for ages before I could come up with the relevant piece of equipment. The Boys tried to help, but it was too difficult to explain telephoto lens, or the Minolta wide-angle, or the 24mm lens, particularly when I was in a hurry, and especially when running out of film, which invariably happened at the worst moment in the middle of an interview.

And then there was the tripod. Because it was so obviously an expensive and strange piece of equipment, the Boys had decided that it would be safer to put it into one of the plasticized gunny sacks that now enveloped all the bags of clothing and equipment. They reasoned that if we were stopped at a checkpoint and the Chinese soldiers gave a cursory glance inside the van, they would see sacks which were similar to those that all Tibetans, in the absence of suitcases or grips, travel with. But finding the tripod and extending it from the bag was a hassle each time. And my impatience, aggravated by cold, altitude and fear did not help. So eventually Thondup decided to put it up, align the spirit-level, and then either he or I would clip the camera onto the tripod-head and readjust the level again. It was an unwelcome chore.

We had decided to travel to Chamdo, the third largest city in Tibet, by the northern route in an attempt to avoid most of the Chinese army lorries that used the southern road to Lhasa. But even on the northern route there was still a considerable number of three-tonne lorries and I soon learnt to read the licence plates' prefixes. These were in Roman numerals with the letter U or S or another letter of the alphabet as a prefix – usually in red or white – according to where the vehicles were stationed. A rapid scrutiny of the plates meant that if it was a civilian truck, I could relax and not worry about the van being pulled over for a spot inspection – until the next truck came round a corner.

Everywhere on our journey there were the neat little white tents of the Chinese army road-building brigade. It must have been a miserable life for the troopers, who in the cold and rain, without protective clothing over their thin olive-green uniforms and piti-fully flimsy plimsolls, had to build roads through those unyielding mountains. They were mostly young soldiers and looked thoroughly miserable stuck on a bleak mountain in the middle of nowhere without any heating, diversions or any form of recreation and without any of the food that they were used to in China. The gradients in the mountains were vertiginous and very often we saw trucks and even earth-moving caterpillars stuck deep in the glutinous mud. From the volume of military traffic seen on Tibetan roads throughout our journey, I have to admit that the Tibetans' claim that the Chinese were building roads inside Tibet for military purposes to move men and material from one army garrison to another was completely substantiated.

We drove for hours. I was totally captivated by the ever-changing scenery. At 16,000 feet we were above the tree-line and the rough road hugged the side of the barren mountains, within touching distance of the clouds, and then dipped into the valley, green with lichen. The mesmerizing play of light made me think I was driving through a giant kaleidoscope that was constantly changing into a myriad shades of blues, greens and browns. Everything was on a more monumental scale than I had ever seen anywhere before. Not even the Altiplano of Bolivia, Peru or Ecuador could compete. And the emptiness was staggering.

Throughout our journey in Kham, the mountains surrounded us everywhere; there was no pattern, no north–south bearings; they seemed to run in all directions at once, and at times it seemed that all the mountains of the world had been tipped into Tibet. The sun appeared to hover continually overhead, and it occurred to me that if we went over one of the vertiginous drops that seemed to accompany practically every corner, Channel 4 would never know where to find the wreckage – or me.

Looking at the maelstrom of mountains, I felt no sense of fear or foreboding as one often feels at looking at uncharted territory; there was just a sense of absolute timelessness, as if the mystery of eternity might, one day, be unravelled right here.

Tenzin caught my arm, pointed to the horizon to some snow-capped mountains and said '*Ionsher*'. Thondup translated, telling me that there was a famous complex of caves there where holy Buddhist monks (*gom-chenla* – very religious hermits) spent years isolated in prayer and meditation without light or heat and just a handful of barley, which now and then might be left at the entrance by a passing nomad. After decades of *Tsa-Lhung-Gom* – special spiritual exercises, a form of prayer and penance for all sentient beings, rather like those practised by the desert hermits in the early centuries of Christianity – with barely a pulse and respiration rate, many hovered on the edge of life and the threshold of that higher understanding that leads to Nirvana, the ultimate release from suffering.

The Chinese called this 'parasitic and reactionary'. They dragged all the hermits from the sanctuary of the caves into the daylight (which blinded most of them, after years in the dark), interrogated and tortured them. In a weak physical state, unused to even the exertions of eating, not many hermits survived, Tenzin told me. The Chinese also destroyed the sanctuaries which, like the ancient 108 caves of the eighth-century saint, Padmasambhava, at Samye Chigo, were of particular religious veneration for Tibetans. It was not the only such story I was to hear in Tibet.

In the early afternoon we crossed the Shonkula pass into yet another bowl of mountains and valleys. At the top a nest of twigs and prayer-flags fluttered in the stiff wind. I nearly jumped out of my skin as the Boys let out a whoop that sounded like the war cry of a band of Apaches about to attack a wagon-train. It was followed by a loud muttering in Tibetan from all of them: '*Kiri soso lha-gyal lo*'. Thondup explained that every time Tibetans crossed a mountain pass they called out for the victory of the gods over evil and to speed the word of the Buddha that was inscribed on the prayer-flags to all mankind.

I had to get footage of the van driving through various parts of the countryside to superimpose over a map to chart our journey for the viewer at home. I tried to explain, to Tibetans who had never seen a television documentary, the rudiments of filming: that if a car exits right of frame in one scene it has to come right to left in the next scene. They shook their heads, and I suspect that they thought I was somewhat insane to worry about the niceties of film grammar when at any moment a Chinese patrol might come round the next corner. But we devised a system so that when we were filming, one of them would keep a look-out on the road behind and one in front to warn us of approaching vehicles and people. I tried to involve them in the filming, asking them to look through the view-finder at what I was trying to do and running it back later for them to see the results. At first it was a big game. But soon they tired of it and as the journey progressed the more irritated they were with their English *mola* (lady).

But that day they were wonderful: they even waded into an icy stream of alarming force because I wanted to film from a boulder in the middle to catch the effect of the sun sparkling on the cascading water as it tumbled down into the valley. The refraction of the light on the dancing white-water rapids looked as though the whole stream had been strewn with diamonds that were erupting into star-bursts. In a studio you can get the same effect by using star filters so that every light you shoot erupts into a star. In Tibet the combination of rarefied air, magical light and effervescent water turned every mountain stream into a cascade of jewels on fire.

Tibet's hydroelectric potential is phenomenal. The country is criss-crossed by thousands of rivers and streams. But after the first five hours, after we had crossed thirty-three rivers, I simply gave up counting. With independence and a loan from the World Bank, Tibet could easily harness the wasted energy of those wild rivers shooting untamed down steep gradients to supply the energy needs of most of her neighbours. Tibet has the potential, an Indian hydro-engineer told me, for the equivalent of 500 Iguaçu Falls projects (the gigantic hydroelectric scheme on the Brazil–Paraguay border).

When we approached a bridge over a river or stream, unless it was a large concrete Chinese army bridge, the Boys invariably slowed down, turned off the road, drove down the embankment and forded the shallows. For on closer examination, these bridges proved to have more holes than logs spanning the water. Very occasionally, there might be a pile of stones in front of the bridge to warn the unwary traveller. Away from the main road we saw the bridges that Tibetans have traditionally used for hundreds of years. Picturesque rough logs bound with rope spanned the small rivers; sometimes there would be a rope bridge, and for the wider ones a rope-and-pulley system spanned the turbulent water. In the upper reaches of the Yangtse, Salween, Mekong, Brahmaputra and other major rivers, Tibetans still use *ko-du*, their traditional round coracles made of yak hide which they navigate skilfully in the vicious currents. But throughout our journey we saw only a few in use, and I was not looking forward to going in one, when we had to be smuggled across the Yangtse river at night to avoid the notorious Tibetan Autonomous Region border checkpoint.

At 3 P.M. we drove through Sharchuka which marks the boundary between the provinces of Nachu and Birzong. It is a scruffy little hamlet of Tibetan mud-brick homes along one side of the road and on the other low white concrete buildings with tin roofs – the Chinese army barracks and a Chinese tax-collection point. The disparity between the Chinese and Tibetan houses was striking. The Tibetan houses, huddled together in a muddy swamp, had none of the farm machinery, or vehicles, or piles of firewood, or vegetable plots that were in the yards of the Chinese compounds. There was not even a flower in a rusty flower-pot. And once again the electricity supply blatantly by-passed the Tibetan dwellings. It was the same all over Tibet. And in those Tibetan yards, I saw piles of yak dung waiting to be dried for fuel, whereas in the Chinese yards (which I could peer into from the height of the van) were large stacks of roughly chopped wood.

The few children playing in the Tibetan yards wore ragged and muddy Western track suits and more often than not had no shoes on their feet. The further east we travelled towards China, the more noticeable it became that the clothes of the Tibetans gradually changed from the traditional *chubas* to shapeless Chinese trousers and shirts. And even those who did wear *chubas* (but never in the towns) wore Chinese-made nylon track suits under them. Toddlers sported the Chinese kind of trousers which were slit from the navel in front to the top of the buttocks at the back so that a child could quickly urinate or defecate. Further east, Tibetan toddlers even wore miniature Chinese army uniforms and caps, like the Chinese children. As Sonam had told me earlier in Lhasa, 'You see in China God is the State and the army is its servant. And therefore all must appease and emulate the army if we are to get on!' But it was an affront to see a chubby, bright-eyed Tibetan toddler in a minute green uniform complete with two yellow bands on the sleeves; I wondered what Tibetans, like Tenzin, who had fought the Chinese in those very uniforms and had spent the best part of their manhood being imprisoned by men wearing similar uniforms, thought. Tenzin had no words: his contemptuous look, a mixture of impotent anger and pain, said it all.

I asked the Boys, and later the Tibetans who hid and sheltered me, why they wore Chinese clothes. They all told me that not only had they had no money to make their traditional *chubas*, but more importantly, if they wore Tibetan clothes they were ridiculed and discriminated against by the Chinese. As jobs were difficult enough to come by, they had no option but to comply. Of course, I did not want to see Tibetans in national dress as a tourist 'attraction'; but many Tibetans were being coerced, and covertly penalized, by the Chinese into abandoning their right to their national dress. As Sonam had said to me in Lhasa: 'That too is a form of cultural genocide.'

Later in the afternoon, after we had crossed the Kongu river, we plunged 2,000 feet into a gorge where, at the lower altitude, the hillsides were covered with lush grass and miniature larkspur in every shade of blue and pink. Small fields of barley appeared on the hills and in other fields something green was growing. They told me it was *labug*, a sort of large white radish which is apparently full of vitamins. There seemed to be no systematic planting of the fields and very often there was just a sickle-shaped strip high on the mountain near the skyline. I asked the Boys why Tibetans did not follow the example of the Chinese, who energetically cultivated every inch of land.

The Boys smiled at my ignorance and said that, in keeping with Buddhism, they grew only what they needed for themselves. It was *chok-shie*. They did not have the same acquisitive tendencies as the Chinese. I pursued it, suggesting that if they grew a surplus, then the extra cash could help pay for the many things they obviously needed. Again they smiled and said that when they needed more, they would grow more. I gave up. It was impossible to argue with such genuinely unworldly people, who though far from naïve, and tough when necessary, seemed more motivated by the tenets of their faith than by economics.

As we drove towards Kongmed, a small Tibetan hamlet set deep in a wide valley surrounded by ripening barley, I saw a group of men and women in colourful Tibetan dress. It was a perfect picture-postcard scene. They were chuckling and teasing each other, flirting, and as the French would say, '*ils sont des gens bien dans leur peaux*'. The men – and some of the women – were on the sturdy horses, the *khamta*, that Kham is so renowned for. They sat well and proudly in the saddle. Immediately I thought of all the romantic folk tales I had heard about Kham. The men in their short *chubas* had one arm free and their long hair was wound with the traditional red *tap-shu*. The women's dark *chubas* were lit up with bright pink and turquoise or green blouses that toned perfectly with their rainbow-striped aprons. And bits of turquoise and coral (*yū* and *jeru*) studded the long plaits that hung down their backs to their waists. Many women also wore colourful semi-precious stones studded in the long leather thong that dangled from their belts. Some of them also wore traditional Tibetan boots made of colourfully embroidered felt with leather soles and upturned toes.

It was a scene that cried out to be filmed. But no, filming was out of the question. I was not even to get out of the van! The Boys explained that it was too dangerous. Tenzin did not recognize any of the Khampas and as we were not very far from our destination, it was much wiser not to take the risk, in case anyone informed on us. Reluctantly I looked back on the group and its infectious gaiety as the van climbed once more into the mountains.

For the past few hours I had noticed several mountains where the whole mountainside was of green or red or amethyst-coloured rock, and it occurred so often during our journey that I asked the Boys what it was. 'Minerals,' Tenzin said, 'but I do not know the names. We have many minerals in Tibet.' I then remembered reading transcripts of some Radio Lhasa reports that had been monitored by the Tibetan Government-in-exile of discoveries of minerals in Tibet. The list is quite staggering. Apart from the Chinese-certified discoveries of over sixty different minerals, one excerpt perhaps gives some indication of the vast mineral wealth that has already been exploited – and of the colossal reserves waiting to be tapped. In the Radio Lhasa broadcast of 24 October 1984 at 20.37 hours, Wang She Yue, the Beijing Geological Institute-trained Director of the TAR (Tibetan Autonomous Region) Geological Mineral Department, said: 'Eminent scientists have carried out exploration work for over ten years and discovered ninety mineral deposits and, of them, sixty contained huge deposits and they account for 40 per cent of the mineral deposits of the entire country [China].'

What is quite amazing is the geographical spread of the minerals all over Tibet. For example, in February 1982, Reuters reported from Beijing that the largest deposits of uranium in the world are in Tibet and copper deposits (the world's third largest) are found in Lholhak, Riwoche, Tingchen, Dakyab, Pasho, Gojo, Derge, Jodha, Dunbuk-chu in Dungkar, Karze Poyul Dzong, Chamdo,

Amdo-Tongchuk, Nemo Thingkyi and Dara. In fact so many of the metallic and non-metallic ores like petroleum, lithium, coal, iron, platinum, diamonds and dozens of others are found in such profusion that on 14 January 1986, Dorje Tsering, head of the Economic Delegation and Acting Chairman of the Tibetan Autonomous Region, in a speech in Hong Kong, when soliciting investment, said: 'Tibet is a land of treasure, a virgin land where everything is available and waiting to be undertaken.'

Tenzin told me, as did other Tibetans I met, as well as refugees outside Tibet, that the Chinese had used forced Tibetan labour in the mines, particularly in the years from 1955 to the late seventies. Conditions were so harsh that many of the men died. We had decided to interview survivors of the mines – both past and present – in Amdo, Tibet's north-eastern province where the richness of the mineral deposits had made it a prime target for early annexation by the Chinese.

As the sun moved almost imperceptibly towards the west, the shadows of the mountains crept slowly across the valleys. After a day when the temperature in the sun must have touched 75°F, there was a distinct chill in the air.

I had noticed that most of the Tibetans we saw in this region seemed to be women. Tenzin explained that the people of Kham were the first to come into contact with the Chinese occupation forces in the early fifties, and Kham soon became the centre of resistance. The Khampas, following their clan leaders, attacked the Chinese and their bases in Kham and Amdo. They had only swords, pistols and antiquated rifles and, despite the advantages of the wild countryside which was ideal for guerrilla tactics, they were no match for the Chinese heavy artillery and air-strikes from planes based in Chengdu. The fighting continued from the late fifties to the early sixties and also during the Cultural Revolution, and because of the prolonged fighting most of the Tibetan males were dead.

Throughout our journey in Kham, Tenzin told the Boys the heroic and tragic tales of the doomed Khampa resistance. Tales as epic as any Arthurian legend – and as tragic a betrayal by the West as any cause that has ever been buried by the pecuniary interests of a world which allowed the Chinese to slaughter the flower of Tibetan chivalry.

When the PLA invaded in 1949, the ill-equipped Khampas along with the rest of the minuscule Tibetan army were soon smashed. They had no modern weapons at all; their ancient *Bonda* flint-lock guns were no match for Chinese tanks and artillery. Thousands of Tibetans were simply mown down and monasteries razed as the Chinese installed military law in Tibet.

The Tibetans soon realized that a conventional war was out of the question and that they should make use of the wild terrain for hit-and-run tactics. In the summer of 1956, in Jomdha Dzong, a fortress deep in Kham, 210 Khampa fighters were being held prisoner by the Chinese. Managing to escape, they fled to the mountains, mobilized the clans, and the guerrilla movement was officially born.

After the Khampas' first victories, the legendary chieftain Gompo Tenzin Angdrugtsang took over the command of Chushi Gangruk ('four rivers, six ranges' – the traditional epithet for Amdo and Kham) that was now the name of the united guerrilla movement of all the Tibetan resistance forces. In the meantime Gyalo Thondup, the Dalai Lama's second eldest brother who lived in Darjeeling in India, had stepped up his intelligence-gathering operation with the help of the CIA, with whom he started liaising in 1951.

Guerrilla activity, despite the overwhelming odds, increased. Fighting escalated and the Chinese had to send in fourteen divisions of men (over 150,000) to Tibet. Tenzin also told me that some of his friends (in fact many of the guerrillas) had been smuggled secretly to Guam via Thailand, India and Pakistan and had been trained by the CIA to use modern weapons and commando tactics in US bases in Guam and in Colorado; afterwards the guerrillas, supplied with arms and radios, had been parachuted at night into Lokha in central Tibet and Markham Chari-Pena and other locations in Kham. Sok Tsenden Dzong, the village where we were going to spend the night, was one of the places the Khampa guerrillas had been dropped by American C 46 planes flying from secret bases in Taiwan. (The planes had refuelled at clandestine airstrips in what was then northern East Pakistan.)

It is one thing to read dry accounts of history in a book, but quite something else actually to drive through the land that saw such an epic struggle. The evening sun warmed the ripening barley to a burnished gold, red poppies swayed in the faint breeze, while a pervasive sense of languor totally disorientated me as Tenzin's tales fired my imagination. As he pointed out various vantage points in the high hills, I vividly imagined a charge of Khampa horsemen yelling their blood-curdling cries '*Ki-hi-hi*!', brandishing their long swords (*tipathangs*) and firing from the saddle. It is the stuff that legends – and films – are made of.

Of course, although I am fully aware that Tibet and its struggle are not fashionable in the West, it seems so unjust that practically any liberation movement that grabs the world's headlines by hijacking a plane or using senseless violence on innocent victims, like the Beirut hostages, is then automatically guaranteed absolute saturation media coverage; yet, here in Tibet, the valiant struggle of an amazing people has passed unknown and unsung to the majority of the planet.

I was quickly jolted back to reality by the sight of an electricity pole. '*Gyami*,' the Boys said quickly. 'Chinese!' It was a pretty good rule of thumb, I found, that whenever you saw electricity poles you knew Chinese were near or that you were approaching a Chinese settlement. I stiffened with tension and pulled my hat further down over my face.

We were by now driving along a wide valley with a ribbon of river running through it and surrounded by tall mountains sloping into a darkening sky. On the lower slopes yaks were grazing. Then, without any warning, as we rounded a bend, a fortress-like monastery stood on a rocky promontory rising from the middle of the valley floor. Perched on a mountain in a bend of the river, it was as dramatic as any Scottish fortress or Rhine castle. In the fading light it conjured up all the romance of a bygone era.

Tenzin told me that it had been bombed by Chinese Illyushin planes in July 1957, with the loss of nearly 1,500 pilgrims who were at their prayers. 'But maybe the Chinese thought the guerrillas were sheltering in there?' I suggested, playing the devil's advocate. 'You know nothing about fighting,' he said. 'That is a sitting target, you can shoot at it from anywhere. It sticks up like a boat in an empty lake. No, we were in the caves above the road there,' and he pointed above my head. 'They were pilgrims at a prayer festival. They had no guns, nothing. The same thing happened in

Batang and Lithang and Derge in 1956. In Amchokgon, Kyigndo and Labrang Tashikil in 1958, and in so many other places like Nyarong, Chatreng, Markham, Drayab, Gyalthang, Gonjo, Nangchen and Lingtsang. You will see for yourself. We are going there. You will speak to people there too.

'Our people have been repairing this monastery, and other ones for years, little by little. You see, it is very important in our lives,' Tenzin said simply. I asked them to stop the van and with daylight fading fast I tried from the window to plan how I could film the interviewees. I decided that we would do it from the road, with the castle in the background. Dangerous, but if the Boys kept look-out, perhaps it might be OK. Tenzin suggested the other side of the valley would be safer. But I could see no road, or even a track snaking up the mountain. And an odd group of people pulling one strange-looking woman up a mountainside did not sound like too great an idea.

It was getting late and we had to find the safe house in a small village eighteen miles away, on the other side of the Tibetan quarter. The Boys decided to drive down through the town to see the layout so that if necessary we could make a quick getaway. The Chinese end of the town had its customary concrete houses, electricity, tinny music and a considerable number of army trucks and small green jeeps. We also located the petrol pump. Although we had several barrels of petrol under my luggage at the back, the Boys told me you should always try to buy petrol, which was rationed, wherever and whenever you could. Of course the Tibetans did not have the right papers and the pump sold only to Chinese.

As the dusk shaded into night, we drove slowly, without lights, through alleys so narrow that the mud-brick dwellings scraped the sides of the vehicle. The 'road' was an unlit muddy track that meandered between high mud walls. The brisk wind wafted the sound of Chinese music from their tin-roofed houses at the other end of the town. In the van no one spoke. It was dark and I found it impossible to learn the landmarks as I usually tried to do before going into a potentially dangerous situation. That way there was the faint hope that I might be able to find my own way out, if necessary.

After half an hour, the van stopped. Tenzin got out and disappeared through a dark doorway. Ten minutes later, he returned and without saying a word tugged my arm to get out of the van. After ducking through four courtyards and several doors, I found myself in a largish dark room which felt full of people. It was pitch-black. Every muscle in my body tensed. I tried to quieten my own breathing. After a while there was a shuffling at the door, low voices in Tibetan and the sound of something being dragged in. A match flared, a hand lit a small candle and Tenzin's face smiled reassuringly at me as though he sensed my fear of the darkness.

Tenzin did the formalities, introducing me only as *mola* (the lady). While the others had butter-tea, Thondup got me some hot water and mixed me a black coffee. By the time we had finished talking to the interviewees it was 11.30. I asked Thondup to assemble one of the kerosene pressure lamps that we had bought in Lhasa, as I needed to see to reorganize the bags. Almost before Thondup could light the lamp, Tenzin had extinguished it with a swift movement. 'The light is too bright,' he said. 'No one in the village has a lamp like this. It will draw attention.'

I was more than tired. I sat on the bench-bed that ran round the room with its low ceiling and earthen floor, and leaned back against the mud wall while Thondup said that the lady of the house would shortly bring us some food. The others were sitting on the floor talking in low voices. Around us were strewn my interminable bags. I must have dozed off. Suddenly there was a shuffle of feet, and Tibetan voices were whispering something. Even without a translation the hair on the back of my neck began to stand on end. Tenzin snuffed out the candle. Thondup grabbed my arm and pulled me quickly towards the door. The night sky was full of stars and the sound of running feet. 'Chinese! House-to-house search! Run!'

12
Phagpa

Hands grabbed and pushed me towards the door. In the darkness I tripped and crashed with the camera-bag to the ground. There was an urgency in the scurrying feet inside the room. From outside came the sound of muffled voices with that unmistakeable pitch that heralds catastrophe. Inside, the dark was dense with moving shadows that pulled and dragged me along the floor. There was that sharp hiss of breath as one hovers on the brink of disaster. No one spoke a word. The tension was electric.

I was bundled from hand to hand and finally stumbled into the yard. Figures, dark against the starlight, rushed me down an alley and dragged me into the van. Sumpa switched on the interior light. I nearly screamed for him to extinguish it as we were sitting targets. For what seemed an eternity, our existence was in the balance. Frozen in my seat, I peered into a night that was heavy with menace. I could not marshal a single constructive thought and knew that I should be preparing some sort of an alibi. But all I could do was listen with an intensity that hurt my ears to the sounds that surged round the van. For the second time in less than twenty-four hours I was a pawn of fate. I thought I was going to throw up.

Sumpa rammed the van into gear. Doors slammed and we crashed through four or five twisting alleys so narrow that the side mirror was torn off and later we found the front bumper dangling from the end of a metal hinge. We sped through the village and as we passed the last mud wall a resounding clap reverberated around us. Thondup looked horrified and I tensed every muscle in my body in apprehension, unsure whether it was the crump of incoming artillery or a clap of thunder. Sumpa kicked the accelerator and the van ricocheted in the blackness and up the side of the mountain without a road or track in sight.

For an hour I was too afraid to look behind, superstitious that I might be tempting fate. Forked lightning slashed the raging sky every few minutes and in the brief electric-white light I made out the bleak mountains that loomed out of the blackness and towered around us. Thunder crashed around us on every side. It was so near that we could almost feel the sound waves buffeting the van. It was just like being on the receiving end of a murderous artillery barrage in Beirut.

My eyes were mesmerized by the twin-beam of the headlights, now pointing almost ninety degrees upwards into the sky, now plummeting down into the grassy mountainside, as we lurched up and down hillocks and plunged into valleys.

Suddenly, I was no longer frightened and actually found myself enjoying bouncing around the mountains in sheeting rain with the elements erupting in the most spectacular pyrotechnic display that I had ever seen. The adrenalin raced. I almost laughed. The setting was unbelievably histrionic: raging winds buffeting a little van of crazy people fleeing from the 'baddies' in the dead of night! What a terrible scenario, I thought. It was like a bad B-feature movie. Only, I reminded myself, this was 'real time', our situation was critical and we were not out of danger yet. At any moment, round the next bend, a patrol of Chinese soldiers might put an end to the turbulent odyssey. But for those few wild hours I knew that I was intensely alive: every nerve in my body was unashamedly tingling with an uncontrollable excitement.

It was the same adrenalin that I felt under gunfire. All correspondents under fire, if they are honest, admit that there is an 'exquisite' heightening of the senses, when your life is suspended between 'incoming' shells, over which you have absolutely no control. It is an agonizing exhilaration of not knowing whether you will survive or not.

Like any other correspondent in a war zone, I too have experienced this paralysing uncertainty. In that extraordinary fraction of time you go beyond fear: everything is crystal clear, there are no more pretences, no façades and, in a macabre way, you actually enjoy the intensity of the moment. I vividly remember one such time in Vietnam during the An Loc campaign in 1972.

We were filming on Highway 13 (from Saigon to An Loc near the Cambodian border). My cameraman, new to war, dropped his battery belt which powered the camera as he came under fire. Furious because I could not get spectacular pictures of burning tanks, I decided to crawl back to recover the dropped belt. As I

got to a tiny hillock all of a foot high, there was a furious small-arms
fire barrage as the Vietcong closed round and cut me off. At almost
the same time an ABC-TV correspondent dived under the same
tuft of grass and we collided head on. We both laughed as AK 47
fire whizzed round us. Neither of us knew if or when we would
be hit and, as happens when extinction is a hair's breadth away,
we chatted with an instant intimacy for that long hour pinned
down by the Vietcong in the burning sun on Highway 13. We
exchanged confidences that normally would take years of friendship to divulge and flirted outrageously. A few months after the
incident, I read in the *Stars and Stripes* – the US army newspaper
in Vietnam – that he had been killed in an ambush, covering a
story near the Cambodian border.

Back in the van, the Boys were tense with apprehension and
preoccupied, as I was, with not hitting their heads on the roof or
being thrown to the floor as the van broncoed over the rough
terrain. Sumpa was amazingly cool. A slight shy boy, he would
be unremarkable in a crowd; but as the trip wore on and the
hazards multiplied Sumpa grew magnificently into the situation
and with a face showing absolutely no emotion he threw
the steering wheel dextrously around and kept the van upright.
After two hours bouncing over the trackless mountainside, without even the stars for navigation, the van slithered to a halt.
Tenzin and Jigme got out in the pouring rain and with torches
examined the ground closely. Thondup told me that they were
looking for the way. When I got down to go discreetly to the
loo, I wandered to the edge of the beam of the headlights and
was aghast to realize that we had stopped within six inches of
a steep ravine with a torrent raging around rocks that looked
jagged in the torchlight. How Sumpa had the sixth sense to
stop just then, I will never know. There had been absolutely no
warning signs, just an undulating stretch of bleak mountainside.
Some guardian angel or deity must have been doing overtime
on our behalf.

About 3.30 in the morning Sumpa slowed down and switched
off the headlights. After a few minutes I saw the first tell-tale
electricity pole and felt everyone tense once again. We were
approaching a Chinese area. With the engine still running, Tenzin
got out quietly, leaving the door slightly ajar. He squelched

through the mud and disappeared round the corner of a wall. No one in the van spoke. The only sign of animation was the glowing end of Sumpa's cigarette.

Fifteen minutes later Tenzin came back, got into the van and spoke quietly in Tibetan. Thondup translated as two of the Boys slid out of the van and silently disappeared into the night in opposite directions. Thondup told me that we were going to spend whatever remained of the night with some friends of Tenzin's but as we were in a Chinese area we had to be very careful. The two on look-out would signal to us if it appeared clear: then I was to go with Tenzin into the house and they would bring the bags after us. There was an almost inaudible whistle from the darkness where Jigme had disappeared, followed by another one from somewhere in the front of the van. Tenzin took my hand and as we got out of the van into the rain, he tucked me under his coat. With my head almost under his armpit I stumbled through mud to a yard strewn with straw, then through a creaky door in a mud-brick wall into a smoke-filled room. Outside in the yard the dog had awakened every other dog in the neighbourhood.

When my eyes grew accustomed to the faint light from a small candle, I saw that we were in a small room with a low ceiling and an earthen floor. At one end an old man lay, breathing heavily, under a jumble of coverings. Tending the stove in one corner of the room was an old lady in a dark *chuba* and tattered plimsolls. Her face creased into a thousand wrinkles as she shyly smiled at me and folded her hands in greeting. Tenzin motioned me to sit down on one of the four bench-beds that lined the walls and as he talked I looked round the room. The old lady moved slowly as she piled dried yak-dung 'patties' into the blackened stove and put a kettle on. Her grey hair, wispy from sleep, hung down her back in two plaits. She stooped slowly and fetched a couple of cracked cups from under one of the benches, unscrewed the vacuum flask that was resting on the top of the stove and offered Tenzin and me some butter-tea. Her clothes looked dirty and as I looked round the room it became obvious that the couple were very poor.

The rough walls were covered with yellowing Chinese news-papers, pasted over the cracks to keep out the winds which howled with the storm outside. If it was freezing like this in summer, how infernal would the winter be, I wondered, when the temperature dropped to minus 20°C? The old man in the corner suddenly coughed into life. It was that deep racking cough I recognized as unmistakeably tubercular from my days as a nurse. However, I was puzzled because the TB bacillus does not normally survive above 10,000 feet and we were at 15,000 feet. Another paroxysm of coughing rent the old man and he reached for a small tin and spat into it. The phlegm was bright red with blood and frothy – the classic signs that it had come from the lungs. The man obviously had open and highly contagious TB.

When Thondup came in, I asked why the man was not in hospital, as he was clearly very ill. The man, sweating profusely and his eyes bright with fever, spoke in a whisper and with great effort as his thin chest heaved under his grimy shirt. I immediately felt guilty at having exerted him. I suggested we stop, but the old man was adamant and spoke, as Solzhenitsyn would say, 'with the unhurried dignity of a dying man'.

'No, no!' he insisted. 'There is not much time. Nobody from outside has come here before. I must tell you what is happening. Tell the outside people. Tell them what is happening in Tibet. Tell them to help us! *Kuchi! Kuchi!* Please! Please!' he implored with heart-rending desperation, his hands knotted with emotion. It was the same touching belief that everyone I met in Tibet held – that I would carry their message to the outside world. How could I possibly shatter their fragile hopes and tell them that 'the outside world' was more interested in the trade potential in China's vast new markets? How could I explain the conspiracy of silence to the dying man who was risking the only thing he had left – his life – in talking to me?

Thondup continued translating. He told me that the old couple had no money for hospitals or medicine and, as the old man said resignedly, even though they were near a large Chinese settlement where there was a clinic, they were Tibetan and could have medicine only if they paid what would have been, for them, an exorbitant price. I told them that the Chinese Government insisted that some of the major benefits they had brought to all Tibetans were medicine and hospitals. The old man gave a rasping laugh. 'Go,' he told me through Thondup, 'go throughout our land, and see for yourself in the countryside. We don't have enough money for food. How can we buy Chinese medicine? Go and see the *drogpa* [nomads], see how our people suffer.'

He shook his head slowly, and in the candlelight his face was ashen. I looked at his thin face with its almost transparent skin, and wished that I had the right drugs to help him. The medicines for TB are so simple and effective, but I knew I did not have the specific ones, and I suspected that the old man was beyond help. I hoped that in the light of his faith his rebirth would be in happier circumstances. 'Remember, child,' he said, turning his face, which was beaded with perspiration, towards me, 'what the Chinese say and what the Chinese do are not the same thing.'

The Boys came in, sat down to butter-tea, took some *tsampa* out of their pouches, and mixed it with the tea. Before they started to eat they first offered some to the couple, who were too poor to observe the most fundamental of all Tibetan courtesies – offering your guests whatever food you have, however little that might prove, first. Thondup opened one of the food-bags and we took out some dried noodle soup. While that was boiling in a pan, I opened some tins of tuna and offered it to the couple and the Boys, who gingerly accepted some.

It was nearly 4.30 in the morning, the night was pitch-black and the rain splashed noisily into the mud outside. I wondered whether the water would overflow into the shack as there was no drainage, or crumble the mud walls as I had seen happen during the floods in Bangladesh. But I was too tired and had gone through too many alarms in one day to worry about even more terrors; at that moment all I wanted to do was to close my eyes and shut out the problems and the cold. The old man was asleep and breathing laboriously. I found my sleeping bag, opened it on one of the bench-beds, discreetly removed my trousers and top sweater and blessed the warmth of the Arctic-rated down. The old lady got into the bed with her husband – top to tail – and the Boys shared the other two benches. Thondup asked whether he could share my bench. At another time it would have been hilarious, but I was too tired to find the energy to joke. So he climbed into his sleeping bag and we lay sardine-fashion on the same narrow bunk. Outside the storm still raged and as the candle flickered I heard the deep breathing of the Boys as they fell into deep sleep. It had been a long eventful day.

I woke with my stomach in a spasm of colic. I lay still as long as I could but finally had reluctantly to wake Thondup to take me outside to the loo. As there was no running water in the shack, I presumed that nature took its course outside the yard; but as the last thing I needed was to stumble on a Chinese patrol, Thondup patiently escorted me on the first of the 'loo patrols'. It was still raining as we tried to dodge the puddles.

Back in my sleeping bag in the shack, my gut rumbled and I felt distinctly unwell. I took my pulse and found my temperature was raised. I assumed that I had a gastric infection. I decided to wait until light before starting a course of tetracycline from my medical kit. It was all I could do to cope with a slipped disc: I just had no time – or energy – for any more personal problems.

A loudspeaker screeched into life with a harsh stream of Chinese. I lay perfectly still, unsure whether it was an announcement that we were surrounded and to come out quietly – or whether it was simply the ubiquitous Chinese system of making sure the citizenry are well motivated to start the day with a diet of propaganda and martial music. But nothing happened, and as the tinny din went through the decibel level I relaxed and wondered why the Chinese had to do everything so loudly.

As the room stirred and we packed away the domesticity of the night, I rummaged with increasing anxiety in the plasticized bags looking for the medical kit. It contained all the medicines, most of my make-up, all my toiletries, undies, twenty rolls of video tape, my precious books – without which I was sure insanity would follow within a day, and my box of Tampax – including the one containing the miniaturized details of what to film where. If the Chinese found the case, it would surely only be a matter of time before they either caught up with us, or radioed ahead to have us arrested at the next checkpoint. But it was nowhere to be found and I could only think that in the confusion of the alarm and the dark of last night it must have got left behind.

While Thondup explained the importance of retrieving the case to Tenzin, I fumed at myself for my incompetence. Tenzin was reluctant to return as we were low on petrol and only had sufficient to get to the next 'store' to fill up. Eventually he agreed, but warned Thondup to get me out of the room and into the animal shed, as our van with Nagchukha number plates was bound to have attracted attention. He told us they would be gone for four hours.

With my hat pulled well down over my face, Thondup guided me to an adjacent mud-brick shed filled with bales of hay and a few rusting tools. I settled down to sorting out the bags. Then I poured some hot water from the flask into the saucepan of the night before and had a wash. Unthinkingly, I also washed my undies and socks and hung them out to dry on some straw in the yard in the bright sun which had at last begun to shine. Then, feeling nauseous and weak with my gut rumbling in colic, I just curled up on the hay and tried to sleep.

I awoke with Thondup coming softly into the shed carrying my undies in his hand. 'Poor people don't wear white!' he said. 'And our people don't wear white silk undies!' he laughed as he handed me my bra and panties. I blushed scarlet at my stupidity in putting them out to dry in such an obvious place. While he went to get me some noodles, I decided that for the rest of the trip I had better decline any food from the Boys and stick to a bland diet of noodles, for by now I had full-blown diarrhoea.

Thondup had been talking to the old couple. He told me that they had been small farmers in the valley, until the Chinese came and confiscated their smallholding and those of the rest of the small Tibetan community. Chinese farmers had been installed on the land, and the Tibetans left to fend as best they could. The couple, with only one yak, had at first tried to get work as casual labourers, but after an accident had injured the woman and the man had developed a 'bad chest', their meagre and precarious income had dwindled to nothing. At the moment they were living on the milk of the yak and on the small, occasional gift that their daughter brought them from Riwoche where she was working for the Chinese. They told Thondup that all over Tibet the same thing was happening. The Chinese would come and take the best land, pushing out the Tibetans, who now had to eke out a tenuous existence as landless nomads in the infertile high mountains. When the old man's condition had deteriorated two years ago and he began to spit blood, the couple were lucky enough to get the use of the shack from friends who, by collaborating with the Chinese, managed to earn a reasonable livelihood. In return, the old lady looked after the friends' yaks and helped in the fields. Although

Left: Lobsang Norbu, a monk from Sera Monastery who was imprisoned for twenty-two years, told me of prison conditions, including the presence of cannibalism.

Right: Two nuns, arrested for peaceful demonstration, who described how in detention they were stripped naked and tortured with electric batons.

Left: An ex-monk from Batang, who spent nineteen years in prison, also spoke of prison conditions, describing suicides and mass graves.

Above: Chinese loggers carrying off timber to China. Tibetans claim that their timber has earned China $54 billion in the period 1957–1987.

Left: Rapten, a Khampa, spoke of the massive Chinese programme of deforestation in Tibet, which has resulted in dangerous soil erosion, flooding, the near extinction of flora and fauna, and, Tibetans claim, changing weather patterns.

Right: Tenzin and Jigme push our van over a landslide, 18,000 feet up the Yila Mountain in Kham.

Right: Wangchuk, a farmer from Kham, witnessed mass starvation due to Chinese mismanagement of Tibetan agriculture and the usurpation of Tibetan farmlands by Chinese settlers.

Below: Kham, eastern Tibet – one of thousands of idyllic mountain valleys.

Rock paintings and
prayer-flags behind
Sera Monastery on the
outskirts of Lhasa.

Above: Monks rebuilding their monastery in Tashikil. This was one of 6,246 monasteries and temples looted and destroyed by the Chinese.

Below: Vandalized statues and religious objects from the sacred monasteries and temples of Norbulingka in Lhasa.

Right: Tibetan workers outside the Potala scavenge for fragments of sacred scriptures destroyed by the Chinese fourteen years after the Cultural Revolution was officially declared over.

Right: A nomad family in Amdo, north-east Tibet, stretch yak hides for clothing.

Above: Lhasa – a view of the Potala from the roof of the Jokhang.

Right: Seán Bobbitt and I posing as tourists in Lhasa after having been deserted by our first interpreter.

Below: Chinese communications antennae opposite the Potala. Visible all over Lhasa, these antennae are a potent reminder of omnipresent Chinese surveillance.

the couple looked as though they were well into their eighties, Thondup told me that they were only in their late fifties.

I gave Thondup a wad of notes for the couple – the equivalent of at least three years' income. As we had no space in the van, we could not take the old man to hospital, but I asked Thondup to make sure that someone took the old man to a doctor. A few minutes later he returned with the old lady, who hobbled in, her face bathed in a wonderful smile. She took my hands in her gnarled, cracked ones, touched them to her forehead and said, '*Thu che che* – Thank you,' and returned the bundle of money to me.

Astonished, I asked Thondup why. He explained that while they were very grateful for the gesture, they could not take any money from someone who had come to help Tibet. I tried for ages to argue, explaining that it was not my money, it was Channel 4's and would have been spent anyway if I had been in a hotel . . . It was no use. Thondup just said quietly: 'Please understand; we Tibetans are a proud people. We are not used to begging or taking things.' I stopped arguing and before I left I hid the notes under the tin containing the salt, where I knew she would find them the next time she went to make tea. I wished I had also been able to give them a picture of the Dalai Lama that they had timidly asked for. I felt that the comfort that such a picture would have given them would have far outweighed all the money and creature comforts in the world.

It was 2.30 by the time the Boys got back. Tenzin told us that he had searched the house we had been in and questioned everyone he dared, but the bag had not been seen. Whether someone was lying, or whether, more likely, we had dropped it in the alley and it had been found by the Chinese, we would never know. But it was dangerous to remain in the shack. There were a lot of Chinese in the village and in the fields. Also, if the Chinese had found the bag, they would know that a foreigner was in the closed area. And as it had been on a route far removed from any area that a tourist could possibly have got lost in, they would immediately be suspicious and put out an urgent alert to the considerable number of military between Nagchukha and Chamdo. Our only safety now was to move as fast as we could and not sleep in the same place twice.

Not only had I nothing for my stomach, which by now had developed the symptoms I recognized as gastro-enteritis, I did not even have an aspirin for any of us. All I had was my make-up bag with mascara, eyeliner, lipstick, comb and a carton of Wettex for wiping babies' bottoms and excellent for wiping away the grime and dust of the journey. Worse still, I had only the underwear I stood up in. Without moisturizer in that bone-dry atmosphere, my skin was already feeling uncomfortably taut and stretched after only one night. Later the Boys with deadpan faces suggested that I use yak butter. But the smell made me retch and I had politely to decline. The worst calamity of all was that I now had no scent. I had left a large bottle of 'Nahema' in one of the bags. Enough not only to see me through my journey, but also to sprinkle away my worst depressions. I knew scent and frilly knickers were totally irrelevant in my situation, but in the past, however difficult the location I had found myself in — even up to my thighs in mud in the Bangladesh monsoon covering the guerrilla war — I had always travelled with two essential fripperies: silk underwear and scent. For, when I felt miserable and everything was going wrong, to wash, put on pretty undies and douse myself in scent made me feel human again.

The Boys started to load the van. I said my goodbyes to the kind couple who had sheltered me, at enormous risk to themselves, right under the noses of the Chinese; then, tucked under Tenzin's arm, I got back to the van. As we left Madzu I looked at my watch. It was 3.30 P.M. on Saturday, 3 September. I had twenty-seven days before my visa expired and over 3,000 miles still to do. Not to mention all the filming!

We left behind the neat fields of ripening barley and the Chinese harvesting the crop with farm machinery and started climbing again to a pass to drop into another natural amphitheatre of mountains on the other side. The sun was so warm that I began peeling off layers of sweaters, but then it got darker and colder, and I slipped them on again. It was a daily ritual with all of us. We climbed again into the high mountains covered with green, tundra-like scrub, for we were now again above the tree-line. The mountainsides were dotted with yaks and occasionally I saw a nomad. But curiously enough there was not one eagle or bird of any kind in the blissfully peaceful, cloudless sky. In Lhasa I had looked for the wild geese and cranes that Tibetan friends had told me flew over the Potala, but I had never seen them. Later, when we were in the valleys and in the heavy foliage of lower altitudes, and even when we slept in the open, I did not see or hear one bird. Not even a sparrow. I asked the Boys why. They told me that when the Chinese came to Tibet, Mao had issued an edict that all birds were parasitic and therefore should be exterminated. And the Chinese made certain they were. In the 4,000 miles that I travelled in Tibet I never saw one single bird or heard one sing.

We drove down from a pass into a perfect Alpine setting. Undulating green mountainsides with, in the distance, snow-capped peaks glistening in the late-afternoon sun, sparkling streams, pure mountain air – it was all so perfect that I expected Heidi to come tripping through the grass complete with immaculate dirndl, frilly pinafore and blonde pigtails, and leading a cow with a bell round its neck. Instead, the black dots on the hills turned into yaks, the dark blobs into *ba-gur* – nomad tents – and instead of picturesque Swiss cowherds and lederhosen, there was a gaggle of ragged urchins with runny noses that looked after the yaks. They played with each other in the same boisterous way that children all over the world play when left on their own. I told Tenzin that I wanted to interview some *drogpa* and he agreed, telling me to wait until we got through to the next valley where he knew a nomad leader.

We left the road, and again bumped over the mountainside. The yak continued munching, with scarcely a glance at the strange antics of the rickety van cavorting wildly among them. We finally tracked down Phagpa, the nomad leader. He was a giant of a man, with a deep voice that instantly commanded respect. It was only when he walked over to the van that I noticed his pronounced limp which, Tenzin told me, was the result of a severe beating he had received in jail when he refused to renounce his faith and his aspirations for an independent Tibet. His leg had been broken and because he received no medical treatment in jail, it had healed badly and left him with a permanent and painful limp.

Phagpa's story was quite extraordinary. When the Chinese arrived and started to brutalize the Tibetans, because Phagpa could read and write he was accused of being a counter-revolutionary and thrown into jail. On his release, instead of keeping a low profile, he continued to stand up for the rights of the nomads, the most disadvantaged of all sections of Tibetan society. Then followed an appalling cycle of imprisonment, release and re-arrest. In all, he had so far spent twenty-two years in jail. And in one prison he had met Tenzin. Talking to Phagpa, I was suddenly reminded of Chico Mendez, the Brazilian leader who was murdered for defending the rights of the Amazon Indians and for protesting against the destruction of the rain forest. Sitting in the lee of the van surrounded by the mountains of Tibet, Phagpa's struggle against the Chinese was so monumental in its inequality that, filled with admiration for the man's extraordinary courage, I feared he too would soon suffer Chico Mendez's fate and be murdered in the night.

I asked him why, in view of his long years in prison, he went on protesting. He told me that his aim was not to overthrow the Chinese, which was impossible for one man to do; he was not interested in power, but to fight to defend his land was his birthright. It was his duty to help make others aware of what the Chinese were doing, whatever the cost. 'It is the only way to escape living a lie,' he said simply, echoing Vaclav Havel, the Czech playwright – and now Czechoslovak President.

Phagpa agreed to be interviewed on camera, but suggested that it would be better if he was not recognized. 'Not that I am frightened of prison any more. What more can they do to this old body of mine that they have not already done? Once you have been tortured you know what to expect and, although the pain is terrible, you no longer have any fear. But I still have work to do while I am at liberty among the people.' Dressed in Tenzin's *chuba* and big felt hat, he sat on a rock, with the mountains behind him. I set the exposure for the bright sky to put him into deep silhouette, so that even the Chinese would not be able to identify him. Proper obscuring of identity was important because I had been warned that once the programme was shown, the Chinese would attempt electronically to decipher every frame of tape. I filmed a few minutes of him sitting on the rock, stopped, rewound the tape and ran it for him through the view-finder. 'There was no need to prove it,' he said gently. 'We trust you.' But he did not know me, and I wanted to remove even the tiniest doubt that could worry him for years, wondering whether the silhouette was impenetrable, wondering if – and when – the Chinese would come for him . . .

Phagpa told me about the miserable conditions in which the *drogpa* lived. I had seen these earlier when he had taken me, with Thondup and Tenzin, into the yak-hair tents to talk to the *drogpa*. 'It is true that before the Chinese invaded, the *drogpa* were not well off. But you must first understand what the yak means to a *drogpa*. They had their yak and sheep – one family sometimes had up to one hundred head of livestock from which they were able to earn a reasonable living. The yak gave us milk, some of which we drank and made into butter and cheese, some of which we bartered for other necessities. Then apart from meat, the yak provided hide for shoes and saddle-bags. Its long black hair was woven into tough fabric for tents and even made the ropes that tethered the tents against the fierce winter gales. And of course, its dung provided fuel for fires. It was also the main means of transport before vehicles came to the mountains. So you can see how indispensable the yak is to the life of a *drogpa*. It is to us what the camel is to the nomads of the desert. Most *drogpa* were – and still are – illiterate, but those who wished to read and write were free to go to the local monastery to learn. Of course, the *drogpa* and everyone in Tibet want to better themselves and their children.

'For centuries the *drogpa*, who make up 40 per cent of the population of Tibet, never had an easy life. But do not judge their life by the luxury standards of your own country. Despite the hardships of the climate and their lives, no one starved in Tibet. Our people always had enough to eat – and a little over for a bad period. Tibetans were content with their life, what we call *Chok-shei*. It was a simple existence, herding their flocks, moving pastures, but they were not unhappy. It is true that they did not have schools or hospitals in the remote parts, but Tibet had only just come into the twentieth century after hundreds of years of isolation. Things like Western technology were unknown in Tibet until only a few decades ago. And then only in Lhasa and the main towns near the Indian and Chinese borders. But the Dalai Lama had already drawn up detailed plans for the development of the country, for reforms in land holdings and redistribution, and for reduction in taxation and debt relief and so on, when the Chinese invaded and he could not put them into practice.'

I put to him the Chinese claim that they have brought health, education, roads and a much better life to all parts of Tibet for all Tibetans. He laughed cynically, but without bitterness. 'Look around you. Travel all over Tibet as I have done and then come back and tell me what "better things" the Chinese have brought for us. Schools? Yes, in the big villages there are Chinese schools for Chinese children. But up here, in the mountains, and most of Tibet is high mountains – very few of our people live in cities like Lhasa where there are schools – here in the countryside, where are the schools? There are none. The Chinese have made no provision for our *drogpa* children. And today our children are illiterate.' Despite the fact that the Chinese insist that there are schools for the Tibetans in the rural areas, in all the 4,000 miles of my journey in Tibet, I met only one *drogpa* child who was going to school – and sporadically at that.

I asked him about hospitals and the 'barefoot' doctors that the Chinese talk of. He replied: 'Where are they? Go and ask our people what happens if they are sick. If someone is injured in the countryside, we have no lorries, no transport; when people are sick, we either put them on a yak, or a horse if we have one or can borrow one, or put them on our backs and carry them, sometimes for weeks, to the nearest Chinese town. And then if we do not have money for Chinese medicine we have wasted the journey. And most often the person does not survive the journey. How can a woman in breech labour travel for a week over our rough mountains?

'Before, we had Tibetan medicine which has cured our people for hundreds of years. The monks had practised and given us medicine from the monasteries. Now we have nothing because they have destroyed the monasteries, and the monks that are left are not allowed to practise. The Chinese call it superstitious rubbish. But they still steal the herbs that we grow here in Tibet, herbs from which for hundreds of years we used to make our medicine. They come now and cut them and take them back to China. You came through Nagchukha, that was a big centre for our herbs. Now nothing. It has all gone to China. So our people are robbed even of their herbs! And the Chinese call this "beneficial"? Next they will decide that the air belongs to the Chinese! Maybe they will try and take that back to China as well.

'Also, another thing. "Those dirty, primitive and barbaric

people", as the Chinese call us, were very healthy before the Chinese came. We were almost never sick. Now we have diseases that we never had before. Like the coughing disease and other ailments. Things absolutely unknown before. And even our children are not as healthy as they were. Look at the teeth of the adults – they are still strong and white and even old people have their own teeth. But look at the children. Their teeth are brown and rotten.' This was confirmed later by the doctors and nurses that I spoke to as being due to the malnutrition that was now endemic in Tibet.

He jerked his head in agitation, and I tried to follow his movements so that he would always remain in deep silhouette. 'You see, before we might not have had much. But what we had was our own – and we were free. When the Chinese came they confiscated all our herds, allowing us only one yak and a sheep. They then made us look after our own herds – *for them*. They took all the produce; they took all the money from the sale of the herds, from the wool, from the meat – even from the milk. They were bad times for our people. Many of them starved. But then a few years ago in 1980, they relaxed their policy here in Tibet and gave us back a few of our own herds, a small number to each family, but not as before. And still, today, we have to look after our own animals for the benefit of the Chinese! And they make certain that they get it all – have you seen the small white houses in the countryside? The ones with electricity? Well they are for the Chinese tax-people. They come round in their jeeps checking up on us, to see that we are not taking even a cup of milk more than they allow us – *from our own herds*!

'Also, we are a nomadic people who like to – and need to – wander from pasture to pasture when it is necessary for the animals. Before we were free to go wherever we wanted to. There were no restrictions. Now, since the Chinese came, we have to be registered in one area and are not allowed to move without special permission from the Chinese – which they never – or very seldom – give. Even if we want to go to the nearest town to buy *tsampa*, or if someone is sick, we have to get many permissions from our "work unit", from the Chinese army sometimes. This is not a life. The animals do not recognize boundaries. If you are sick, you do not have time to go three days' journey for permission . . .

'And another thing: others are now coming to live on our land. The Chinese are pushing the farmers out of their valleys. Taking the land to give to the new Chinese settlers that are coming in great numbers from China to Tibet. They give them special money and work points and they give them Tibetan land! So where do the people who have been pushed off from their own land go? Where else can they go but to the mountains with maybe one yak and a sheep? This is terrible for the farmers. They are not used to the high mountains. And it is bad for us. Although we have a big country, there is not that much good land . . . And when will the Chinese push us off this high land and start using that for themselves also?'

The shadows were lengthening in the valleys. Tenzin was anxious to move, as it was more prudent to try and find some shelter for the night than to sleep in the van. Delayed by the mislaid bag, we would not now reach the designated safe house by nightfall and would have to risk trying to stay with a *drogpa* family, or a farmer further east.

I quickly pulled the tab of the exposed tape to prevent accidental re-recording (one of my recurrent nightmares). I sealed the cassette, stored it in a double plastic bag to protect it from the dust, and put it with a small pile of exposed tapes in a bag behind my head so that if we had to run I had all the exposed tapes in one place. As I said goodbye to Phagpa, I wondered for how much longer the Chinese would leave him at liberty. And for how much longer he would survive. One day, I promised myself, I would return to Tibet and make a film of that extraordinarily courageous man's struggle to concientize the *drogpa*. He reminded me of so many Catholic priests and peasant leaders in South America, who, as part of the Theology of Liberation Movement, tried to make the peasants aware of their rights – often at the cost of having their own lives brutally extinguished by the soldiers and secret police of Latin America's dictators. I wondered whether the Buddhists had an equivalent of the Peruvian theologian, Gustavo Gutiérrez, or their own version of the Liberation Theology that throughout the Third World was teaching the peasants – and the disenfranchised – their rights?

Several passes and valleys later, I had somehow dozed off in a half-sleep when I heard one of the Boys say '*Gyami*' (Chinese). I sat bolt upright and looked out of the window. It was almost dark. We were in a wide valley with a river running down the middle and there were fields of barley on either side of the road. But also running alongside the road were electricity poles: we were approaching a Chinese settlement.

With the light practically drained from the sky, we pulled into a compound of low concrete houses set under the lee of a mountain. Tenzin got out and disappeared into one of the buildings. Sumpa and the other Boys lit up their cigarettes somewhat nervously and I asked Thondup where we were. When he told me I nearly jumped out of my skin. We were *inside* a Chinese army camp and Tenzin had gone to ask if we could rent a room for the night. My bowels turned to water. Stuck in the van with no release, I thought that I just had to be in the middle of a very bad nightmare. I clutched the video camera to my rumbling gut and the hard cold contours jogged me back to sense. I carefully pushed the camera, the 'operational' bag with my stills cameras, film and exposed tape under the front seat in the unrealistic hope that if we were discovered it might just escape notice – and sat quietly clutching my stomach.

After an age, when it was dark, Tenzin came out of a lighted room with a Chinese soldier. Tenzin was laughing. It was a great bravura performance. Still talking to the soldier, he casually walked over to the van and got a bag out of the back. He beckoned Sumpa to follow him with the van and we drove round the corner to where the soldier opened a door in another low building. Through a tear in the van's curtains, I saw a naked bulb dangling in a bare room with a bed in the far corner. Tenzin and the soldier disappeared round the block, and Thondup took the opportunity to bundle me out of the van. He told me to lie down on the bed and covered me with blankets and bits of clothing. He and the Boys sat down on the floor and proceeded to play *Sho*, the Tibetan game of dice. Unable to move because of my back, my gut, my head and practically everything else hurting, I closed my eyes and drifted in and out of sleep.

It was nearly eleven when Tenzin pulled back the covers, grinned and made motions for me to join the Boys, who were sitting in a circle round a cooking pot full of bits of meat that I recognized as the hunk that Tenzin had managed to buy earlier in the day from one of the nomads. It tasted good but, for me, it had been cooked in too much butter. While they were eating I decided I would change for the night. So Thondup escorted me to the van which was parked immediately outside the door, let me in and with half a thermos of water, a mug and a box of Wettex I proceeded with my ablutions, contorting myself into amazing positions in the narrow space between the back bench and the driver's seat. I had to hide behind one of the front seats because if one of the Chinese sailed round the corner I was in full frontal view of the windscreen.

Fifteen minutes later Thondup came and knocked softly on the door. I got out, careful to avoid the puddles, and walked into the room in my pink track suit and bedsocks. The Boys looked up, amazed. Curiously, there was absolutely nothing sexual in their look and it did not bother me to hang up my only set of undies to dry and get into my sleeping bag with five strange men in the room. As I scribbled in my diary the light went out – it must have been midnight. The Boys got up, dusted themselves, pulled out some threadbare blankets from one of the bags of sacking and wrapped them around themselves. Three of them slept on the other three beds, while Tenzin and Sumpa just stretched out on the earthen floor as casually as a sultan would recline on silken cushions in a harem.

At five the next morning Tenzin shook me. We had to be away long before light to avoid awkward questions about our papers and the risk of a search. At six they would be changing shift and we had to be out of the gate, which Tenzin had bribed one of the Chinese to leave open, by then. I did another imitation of Houdini in my sleeping bag and emerged fully clothed. By the end of the trip I had really become quite dextrous at lightning changes in the most extraordinary of places.

Sumpa started the motor. We quietly squelched out of the open gate, through the small village and then, with the headlights now on, Sumpa put his foot on the accelerator. As we turned a blind corner we ran headlong into a quagmire of mud where the land had slipped off the flanking hill right onto the road. Sumpa tried to reverse, but got embedded further in the mud. The Boys got out to push, but the van was axle-deep in mud and the only thing to do was to find some stones to build two tracks out of the rut.

The morning star was shining and the moon hovered over the torrent that raged white a few feet from a precipice, just nine inches from the offside wheels. Behind us there were sounds of activity from the camp. Tenzin and Jigme got into the van and Jigme began reciting his Tara mantras. I was very nervous that the Chinese would appear at any moment round the bend and I gave Tenzin a small incense stick which a holy lama had given me to burn in time of danger. Tenzin reverentially lit it and waved the stick round our three heads and all over the van. Then he went outside to 'anoint' the heads of Thondup, Sumpa and Tsering. The lights of a Chinese three-tonne army truck bounced off the nearside mountain and from the revs I could tell that it was coming up the road towards us. Sumpa got in, and with the others standing by the precarious piles of stones in line with each wheel, they guided Sumpa as he balanced the van inch by inch along the stones on top of the rut.

I looked at my watch and saw that it was 8.15 on Sunday, 4 September. Again I wondered about my sanity and told myself that all well-balanced people were in a warm bed safe at home, reading the Sunday papers and indulging in piping-hot coffee and croissants – not shivering on some God-forsaken mountain somewhere in the middle of Tibet. For the next hour the Boys had to dig us out of the ruts every thirty yards until we hit the harder bed-rock several hundred feet above the village of Rongbochue. As light flooded the sky, people started to walk from their mud-brick homes to tend their fields of barley scattered across the mountainside. It was a grey damp day and the hills were green with just the odd patch of cultivation which disappeared as we climbed higher towards the Yila mountain. Wisps of mist smoked up from the valleys and clung to the crags of the jagged mountains. Too raw, too wild and too monumental in scale, it was not at all like a delicate Chinese painting.

Every time we hit a rock my stomach seemed to hit my backbone and vicious colic ripped through me in spasms. With no hope of medication until we reached Chamdo – a couple of days ahead – I was not the happiest sunflower on the planet. By 9.15 it was getting cold, a bitter north-east wind was blowing and the van had started to climb. There had been no mention of a mountain in this stretch of our journey, but I shrugged and put it down to my incompetent map reading. I tried to scribble notes as we lurched along a road that was getting progressively worse. We soon left behind the Chinese, harvesting what had once been Tibetan land, and drove past scores of little groups of *drogpa* plodding along precipitous tracks that disappeared into the high mist.

As we climbed higher, the track disappeared into a swamp of sticky mud churned up by the Chinese lorries. As we skimmed the edge by inches, the only way I could cope, when I saw a corner coming up or a truck approaching and we were on the precipice edge, was to close my eyes. Every few miles we saw the neat white tents of the Chinese military responsible for building and maintaining the roads. The soldiers looked sullen as they wandered round the muddy compounds in plastic slippers. They wore red or blue nylon track suits under their green uniform trousers which were rolled up to their knees.

We had been climbing for more than two hours with the engine straining noisily when, turning a blind hairpin bend 18,000 feet up the Yila mountain, we ran straight into a fifteen-foot mud landslide.

13

Nightmare on a Bald Mountain

Just how many times, I wondered, could one 'die' in three days: the Chinese patrol in the Nagchukha street, the house-to-house search, the night in a Chinese army camp, and now doing a high-wire act 18,000 feet up a mountain in Tibet.

'Hei! Hei! . . . Stop!' Tenzin shrieked. While I held my breath, he gently pushed the van over the top. As the wet mud of the precipice rushed up to meet the windscreen, Sumpa threw the wheel over to the right, let out the throttle and we swerved round the corner and charged up fifty more feet of wet mud before getting stuck again. However, this time we were at least fifteen yards from the edge.

My hands were so slippery with sweat that I dropped the camera. I grabbed my knees tightly to stop an uncontrollable tremor that had invaded my whole body. In the front Sumpa lit up another cigarette and took a swig of water from his water-bottle jammed between the gears and the dashboard. His face showed absolutely no emotion.

An hour later the Boys inched the van up the 75-degree slope. With only 300 feet to go to the summit of the pass, it slithered back through the mud. Only Sumpa's quick-wittedness in swerving the steering wheel so that we were broadside to the mountain saved us once again from going over the edge. While the Boys jammed stones under the wheels, Tenzin and Thondup exchanged a few terse words. Then Tenzin went to the back, opened the door and started off-loading all the luggage. Thondup very gently opened the door near me and told me to get out carefully as we were in danger of going over the edge. What, I wondered, had he thought that terrifying balancing act on the mud-slide had been? A dress rehearsal?

I carried the video camera in one hand, slung the small camera-bag with my film and exposed rushes and my two Minoltas over my shoulder, and got gingerly down, trying to avoid the foot-deep ruts in the wet mud that the van had made. As the Chinese were round the last bend and somewhere behind the pass, I kept my ski-mask over my mouth and nose. I tugged Tenzin's hat (my straw one had by now disintegrated) down over my face and set out to film from above the van so that I could get a good general view — wide shot — of the van and the whole valley and mountain complex to put the scene into perspective.

But I had not reckoned with the altitude. We were now at nearly 19,000 feet and I was somewhat debilitated by two days of non-stop gastro-enteritis. Suddenly, after taking only four steps, I found that I had enormous difficulty in breathing. I was gasping for breath with a terrible air-hunger that I had never experienced before. I tore the mask off my nose and sat on the ground panting.

After a rest I struggled to an outcrop of rock and sat cradling my camera in my lap. I looked into the valley. It was so beautiful and so peaceful that I ached to share it with someone. Again, I felt a terrible loneliness. Below and all round me was yet another breathtaking panorama: a complete little universe, a mottled green valley with a sparkling river winding playfully through it. The mountains again rose green from the valley floor, transmuting to infinite shades of blue as the shadows modelled the tributary valleys. Finally, above the snow-line, they became more masculine and menacing with vicious brown scars of the landslides excoriating the tapering slopes, devoid even of lichen, as they thrust their jagged peaks into the unbelievably blue sky. It was a wonderfully graphic way to learn physical geography!

Apart from the valiant Boys pushing the van up the mountain, there was not a single living thing anywhere in sight. The sun was still hot at six o'clock in the evening and a faint breeze lulled me into soporific doze.

One hundred feet below the Boys were now taking a break. The burner was brought out, tea made and while the others sat chatting and smoking, Tenzin had lain face down on the mountain and fallen asleep. I marvelled at their strength. Even Thondup, who had lived in lower climes for the past thirty-eight years, seemed to show no fatigue. It had something to do, I was later told, with the especially large lung capacity and the extra red blood corpuscles that Tibetans develop to accommodate the rare atmosphere and oxygen deprivation of high altitudes.

I pointed the camera at the Boys, zooming in on detail like

hands pushing the wheel: such 'cutaways' would be useful when editing to cut smoothly from one wide shot to either another or a different angle. But I was always careful when filming to keep their faces in silhouette or to show only the back of their heads. I wondered what would happen if the van did go over the edge. There would be no way that we could walk off that mountain with all our gear through hundreds of Chinese soldiers. A thought kept niggling me. The Controller had made no mention of this mountain in our plans. Or the absence of roads. In fact a six-hour journey had been scheduled from Rongbochue to Kongpo, our next stop.

Seán's warning about someone sabotaging the trip kept recurring. The why was obvious. But who and to what degree had the infiltrator, if indeed there was one or more, managed to wreck our plans? And was it just a question of time before, as Seán suggested, we were arrested?

As often on the trip, I began to wonder what the Chinese would do to me if I was caught. I could hardly draw myself up to an imperious five feet and one and a half inches and glacially declare: 'Go away, you nasty little man, I'm British!' I regretted that I had forgotten to bring *Teach Yourself Chinese*, the small book I had bought in London specifically in case I was captured and put away for a very long time.

The light was a warm liquid gold. It might have been the altitude, but it engendered a wonderful sense of well-being. My thoughts wandered to languorous tropical palms swaying gently above an immaculate beach, with nothing more arduous to concern myself with than saluting the dying day with a sundowner. About 7 P.M. the Boys clustered around the van for another go at pushing it. I asked them to wait and dragged myself to the other side so as to vary the shot. When I was focused close on the wheel, I started filming and asked them to start. The van revved and I prayed that this time it would actually get going and climb the last sixty almost perpendicular feet to the top.

Fortunately I was filming when the van moved. (So often after waiting for hours for a particular shot, the camera is not running, or jams, and the irreplaceable shot evaporates without being recorded!) Again, the van lunged at the mountain. For a semi-quaver of time it hung in its tracks, defying gravity as though some fiendish spirit was torturing us with indecision. Through the view-finder I saw the Boys freeze and collectively hold their breath; the back wheels spun a tarantella and the van spurted up the last few feet. At the top the Boys cheered wildly, delirious with their achievement.

I clambered up, grateful that another disaster had been avoided. I was looking forward to getting off that mountain as soon as possible. The sun was slipping behind the far rim of mountains and the valleys were cloaked in their mysterious evening blue. I took some photographs of the Boys, who posed triumphantly by the gaily coloured prayer-flags at the top of the pass. They grinned and looked every inch as victorious as Hilary and Tenzing when they stood on the summit of Everest. For the Boys it certainly was an extraordinary feat of courage and perseverance.

When we reached the top of the pass and I looked into the next valley complex I could have wept. The whole mountainside – all 4,000 feet to the valley floor – was crawling with Chinese soldiers and earth-moving equipment. There was no road down the mountain – just raw gashes – and the Chinese were blasting rock to build it. In front of us, four three-tonne army trucks were firmly embedded deep in the mud. With no way back, we were well and truly stuck on the top of a bald mountain – with no Mussorgsky – in the middle of Central Asia. It was one of those times when strong men take hemlock.

It was 8 P.M. and dusk was already softening the contours of the mountains. Tenzin and the Boys went to investigate, while Sumpa inched the van onto the top of the deep ruts left by the trucks' heavy wheels. I idly wondered whether, if we slipped off the ruts, the weight of the trucks would be enough to stop the van or whether we would end in a sticky mud ball at the bottom of the mountain. The Boys returned. There was no way off the mountain. The Chinese were packing up for the night. As I watched the soldiers in their green uniforms climb down to the neat little white tents that dotted the mountain, I could have cheerfully thrown a truck-load of dynamite after them. I was more than somewhat irritable. The last thing I wanted was to spend the night on that infernal mountain.

We had inched down another hundred feet to be followed by two trucks which had been waiting in a cutting above. Wonderful,

I thought: not only were we surrounded by hundreds of PLA soldiers, but we would now have to spend the night literally sandwiched between them as well. I fumed impotently in the van. Thondup came in with a mug of hot noodles. Outside the Boys were sitting happily on the ground. The burner was blazing, the kettle was on and, going by the gales of laughter, they were having a ball. Once the sun had gone there was no lingering twilight, as in the temperate zones, and night fell quickly with biting cold.

As I could not get out of the van, had nothing to read, and could not listen to the radio with all the Chinese passing backwards and forwards on the other side of the window, I decided that I might as well pack it in and get into my sleeping bag and at least be warm. I really felt deprived at not listening to the BBC's World Service, but Tenzin had warned me not to put on the radio, because the Chinese would pick it up and locate us quickly. I didn't quite follow his reasoning, but it was something to do with radio waves bouncing off the mountains.

He explained that it would give us away very fast. Most Tibetans could not afford a radio, although in the big towns many saved for ages to buy a rudimentary Chinese one on which they could listen to All India Radio's Tibetan Service broadcasts. However under Chinese law they were forbidden to listen to any foreign-language broadcast, as the Chinese considered them all counter-revolutionary. There were severe penalties for anyone caught. 'Why else,' Tenzin said, 'do you think that in Tibet you find no newspapers, magazines or foreign books? It's not only censorship, it's more: it's China's deliberate policy to keep our people ignorant – not only about their rights, but about the outside world. If you asked most Tibetans, they would not even be able to show you Britain on the map. Most of them have not even seen a map. The Chinese are trying to turn us into living vegetables. Much easier to manipulate an entire population that way.' Tenzin spat on the ground.

In the darkness Thondup escorted me round the next corner. It was quite extraordinary to attend to one's bodily functions surrounded by a cacophony of strange voices and unfamiliar shapes. Privacy, I decided, was something I was going to have to learn to forget. Back in the dark of the van, Thondup and I rearranged the bags at the back, spread the foam rubber ground sheet I had bought in London, and opened our sleeping bags top to tail on the top. Sumpa, looking exhausted, spread some sacks across the two front seats; Jigme and Tsering decided to sit/sleep on the back bench and Tenzin said he would sleep outdoors.

While they were eating and chatting, and because there were no baths or bidets on that mountain, I began the first of my nightly contortions with the Wettex to get clean, and by the end of the trip I had perfected it to a fine art. The most difficult part was to wash my smalls in one mug of water. Without, as the French would say, any *pudeur*, I hooked my bra and panties along the inside of the window and prayed that they would dry by the morning.

Getting comfortable inside my sleeping bag on top of drums of petrol, bags sharp with batteries and tins of food was a feat I never mastered. But for me it was the best part of the day: for a few brief minutes, I could be on my own, be clean and warm and snuggled into the down sleeping bag. In that blissful cocoon I felt almost human. Above all, for a few hours there were no more decisions to make – should I film this or that – no more questions to ask.

But, unable to sleep, I drew back the curtain and there in a velvet sky the firmament blazed with a brilliance that is hard to describe. The sky was carpeted with so many stars that there seemed hardly a pinprick of space between them; it seemed that night as if all the stars of the world had been strewn across the sky. Long after the Boys were asleep, I lay totally mesmerized.

Sleep was elusive that night. Worried about disturbing Thondup, whose head was near my feet, I tried not to move. Sumpa, who had no blanket, just pulled his thin blue coat, padded with cotton, over him and, uncomplainingly, fell sound asleep wrapped round the van's gears. It was the same for Jigme and Tsering. They too just pulled their collars up, and grunted into sleep. Tenzin wrapped himself in his *chuba*, put his hat under his head and slept on the frozen ground outside the van, where that night the temperature must have dropped well below zero. I resolved to do something about buying blankets for the Boys at the next stop. I was very humbled by their total acceptance of the situation and the fact that not once during the whole trip did I hear them complain about anything – apart from my continual bleats to be allowed to film! It was just another characteristic of the hardy Tibetans.

It was still dark when I decided to give up the struggle. It was bitterly cold and my underwear had frozen solid. The Boys were sound asleep and Sumpa was snoring gently. Outside it was pitch-black; the only sound was the faint moan of the wind, and in the sky the morning star shone brightly. I knew dawn was not far off. Much to the chagrin of loved ones, I adore the dawn. For me it is the most magical time of day. At home in London, awakened by the birds, I watch the sky lighten across the trees and turn the Thames to silver. The daybreak on Monday, 5 September, was the first of a series of bewitching dawns and the most spectacular I had ever seen.

Previously, I had watched the day break on the mountains from below the peaks, and seen the dawn outline their contours with the silver filigree of day. But on Yila we were on the crest of the mountains and that morning dawn crept majestically and unforgettably into the sky. One moment earth and sky were cloaked in night, and then, without warning, suddenly from the east a shaft of rosy light lit the nearest mountain. It was as though a laser had exploded on to it. As the peak flamed, a cascade of light glided languorously down, caressing the sleeping mountain into life. As one peak caught fire the one behind it also became incandescent. It was like being inside Stanley Kubrick's *2001: A Space Odyssey* watching the day creep up on the planets, on one world after another. It was impossible to take my eyes from the unfolding panorama as mountain upon interlocking mountain seemed to erupt into light. It seemed to go on and on as the horizon receded with each new revelation. All that was missing was the Strauss soundtrack!

Monday was not to prove my happiest day. My anxiety was mounting. Surrounded by Chinese and days behind schedule, I knew we had to get off that mountain. But by ten o'clock we were only another 200 feet down. The earth-moving machine in front of the trucks had itself got bogged down. The Chinese seemed unconcerned. As Tenzin explained, the soldiers were paid whatever happened, and on their pitiful salaries why should they exert themselves? Better to go back to their tents and wait for the weather to harden the sodden ground – and that could take up to two weeks.

I gave Tenzin a bundle of Rmb and suggested that he tried to coax another Caterpillar from the Chinese. He disappeared and the others were brewing tea outside when a swarm of Chinese soldiers seemed to move uncomfortably close to the van – the only one with Nagchukha plates in the whole Chinese convoy. Thondup hurried into the van and suggested that I lie flat on my back to avoid any questions, and proceeded to put a blanket and Tenzin's *chuba* over me. So, clutching the Sony to my belly, I pushed the camera-bag under my head, pulled the hat down over my face and pretended to be sleeping.

Breathing was very difficult with the ski-mask over my nose and mouth and I alternated between panic when the Chinese leaned talking against the van, and gasping in sheer physical air-hunger. It was 10.30 A.M. Thondup quietly passed me a cup of hot noodles. I was reluctant to drink any liquid, for with Chinese so close to the van, to have gone outside to the loo would have been to court certain disaster.

Several more Chinese soldiers came up to the van to chat, and although quite friendly, each approach seemed to swing the sword of Damocles more perilously near my head. The last time I looked at my watch it was 2.15. The Boys had disappeared down the mountain to scout out another way round the impasse. And every time Thondup left me alone to stretch his legs, I found myself straining apprehensively at every extraneous sound until I heard his whistle as he returned to the van. For most of the day, immobile on the back seat, I drifted in and out of a light doze. Without being able to read, listen to anything, talk to anyone, or even watch the ever-changing scenery, I began to get an inkling of what solitary confinement would be like. I also realized that I might not be too good at coping with it.

I suppose I must have dozed off, but I woke with the driver's side door being opened. Just as I was about to call 'Sumpa', I saw a green-uniformed arm with two gold bands grab the steering wheel and haul a Chinese soldier into the van's driving seat. Neither Thondup nor Sumpa nor any of the others was in sight. I was alone in the van, lying a few inches away from a Chinese soldier. It seemed that there was no one and nothing in the world that could help me. I thought that I knew what it was to be scared. But at that moment I went through the fear barrier. I was literally paralysed with terror. My heart seemed to rise in my throat and choke me. I couldn't breathe. Panicking in an immobile body seemed to compound my impotence. I thought I was going to die – or at least have a heart attack.

Peeping from under the brim of my hat, I watched every breath the soldier took. I can even now visualize the back of his neck, placing every hair correctly. I waited for forty eternal, agonizing minutes. They say a drowning man sees his life flash past just before he goes under – all I saw was the short back and sides of black spiky hair under an army cap. I was waiting for the soldier to turn round. For his hands to whip the covering off me. I could not string two coherent thoughts together. After an aeon, the other front door opened and Sumpa got in and started merrily chatting to the soldier in Chinese. Then Thondup came up and I heard the alarm in his voice as he spoke sharply to Sumpa in Tibetan. After interminable bonhomie, the soldier got out of the van and slammed the door. I broke into a fit of trembling, realizing how close to catastrophe I had come. To this day, I do not know why I was not discovered. There is no logical explanation. But I have a strong conviction that a sacred Buddhist thread, that had been blessed by a holy lama and placed round my neck, protected me.

When the rest of the Boys returned, they were sobered when Thondup told them what had happened. It brought home to them that we were in considerable danger and had to get off the mountain and away from the Chinese military as soon as possible. About six o'clock in the evening the bundle of notes Tenzin had given one of the Chinese appeared to have some effect. A bright orange Caterpillar started dragging the three trucks in front of us out of their ruts and by eight we were dragged out of the morass with a sickening screech of tearing metal that did not augur well for whatever remained under the chassis. An hour later we were finally moving slowly down the mountain under our own steam. By 10 P.M. it was almost dark, and Sumpa switched on his lights. Nothing happened. The electrics had packed up. For the next four hours the Boys, in relays, walked in front of the van roughly in line with the wheels and shone the weak beams of their torches on the ruts for Sumpa to decipher the path off the mountain.

In the early hours of the morning we hit another rough patch when the van shuddered to a halt in a particularly deep rut. It had started to rain heavily again. The Boys got out and pushed, and as the van finally pulled free of the mud, Sumpa seemed agitated about something. He got out and lay on the ground to look under the bodywork with a torch; he yelled something to Tsering who handed him some tools and then himself also got under the van. We had lost our entire exhaust, the oil seal had ripped off and the electrics for the rest of the engine had just died.

Outside there was only blackness beyond the beam of the torch. There was no moon, and not a star in sight. From further up the slope came the noises of other vehicles stuck higher up than us, and also in trouble. I was too exhausted to care. Although it was cold, and by now damp, it was easier to breathe at the lower altitude. I just sat numb with cold, inanimate and subhuman. I hardly dared to think what more could go wrong.

14

Testimony in Kham

The sound of Chinese voices a few inches away woke me with a start. In the grey light of a drizzly dawn I peered through a tear in the van's curtains near my head and saw two Chinese soldiers slowly walking by and looking with some curiosity at the van. When they had passed, I sat up, looked through the mud-splattered windscreen and almost had hysterics. After the fatigue of last night, having to cope with the mountain, rain and practically everything going wrong with the van, the Boys had understandably parked at the first convenient flattish spot. On one side was the fury of a mountain torrent in spate – only a few yards from the front wheels – and on the other three sides were the white tents of a Chinese army camp.

In the van everyone was sound asleep. It had been a long hard night – especially for Sumpa, who had worked miracles driving us off the mountain. As the light got stronger more Chinese soldiers passed by the van: we were obviously parked in the middle of some sort of pedestrian walkway from the camp to somewhere beyond the bend in the river. The Boys stirred, got up and started to make tea outside. Poor little Sumpa just could not shake awake and pleaded to be left alone.

The domestic necessities completed, I asked Thondup when we were going to move. Tenzin sent the others ahead around the spur of the mountain that was jutting out into the river to see if they could find another way. For the track from the camp ended in the rock-face of the mountain and it would take weeks to blast a road through that.

While they were gone, I tried to clean the equipment. It was not an easy task because the floor of the van was awash with mud. Everything was covered with mud. Sumpa's and Tsering's hair was matted with dried mud and their coats looked more mud than fabric, from their endeavours under the van. The bags too were covered with caked mud. We were surrounded by a swamp of mud – even the coffee tasted of mud.

As I scribbled my diary, I idly looked up and saw two Chinese soldiers in uniform and in knee-length black boots, with AK 47s in their hands, walking in the near distance. The cut of their uniform and their boots led me to suppose they were officers. They were laughing and obviously having a good time. I asked Tenzin why they were going up the mountain alone. 'Hunting!' he snarled. Surprised at his ill-humour, I asked him what he meant. As a Khampa, he had an almost mystical attachment to the land, and as a Buddhist, he had respect for all life. He spoke with raw emotion at the way the Chinese had ravaged his land. Not only had he and his people been dispossessed, but the Chinese had also indiscriminately slaughtered the wildlife that once abounded in the mountains. Rare animals, like the snow leopard and the blue Himalayan bear, had been shot to extinction.

'That's what they do!' He pointed to the soldiers disappearing up the mountain. 'They go with their machine-guns, sometimes on foot, sometimes they fire from a jeep. They do not observe the mating times, or when the animals are with young. Nothing matters to them. It's not their country, why should they care if they destroy our precious animals? You will probably find that they will wave Mao's little red book at you and tell you that they are only obeying orders. But you saw the look on the faces just now: you heard the laughter. Often, and I will show you one of the places on our route, the Chinese build low corrals – you can see them snake over the hills – to trap what little is left of our wildlife. Some foreigners in Lhasa told me that outside Tibet you have world-wide organizations that impose very strict penalties on poachers for killing wild animals, such as elephant and rhino. But why is it no one says – or does – anything when the Chinese have, for years, shot our wildlife to extinction?'

It was always very painful when Tibetans, trusting and often touchingly naïve, continually asked me why the world had done nothing to help them. The further I travelled in Tibet and the more simple the people, the more the question became almost unbearable.

Throughout my journey in Tibet, even at night, when animals move, I never saw any wildlife. Not even a rabbit or pheasant or rat. Neither in the fields, in the mountains, nor even running across the road. I did not see a snow leopard, bear, gazelle or deer – not even their tracks.

It soon became clear that to get off the mountain we had only one option left. We would have to drive through the shallows of the torrent, around the spur of the mountain and somehow forge a way down till we picked up the main Riwoche–Chamdo road. Waiting for the Chinese to blast a road was just too impossible even to contemplate. The Boys washed the mud off the windscreen, packed up the burner and tied everything down. Sumpa once again charged the van into uncharted waters.

If I had not been so preoccupied with stopping myself from going through the windscreen as we hit rocks hidden by the swirling water, I might have enjoyed the ride more. For plunging into a raging river that exploded white round submerged rocks and foamed into sinister whirlpools was enormously exhilarating. With the water swirling round the wheels and trickling through the doors, I held onto the seat and felt like an excited ten-year-old on a Disneyland adventure ride.

By five o'clock we had finally got ourselves off Yila mountain, and amid perfect Alpine scenery the Boys decided to camp for tea beside another fast-flowing stream. I was overwhelmed by an uncontrollable desire to feel the water on my skin. I borrowed some soap and toothpaste from Thondup and rushed like a demented banshee to the stream. The Boys looked at me in amazement. 'But it's cold,' Thondup called out. I just did not care. It had been five days since I had washed properly – and heaven only knew when I would have the opportunity again!

It was a deserted spot and we could see anyone approaching for miles. I clambered down the bank to the water's edge, and with modesty thrown to the winds (the Boys were out of sight), I stripped, washed everything I stood up in, laid it out on the scrubby bushes and proceeded to pour water over myself from my only mug. The water was brown with silt, and freezing. As I stood with my feet in the water – it was too dangerous to actually go in deeper as the current, fed by the steep gradient, looked vicious – my toes, and then my feet, began to turn blue with the icy water.

Hurrying to put on the bare essentials before they became stiff with the cold, I mused at how little, when it comes to the crunch, one can make do with. But I still, unashamedly and desperately, hankered after a splurge of restorative scent! With bedraggled hair, I scrambled up the bank to join the Boys for tea. Thondup told me that they thought I was completely mad. It was almost a perfect scene from *Déjeuner sur l'herbe* – Tibetan-style! For half an hour the horrors and alarms of the past few days evaporated as the sun came out of the cloud and warmed us.

Then the gods again smiled on me: delving into the depths of one of the bags to find some more coffee, I discovered a secret store of three paperback books. I was delirious with joy and could have almost taken on the whole Chinese army single-handed! The Boys must have thought I was very strange indeed, but for the rest of the daylight hours, in between looking for locations to film, I was oblivious to the bumps and pains, the mud and the cold. I was just blissfully happy with my nose in a book!

We drove through farming country where Tibetans were harvesting the barley. The men were stripped to their shirt-sleeves with their *chubas* tied round their waists, and the women had rolled up the sleeves of their blouses and tucked their hair into bright scarves. There seemed to be an infectious gaiety in the snatches of laughter that wafted through the open windows as we drove past. I wanted to film, but Tenzin said there were too many Chinese around. And indeed, half an hour later, while climbing out of the valley, we saw the white tents of the Chinese harvesters. I could not help noticing that there was no laughter, no amused calling to each other like with the Tibetans. But I also noticed once again that the Chinese were using modern farm machinery to harvest while the Tibetans were still using antiquated scythes.

By nightfall we reached the village of Den Chen, still a day's hard drive away from Chamdo, where we should have arrived a week ago. As it was an unscheduled stop, Tenzin had no safe house arranged, so we pulled up at a Tibetan farmhouse above the road. As Tenzin did not know the people, it was decided that I would sleep in the van, and the Boys, after the past two difficult nights, could at least have the comfort of stretching out in some hay in the shed.

After the nightly ablutions, I settled down to read *A Princess Remembers* by Gyatri Devi, the Maharanee of Jaipur, by torchlight hidden under the cover of the sleeping bag in case the beam attracted unwelcome attention. The countryside was noisy with a cacophony of barking dogs and the fury of a rushing stream further down the valley. The night sky was resplendent with stars, but not as scintillating as the display on Yila. As ever, mesmerized by the firmament, I was day-dreaming when Thondup and Tenzin came up.

'Tenzin is worried about you sleeping alone in the van, so he is going to sleep here too – just in case,' Thondup said. I was very touched at Tenzin's generosity in giving up the opportunity of sleeping completely horizontal in order to guard one strange English lady, and I felt reassured at the thought of his curved dagger which, ever ready at his side, I knew he would put to effective use if necessary.

We were away before daybreak. As the light flooded the valley we drove through farming land with curious mud-brick, fort-like houses. Typically Tibetan, they curved upwards and inwards and ended in squared crenellations at the top. I was extremely irritated that Tenzin would not let me stop and film, but we had to reach Chamdo by nightfall as he had the times of the changing of the guard at the checkpoints, and the information, already a week old, ran out at midnight. So I could hardly argue.

By ten the van had started to climb up the most spectacular gorge I have ever seen. A raging stream, hurtling boiling white water down between massive boulders, seemed to come from somewhere beyond the cliffs high on the skyline. Flanking the torrent, the track snaked perilously upwards hugging the contours of the mountain on one side, while on the other the mountain soared rose-red into the sky. Dotted on the perpendicular rock-face were many caves – some as high as a four-storeyed house. It was a sort of compact Grand Canyon and rose-red Petra rolled into one. The grandeur of the gorge was accentuated by its emptiness. Just the towering gorge and the silence broken only by the thundering cascade. A solitary Khampa on horseback was the only human being we saw for hours, and our straining little van made an unholy row without the exhaust and silencer. If anything cried out to be filmed, if anything begged to be allowed the time to be explored and savoured, it was this wild precipitous gorge without a name. We climbed for over two and a half hours and the stream became less tumultuous as we approached the top of the gorge. When we crossed a more tranquil river, I was allowed out to film.

Half-sitting in the sparkling water, I focused on the light refracting into tiny rainbows on its surface; then, zooming back to the wide shot of the mountain and the river, I cued the van to ford the river from left to right. It is always more interesting to have some action in a wide shot, and the van would put the scene into perspective. It would be a useful transition shot. As I walked back, I saw a stone, about six inches long, in the grass. It had lettering on it.

Tenzin took the piece of grey slate, dusted it, and showed me the elegant *U-chen* script which Tibetans use in all printed and religious documents. It was a fragment of a religious text that testified to the destruction of a nearby monastery.

'But I don't see any ruin.'

'Of course not,' Tenzin scowled. 'The Chinese remove most of the evidence nowadays.'

'What do you mean? Why here? We are miles from anywhere. Who on earth would bother to hide anything here?'

'You don't think like a Chinese!' Tenzin said curtly. 'First they don't want evidence of the destruction around any more. Second, why should they cut stones from the mountains for their houses when all they have to do is to take the stones from our monasteries and from our houses? Much easier and quicker. And they don't have to spend any money on it, either!' He spat on the ground with frustration.

Throughout our journey I saw several bits of sacred scriptures lying derelict in the fields and in the streets. I had been told several times in different places stories of how the Chinese had desecrated the monasteries and chapels, burnt the sacred scriptures or laid them on the ground and made Tibetans and their cattle walk over them. It was as heinous an offence for the Tibetans as if the Bible, or the Torah or the Koran had been desecrated in the same way. It was a similar story with the Mani Stones – pieces of rock carved with verses of the Buddhist scripture, particularly with the prayer '*Om Mani Padme Hum*' (Hail to the Jewel in the Lotus). Stones carved or painted with sacred verses used to be found all over Tibet as wayside shrines. Tenzin told me that the Chinese, with their finely tuned sense of degradation, had forced the Tibetans to build toilets with the sacred stones.

'And,' Tenzin said, with a sharp tongue that became more

acid as he got to know me better, 'another particular refinement perfected by the Chinese was their habit of converting monasteries into abattoirs. Look what they did to the Jokhang in Lhasa. But also all over the country there were – and still are – examples of this particular barbarity. Like the former monastery at Chokhorge near Gytsa in Dghagpo. And then the Chinese call *us* barbarians!'

As we climbed towards the Nyela pass I saw the first evidence of deforestation. Once, Tenzin told me, there had been thick forests of pine and rhododendrons, but now only a few trees remained amid ugly mutilated tree-stumps. There were no signs of re-afforestation. Not even one tiny sapling. Several times along the road I saw white notices attached to the trees. I asked what they said. 'Tibetans not allowed to cut trees,' Tenzin said flatly.

As we climbed higher, it began to rain and the windscreen wipers packed in. Then about 1.30, near the summit of the pass, it began to snow hard. All the Boys remarked then, and several times during the trip, that the weather patterns were changing dramatically and they did not know why. They told me that normally the rains were finished by early July (which is why I had decided to travel then) and that the snow was not due until November. Everywhere I went in Tibet, Tibetans kept remarking on the strange weather. It was grey and sludgy and every time we got out of the van so as not to strain the engine too much on the very sharp gradient, it reminded me of a gloomy miserable London day in mid-winter. My feet were like blocks of ice despite the thermal socks.

As we approached Riwoche, a fairly important provincial town, the houses became somewhat more substantial than the bracken-and-twig dwellings lashed together with straw that the Tibetans lived in higher up the mountain. Bits of stone and timber were now used, but the Chinese of course had their statutory concrete blocks as well as many substantial houses made from chunks of well-rounded stone. And the first trees I had seen since Lhasa were planted round the Chinese houses!

Riwoche saw many bloody battles between the Chinese and Tibetans in 1917 and 1932. After the invasion in 1949 fierce fighting erupted again in the area and most of the monasteries, including the famous Dokhang monastery, were destroyed.

I had particularly wanted to see the ruins of the Khumgpo Teng

Chen monastery, which were between Riwoche and Nagchukha, because in the summer of 1959 thousands of Tibetans had been slaughtered nearby. That summer, fighting between the Chinese and local Khampa guerrillas under the chieftain Karupon Tsewang Topgyal was fierce. The Tibetans had only ancient muskets, which had been bought in India at the turn of the century, their *tipa-thang* (long swords/knives) and their valiant Khampa horses. For two weeks in high summer the Khampas saw, every day, Chinese planes flying low overhead and noting their positions. Then on the 15th morning of the 12th Tibetan month of 1959, while the Tibetans were engaged in a skirmish with the Chinese, the Chinese planes flew low out of the rising sun in the east and bombed everything in sight – the guerrillas, the houses, innocent villagers and the monastery. The Tibetans' muskets had neither the range nor velocity to attack the planes, and as Tenzin, who had fought there, remembered: 'There were more bodies of dead and dying lying in the valley than there were summer daisies. It was a question of gunpowder against bombs.'

The Khampas, seeing that there was no way in which they could win the battle, and knowing the gruesome torture that the Chinese perpetrated on any Tibetan they caught, tried to escape. The few who were uninjured left with as many of the wounded as they could carry on their horses to regroup and fight again. But many who had been seriously injured in the field and had no hope of escape gave the old Khampa war cry *'Ki-hi-hi!'* and slit their own throats. Although *rangshi* (suicide) is expressly forbidden in Buddhism, the injured fighters found it preferable to being captured by the Chinese or being left to be eaten by the dogs that were already devouring the corpses of the dead strewn around the valley. After the battle and bombing that day alone over 3,000 Tibetans died.

Tenzin told me that the few villagers who were uninjured dragged as many corpses as they could to the monastery, but by nightfall the dogs and wolves had got to work on those left outside. The next day the Chinese returned and threw all the dead, and some of the wounded who were not dead, into a large shallow grave not far from the monastery.

'Do you mean that they buried human beings alive? Why? And what proof have you got?'

'Why should the Chinese waste time and medicine on Tibetans?' Tenzin replied. 'It was a tidy way to get rid of the problem. And if some were still alive – so what? Who could complain? But if you don't believe me, I will take you to a man who survived, who crawled into a small cave near the monastery where he saw these things.'

Tenzin drew me a map of the area on the ground and said that we could go there; and if I did not believe him, we could dig up the mass grave, as all the bodies were still in it. 'And,' he added 'there are many, many of these mass graves all over Tibet. They have done worse things to our people. I will show you. You can take back part of a skeleton to have your people see if it is not the truth.'

All remnants of the monastery and the village had been dynamited and bulldozed by the Chinese. For twenty-four years it had remained a deserted, haunted place where nothing would grow; then in 1983 the Chinese built new Chinese buildings for new Chinese settlers.

Tenzin went on to cite examples of other mass graves like Khumgpo Teng Chen and gave me details of another eight between Riwoche and Chamdo.

But for the moment I was looking for a monk who, I had been told, had survived the horror and who could guide us to Khumgpo Teng Chen and tell us about the destruction of the other monasteries in the area. We found him waiting in the shell of another ruined monastery on the road down into Riwoche. We sheltered from the rain in what had once been the main hall, but which now looked like a pigsty. Walls that had once been painted with exquisite murals were stripped to the stone and in some places where the sledge-hammers had not quite managed to smash off all the frescos, half a halo or a hand in peaceful benediction still survived on a patch of crumbling plaster. In one corner a makeshift ladder led to the gutted second floor. 'We are making repairs ourselves. But it takes a long time as we have very little money,' the monk said.

'The Chinese say they are spending a fortune on repairing the monasteries. Four hundred and nineteen are supposed to be under construction in Kham alone,' I said.

'The Chinese are giving some money to rebuild the monasteries, but only where the tourists can see them and they can bring in foreign money. But deep in the country it is our people who put in the time, effort and what little money they have to rebuild our monasteries. But,' he said and smiled with the sad resignation that I was beginning to recognize in a people who had seen the things they held most dear in life shattered, 'how do we "repair" the irreplaceable?

'In 1966 they [the Chinese] destroyed the Dokhang Th'e Gelma monastery. But more important than the building, which was indeed old, were the most beautiful scriptures painted in gold and silver on palm leaves. They were very ancient. Very special. But the Chinese came and tore them from the shelves where they had lain for hundreds of years and threw them on the fire they made in the middle of the temple. When some monks pleaded with the soldiers saying, "Please don't. They are very old and mean everything to us," the Chinese pushed them to the floor and said, "Rubbish, religion is bourgeois poison!" They proceeded to pour kerosene on the priceless scriptures and then put a match to them, as though they were useless refuse. Now how,' he asked me gently, 'can we replace that?'

As the question hung in the air, I thought of the outcry in Britain when national treasures such as the Mappa Mundi (the same age as these scriptures) or a Gainsborough or a Constable are in danger. But where were the art curators, the Ministers of Culture, UNESCO (United Nations Educational, Scientific and Cultural Organization) and all the international agencies that are supposed to be concerned about saving the artistic heritage of the world, irrespective of culture, language or creed?

'Many of our people went to prison resisting the Chinese,' the monk said. 'Near here I can take you to a man who survived the Nak Dzong Sheu prison, where he saw terrible things done to Tibetans. During the Cultural Revolution there were over 5,000 prisoners, of whom only about 200–300 survived.'

'But how do you know? How can you be sure of the figures?' I asked.

'Oh, the Chinese do not give figures, of course. In fact they deny most of the things they have done. I know because my oldest brother was in that prison for many years. He survived, but today he cannot walk because of the way they tortured him. I can take you to him: he is a *drogpa* and lives two hours from here.'

I looked at Tenzin and asked Thondup if there was any way we could get there and also be in Chamdo by nightfall. Tenzin shook his head. Chamdo was probably the most dangerous of our locations, as it was a military headquarters and the town was full of Chinese soldiers. Also the doctors waiting there could not stay long. We dare not risk it. It would be better to try and return to Riwoche after we had finished in Amdo, returned to Lhasa and evacuated the exposed tapes. Only then could we return. By that time I reckoned I would well and truly be out of visa time. As it was, I had only nineteen days left on my visa and still another 3,000 miles left to do.

I asked the monk about reports of considerable mineral deposits in the area – coal, gold, silver, borax, copper, iron, *shache* (similar to aluminium), *mu* and salt. He told me that the area was indeed very rich in minerals. I explained that I wanted to check for myself the conditions in the mines and asked him to arrange for me to talk to miners. He agreed to make such arrangements for my return.

Tenzin reminded me that we had to move quickly to Chamdo as otherwise we would miss one of the Lhasa doctors, who was on his way to an obstetrics course in Chengdu. 'But is there a way back other than through that infernal mountain?' I asked. Tenzin laughed: 'Yes, the southern route!' I thought I showed remarkable restraint by not asking why then we had had to go on that crucifying journey up the infernal Yila mountain.

For two and a half hours we drove down through interlocking mountains and valleys. Suddenly, about an hour from Chamdo, the road improved dramatically. There were fewer ruts, and as we approached the outskirts it became graded, but not tarmacked. And the ubiquitous electricity poles appeared again. I tried to remember what I had heard about Chamdo.

The capital of Kham, Chamdo is the third largest town in Tibet and has always been an important administrative and military centre. It is situated between a tributary of the Ngomchu and the Zachu which join together at the foot of the town to form the head-waters of the Dachu (Mekong). It has always been strategically important and since the turn of the century it had been coveted and occasionally occupied by China. Chamdo was considered such an important listening post in China, that the British Government in India had seconded Robert Ford, a wireless operator, to the Tibetan Government in August 1949. When the Chinese invaded Chamdo on 19 October 1950, Ford was captured by the Chinese and spent five very difficult years in a Chinese jail in Chunking. He graphically describes his imprisonment and the turbulent history of that period in his excellent book, *Captured in Tibet*.

In 1949 when the PLA soldiers invaded Tibet, Chamdo had a crucial – and disastrous – role to play in the struggle against the Chinese. In the week before the outbreak of the Korean War, news reached Chamdo that Dengkok, on the Upper Yangtse, had been attacked and over-run by the Chinese. Instead of uniting against the common enemy, regional and clan rivalries that had for centuries embroiled Kham in bitter vendettas, skillfully manipulated by the Chinese, threatened the very roots of Tibet's eastern defences which were centred, somewhat precariously, on Chamdo. Instead of capitalizing on Tibet's greatest assets, the impregnable mountains and the lack of roads, which would have halted even the most efficient of armies, the new Governor of Chamdo vacillated. Instead of mobilizing the clans of the Kham alliance, he spent time attending receptions in honour of his arrival.

The Tibetan army itself was hindered by the Government's incredible inefficiency and failure to reply to a telegram reporting the situation and demanding instructions (unbelievably, news of the invasion was kept from the Tibetan Cabinet for nine days while they caroused at an annual picnic). With the Tibetans disorganized and indecisive, the Chinese armies advanced.

Early on the morning of 7 October, the Governor fled, Chamdo erupted with panic and the PLA walked into Chamdo and accepted the surrender from a force twenty times their own size. The war lasted eleven days. On 25 October the newly formed People's Republic of China announced on Radio Beijing for the first time that its troops had entered Tibet, 'to free' Tibetans from 'imperial oppression'. The Tibetan Government in Lhasa sent an impassioned plea to the United Nations. China replied by resolutely maintaining that Tibet 'is an entirely domestic problem of China and no foreign interference will be tolerated'. The United Nations was silent and not one nation responded.

Today, Chamdo is 80 per cent Chinese with a small Tibetan ghetto. It is also the headquarters of the Chamdo Military Region and is pivotal for supplying men and equipment to the troops stationed on permanent alert on the border with the Indian territory of Arunachal Pradesh. Security is extremely tight in Chamdo. I had been told in Lhasa that it was suicidal even to try to get into the town, and that I would almost certainly be caught, arrested and imprisoned if I did.

Chamdo was therefore the one location I was really frightened of. The Controller had told me that Tenzin would decide how and when we would cross the checkpoints into the city and that he was totally in charge. The other possibility was to cross one of the rivers at night in a *ko-du*, the aforementioned Tibetan coracle made from yak hide. But as we drove towards Chamdo, the river broadened and the current looked vicious. In fact, I would rather have been anywhere in the world than driving relentlessly down the mountains to Chamdo. I was more frightened than I cared to admit and as signs of habitation appeared and the fields gave way to houses, my mouth dried and my eyes were glued to the red dirt road.

In the van the Boys were looking rigidly in front, their bodies taut with tension. No one spoke. Sumpa smoked his fourth cigarette of the hour. The van seemed to make an even louder noise. It was just after eight in the evening, the light was soft and it had stopped raining. After we passed an electricity sub-station on the east bank and some sort of factory, we crossed the river by a concrete bridge with sentry-boxes at either end, which mercifully were empty. The river, brown with silt, ran below the road on the right. Soon more factories and cyclists appeared. From the snatches of conversation that we caught as we passed, it was obvious that the cyclists were all Chinese; they were dressed in blue or green Chinese Mao suits and sporting Mao haircuts. The very normality of people returning home after work seemed to heighten the vulnerability of the little van chugging away with its dubious cargo.

I started counting the small suspension bridges for pedestrians that spanned the river to the right and tried hard to memorize the details of the route, just in case I had to get out on my own. I also tried to look for the 500-year-old Geden Jampaling monastery that had been savagely attacked in 1959 and further damaged in the Cultural Revolution. It had seen brutal repression and served as a notorious jail where those who survived the fighting against the Chinese (and over 5,700 were killed in Chamdo alone) were held. The Tibetan Government-in-exile told me that their records showed that over 2,000 Tibetan prisoners died as a result of torture and maltreatment in the monastery-prison. Our contacts in Chamdo were also to take us to the notorious Sertok-thang prison, the biggest in the Chamdo administrative region and a few miles to the east of the town. Hundreds of Tibetans had died there in terrible circumstances during and after the Cultural Revolution.

Several red and white barriers marked the road at intervals of about a mile. When we approached the first one, it was up and unmanned. But every time we saw one in the distance, and not being able to discern whether a soldier was sitting out of sight on duty, the tension in the van reached almost breaking point. After forty-five minutes I lost count of the number of the barriers and I was bathed in sweat. I had decided to take the risks involved not only in being in Chamdo, but in attempting to film in such a high-security area to check our reports about forced abortions in one of the most notorious hospitals in Tibet, the Chinese-built Manama Hospital. In 1987 reports said that over 600 forced abortions had been performed there on Tibetan women since 1980. Other reports told of 3–5-month-old foetuses – and sometimes older – being regularly found in the hospital's dustbins and in the storm drains. There were overtones here of Hitler's racial policies and I had to have first-hand witness to allegations that I was sure the West would find difficult to believe. I wanted, if I could, to talk to doctors, nurses and especially to Tibetan women who had been forced to go through the traumatic procedures. Forced abortions and sterilization of Tibetans had been reported in many places in Tibet, but it was in big urban centres where it seemed that they were being conducted on a large scale.

It had not been feasible to film interviews in Lhasa, as we had been running late for the Nagchukha interviews, so we arranged with the few brave doctors and nurses from Lhasa who had agreed to speak out to meet us in Chamdo. Ideally, I would have liked to film the interviews with the hospital in the background, but as that was impossible inside Chamdo, Tenzin told me that he knew a place downstream where the hospital was still visible and we could film in the security of a friend's compound overlooking the river and the hospital.

When confronted with allegations of mistreatment of Tibetans, the Chinese usually retort that these are lies spread by 'just a few counter-revolutionary "splittists" of the Dalai Lama's clique, who are found only in Lhasa and not anywhere else'. I hoped, by recording interviews in different parts of Tibet (if indeed the allegations held up under cross-examination), to challenge the Chinese contention.

Just before the confluence of the two rivers, I saw some big, institutional-looking buildings on the right, and wondered whether they were army barracks. The van swerved sharply right and Thondup told me to make myself invisible, which was not easy as by now I was sitting between Tenzin and Jigme (just in case either door was opened by the Chinese) and in full view of anyone who cared to look through the windscreen.

I slumped down, crushing my lumbar disc into spasm, pulled the hat down over my eyes and felt the quality of the road under the wheels change. The van twisted and turned, then slowed to almost a stall and I heard the noise of other cars and cyclists' bells; Chinese voices became distinctly audible. I presumed we were in the town centre. After what seemed a long time, though in fact it was only twenty minutes, the van stopped. I heard Tenzin say something in Tibetan, the doors opened and slammed and two of the Boys got out. Somewhere to my left I heard someone shouting in Chinese and what sounded like a lot of feet stamping.

Unable to contain myself any longer, I pushed up the brim of the hat, carefully squinted out of the tear in the window curtain – and freaked! I could not believe what I was looking at – we were in the middle of a Chinese army barracks parade ground! On the left a soldier was barking orders at a platoon of other soldiers and putting them through a drilling routine. In front of the van – and obviously that was the way we came in – was an iron-grille gate set into a high wall, and behind and all around us were the barracks and buildings of a very large army depot. Seeing my agitation, Thondup told me that the Boys had gone to enquire about accommodation from someone in the building behind us. When the Boys returned and calmly sat in the van discussing the problem – with soldiers only fifteen yards away – I lost my temper and told them to get the hell out of the parade ground before someone on guard duty came over to inspect the van.

Sumpa accelerated with infuriating slowness out of the parade ground, just as the platoon broke up and started to disperse in our direction. With shrill Chinese voices and the thud of heavy boots running on tarmac coming closer and closer, I pulled the hat down over my face again, slumped almost to the floor, and prayed to everything under the sun to get us out of there before either the gates were shut or a hail of bullets showered the battered van!

We drove round for an hour looking for accommodation for the Boys. For once I was glad about the darkness of the night. Chamdo – or what I saw of it through the slit in the curtain – was brightly lit and the streets were lined with lots of stalls selling tins and bottles of things I could not decipher. The houses were of three and four storeys and had concrete balconies hung with washing. The tarmac road-surface, the black Chinese ideograms on the gate-posts and the Chinese music blaring loudly from open windows and shops told me that I was in the Chinese quarter.

Later that evening, when the streets were practically deserted and all the stalls had shut down for the night, Sumpa stopped the car and Thondup told me to do exactly what Tenzin said. Before I could ask how on earth I could understand the man, Thondup was suddenly very earnest and his voice was high with tension. 'Please Vanya, your life is in danger here. Do what Tenzin says. We are all in danger!' Tenzin motioned me outside. Clutching the Sony to my belly under my jacket, I followed Tenzin's guiding hand that then proceeded to tuck me under his arm. He threw a blanket over both my head and his shoulders, and before I could get my balance, he set off briskly along the wet unpaved streets. As I was dragged along, I sank up to my calves in foul-smelling mud. We were in the Tibetan quarter.

The streets were dark, unlit and so narrow that we scraped the sides of the mud-brick walls. After a few minutes Tenzin ducked – dragging me with him – into a dark archway and through an open door that closed softly after us. We hurried down an even narrower passageway, then Tenzin pushed me into a small room lit with a weak bulb dangling from the ceiling. When I got accustomed to the light I saw four people in Chinese clothes waiting anxiously by the door and looking intently at me. For a split second I froze, thinking that I had walked into a trap. But before I could panic, they smiled, said '*Tashi Delek*' and raised their hands in the traditional Tibetan greeting. I could have hugged them in relief!

They made gestures for me to sit down, got some cups and started to pour Tibetan tea. I was just about to decline, but Tenzin must have explained about my liver, for they poured me a cup of hot water from the flask. Tenzin sat down with them and, in a low voice, was soon deep in conversation.

I leaned back against the rough wall and looked around me. An earthen stove blackened by cooking smoke was built into one corner, and near it a wooden bucket with a ladle. Chipped enamel washing bowls and a jug were neatly stacked on a rough wooden box in another corner. Under the bed-benches I could see various rolls of bedding and bundles of clothes. There were no refinements such as carpets, cupboards or chests of drawers, or even hangers – coats and jackets were hung on a nail behind the door.

The one small window was covered with a cloth pinned carefully with nails completely to obscure the view from the outside. In the centre of the room was a small wooden table and in another corner of the room was a simple shrine to Avalokiteshvara, the Bodhisattva of Compassion. Despite the mud outside, the earthen floor was clean. That small room contained the sum total of the family's possessions – a few pots and pans, a couple of rolls of bedding and a change of clothes for each of them. This room, Khandoo the mother of the family told me, was very different from their own home in Lhasa.

There was no running water and later Thondup told me that the family considered themselves very lucky that the women could draw it from a stand-pipe in a yard seven houses down. The nearest communal loo was five minutes' walk away through muddy alleys. There were only four in the family – usually families of up to eight and more had to share the same amount of space. They later told me through Thondup that they had been merchant traders and, although not wealthy, in common with most Tibetans of whatever social class, they had been used to much more room. But after the Chinese came and took over their houses, Tibetans considered themselves lucky to have even one room. And although many – but by no means all – Tibetans in the towns had electricity between six and ten in the evening, it was very expensive. The Chinese, they said, did not pay for electricity – one of the perks supplied by the Chinese Government to encourage Chinese to emigrate to Tibet. But they were particularly lucky to have electricity as they shared a line with the family in the next room who, because the husband worked for the Chinese, had managed to obtain a supply.

It was nearly midnight when Tenzin went to fetch Thondup. Khandoo put a plate of hot, specially purchased Chinese stew in front of me and ladled some peas on the side. With traditional hospitality she sat with me in case I should need anything. The frustration of not being able to communicate freely, not even to be able to thank her properly, was mortifying.

As I gratefully wolfed down the food, I realized that I had not eaten anything hot and substantial since my last dinner with Seán in Lhasa. It seemed light-years away. With traditional Tibetan courtesy, they asked Thondup what they could do for me. They apologized for not being able to offer me much, but their warmth and concern suddenly brought exhausted tears to my eyes as, for the first time since I had left Lhasa, I began to relax and realize how very tense I had been for so long a time. I was just beginning to feel human with a warm full belly when an infuriating spasm of pain convulsed my gut. It was then that I discovered the delights of the loo – Chamdo-style.

Khandoo guided me through the dark alleys until the smell told me we had arrived. There was no light in the small concrete shelter which housed three holes in the ground. There was no privacy at all as it was open to the street in front. And even though I had a torch I nearly fell into one of the revolting holes. It was a stinking cess pit awash with faeces and without any flushing mechanism; in hot weather it would be a breeding ground for epidemics like typhoid. I wondered about rats as I carefully tiptoed out of the putrid mire. I have experienced filthy toilets in most parts of the Third World, but that one in Chamdo was right out of the Middle Ages and I made a mental note to ask the doctor and nurses about infection, especially among young children and old people. The gastro-enteritis, which had not troubled me too much that day – because I had eaten nothing since my cup of muesli at dawn – was back with a vengeance.

I was in too much discomfort to be embarrassed by the arrangements to accommodate the problem. It was obvious that I could not, as I had in the van, creep out and solve the problem on a mountainside. As Khandoo said, there were so many 'informers' everywhere that even in the dark someone might flash a torch in my face. Instead, she brought me a small tin – the sort that baked beans come in – and took me to a shed across the yard which housed a sleepy sheep. She showed me where she had carefully prepared me a 'bed' in some straw. They had no sheets or blankets, and not realizing that I had a sleeping bag, she had put her only warm *chuba* down as a cover. Seeing that I was covered with dust, she brought a flask of hot water and one of the chipped bowls. Then she went to fetch Thondup.

Thondup had brought me the bag containing my few personal belongings. I spread my sleeping bag and prepared to wash while Thondup told me that Tenzin was out contacting the interviewees and would bring them in relays to the house early in the morning. I shut the shed door and wedged it with a log of wood as Khandoo had shown me. What good that would do if the Chinese raided the place I was too tired even to think about. The sheep just stared at me with blank eyes. It was heaven to be comparatively clean. As I slipped into my sleeping bag, I looked at my smalls drying on the straw and hoped that the animal would not have eaten them by the morning!

I blew out the candle, and luxuriated in the soft straw – at not feeling sharp tins and curious objects sticking into me. It was pure bliss to be able to stretch out fully without knocking poor Thondup senseless with my feet. Hoping that the sheep didn't snore, I fell into an exhausted sleep.

15

Chamdo Agony

From early in the morning on 8 September to way past midnight I listened to doctors and nurses and ordinary women telling me horrific stories of forced abortions and sterilizations.

I was quite taken aback when Tenzin brought in a Chinese doctor, an obstetrician from Lhasa. I asked the Chinese doctor why he had chosen to speak to me when he knew well the penalties for such 'counter-revolutionary treason'. Through Tenzin (who did speak Chinese) and Thondup (who spoke no Chinese and therefore had to have the translation in Tibetan), he said: 'Not all Chinese are bad, you know. There are some of us who feel ashamed at what is being done to the Tibetans, and to other minorities as well. But if we speak out publicly, we go to jail and our families suffer. I am a doctor. I bring new life into the world. To take an unborn life was difficult for me at first. I had nightmares. Now, I am almost ashamed to say that performing an abortion is no longer such a problem. But I am still not at ease with it. Now I have no choice; if I or any other doctor or nurse refused to assist at these procedures, we and our families would suffer.'

There were eleven people in the room to begin with. After I had spoken to each one, they left the room and waited somewhere else safe where Tenzin had arranged shelter until Tenzin called them should I want to interview them on camera – and provided they agreed. There was no point in exposing more people than necessary to the risk of imprisonment by talking on camera. If any of these interviewees were caught as a result of what they had said about abortion on British television, none of us in that room had any illusions about what punishment the Chinese would mete out to them.

And I could not decide whom to interview until I had spoken to them all. Many others came in during the day. Many touchingly spoke to me of their painful experiences, but understandably declined to be filmed or directly quoted. But they were all desperately eager that I took the knowledge to the outside world, because they – sadly – naïvely believed that public opinion might be galvanized to help them. I filled several notebooks with their evidence. The details confirmed what I had already heard about forced abortions, sterilizations and medical facilities available to Tibetans in Tibet.

I told them that I had heard allegations that there was a two-tier medical system, one for Chinese and one for Tibetans. I asked them if it was true.

'That is correct,' said a nurse. 'For example, if a Chinese man is ill, he goes to the hospital and will get good medication and be allowed to stay in the hospital. If a Tibetan is ill, he will not be able to afford the cost of the medicines and treatment. If, for example, he comes in as an emergency – a road accident or he collapses – then he is admitted, but he gets inferior treatment and medicine. Often, and there are examples of this all over the country, the Tibetan is given drugs that are out of date. Sometimes we have had cases where the wrong diagnosis is made and the wrong medication given with most unhappy results.'

'Sometimes,' one of the Tibetan women interrupted, 'they give us medicine, saying that it is for one thing; and when we get sick with a different sickness and go to a Tibetan colleague, we are told that what we have been given is part of an experiment. And I have relatives in Amdo who told me that in some hospitals there they do the wrong operations on Tibetans.'

In every country there have been cases of wrong diagnosis and treatment, often with tragic results; I suggested to them that perhaps these were just a few unfortunate, but isolated, incidents. They vehemently insisted that the malpractice was part of a very deliberate campaign against Tibetans and offered to take me to various victims, whose names and addresses they gave me, who would show me proof to substantiate their claims. It reminded me of Dr Mengele's medical experiments on the Jews in the Nazi concentration camps. It was almost too incredible to believe and I checked with the doctors and everyone I interviewed. They all confirmed that they had heard of similar cases in many different parts of the country.

'But no one outside is ever going to believe this. What proof have you got?' I asked.

One of the doctors smiled patiently. 'I cannot show you pictures of a patient whose right femur was amputated instead of the left one. Nor can I produce at this moment the Tibetan woman who went in for a routine appendectomy and came out without her appendix, but also with her Fallopian tubes tied, without her knowledge or her permission. But there are cases that we all have heard about of medical experimentation on Tibetans. If you had more time or you come back, we can produce these for you or for anyone who does not believe what we say. I know it's difficult for you to believe me – or any of us – but go into the villages, go and visit the people. Talk to everyone. You will find that the truth.'

I then told them that the Chinese repeatedly claim that they have brought great progress to the Tibetan people: roads, schools, hospitals, medical care for each and every Tibetan. And that Tibetans today are infinitely better off than before the Chinese 'liberated' Tibet and found the Tibetans living in 'barbaric conditions'.

They all smiled and shook their heads. It was a story they had heard many times from the Chinese.

'It is true,' a doctor said, 'that in old Tibet we did not have much medical care as you know it today in the West. We had our traditional medicine that coped with most of our problems. We did not have neuro-surgeons, nor did we have renal dialysis units – by the way, we still don't have those facilities. But in the old Tibet you must understand that our people were generally very healthy. As a race, Tibetans were strong. When the Chinese came to Tibet they did bring improved health care, but what good did it do for Tibetans? They say that they have improved the standard of hygiene and medical care: why then is it that today there is a marked increase in the number of Tibetans who are sick? And there is a dramatic increase in the number of diseases, and an increase in the cases of serious illness that Tibetans now have. So how do the Chinese explain that?'

'Can you be more specific?' I asked.

'Yes. To give an example: before the Chinese came, Tibetans, though not rich, ate well. There was ample protein in their diet – yak meat, butter, cheese. And no one had scurvy. It was not the most evolved cuisine, but no one starved and we had no malnutrition. Today, forty years after the Chinese came here, clinical malnutrition is endemic in Tibet. A thing unheard of in all our history. Like the famine induced by the Chinese in Tibet with their mismanagement between 1959 and 1962. In all of Tibet's recorded history there never was a record of famine. It's the same for malnutrition. But unlike the famine, with the malnutrition here there are at the moment no dramatic signs, no thousands of corpses to be disposed of and therefore no visual evidence for Tibetans to talk about after they have escaped to India. No, the effects of malnutrition are much more insidious, and in the end, if nothing is done about it, will prove as deadly as the famine.'

'What do you mean?' I asked.

'Because of malnutrition, there are now a lot of lung-related diseases and about 50–60 per cent of the Tibetan population suffer from them. Tibetans not only suffer from lung diseases, but also from heart and blood diseases, as one would expect. But we are now seeing things that never occurred before – high blood pressure, stress-related coronary diseases and nervous disorders that were simply unheard of before.'

'But why?' I queried.

'Because,' he went on, and the other medical staff concurred when I afterwards asked them individually, 'genetically Tibetans are very robust people. They have to be to survive in these mountains. And some things, for example diseases to do with blood pressure: when people live at high altitudes and are used from a very early age to considerable physical activity, they develop *low* blood pressure. Rather in the way that athletes and professional dancers who train strenuously from an early age develop low blood pressure and slow pulse rates. It is the same sort of syndrome for Tibetans. But now we get many cases of hypertension, coronaries, anxiety-related diseases, ulcers. It was unheard of before.'

'Yes, but why?'

'Because if you are lucky enough to have survived all these years under the Chinese and the system of informers they have very thoroughly introduced, when you do not know if your neighbour, your relatives, or even your own children are going to inform on you for even trivial things like saying your prayers, a fear is instilled in you that is part of the fabric of your life. The insidious but pernicious stress that builds up over the years is incredible.

'And on top of that they have somehow survived all the horror of the Cultural Revolution, and now they have the additional strain of unemployment because of the influx of increasing numbers of Chinese settlers who are pushing Tibetans out of their jobs, their land and even their homes: of course they will have stress symptoms. But the problem is compounded by the medical system here. It is difficult enough to get proper treatment for medical emergencies; but for these symptoms, which in the end are as deadly and more debilitating, there is no hope. Unless a Tibetan haemorrhages from a perforated ulcer or collapses in the street with a cardiac arrest he can't have treatment. Even then the chances of proper treatment are slim; and if this happens in the countryside, especially among the *drogpa*, there is absolutely no hope. Haemorrhaging ulcers cannot wait four or five days for the sufferer to be carried on someone's back to the nearest clinic, you know! And even if the patient does survive the journey, all that the clinics in the country stock are a few aspirins. The 'barefoot' doctors that the Chinese so boast about are not medically trained and are more hindrance than help.'

'But the Chinese say that they have built new hospitals and that in the rural areas Tibetans have access to doctors and hospitals that they never had before,' I insisted.

'It is not true that the Chinese have brought better health care to all parts of Tibet.' The doctor was adamant: 'In the towns it is a little better. Hygienic conditions are better. Let me give you an example.' He lit another cigarette – one of the signs of stress, he told me, among Tibetans, who before the Chinese occupation generally did not smoke. In fact, another doctor told me that the 13th Dalai Lama forbade the import of tobacco over seventy years ago.

'Let's take the case of a Tibetan going for a check-up to the doctor. Now if he is a high official and has good connections with the Chinese, he will get a check-up and go to hospital if necessary and be given the same medicines as the Chinese get. And if necessary he can be treated in an area other than the one he is registered in if it has better facilities.

'But if an ordinary Tibetan wants a check-up, as you in the West would go to your own doctor for, if he has not the right Chinese connection – and how many Tibetans do? – they will get absolutely no help at all.

'There is a system of permits for medicine whereby a Tibetan in the rural areas is allowed only a specific amount of medicine for the year. Now if he uses up the allocation and is still sick, or gets sick later, that's it. There is no other means of receiving health care, no matter what disease or ailment you have.

'Even if the Tibetan does somehow manage to see a doctor, he cannot be sure that the diagnosis and treatment will be reliable. Alarming stories are coming in from all over Tibet, and they report similar things from different parts of the country. It is too much of a coincidence and we need to investigate these disturbing things.'

'Like what?' I asked.

'So often we hear of Tibetans being given the wrong medicine. Sometimes – and the women will tell you themselves – they go for some unrelated complaint, and the doctors, seeing that they are pregnant, give them, without their knowledge or permission, medication to induce a termination of pregnancy.' I turned to the women present and asked them. They all agreed that what he had said was true and that they all personally knew several women to whom this had happened; they could give me their names and addresses and if I wanted I could travel to the area to interview them.

'Other cases are more difficult to prove with our limited facilities, but are very disturbing. Patients tell me that in some rural areas the Chinese put something into the water, and many Tibetans have subsequently gone blind and others have been near death with gastric problems. In other areas, Kongpo Nyitri for example, babies are being born deformed – which has never happened like this before.' The two women who had come from Kongpo Nyitri confirmed this, with names of women whose babies had been deformed. And when I asked them if this was so unusual – babies sometimes do have genetic irregularities – they were adamant that this had never happened before in the memory of their families and even in their grandparents' time. One said: 'I think it is something to do with the medicine that they give our women when they are pregnant.'

'It is also being reported from other areas too,' another doctor said. 'We are now commonly seeing in Tibet diseases that never occurred before – like tuberculosis. TB is not complicated to diagnose, but for other symptoms that need specialized equipment it is not so easy. Yet the reports still keep coming in.' Doctors outside Tibet confirmed to me that although TB is rampant in most poor, underdeveloped countries, in Tibet – with its altitude, dry climate and robust people – it was unknown before the invasion.

Ever since we started, before light at seven o'clock, Khandoo's husband and their twenty-one-year-old twins had kept watch. One on the roof, and one at each end of the alley, to give us warning of anything strange, or if the Chinese came. Though if they did, I could not see where we could hide – or run – as the house appeared to be in a cul-de-sac; but maybe, I thought, it was just possible to escape over the roofs.

I then turned to the question of forced abortions and sterilizations. I knew that in China, as in many other Communist countries, abortion is the most common form of birth control. With its population explosion out of control and with 2,500 babies being born every hour (1988 figures), China's one child per family policy has not proved a resounding success. Its hopes of containing the population to 1.2 billion by the turn of the century seem, to informed sources, unrealistic. The Chinese constitute one-fifth of the world's population but live on only 7 per cent of the world's land area and much of that is barren. It is understandable that the Government had to do something about it, but the penalties for having more children are extraordinarily severe. People having more than one child are fined, they often lose their jobs, lose bonuses and preferential access to housing, health care and education. In the minorities areas, like Tibet, the birthrate is limited to two per family.

'I can understand the Chinese need to limit their population. They have very little land space,' one of the nurses said. 'But here in Tibet, we have so much space and such a tiny population. Why should we have to limit our families when traditionally we have four or five children, sometimes more without any difficulty?' In fact the doctors pointed out that the population density in Tibet – by Chinese statistics – was only one person per square kilometre, as opposed to China where, for example, in Shanghai there are 1,987 Chinese per square kilometre.

I asked what they did about contraception in Tibet. 'In the past, we never used it,' a doctor said. 'Now there are contraceptives available for high officials who work for the Chinese, but not for ordinary Tibetans. The only way now is abortion and sterilization.'

But another explained: 'You must understand what children mean to Tibetans. Of course all people love their own children, but here in Tibet with our Buddhist philosophy, children are a gift – *soere* – a special blessing on the family. We have a different attitude to children from yours in the West. For instance the word "illegitimate" for a child born out of wedlock does not exist in our country. If a child arrives it is welcome and loved by the family, by the whole community, and it grows up knowing that it is loved and wanted. There is no such stigma as illegitimacy in our country.'

'Another thing,' Dolma, a nurse from Amdo, said, 'there is no word for abortion in our language. Even now the word we use is *ke-go-kak* – which means to block the door of birth . . . For Buddhists, to take any life, even that of an insect, is a *dhig-pa* – a sin – and to take human life, that of an innocent unborn child, is a terrible sin, *mi-sey-pai-digma* – murder. It is against everything we believe. For a Tibetan woman to have an abortion is a terrible emotional pain for her, to have a living baby taken from her womb – and with it all her hopes and dreams for that unborn child. The physical extinction of a life within your own belly is a nightmare – but how can I describe it to you? It is difficult for you, because you are not Tibetan and not a Buddhist, to understand the psychological trauma for a Tibetan woman to commit this crime – even if she is not directly responsible.'

'But doctor, is it true that Tibetan women are forced to have abortions?' I asked one of the obstetricians on camera.

'That is correct. It is true that Tibetan women are coerced into limiting their families to two children.'

'But how can anyone, let alone the Chinese Government, force any woman to have an abortion?' I asked.

'Although the Chinese do not use actual physical force, they impose such measures – like implementing economic and political sanctions, and then the woman has absolutely no choice.'

'Like what?'

'On the political side, they do not allow Tibetans to leave Tibet. If you are working, they will not increase your salary. Sometimes you can even lose your job. Any child after the second – and sometimes the mother – will not be allowed to have a ration card, and without that you cannot buy any food in the state stores. The child will be denied medical permits, so that the child cannot get medicine or see a doctor or go to a hospital in an emergency. In fact the child becomes a non-person and the parents are ostracized. Sometimes they are evicted from their homes. Other than that there is a heavy fine – 500–1,000 Rmb, many times the monthly salary, and sometimes a year's income for a Tibetan family, which is impossible to pay.'

'But what are the mechanics of this forced abortion? How does it work?'

All the Tibetans had their own evidence to relate. Most, understandably, declined to be on camera. But they all told me that Tibetan women who already had two children are pressured to have sterilizations. Often if, as others had already told me, they are admitted to hospital for another surgical procedure, while they are under the anaesthetic they have their Fallopian tubes tied or cut – without their knowledge or consent and in such a way that the operation is totally irreversible. Sometimes the women who go into hospital for a normal delivery (of an allowed child who therefore has a permit to be born) are anaesthetized during labour and wake up later to find that they have also (unknown and unauthorized by them) been sterilized.

Mrs Pema Gyaltsen, from a village in Dechen District of the Sene sub-district, gave evidence that in Village No. 2 in the Toelung Chue sub-district twelve families lived. Of them, the following women were forcibly sterilized by the Chinese: Khandoo, Pema Tashi, Tsering Chozom, Pasang Dolma, Dawa, Yugden Lahmo, Dawa Tsering, Dekyi Tsamja and Dalkar. And in Village No. 1 of the Dongkar sub-district, Toelung Dechen District, fourteen women were subjected to forcible sterilization including Tashi Anu, Yugden Wangdu, Lapka, Dolma Tasam, Lapka Tsering and Dawa Tsamja.

They told me that surveillance begins in the community or in the work-place where charts are put up recording the women's menstrual cycles. Menstruation itself is checked. Then, with the highly developed system of informers and the close proximity in which Tibetans now live, even the most private area of one's life – making love – is noted and reported on. So that if a woman misses her period, it is not likely to go unnoticed by the head of the group, who then informs the *kapo* of the unit, who talks to the woman and her family and brings enormous pressure on them.

Another woman from Amdo told me that the Chinese sent a truck to round up the offending pregnant women in the district and drove them to hospitals for abortions. She said that at Amdo Tsekok, the Chinese doctors have now started to go into the nomad areas, where they pitch tents and 'herd up the *drogpa* women, like cattle', and perform abortions in the tents. Other Tibetans present confirmed that they too had heard similar stories, but as they did not directly know the people involved they could not confirm it from their direct experience.

I asked them, and in particular the doctors, about the report of a Chinese doctor, Dr Bao Fu, that I had read in *China Spring Digest* the previous year (1987). The doctor, who is now studying in Canada, said in an article about abortion in China that:

In the case of a pregnancy of more than sixteen weeks, a frequent method of abortion is to introduce into the uterus an expandable rubber bulb which is then filled with sterilized water. Within a few hours premature labour is induced and the foetus is expelled ... recently a traditional Chinese medicine, Trichosanthes Kirilowii, has also been injected to induce premature labour.

... Since 1976 many articles have appeared on the various methods of terminating pregnancy, from hysterotomy [cutting into the uterus to remove a foetus too large for vaginal evacuation], prostaglandin injections etc ... But in many hospitals a more humane way [instead of suffocating the newborn baby] has been found. A long needle is used to inject pure alcohol into the foetal brain through the fontanelles when the baby's head presents itself at birth. There is no cry, no breath is taken. The newborn without a 'birth permit' falls into eternal sleep before his eyes can open to see the world that rejects him.

I asked those present whether anything like that happened in Tibet.

They all confirmed that women had been subjected to abortions performed in various ways and that foetuses of three and five months, and some even older, of seven and a half months, were regularly found in dustbins in Chamdo, in Lhasa, Rekong and other parts of Amdo. The usual method was oral medication that induced premature labour. Other times vaginal evacuation was effected by an injection into the uterus through the cervix.

One of the women, Jigme Pema, who lives in a village near Kumbum, in Amdo in eastern Tibet, told me that she had seen many abortions. She worked near the local hospital at Kghena Dhu near Chapcha Dzong and her cousin was a nurse there. She told me she had often asked her cousin to let her watch in the operating theatre: 'Many women up to seven months pregnant were aborted. Sometimes they were given an injection. Sometimes an electric rod was put up them and the baby taken out. Often, if it was a big baby inside, they would put the woman fully conscious onto the operating table, put a stethoscope on her stomach to see where the head was, then put cloths round the stomach and take a big syringe filled with yellow fluid and with a long needle inject right through the stomach near the belly button. It was very painful. The women used to scream very much. After about twelve hours the woman would have unbearable pains and they [the Chinese doctors] would feel round her stomach again and give her another injection into the side.' Jigme Pema placed her hands into the side of her abdomen, just above the pelvic girdle. 'Then after a while the woman gave birth to a dead baby. Afterwards she was sent away from the hospital. I saw many of the women in a small hotel nearby. They could barely stand. They were bleeding and in a very bad state. There was no after-care. Often they would lie there for a week.'

Choezom Pema and Pema Tsering came from a village between Markham Gartok and Chamdo. They told me that they had been forced to have abortions. In tears, Choezom Pema said, putting her hands to her stomach, 'They took my baby from my belly. There are no words to tell you how it was. I so wanted my baby . . . I am thirty-seven now, and my time for having more babies is running out [malnutrition affects fertility and there is some evidence that it can bring on an early menopause]. We live in the mountains, where life is hard. Often there are accidents and a child slips and is killed. What will we do if that happens to our children?' It was the most understandable fear for mountain people and one of the reasons, they told me, that they had large families.

'And many of the women in our area have died after the abortions,' she continued.

'Why?' I asked.

'They [the Chinese] never give us reasons. But we think the young Chinese doctors do not have enough experience in their job. Some women also say they experiment on Tibetans. Some women also tell of going into the hospital to have their baby delivered and when in labour they say that the Chinese doctor gives them an injection and the baby comes out dead.'

'What do you and other Tibetans feel about the doctors who do the abortions?' I asked her.

She shrugged. 'The medical people have their job to do. If they refused, they too would be punished.'

I asked the doctors and the other women how representative Jigme Pema's story and that of the Markham women were. They all told me that they knew of similar cases in their own part of Tibet and had heard of cases in other areas. One of the doctors added: 'After the abortions many women suffer from septicaemia and often the infections linger for a long time afterwards. Sometimes it is so bad that they collapse and are taken in to hospital to have further surgery; sometimes the original abortion was done so badly that the uterus prolapses. Very many of the women should take constant medication for a considerable time, but few can afford it, so they have chronic problems. Others subsequently suffer from eye diseases, from chronic bodily fatigue, from anaemia from the loss of blood; others have constant headaches.'

Jigme Pema went on: 'Chinese officials toured our area and other women I know tell me they go round their areas, too. The officials look at the records of how many children one has and at the charts and tell us, "You have had your children. If you have any more, your husband will leave you and you will go to prison." And I have seen with my own eyes what happened to some Tibetan women who got pregnant by accident because we have no method to stop pregnancy or because they badly wanted another child – the Chinese came with a truck and dragged these women into it and took them to hospital for abortions. I have seen this with my own eyes.'

I asked her why she didn't protest.

'We can't protest. If we complain we are punished. We lose our jobs, the ration book is taken away, the children are not allowed to go to school. Sometimes they even take the roof from over our heads. The punishments are so severe that Tibetans dare not complain.'

'There is not much we can do,' another doctor said. 'The Chinese have all the weapons of intimidation.'

It was extremely difficult for me to ask the next question. 'Forgive me, but how do I know you are not lying and all this is not just propaganda?'

One of the doctors spoke for them all: 'It is difficult for you to believe me, or any of us. Go yourself and visit the Tibetan people, the villages, the hospitals. Go and talk to everyone, you will see we are not lying. Go and see for yourself, otherwise you will not know. The reason that I say this is because this is your first time here. No foreigners are allowed here at all. You are the first to come and find out things for yourself. The Chinese say one thing to the outside world and they say another thing to the Tibetans. They say they have a political policy to outsiders, but the implementation of that is different inside Tibet. What the Chinese are trying to do is to exterminate the Tibetan race.'

The room was silent. Only the kerosene lamp, hanging from a nail in the ceiling, hissed. 'Time is running out,' he said. 'Tibetans are under the total power of China. They have no power, no means, few educational skills. If the world does not help the Tibetans, then there is very little hope . . .'

It was gone midnight and we had been interviewing for seventeen hours. I felt completely drained. I started to pack up the camera and to try and thank that very brave group of people who had risked everything to come and bear witness to what was happening in Tibet. Words were so grossly inadequate. Because there are very few doctors and nurses in Tibet – of either nationality – I decided to film the interviewees in silhouette and disguise their appearances to limit the chances of recognition.

When the last Tibetan had left, Khandoo showed me the flask of hot water and the bowl she had already, thoughtfully, put near my 'bed'. She had been incredibly supportive. Not only did endless cups of tea appear at regular intervals, but when the women broke down with emotion, she was the first to comfort them, allowing me to go on interviewing, as time was running out. She had also managed to send out for a pair of new green trousers, as my existing ones were perfectly disgusting.

My gastro-enteritis was still an embarrassing problem, for although I was surrounded by medical staff, I could not get any medication. In Tibet doctors do not carry 'black bags' with a mini-pharmacy of contingency drugs. Nor could they just write out a prescription and send someone to the chemist to collect it. Apart from the fact that there is a shortage of basic drugs in Tibet, there is a complicated and lengthy queueing procedure at the pharmacy whereby the patient has to produce his or her residence and medical card. It was just too complex and I decided to wait until Chengdu for some antibiotics.

Khandoo had also, without me even asking, washed my pink track suit and laid it out on my 'bed'. I looked at the kind woman who had taken — and was still taking — the most awful risks in sheltering me and allowing me to film. I felt very close and just put my arms round her and hugged her with a gratitude and affection that I was never able fully to express.

There was a soft tap at the shed door. For a moment, roused from a deep sleep, panic seized me. It was four in the morning. Khandoo softly called my name through the door. Fumbling, I lit the candle and opened the door. Khandoo smiled and gave me a cup, a flask of hot water and some coffee and dry biscuits that Thondup had brought for me the night before. Outside the sky was dark.

Tenzin and Thondup arrived shortly afterwards. Tenzin wanted to leave early as we had already spent two nights in the same place, which was dangerous. I protested that I had not even filmed anything in Chamdo. How could I convince anyone that I had been there? I had to have visual proof otherwise the Chinese would say, as they had on other occasions when confronted with unpalatable evidence, that I had filmed the interviews in India or London.

As security was tighter than I had imagined, it had been out of the question the day before to film the interviews with the hospital in the background. So I had filmed in the room of the safe house. Earlier in the day I had managed to do one interview using the light from the courtyard to silhouette out the interviewee; but as the day progressed, and delayed by the camera breaking down all the time, we had to resort to filming inside with the help of one of the lanterns we had bought in Lhasa, for the room's weak

40-watt bulb was insufficient to give me enough illumination to get a silhouette. I deliberately obscured the background, using plain material, which my hostess had sent out for, stretched over the wall so that no tell-tale signs like colours, or a calendar, or a distinctive detail could give away the identity of the people when the Chinese came to analyse the film, frame by frame, after the transmission.

But realistically, judging from the anonymous backgrounds, the interviews could have been filmed anywhere. It was vital to have visual evidence to prove that I had actually been in Chamdo. After much heated discussion with Tenzin, who quite understandably could see only the dangers, we agreed that early in the morning we would drive to the top of a hill from which I could film the view of the confluence of the two rivers, the remains of the monastery and part of the army barracks. He emphasized that we had to be out of Chamdo very early to avoid the checkpoint inspections.

I also wanted to interview some of the monks who had witnessed the destruction of their 500-year-old monastery and had suffered considerably during their subsequent imprisonment for refusing to renounce their faith. That morning they were going to come to Khandoo's room. The monks had come a long way. Two were now living in Derge, several hundred miles north of Chamdo, and the third was working as a casual labourer in Markham where he had an aged sister. So while Tenzin ferried my bags to the new van – the old one had finally collapsed, and anyway it was better to change the van so that the Chamdo number plates would be less noticeable than the Nagchukha ones – I talked to the monks.

Another, an ex-monk working as a farm labourer in Batang was enormously articulate and I suggested to Tenzin that we try and squeeze him into the van and take him to the top of the hill. I thought it would give considerable emphasis to his story, if he could point out the places in Chamdo, and in his monastery, where he had seen atrocities and where he and the others had suffered.

It was still dark when Tenzin tucked me under his arm again and hurried me through the slippery alleys to the new van, where Sumpa had the engine running. We got in and quickly drove off. Chamdo was still asleep, the streets were deserted and in the east there was a glimmer of light in the sky. Yet despite the somnambulist calm, I felt, the hairs prickled at the back of my neck. The Boys too, although looking better for a couple of nights' sleep, were tense and withdrawn as we drove through muddy back streets, for we all knew that at any moment we could run into a Chinese patrol. After ten minutes we came to the base of a hill, Sumpa changed gear and charged the van up the steep gradient. On the way the ex-monk pointed out the bottom walls of his old monastery, the Geden Jampaling, which had been built in 1444 by Jangesem Sherab Sangpo. After another ten minutes of winding our way up the hills so as to avoid any early-morning Chinese, the van emerged on the grassy top of a high hill that overlooked the town.

'Hurry! Hurry! Film quickly, we must go!' Tenzin said, more agitated than I had ever seen him before.

I looked at the sky and knew that even with the remarkable Sony there was not enough light to get an image: to be able to pick out the definition of the buildings below I needed the sunrise. 'I can't yet, Tenzin – there's not enough light.'

'But last night you filmed with no light,' he said impatiently.

'Tenzin, last night I had artificial light, which is a different setting on the camera.' It was no use trying to explain to someone who had never even seen a documentary film or been in a studio the problems of colour temperature, which governs what you can film and where and with what filter. I gave up, told Thondup that it would probably take another twenty minutes and started talking to the ex-monk.

He pointed out the monastery in the hill below, now slowly becoming visible as dawn began to streak the eastern sky beyond the confluence of the two rivers.

In March 1959, after the Dalai Lama had fled to India, in the fourth month of the Tibetan calendar, the Chinese began their 'democratic reforms' inside Tibet, the ex-monk told me, keeping his voice to a whisper: 'They were out to destroy the religious and secular systems of Tibet, so they started by destroying those monasteries that had not been bombed in the fighting earlier. They first of all marked out all the learned monks, the teachers, the reincarnate lamas, the administrators and reserved them for special torture. See that building on the left?' He pointed to the outlines that were beginning to emerge from the gloom. 'The monks were locked up there in what used to be the school for dialectics. Then the Chinese went through the monastery stripping out all our sacred objects. They dumped all our statues and scriptures there in the front in a huge pile and stripped all the statues of their ornaments. Then they made some of the monks make fires to melt down the gold and silver from the butter-lamps and the statues into just lumps of metal. Some of the statues had been made over 500 years ago! But it did not matter to the Chinese. For us it was indescribable . . . I cannot tell you what I felt.'

Wiping tears from his face, he went on: 'The Chinese loaded the things into big trucks that came at night and took our treasures back to China. Our monastery was very well endowed and they filled over 300 lorries . . . Then they rounded up all the monks and made them burn thousands of our precious scriptures that had been written long, long ago in gold and silver and turquoise ink. The monks were forced to do this, but we were all crying. And then they made us break the monastery with our own hands so that later they could say that it was Tibetans who broke the monasteries. All the time the soldiers held the guns over us and if we hesitated we were beaten with the guns, and with sticks. Then they put us in the part of the monastery that was left. We suffered so much . . .'

Just as the ex-monk was pointing out another mass grave at the side of the monastery, Tenzin came up to the van window and spoke urgently to Thondup, who turned to me and said: 'Please hurry and take pictures. Tenzin is very worried. We are in great danger here.' So telling the ex-monk that we would talk later, I left him in the van and set up the camera ready to record. With the camera covered by my spare sweater, I got down on the far side of the van and walked the last hundred yards up to the top of the hill, where I immediately dropped to a crouch. The sight was indeed spectacular. The mountains on the horizon were still slumbering in the smoky blue of early dawn. In the east the early sun had back-lit the mist that wafted like wisps of gossamer in lazy arabesques between the hills and hovered over the valley. It was ethereal, and the water of both rivers shimmered from pale silver to liquid gold in the diffused light. It had all the luminosity of an exquisite Turner waterscape. But down towards the base of the river I could see forbidding-looking buildings and heard a loudspeaker blaring something in Chinese that sounded suspiciously like a sergeant-major barking orders . . . I also realized with considerable trepidation that on the skyline above the town we were dangerously visible. There was not a tree, not a shrub, not a building to shelter us and there was no one else in sight. A group of strange figures on the skyline above major military installations would soon arouse suspicion. I began to tremble, thinking that at that precise moment we were probably fixed in the sights of some powerful binoculars.

'Hurry! Hurry!' Tenzin hissed in Tibetan. My hands were shaking so badly that I could not find the start button. There was no question of putting up a tripod. It was also highly risky to put the camera to my shoulder to see through the eye-piece. Who in their right mind would ever believe that I was not a spy filming Chinese military installations below? I tried to do what I had seen many cameramen do in similar circumstances when they wanted to 'turn over' without appearing to film. I put on a wide-angle lens; then, holding the camera in my right hand at thigh level, I switched on and 'squirted'. As I made a 180-degree pan, hand-held without seeing what I was doing – I could well have been pointing to the sky – I prayed that it would give some idea of what the town looked like. Then I tried to give some more static 'squirts' onto buildings below so that Chris Lysaght, the film editor in London, would be able to make some semblance of a montage, as I was sure that my hands were trembling so much that the pan would be unusable.

The light was growing stronger in the sky. Martial music from the loudspeakers below drifted up to us and in the streets people were beginning to move and start the day. Thondup held the Sony, while I took some stills with the Minolta. If I had completely messed up the shooting, I could maybe salvage the situation by doing an 'action-stills' sequence using zooms and pans to give it some animation – which is the cheat's way round not having got the actual live footage! That is *if* there was anything but sky on the film.

I lay on my belly trying to be as unobtrusive as possible on the hill. With shaking hands I tried to focus the Minolta with a long lens to my eye, reckoning that as I was nearly flat with the hill it would be more difficult to pick me out from below – or so I hoped. I kept remembering terrible stories of how journalists and film-makers had often nearly been shot when the 'opposition' mistook their long lenses for the barrel of a gun. I was about to invoke every protective deity I could think of when Jigme, who had been on look-out just below the brow of the hill, shouted '*Gyami!*'

I froze to the ground. As Tenzin ran up and dragged me back to the van, I saw the Chinese army licence plates on a green jeep, its radio antennae waggling behind, come up over the crest of the hill.

16

A Bitter Harvest

I had reached the door of the van when the army jeep drew up and stopped with its engine still running. Inside were four men in uniform. The Boys were magnificent and continued chattering to each other and discussing a non-existent problem under the bonnet – which Sumpa had put up when we arrived to give us a flimsy excuse should we be questioned.

Finally, Sumpa banged the bonnet shut, and all of them, still talking, got into the van. As we drove past the jeep whose occupants were also still deep in conversation, Sumpa actually waved his hand in greeting!

Once round the corner Sumpa accelerated so fast that we almost flew off the mountain. As we were going round the base of the old walls of the monastery, the ex-monk pointed up to some windows in the new building and told me that the Chinese had now installed eleven Chinese soldiers there. When I asked why, he told me that it was common practice in any monastery that was open and even partially functioning to install PLA soldiers, PSB and civilian informers to keep an eye on the monks . . . However, in Chamdo's Geden Jampaling monastery the Chinese were now also making a tidy profit from a thriving kerosene business and from importing agricultural equipment from China.

As I was uncertain whether I had any image other than expanses of sky on the tape – I had not had time to rewind and look at it through the view-finder – I just had to get some footage, however terrible, of Chamdo. So I switched on the camera, pressed the record button and put it to my shoulder as we drove down the street. It was then Tenzin's turn to have hysterics. He exploded all over the van! Thondup translated the gist: that I was mad, if anyone looked into the van and saw me I would be arrested – and worse. I just nodded, now not only frightened by the threat outside but also by the internal tornado. After five minutes with a convoy of army lorries coming straight at us, my courage gave out and I happily switched off.

It was the rush hour and swarms of Chinese were flooding into town. The barriers on the checkpoint were mercifully up. The buildings were the same unremarkable 'barracks'-style architecture that the Chinese seem to favour. As we turned the bend in the river, the Manama Hospital came into view across the water. It was a substantial square multi-storeyed building. At the exit to the town, I changed places with Tenzin and tried to film out of the window as the van was moving, but my anxiety, the bumpy road, and the sliding windows made it virtually impossible. Around the next bend I asked Sumpa to stop. Thondup stood on the traffic side to shield me from prying eyes, I crouched down and tried to film through the open door.

I remembered Chris Lysaght, with whom I have worked on countless films over the past fifteen years, saying to me, 'Tell the cameraman to give me a sequence. I don't want just a bleeding building – put it in context. Show me where it is, otherwise a building is a building is a building!'

Chris, who is in fact one of the most sensitive editors I have worked with, was also forever reminding me before I went off on location to 'get that cameraman to give me some cutaways for the interviews. I can't produce them out of the Steenbeck' – the editing machine. When you are shooting an interview, you never know which bits you are going to use. You try and vary the size of the shot, from a close-up of the face to a mid-shot of the interviewee which will include some air above his head to a wide shot of the whole person and some of the room. When you cut from one part of the 'synch' (speech) interview to another 'synch' segment, the picture should 'flow' if it is from one size to another. But as often happens, when you join up the pieces of speech you find that they are irritatingly of the same size framing. If you transmit that, the picture will physically jump in the frame, look terrible and jar the viewer. To avoid this, you overlay the sound of the interview over a 'cutaway' or 'noddie' of the reporter idiotically nodding to the camera (shot after the interview). The editor can then cut back to the rest of the interview – in the same frame size – with a smooth transition. If you don't have a reporter in vision – and I had more than a few things to organize other than teaching Thondup how to shoot reverses of me asking the questions – you use some visual that is relevant to the interview. In this case, because I could not show the faces of the women who had undergone abortions, nor was I there at the operating theatre, the only visual available was of the hospital. My hands were still shaking as I tried to focus on the swirling eddies of the fast-flowing muddy Dachu river, hold it for at least fifteen seconds – so that Chris could get the scissors (metaphorically) into the shot – then, tilting up to the hospital, hold it and do the reverse. But as I was hand-holding again – using the tripod was out of the question – I was very dubious about the quality or usability of the shot.

I asked whether we could get nearer the hospital and maybe drive round so that I could do a tracking shot from the van. Tenzin withered me with a look. Thondup gently explained: 'Vanya, please. We have been very lucky so far, don't push the luck. We can't go back, Tenzin does not know the times when the checkpoints are unmanned and it would be suicide to go across the bridge on foot. It's not only your life, but all of ours as well . . .' I could not argue. In a way I was rather relieved, as I was not relishing the thought of walking across the bridge. Even the precarious protection of the van was Fort Knox compared with the total exposure of walking the bridge through the checkpoints with hordes of Chinese. But there was still so much that I had not filmed in Chamdo. Where, I asked Tenzin through Thondup, were the mines? Chamdo had copper mines of very high quality and iron . . . And then what about the interview with the Tibetans who demonstrated in December 1987 and March 1988?

'Please . . .' Thondup said, somewhat exasperatedly.

'But Thondup, if I don't film that now, we never will. And the whole point of doing this insane journey was to examine what was happening *outside* Lhasa! The fact that there have been demonstrations in Chamdo and further east is very important – also, we still haven't visited Sertok-thang prison.' But I need not have bothered. Tenzin was not going to give in, so I looked out of the window and again wished I was anywhere but in that rattling contraption.

As we drove down towards the floor of the valley, it got warmer. The Dachu river, heavy with silt, cut its way deep through terraced hillsides densely cultivated and neatly partitioned into parcels of green, brown and ripening yellow. Curiously, although at the lower altitudes there should have been trees, there was not a single one in sight.

Looking at the furious current of the Dachu river reminded me that a member of the Tibetan Youth Congress-in-exile had once remarked to me that if the Chinese built a dam across any of the head-waters of any major Asian river, they could hold Asia to ransom. At the time I thought it was a piece of frustrated rhetoric, but driving above the dramatic narrow gorges of Kham, which so easily could have been spanned by a series of dams, I saw not only the hydroelectric potential, but more sinister possibilities as well.

By eleven o'clock that morning we had started to climb out of the valley and, after several hours of winding in and out of a bleak landscape, we came near the nest of prayer-flags on the Takima La pass. Tenzin pointed to the right: on the summit of an adjacent peak, a few hundred yards from the road, was an incongruous jumble of sophisticated and powerful radio antennae. They were oddly shaped and somewhat reminiscent of the radar scanners scattered on the approach road to Sirte, Gaddafi's missile base between Tripoli and Benghazi in Libya. But the Chinese ones in Tibet had additional round and long shapes, and it looked as though celestial deities had been playing cat's-cradle with tons of wire cables. I also saw powerful transmitting/receiving dishes and wondered whether they were for radio transmission and reception, radar tracking or a satellite feed?

China, despite its Third World image, has a sophisticated system of electronic surveillance in Tibet. It has built a series of radar-tracking stations (fourteen are known) in the country stretching from Rudok in the Ngari region of western Tibet near the Ladakh –Pakistan border, all along the Himalayan boundary, and scattered throughout the interior of Tibet, for example at Golmud, and also in the north. According to various reports of the British and Indian Strategic Studies Institutes, China has put a number of communications satellites into space. Tenzin said that this was a radar tracking station, but would not let me stop to film. He told me that there were more listening posts on our route and it would be safer to take pictures later. It was a graphic but eerie reminder that Tibet was occupied territory and that all movements were being watched closely by 'Big Brother' to the east.

I must have fallen asleep, lulled by the comparative warmth of another body, the ex-monk's, squeezed onto our bench-seat. I woke feeling that the road-surface had changed. We had just crossed a concrete bridge over a minor stream and running along-side the road, only a few yards away, was another perfectly straight road disappearing into the distance. Since the crazy contours of the topography of a country like Tibet make a straight road a virtual impossibility, I was extremely puzzled, particularly as the wide valley, about twenty by thirty miles, was utterly and totally deserted. There were no trees, no buildings, no *drogpa* and, most surprising of all, no sign of even one yak. It had a menacing sense of suspended animation. Inside the van the Boys looked tense and kept looking around to see if anyone was following. We were at the Tsawa Pomda airfield and the parallel 'road' was in fact the runway.

Reluctantly, the Boys stopped. Sumpa put up the bonnet and two of them got out to fiddle around with the engine. I opened the door and tried to film from the car, but again my hands were shaking. We were on a very high and windy plateau and the wide desiccated flat valley, framed with low dry brown mountains on the distant horizons, was completely empty. It had an uncomfortably spooky feeling to it and I felt my hair rise on the back of my neck. I could not understand it, since the place was not overtly bristling with military. In fact I could see no sign of movement, no personnel, no vehicles, no hangars and apart from some low buildings in the distance, it looked distinctly deserted. No radar scanners were visible, although Tenzin said it was a radar station. The whole area looked utterly deserted, dead. I could not detect any underground silos or hangars – just a clump of low buildings in the distance. But the road was in excellent condition and the bridge over the stream was of good-quality concrete. There was not a sound except for the low moaning of the wind.

I could not shake off the unnerving deadness of the valley. It was as though every move we made was being tracked on a monitor.

Tsawa Pomda is part of a series of airfields (and strategic roads) that China started to build shortly after its invasion of Tibet in 1950, as part of a rapid deployment programme to move troops and equipment as quickly as possible to wherever there was trouble. And after the outbreak of hostilities with India in 1962, the ease of movement of military personnel and equipment from bases in China (Chengdu and Lanchow) became even more important. What was certain was that the runways were the longest I have ever seen in my life. High altitudes (Tsawa Pomda is about 12,500 feet above sea-level), with their rarefied oxygen, necessitate a much longer runway than normal to compensate for the thin atmosphere, but this looked long enough to land a space shuttle.

The ex-monk, who had been watching the area with intense concentration, started speaking. Thondup told me that the ex-monk was saying that there had been a monastery here before the Cultural Revolution. After some time in the Geden Jampaling monastery prison in Chamdo, the ex-monk himself had been transferred to the ruins of the monastery here in late 1961, as they needed labour in the fields. He told me that the Pomda monastery had been turned into a prison by the Chinese in 1961 and that about 5,000 Tibetans had been imprisoned there. Most of the prisoners died of exhaustion and starvation within two years and by 1963 only about 700 prisoners survived.

'Although the prisoners everywhere in Tibet had to undergo the same terrible treatment, here in Pomda we had the added hardship of this terrible wind. There was nowhere to hide from it. No shelter. Tibetans know about the cold and the wind. But at that time, in these fields, it was like having pieces of broken glass blown through your body. In the frozen weather of winter the Chinese would beat us into the fields and make us plough the fields by pulling ropes. We had no warm clothes; we had food that even pigs and dogs would not touch. Sometimes we even had to eat human waste . . . We were very weak and many times we fell to the ground and the Chinese would beat us until we got up. The ground was like rock. We had to pull the plough by thick ropes that burned into our hands and into our backs, and when the blood froze, making it more painful in the wind, the Chinese soldiers used to laugh and say, "It is the human mind that should be left unploughed, not the lands." Very many times I wished I had died. The suffering was so bad that some cut their own throats with pieces of ice. Today I still have pain from my hands,' and he turned them over to show palms horribly disfigured with thick white scar tissue that had contracted the fingers into claws.

One day, maybe, there will be a Tibetan Solzhenitsyn.

*   *   *

By 9.30 that evening we were nearing the top of the pass to Tsagochen Thang when the van spluttered and 'died'. It was infuriating that throughout the trip the van inevitably broke down near the top of a high and windy pass. If only for once we could have had a change and had a breakdown in a warm valley near water and possibly someone selling real food! It was not to be.

The Boys stretched out on the lichen and slept. I wandered off down the hill and collected a bunch of brilliant turquoise-blue gentians. Apart from the view, one of the few pleasures of the high pastures was the extraordinary collection of tiny wild flowers. Gentians that I had only previously seen in deep blue, in Tibet were every shade of blue from pale powder-blue, through lilac, to the bright turquoise that I had just picked. Even little buttercups and miniature larkspur and Michaelmas daisies were of unusual colours.

By nightfall Sumpa was still labouring and the rest of the Boys were snoozing. The relentless driving, the tension and the fatigue of the trip were beginning to tell. Only Sumpa seemed to be on automatic pilot and able to go on driving without a word of complaint or apparent fatigue. By one the following morning, Saturday, 10 September – and by now I had to look at my diary to remember the day and the date – the van was mended. I awoke from a half-sleep to find the air was warmer. In the headlights I saw we were driving down through trees – green, broad-leafed deciduous trees with branches and leaves – and I was not dreaming. Trees of the sort you see in most countries anywhere in the world, but after ten days of verdant deprivation, I was ecstatic.

Lulled by the warm air coming through the window and watching the light from the yellow headlights bounce along the rough road, it reminded me of driving through the Terai jungle at the foothills of the Himalayas with my father as a child and watching, with excited anticipation, for the surprise of the unexpected. Then, there was the very real possibility of seeing the slit eyes of a tiger or leopard glowing green in the gloom, but on that September night on a mountain in Kham, though I felt the same excitement – brought back by the warm night, the trees and the dancing beam of the headlights – I was just relieved to have survived so far with the film I had shot intact.

It was just gone two when the van bumped round a corner and I was jolted awake by the sight of several low buildings round a dirt courtyard, brightly lit and with a barrier at the gate. It looked like an army outpost, but Sumpa drove straight in and parked under a row of naked bulbs that were hanging outside each and every doorway lining the yard. Tenzin, followed by the rest of the Boys, jumped out. I asked Thondup what was happening. He told me that we were at a Chinese 'hotel' and were staying the night.

'But it's insane! If I have to be caught, OK, but I am damned if I will put my head in a noose and walk into a Chinese hotel!' Thondup was sleepy and looked bewildered at the fuss.

'Thondup, look, you might smuggle me in like at the Chinese camp, but that place was pitch-dark outside and we got away with it. It's as good as broad daylight here! And what happens when I have to go to the loo one hundred times a night? How do I get in and out without being seen with all these lights?'

Thondup went to look for the Boys who had settled down inside and were brewing tea. Then started a pantomime with Thondup scuttling backwards and forwards with messages. They were tired; they wanted to stay; I was making a fuss . . . The sixth sense that I have relied on all my working life told me it was too dangerous to stay there that night, and there was something deeply disturbing about the barrack-like buildings and the four army trucks standing in the yard. The Boys finally acquiesced grumpily, and we drove on, arguing, until four in the morning. I felt bad about preventing them all from sleeping comfortably, but my first priority had to be our safety, and that of the film and the interviews I had already recorded.

While the Boys were brewing up on yet another freezing mountain top, Tenzin and I had a blazing row. He accused me of not trusting him and threatened to go back to Lhasa. There followed several hours of ill-feeling in the van and at 5.30 we crept disgruntledly into the darkened town of Markham Gartok. There were no street-lights or any light anywhere at all. Only the cacophony of dogs' barking, as they sensed our presence, told me that there were Tibetans around. The odd time that we put on the sidelights to find the way, the sleeping town looked like a jumble of concrete houses without pavements or trees – rather like Chamdo, but much smaller.

Markham Gartok, situated near the Drichu (Upper Yangtse) river, was an important military headquarters and market town, the crossroads of trade from Tibet to Sichuan and Yunnan. The Chinese merchants traded rice, tea, molasses and the fabled silks and colourful brocades for which China was famous, for special Tibetan cheese, small goats much prized for their soft cashmere wool, leather, salt and expensive and recherché merchandise such as *latse* (a rare musk) and highly prized *yartsa gunpu* (ginseng).

As we turned into a muddy alley at the beginning of the Tibetan quarter, I thought what a disappointing entrance it was to the capital of the legendary King Ling Gesar Gyalpo – a Tibetan King Arthur – who centuries ago waged heroic wars and held court amid chivalrous Khampa warriors and beautiful women. It was around King Ling Gesar Gyalpo that myths and legends as luminous and romantic as any Arthurian saga have grown and multiplied. But all I saw that night on my unheralded arrival in Markham Gartok was yet another stinking muddy alley, viewed from the most sought-after vantage point in all Tibet – Tenzin's armpit.

Tenzin dragged me through a doorway and pushed me up a rudimentary pole-ladder leaning against a mud-brick house. At the top, hands reached out to me from the dark and pulled me inside. Tenzin and then Thondup soon followed and I heard a door bolt shut. By the light of a spluttering candle I looked at a scene that was straight out of the Dark Ages. There were piles of straw or hay everywhere and huddled asleep in it were three families separated only by torn pieces of gunny sacking suspended from string and nails in the ceiling. Around them, and hanging from more nails in the walls, were a handful of pathetic belongings – a kettle, a blackened pan, a few bits of clothing. On the floor were a few pieces of kindling wood and a couple of blackened stones that served as a stove.

In the dark beyond the candle-light a bundle of rags stirred, shook itself and hobbled towards us with hands raised in peaceful greeting. Thondup told me that the old lady, with more wrinkles than face, had told me to take her place as it was still warm. Gratefully I accepted and when I got to the dark corner I found that she had been sleeping on an old plank that was still warm. When you are so poor that all you can offer is the warmth of your body, it becomes the most touching sacrifice imaginable.

The old lady, still drowsy with sleep, stumbled to another corner and lay down in the straw. Her daughter brought me a candle and gave me a rusty tin for the necessary – there was no question of slithering down the pole to the yard in the dark. Thondup told me that Tenzin had arranged for several people who had come in from the countryside to come and talk to me in the morning. The Boys and he would go to another safe house, for it would be unwise – in case we were raided – all to be found under the one roof.

It was 6.30 when I blew the candle out and eased my aching back on the flat board – which was exactly what a physiotherapist back in London would have ordered!

Something soft and warm was stroking my cheek. It was so gentle and reassuring that for once I did not panic into wakefulness as I had so often in the van when the slightest noise contracted every fibre of my sleeping body into a state of 'red alert'.

The gentle warmth stroked my cheek again and I cautiously opened my eyes. Two enormous dark eyes smiled at me in the faint light. I sat up and looked at a small Tibetan child who could not have been more than seven or eight. She was in fact eleven, but in common with most Tibetan children looked much younger than her chronological age because of malnutrition. For a few delicious moments I was totally captivated with the enchanting child in her torn and dirty blue trousers and jacket, her bare feet dirt-streaked and cracked with cold. She sat back on her heels and smiled with all the rainbows of the world in her grimy face. Her tiny hands gently touched my face and hands again and again. She had never seen a European before.

She sat and watched me as I dressed and folded my sleeping bag. Her delicate little hands fluttered like bluebirds, asking mute questions in sign language. They explored everything, my cameras, my books, my socks, even the plastic bags to keep the dust out of the equipment. Everything was a source of wonderment. She touched the soft fleece of my track suit, and putting it to her face giggled with pleasure. Like all Tibetans, she had an enormous native curiosity. When I offered her coffee she screwed up her nose at the bitterness, but some muesli was greeted with giggles of delight. I had no toys to give her, no books (but she was illiterate), no ball-point pen (much in demand with all Third World children). I did not even have a sweet to offer the child.

The last of Seán's chocolate and all my spare biros and pencils had been in the case that had been left behind at our first night-stop.

She sat with me all day, even when I was taking torture testimony from interviewees. And what was delightful was that this child, who had nothing, never asked for, or even looked as though she wanted, anything from me. All that little Dolma did that day she sat with me (when she was not helping her mother) was smile. Her mother said they called her 'Smiley' because she was always smiling, and that she had been born with a smile! It was so painful not to be able to give the child something. All I had was money, which, on leaving, I pressed on her reluctant mother to buy her some shoes and warm things.

I was feeling curiously weak and my gut was again, boringly, playing up more than usual. So I was more than glad not to have to jolt around Tibet for one day. Thondup was patience itself translating for me while I tried to find out from the numerous interviewees, who sneaked up to that dimly lit loft, what it was like to live as a Tibetan in Tibet today. And to find out, from those who were old enough to remember, how their lot compared with the time before the Chinese invaded.

I told them that the Chinese repeatedly claim that they 'liberated' the Tibetans from serfdom and unspeakable cruelties perpetrated on them by their masters, the aristocracy or the monastic overlords of Tibet. I asked them what difference it had made in their lives now that they were 'free'.

They explained that I did not understand the situation in Tibet, and that I was judging them as backward by the standards of my own country. Then Lhamo Tsering, an educated old lady who had spent twenty-three years in jail because her family owned a modest amount of land near Markham, told me her story. The Tsering family were not rich, but like any other landowner, however benevolent, or the learned lamas, they were branded by the Chinese as *shamo nakpo* (black hat). The Chinese put all Tibetans into categories and black hat was the worst. People in this category either ended up shot or sent to prison and labour camps. During the Cultural Revolution, many were summarily shot in the back of the head, without any trial, just because they owned land and could read. Lhamo Tsering told me that she was one of the few lucky ones who were not shot; now, after her release from prison, she lived with a daughter, as her hands and feet had been crushed into paralysis under torture during her first year in prison when she refused to renounce the Dalai Lama and her faith.

'Yes,' she admitted, 'we were backward by the standards of the outside world. But we were slowly adapting. The Dalai Lama and the *Kashag* [Tibetan Cabinet] realized that the country needed reform and had started to put plans into operation when the Chinese invaded. Of course there were inequalities. Take land reform, for instance. A lot of land *was* owned by the 200 or more aristocratic families, and the monasteries also owned much land. *But*,' she emphasized, 'although theoretically the land was owned by the State, the nobles and the big monasteries held large estates, and peasants also owned land. But now how can you own the mountains?' she asked. 'Most of the *drogpa* – and don't forget most of the population is nomad – roamed everywhere they wanted as free men on state mountains.

'There were distinct classes of people also in Tibet, the nobles, the peasants who worked on the estates and the clergy. But the landowner – the patriarchal head of his household and land – looked after the people under him. Although there were certainly differences between them, there was no great distinction in their daily lives. Here in Tibet the climate is harsh and it affects all of us. You must understand that ours was not an economy like yours. Only a very small proportion of the payment of taxes to Lhasa was made in money. It was paid in crops and in services, such as fighting in the army, or working in the civil service. The monastery paid with *shabten* [prayers] and performing rituals for the benefit of the State. And the peasants – the Chinese call us slaves, which is wrong – had a strip of land for themselves which they cultivated and then as their "service" to the landowner they would work on his fields and also sometimes work on the roads, serve in the army and so on. But there were also many smallholders who held land directly from the Government.

'Even our big families were not rich by outside standards: not even as well off as some of the businessmen in the Indian capital. And the differences between us were not so great. The nobles had nicer houses and clothes and some of their children had education. But then anyone could go to the monasteries and get education.

It was free and available to anyone. But no matter where in our society we came from, we all had a very precise idea of our customs and duties to one another and no one starved. Today is worse.'

'But how can that be,' I asked, 'when the Chinese have brought electricity, hospitals and new methods of agriculture here?'

They repeated what I had already been told and had observed about the 'benefits' of electricity and health facilities and education for Tibetans. Wangchuk, one of the more articulate farmers, explained to me what the Chinese had done to the area when they first came and how their disastrous agricultural policy had led to the first cataclysmic famine in Tibet's history.

'You have only just arrived, so perhaps you have not seen how fertile our land is here,' he said. I told him that we had had engine trouble and arrived at night and had not had the time to see much.

'All the Chinese and many outsiders think Tibet is only big mountains and cold deserts where nothing grows! It is true we have many, many mountains and in the Chang Thang [Tibet's vast Empty Quarter to the west of the country] not much grows. But we have very many fertile river valleys where nearly everything grows! And many of the valleys are not even used. Look at all the goodness that the rivers bring down the mountains! And they are always changing their course, so they leave big areas of rich fertile soil. There are many such areas all over our country. In the past we have not cultivated them. We only grow what we need.' It was true: I remembered being surprised at the lush greenness of most of the river valleys all over Tibet and how when the aircraft was coming in low to land at Lhasa I could see where the meandering rivers had deposited enormous sandbanks of silt when they had changed their courses.

'So many things grow in Tibet. Barley of course, which I am sure you know. Maize: here on the Drichu we used to have two crops a year. On the sheltered lower lands, wheat as well. But we also grow *tema* [peas], *logo pedsal* [cabbage], *labug* [white radish], *ngugma* [turnips], *petsal* [spinach]. There are so many things! And of course we also have many, many fruit trees and fruits.'

'What?' I asked, not having seen any fruit or vegetables during my two stays in Lhasa – and obviously not since I had been travelling.

'Well, we have *kushu* [apples] of course,' the farmer went on, delighted that there was something he could be proud of, '*targa* [walnuts], *sued* [pomegranates], which is very good for the blood, *gudum* [grapes], which we often put in rice, and we even have *tsaluma* [oranges].'

'But where then are all the crops?' I asked. 'And why are the Tibetans I have met so poor if your land is so rich?'

'Because much has happened since the Chinese came,' he explained. 'Before we always had enough to eat and our store-rooms had enough for more than a year in case we had a bad harvest. Even those people without land never starved. With our system the landowner or someone more fortunate would give food, or the monasteries would help. There was always an open door. No one died of starvation in Tibet.

'But then in 1950 the Chinese came. I remember how the soldiers looked poor, with faded clothes and not many rifles. They had no food so they ate anything – *tsampa*, roots, even dogs. They ate everything we had and never paid. Soon we had nothing left for ourselves; and they did not treat us well, so we rebelled. They had *Phadu* [Russian automatics which were not then found in Tibet] and we had not enough guns, and Lhasa did not send us any so we were beaten,' he said flatly. 'Then they [the Chinese] started sending more and more people in from Yunnan and Sichuan. There was not enough food and the Chinese took away the land, not only from the big landowners, but from small people like me. Then they made us plant *gondo* [Chinese wheat] all over Tibet. We told them it wouldn't grow so high up. They would not listen. They wanted to grow wheat for their noodles because they did not like our *tsampa* made from barley which is well suited to this climate.

'Then they set up their commune system, *mimang kongri lamluk*; the Chinese told us that they were building "the golden bridge to socialist paradise", but it was the beginning of very hard times for us.' The Chinese disbanded the existing agricultural system, confiscated the land, insisted on planting wheat, and organized everyone (from the farmers to the monks who had by now been thrown out of their monasteries) into communes and put them to work on the land. Without respecting the fragile top soil that in most parts of Tibet needed to be nurtured and allowed to lie fallow to regenerate – a practice that the Tibetans automatically observed – the Chinese assaulted the land with intense over-cultivation with the result that the soil became quickly exhausted, sterile and produced nothing.

The Chinese also insisted on the cultivation of pastoral land which Tibetans knew, from centuries of experience, was not suited to cultivation. With the result that nothing grew, and the land for pasture was reduced. The Chinese then also brought in restrictions prohibiting the grazing of yak and even domestic animals, like horses, cows and *dzo* near their newly built military bases and their supply roads. Any animal that trespassed (and as one of the farmers said, 'We do not have enough *yaktse* [herdsmen] to watch all the yaks everywhere in all of Tibet, and how do you tell a yak where not to graze?') was shot by the PLA units building the roads.

The result of these policies was catastrophic: the first famine ever recorded in Tibet's 2,000-year-old written history. Over 70,000 Tibetans died – very painfully – all over Tibet from 1959 to 1962. Further crop failures and fatal food shortages were reported all through the sixties all over Tibet, in places as far apart as Kanze and Drayab in Kham to Dromo and Phari in the southern part of Central Tibet and all over Amdo.

Stephen Corry, Director General of Survival International (an international organization working for the rights of threatened tribal peoples) reported the Tibetan situation as: 'Far from providing the poor with enough to eat, the overwhelming evidence suggests that the Chinese totally disrupted an essentially self-sufficient society and caused, through their brutality and colonialism, massive food shortages and widespread hunger as the masses were put to work to feed their new masters.'

One of the farmers told me what it was like: 'When the Chinese first came here in 1949 they said that they had come to help us, and gave us tools. But then more and more Chinese kept coming here in bigger and bigger numbers from all parts of China. They took our crops and they ate all our food. Life was most difficult for us as they never paid for anything. Then in 1953 they took over complete control, took our land, took our homes, everything, and gave it to the new Chinese settlers that came in bigger and bigger numbers from Sichuan and other parts of China and pushed the Tibetans to the outskirts.

'When they took my land, I had no means of survival. I thought

I would die. It was so bad that two of my family jumped in the river and died from drowning, so that there might be more food for the children. These events should never happen in human existence. I am overwhelmed by this . . .'

The farmer, a man in his mid-forties, broke down and cried. Wiping his face with the back of his hand he continued: 'There was no consideration for Tibetans. Even drinking and eating – basic human rights – were denied us. If we could we would have run away. But we could not even do that. The Chinese stopped Tibetans even visiting relatives in the next village. All our movements were restricted and the Chinese put spies in the communes and they reported on us. If we complained about the shortages of food, we were violently punished by the Chinese as *sarjenyolok*, counter-revolutionary enemies of socialism.' To be a 'counter-revolutionary' is one of the worst crimes in China and is often punishable by death.

But in 1980 the Chinese relaxed their agricultural policy because Tibet was in a shambles. In May 1980, Hu Yaobang, the General Secretary of the Central Committee of the Chinese Communist Party, promised to restore the Tibetan economy to its pre-1959 level within three years – an admission that Chinese economic policies had failed in Tibet. But the promises were broken. Although Tibetans were allowed more say in what crops they grew, and though theoretically loans were available for farm machinery, Tibetans were too poor to buy it and in all my journey in Tibet I never saw any machinery owned by Tibetans or lying in the yards of their houses. When I remarked on the absence, Tenzin told me that Tibetans simply couldn't afford to buy, but sometimes a few of them got enough money together to hire machinery from the Chinese. The Tibetan rural peasant, though better off than the urban Tibetan, today remains worse off than before the Chinese arrived. For a brief time they had relief from paying 40–50 per cent of their produce in taxes to the Chinese, but since 1987 this has been reinstated. A system of ration cards for Tibetans was introduced and is still in force. Grain is issued only on a system of work points so severe that most children, even small ones, have to work in the fields to make up the family's quota.

I asked the farmers and peasants once again why, when there certainly had been relaxations in the laws, and the Chinese proclaimed that production figures were up, they were not better off?

Every peasant and farmer I spoke to had the same story. As Tsultrim, a dispossessed farmer from near Batang, said: 'The Chinese say one thing to the outside world, but inside the story is much different. They say they have liberalized their policies in Tibet and have given Tibetans more freedom and more land. That is partly true. Yes, we can grow barley again. Ownership of some land is now allowed, but if a group works very hard, they are officially only allowed to sell through the Chinese system, and if they exceed the official quota, they have to deposit the profit in the Chinese bank. Once this has been done there is no possibility of the family withdrawing their savings, say for an emergency, if someone has to have an operation. They have to fill out endless forms and get many permissions, and the bank often has the power of refusal. So again it's a question of what the Chinese say and what they actually do.

'Yes, some of us have been given a little land,' he went on. 'But seeds and fertilizers, which we have to buy from the Chinese shops, are so expensive that in the end it is not enough to give a family even one meal a day. We have to buy everything in the shops run by the Chinese: things for the land, the clothes that I am wearing, even my shoe-laces. The Chinese charge us very high prices, but we have no option. And there are many poor people who have no land and no cattle and for them it gets harder to scratch a living.

'It is the Chinese who not only take our land, but also have the cars and the radios, hospitals and education for their children. You have seen our children. You have seen how we live. What we eat. No!' he said angrily, 'We are not better off now. The Chinese have taken everything. You don't believe me? Go anywhere in our country, make a proper investigation into the living conditions of Tibetans in Tibet. Go into the villages and see the living conditions for yourself. Find out how many houses have been built in Tibet – you will find that they are all built by the Chinese for themselves.'

In December 1980, the Hong Kong publication *Emancipation Review* reported:

When Hu Yaobang and Wan Li went to Tibet, what shocked them most was the poverty. China had put in a lot of effort for the past thirty years and invested several billions, but the Tibetan people and Tibet were still in a state of grinding poverty. Hu Yaobang said 'The Central Government have spent several billions (yuan) in Tibet, how did you spend it? Did you throw it in the Yarlung Tsangpo?'

He saw the Tibetan economy, far from being self-sufficient and quite autarkic as before, had swung to the opposite extreme: it was completely dependent on mainland China. All consumer goods had to be imported, even food. Tibet exported some minerals, medicinal herbs and timber. If supplies from mainland China were interrupted, the Tibetan economy would be paralysed and collapse. Hu Yao Bang said one thing that no one in China has ever dared to say: 'This is plain colonialism!'

Western economists acknowledge the appalling state of Tibet's economy, which is a constant drain on China. They claim that Tibet, China's 'Deep South' is in fact a Third World region of a Third World country. When one of the fact-finding missions sent by the Dalai Lama was allowed into Tibet during a brief moment of detente between 1980–83, Phuntsog Wangyal stated in the report made by the delegation of their findings inside Tibet:

> The delegation visited a number of factories during their tour. The dairy plants in Ngapa produce tinned dried milk which is sent directly to Hong Kong for export. All their produce is labelled 'Made in China' and when delegates investigated to see if any Tibetan families were using it, not a single tin could be found. Similarly, the leather factories in Ngapa and Kanze produce shoes, bags and leather jackets, most of which are exported to China, since only a few Tibetan officers (those working with and for the Chinese) can afford to buy shoes, and the majority of Tibetans do not wear leather shoes. Woollen mills in Dhartsedo produce blankets of good-quality woollen fabric. The delegates met only two Tibetans (officers) who wore clothes from the factories, since they are so expensive. In Nepal and Hong Kong one can buy blankets made in Tibet, but once again labelled 'Made in China'.

I asked them about the few Tibetans who seemed well off; who were reasonably dressed and even, in Lhasa, rode motor-bikes. The Tibetans told me that they were *Gyagama* (Chinese-lovers) or *Gynipa* (spies or Tibetan collaborators working for the Chinese), or *Tsakya* (useless) women who had married the Chinese for a better standard of living; these people got better pay than ordinary Tibetans and had access to goods that were denied the ordinary Tibetan.

'But if you talk about the living conditions of ordinary Tibetans – almost 90 per cent of us barely survive on two cupfuls of *tsampa* a day!'

'But why is it that nobody hears about this?' I asked.

'Because Tibetans were not even allowed to talk to one another, let alone to anyone else,' Thupten, another farmer, said almost at the same time, letting out his frustration like a sluice gate opening after monsoon rains. 'We had *thumzings*, and the Chinese police tried to make us think the "correct" way. Many people went to jail from here, and many people to labour camps. And very, very few returned – maybe only about 2 per cent. Although now we do not have to go to political meetings every night – only two or three times a week – we never know who is watching so we still have to be very careful. Even in the countryside you never know who is listening. Who will inform on you. Look at the way we are sitting here in the dark and speaking very softly so that the people next door will not hear. This is why we have to hide you. No one from outside came here before you. You are the first. For years and years terrible, terrible things have been happening to the Tibetan people, here and all over Tibet, and not a word has been said.'

'Please,' Wangchuk said, taking my hand. 'Please take our story to the outside world. Tell the outside people how we have no rights, only hunger and suffering. We have not had the opportunity to tell someone before now. Please do not let the Tibetan people starve to death. Tell the outside people to help us. Because if they do not, and the Chinese remain, there is no doubt that the Tibetan race will be eradicated from Tibet.'

There was a silence in the room and the little girl looked at me with eyes large enough to swallow up her face. The occupants of the next room put on loud Chinese music. Dolma's mother brought some tea as the interviewees prepared to go home. Many of them had come a long distance, and as Tibetans do not own cars and there are no buses, getting from one area to another is a major problem. They have to rely on lorries, more often than not owned by Chinese.

Many of the interviewees during the day had spoken so graphically and with such pain about their experiences. I knew that it would make riveting television, but I also knew that in forty minutes' air-time I would be able to use only one interview about farming. I asked Thondup to explain to them that while I greatly appreciated the enormous risk that they had all taken in coming to talk to me, and although they had all volunteered to be interviewed on camera, I did not want to expose anyone unnecessarily. I had decided to use the farmer Wangchuk, as his pain and passion would touch even the most hardened heart. As he had made a nine-hour journey from his small plot half-way between Chamdo and Markham, Thondup arranged accommodation for him. We then decided it would be safer to drive out of Markham and film the interview somewhere on the way to Batang.

The Boys were arranging for us to get another van with Markham number plates. It was immeasurably difficult for a Tibetan to find any transport, let alone private transport, as one of the principal and effective ways of controlling the Tibetan population was by curtailing their movements. So I was full of admiration for Tenzin and his ability to organize another vehicle.

It was late and we had to be up early again to avoid the checkpoints. Tenzin told me to be ready by 5.30, so climbing into my sleeping bag I set my alarm.

Before it went off Dolma's light touch woke me. How she – or the Boys for that matter – managed to wake, without an alarm clock, before the morning light I will never know. I dressed quickly and packed. It was still dark outside as I shared my muesli with the little girl. Apart from the barking of dogs there was not a sound in the streets.

As Dolma and I sat in the straw and the dirt in the semi-gloom, with the candle that threw more shadows than light, I reflected on the child's future. Ill-nourished, illiterate, inadequately housed and clothed, disenfranchised, a second-class citizen discriminated against on practically every level in her own country, the likelihood of her reaching her potential birthright was worse than nil. But in the half-light of that September morning the child's enchanting warmth and openness not only synthesized for me the essential Tibetan character, but heightened my appreciation of an extraordinary people.

Tenzin and Thondup took my things down the ladder to Tsering who was waiting at the bottom. There were no stars and a chill wind was blowing. I shivered and pulled my scarf more tightly round my neck. Without the sun, and at just under 13,000 feet, it was cold in Markham.

Dolma stood shyly in the shadows. I looked up and waved. There was something about that child I felt I knew well. With my logical Western mind, prone to disbelieve and analyse everything, it did not make sense. I told myself not to be a maudlin idiot, that I was just feeling sorry for an enchanting little girl who had touched my heart. But I remembered a similar incident some time ago when I met the medium of the State Oracle of Tibet at the Nechung monastery in Dharamsala. We met by accident and started talking immediately like long-lost friends, in Hindi, and the subsequent week I met him a few times. Just before I left, he came to see me and gave me a special blessing and a tiny turquoise stone on a red thread that he told me would protect me. I said to him, 'You know, you will probably think I am crazy, but I feel, somehow, that I know you.' He smiled and said, 'I feel the same. We have known each other in another life.' He knew I was a Catholic and believed in an after-life in a different way from Buddhists, but there was a connection that I certainly did not understand, yet felt. It was the same feeling I had with that child. I felt I had known her in another life. I scolded myself, told myself to get a grip on reality and that going into the dark Markham morning was not the time to get metaphysical. I had already said my adieus, but as I put my foot on the ladder, the child came up and once again softly touched my face and smiled.

There are a few very precious moments in life that I will always remember. There was so much joy in Dolma's small face, such openness and trust, despite the harshness of her life, that I will never forget it. And even today, whenever I think of that grubby little girl with laughing eyes, I still smile. One day, I promised myself, I would return to Markham to see her, to try and help open a new world to her and to so many Tibetan children who are growing up illiterate and ignorant, not only of the world beyond their snowy mountains but also of their own world and of their own Tibetan identity.

After once more running the gauntlet of the muddy alley, I was safely ensconced in another van. It seemed to have even more bumps and sharp corners than the previous ones. Then Thondup told me checkpoint timings had been changed. So while Tenzin and the Boys went and had some tea at a Chinese-run 'hotel', I stayed in the van with Thondup and the ex-monk who was returning to his home in Batang with us.

Silently cursing and wishing I was still horizontal in my sleeping bag, I watched the sun warm the valley. Beyond a field of ripening barley, I saw a low building that looked like a small monastery. Through Thondup I asked the ex-monk about it. He told us that in 1959, well before the Cultural Revolution, the Chinese had destroyed forty-two monasteries in Markham; a few were in the process of reconstruction and the small one in front of us was one of the ones the Tibetans had rebuilt with their own time and money. But like all the others they were restoring, it was much smaller than the original. He pointed out the ruins of the Wozel Gompa (temple) which had been used as a prison in the fifties and then looted and destroyed.

The scenery was idyllic. There were some dark-green pines that had escaped the deforestation axe and stood tall amid the logged stumps. Wild flowers blossomed in such profusion that they tumbled down into the road. The air, scented with warm grass, the aroma of pine cones and the effervescence of a pot-pourri of flowers, was magical under the warm sun. Down in the valleys the fields were golden with barley interspersed with the green of vegetables. There was no one on the roads apart from the occasional Chinese lorry. I got out, put the tripod up and filmed the van coming into shot, proceeding apace and then disappearing out of shot round a corner to leave me with a clean frame which would make editing much easier for Chris back in London.

We found a secluded spot off the road by a stream to do the interview with the farmer I had talked to the day before. We disguised his clothes and borrowed bits from the Boys: a hat from Tenzin, a *chuba* from Tsering, a scarf from Thondup and a pair of my cheap Chinese sun-glasses. I framed him standing against a low dry-stone wall, with a field of ripe barley waving gently in the breeze behind. Looking through the view-finder I saw something blue dotted in the barley. I waded into the thigh-high barley and found bright-blue poppies with yellow centres. I had never seen blue poppies before. The Boys looked at me strangely; they could not understand my excitement and told me that the flower was found all over Tibet. I later found out that it was the exotic blue Tibetan poppy. It was yet another perfect day with bright hot sun (all the Boys were stripped down to their shirts), with a few white clouds scuttling around the impossibly blue sky. I never did get used to the intensity of the sky. I so wanted just to lie in the barley and do nothing more energetic than watch the clouds go by, sniff the warm earth and drift off to sleep with the sun on my face. But it was nearly one o'clock and we had yet to negotiate the checkpoint to the Tibetan Autonomous Region (TAR); so I ground on with the interview, as the farmer repeated on camera the points he had made the previous day.

By 1.30 we were on our way again and driving north-east across yet more mountains and valleys. We were coming up to the most dangerous checkpoint at the border of the Tibetan Autonomous Region and China – the annexed part of Kham that now officially comes under Sichuan. There were strict military guards, at either end of the bridge spanning the Upper Yangtse. According to Tenzin, they were very thorough, as they were looking for contraband travelling both ways: electrical goods and food going into the TAR, and skins, wool, hides or timber going east to China.

As we started driving down, it got hotter. The mountains were more arid, which in the harsh white light reminded me of the stark mountain contours of Greece in high summer, but without the chatter of cicadas or the scent of resinous pine that can be such an aphrodisiac on a hot Greek afternoon. The Boys were silent and tense and were watching the road as it snaked round the bends.

After a terse burst of Tibetan, Thondup told me that there were no boats for me to be smuggled across in and that I had to do everything exactly as Tenzin said. I nodded and clutched the Sony tightly. 'Now remember, Vanya, do exactly what Tenzin says,' Thondup warned. What else could I do, I wondered irritably: wander up to the checkpoint in my most fetching bikini? We were on a bend in the road and I could see the river, grey with sediment, running swiftly between bare mountains that came down to the river on the opposite side. Where we were parked, our road dropped to a steep bank of smooth stones that ended somewhere over the edge in the water.

There was no one in sight, yet on the opposite mountain

several trucks were lined up, obviously waiting to go through the checkpoint. Suddenly from around the bend came a tall middle-aged woman in dark Chinese clothes. She had a strong face under her straw hat. She smiled at Tenzin. Thondup later told me that she had been in the Resistance with Tenzin many years ago. They exchanged a few words, then Tenzin quickly talked to Thondup, who told me to get out of the car, take my Sony and my small camera-bag with me and go with Tenzin – quickly!

Before I could ask where and for how long and why, Tenzin grabbed one arm and the woman the other, and the two of them dragged me down the steep slope and pushed me under a thorn bush. Tenzin made sign language for me to stay put and disappeared with the woman out of sight down the rest of the bank towards the river. Behind me, on the road, I heard the van start up and drive in the direction of the bridge. It was blazing hot and the sun beat down on the white stones of the river bed. I didn't dare peel off my green jacket in the heat, as it blended almost perfectly with the scrubby bush I was hiding under. Careful not to get impaled on the long thorns, I looked around and to my dismay I found I was totally on my own, stuck under a thorn bush and only a few hundred yards from a heavily guarded checkpoint. Everyone else had disappeared.

17

Checkpoint TAR

The itching was driving me insane. It had started the previous evening and I had not thought much of it. But huddled under a thorn bush, under a merciless sun, unable to move for fear of shaking the branches and alerting the attention of a traveller or the lorries on the road passing fifteen feet above my flimsy sanctuary, and unable to pull off my sweaters and scratch, I was in torment. I looked at my wrists and scrutinized a welter of small red lumps that itched infernally. Flea bites. That was all I needed.

I must have 'contracted' them from the old lady's 'bed'. The timing was excruciatingly inconvenient. It was bad enough with a slipped disc and gastro-enteritis, but flea bites . . . I soundly cursed all the gods – known and unknown – and wondered when I was going to be 'liberated' from my purgatory. It was now three hours since Tenzin had disappeared down the river bank and the Boys had driven off. Unable to read – I had left my book in the van – and unable to stretch my cramped legs, which were doubled under me as there was not a patch of 'cover' other than the minuscule scraggly bush that I was under, I even tried to construct some iambic pentameter. But I didn't have the patience beyond the first stanza.

There was not a breath of wind. The rocks of the river bank were almost incandescent with heat. On the road on the opposite mountainside the line of trucks awaiting inspection grew. Stick, Lowry-like figures in blue wandered along the side of the trucks – and Chinese voices floated down across the river. Time, like the sun, seemed to be suspended in the brilliant blue sky. I hoped that the checkpoint delay did not mean that something had happened to the Boys . . .

It was about 7.30 and the sun was less fierce, when suddenly Tenzin's battered hat appeared cautiously over the embankment. Without looking at me, he walked on, talking to the woman and eating what looked like walnuts. They laughed and joked with the intimacy of old friends.

If we had been anywhere but at the most dangerous checkpoint in all Tibet, I would have devoured what I was sure would be all the fascinating detail of their eventful years in the resistance. Now there was a film! There were so many stories of the Tibetan resistance's epic courage that it would keep Hollywood supplied for years.

Tenzin and the woman suddenly disappeared over the edge of the road above my head and their voices were swallowed by the roar of a truck coming round the corner. I strained to catch even a whisper of sound that would herald the end of my misery. At that moment I really did not care what happened, as long as I could tear off my clothes and have a good scratch. About 7.45 I heard a vehicle approach the bend and stop. Several feet crunched on the stones, and I braced myself for the worst. Then I turned my head and saw Thondup smiling.

'Now do as Tenzin says,' Thondup told me again, as they pushed me up the slope to where Tenzin was standing in the lee of the van, between it and the overhanging mountainside. He was holding a large gunny sack. As I was unceremoniously stuffed into it, I thought that it just could not be happening to me – that this was the stuff of *Boys' Own* comics. Thondup disappeared. There was only Tenzin, the woman, Sumpa and 'the sack' in a dilapidated van on a lonely mountain in the middle of Tibet. It was so unreal that I broke into a fit of giggles as Tenzin and the woman loaded me into the van and laid me on the floor and then proceeded to put other bags and their feet on top of me. The van bumped towards the checkpoint and then stopped with the engine still running. I heard the unmistakeable heavy tread of army boots approaching and stopping by the window.

By now I had run out of gods to bribe or pray to. But I promised to give up champagne, even chocolate croissants; I swore I would forgo silk nighties, would wear sackcloth and ashes – anything. I held my nose and hoped to God that I would not do something as stupid as sneeze from the dirt and the fluff of my inelegant shroud which seemed to have invaded every pore of my body. That Sunday it was Sumpa's turn to deliver a bravura performance. His Chinese was more fluent than Tenzin's, and I suspect that his youthful looks and mop of curly black hair looked less suspicious than Tenzin's scarred face and towering height.

For yet another aeon, in which I slowly died of anxiety for the umpteenth time on the trip, Sumpa chattered amicably with the soldier – undoubtedly offering him packets of Marlboro and Kent that I had bought in the duty-free shop, specifically for this purpose. Foreign cigarettes are highly prized by the Chinese, especially by the PLA, largely as a status symbol and also because the taste of Chinese cigarettes, so I am told, is not overrefined.

I would have given my eye teeth to be filming. I should have been filming the encounter – that was what I had come to Tibet to do. Not lying like a log in the bottom of a van as though I was in a bad B-feature movie.

As the van pulled away, I was no longer able to bear the suffocating sack – I suffer from claustrophobia – and tore it from my head. I pushed the bags off my chest, sat up, peeked above the driving seat and saw that we were crossing the Upper Yangtse on the first proper concrete bridge I had yet seen east of Lhasa. This one was obviously made for heavy-duty military traffic. Below, the river swirled in a brisk current, but there were no white-caps as I had seen higher in the mountains. The Yangtse looked like what it is: deep and powerful and one of the mighty rivers of the world. We were at the lowest altitude in the journey.

The little van felt very vulnerable, coughing across the bridge (we had lost another silencer) on its own. I wondered if the Chinese had deliberately designed the bridge for single vehicle traffic for easier scrutiny and control? Again, suspended between uncertainty and catastrophe, I felt the same sense of heightened awareness that I felt under fire. It is both exhilarating and terrifying at the same time as you wait, mesmerized, for a fate over which you have absolutely no control. With a dry mouth and sweaty hands, I saw the far bank approaching. Near the sentry box stood a small gaggle of people. It seemed that everyone in the van held their breath. There were the drab olive uniforms of the PLA and some civilian blue Mao suits waiting. Had the last checkpoint radioed ahead? Were they just a group of soldiers talking to the locals, or was it the dreaded PSB who had finally caught up with us? I wriggled back into the sack. Inside the van no one spoke. When we drew level, Sumpa neither slowed down nor accelerated, but kept to a nonchalant ten miles an hour. Turning left off the bridge, he slowly accelerated and turned down a small rough path out of view of the soldiers and the bridge.

The Boys jumped out, the woman said something to Tenzin, picked up her bundle, waved, started climbing up a small track and disappeared. I was bursting with curiosity about the strange lady who exuded a very tangible sense of strength and resourcefulness. I asked Thondup about her and why she was there. He told me it was wiser not to ask too much. The less I knew the better.

But for hours I puzzled over what she would have done had the soldiers inspected the van and found me. Would she have bundled me over the edge of the bridge? Would the Boys have made a run for it? Were they in fact armed, I wondered? I never had any reason to believe so and the only visible sign of self-defence was Tenzin's curved Khampa knife that dangled quite openly from his belt.

I certainly had no weapon and, like most journalists, never carried one. To be found with a weapon – or worse, to use it, even in self-defence – was total insanity. The 'other side' would immediately label you a spy and either shoot you or jail you for a very long time. It also immediately put you in the combatant category and made you a legitimate target.

I put a hold on that unproductive train of questioning and started to write my overdue shot list from the deliberately indecipherable squiggles I had managed to write *en route*. It was absolutely vital to keep some track of shots, otherwise on return to the cutting room in London I would have no idea, after 4,000 miles, of which mountain went where and in what sequence.

While Tsering brewed up some tea, the rest stripped and washed off days of caked mud under a small waterfall at the side of the road. Their splashing and laughter were the only indication of the considerable tension that the Boys had been under. I would have given a king's ransom to have sat under the waterfall and felt water, clean water, wash the dirt and tension from my by now crumpled body. Even for a few brief minutes. But as we never knew when a PLA uniform might come round the corner, and since the strong sun had, during my first sojourn in Lhasa, scattered my hair with suspiciously un-Tibetan blonde streaks, I did not dare take off my ski-mask, so I just washed my hands. Thondup told me that we should arrive at Batang at dusk.

The Boys were full of banter and jokes. It was warm and sunny as the van started climbing out of the valley, which was green with crops, shrubs and small trees. I had to get out and film the lush vegetation by the river bed. It was just so unlike anything one ever thinks of as the barren mountains of Tibet. I started the shot with a hold on the swirling water, filling the frame full of circling currents, so that it looked like an early Khalil Ghibran painting, then I panned up through the dense grey-green bushes that came right down to the water's edge, past some low bushy trees that looked like willow and chestnut in the eye-piece, up past fields heavy with ripening golden maize and finally I ended the shot on the slopes of the mountain above, where it shaded from green to bleak grey without any vegetation whatsoever. 'A picture should make words superfluous,' my supervising director, that wonderful film-maker Russell Spurr, told me as a trainee making my first film years ago at Granada Television. But it should do more.

Theoretically a shot or sequence should be planned – beginning, middle and end – and it should be designed to fit into the sequence of whatever point you were trying to make. But with the Boys' impatience to be off the moment the tripod hit the ground, it was a constant battle just to film. And in the rush I invariably had no time to plan anything. It was the worst sort of filming imaginable – just snatching a shot here and there. It was irritating beyond words constantly to grab whatever I could when I was able. Acceptable perhaps during a fire-fight in El Salvador or during an artillery barrage in Beirut, but that is news coverage and what I was frustratingly trying to do was feature-documentary filming. It made me increasingly bad-tempered as we progressed and the Boys, either bored with playing 'movies' or irritated with the hold-up that filming inevitably involved, had become more and more hostile to the delays. It was all I could do to concentrate on smooth zooms and pans. But now, with fifteen days of practice, I was getting better and the zooms were not as jerky as when I first started. At least not all of them.

I did an end-slate by turning the marker upside down to tell the editor back home that the synch marks were on the end of the shot rather than, as usually, at the beginning. Thondup had become quite expert as a production assistant and at organizing the numbering. At the beginning of each day he put on a piece of Lhasa Holiday Inn paper the day, date, location, camera-roll number and then underneath the relevant slate number, which he then crossed out as we proceeded to the next set-up. Thondup was absolutely meticulous about tearing the tell-tale clapper-board page to smithereens and burning it after we had finished filming the scene. 'You never know,' he would warn, worried about the remote chance that a Chinese patrol might come across a strange piece of paper. He was equally cautious about my loo paper and warned me to dig it into the ground. 'Tibetans don't use toilet paper. If the Chinese saw it, they would be suspicious.' I had to admit that I would never have thought of it.

I looked with alarm at the date on Thondup's slate. Sunday, 15 September. I had less than two weeks to complete the filming and get out of Tibet before my visa expired: and I was not even half-way round. Chengdu, the half-way point, was, barring accidents and delays, more than five days away. The van could not go faster. There were no short cuts – there were no other roads at all – and I could not even suggest that we take it in relays to drive, in case we missed some relevant sequence in the night hours. It was a no-win situation and as we approached Batang there seemed no solution.

Batang is a most delightful town. Small and sub-tropical, it is strung along a shallow valley and surrounded with graceful low hills green with vegetation. Approaching the town we could have been driving anywhere in Provence, southern Italy or northern Greece. The rough road wound between low dry-stone walls with trees and bushes tumbling over them. The river meandered lazily somewhere in the distance and beside the road it had flooded the low-lying fields, forming small lakes that reflected the scudding white clouds in an otherwise perfect sky. The occasional flat-roofed, square, one-storey mud-brick Tibetan houses, in the tra-ditional style, were simple and without any ornamentation or colour. They blended perfectly into a landscape of earthy colours, of every nuance of brown, dung and green. The odd Tibetan in a dark *chuba* and rolled-up sleeves, tilling a field or driving some goats, gave a sense of serenity to the perfect rural landscape. The late-afternoon sun seemed to infuse the countryside with a sense of gaiety and there was a scent of blossom and fruit in the air. I felt ridiculously and inexplicably carefree, as though I was on holiday and meandering down some Mediterranean country lane on a balmy midsummer's afternoon.

'*Gyami!*' Sumpa hissed from the side of his mouth and brought me back to reality with a thud. In front a jeep with Chinese soldiers was coming towards us. Then I noticed the electricity pylons and the predominantly utilitarian-style Chinese houses that jarred with the soft contours of the mountains and clumps of feathery willows. The Chinese are no strangers to Batang, for the town has seen savage battles between Tibetan and Chinese on and off for the past seventy years. It was these obscure little conflicts such as at Batang, where towns and villages changed hands that, Tsering told me, allowed the Chinese to 'trumpet their claim to Tibet'.

When the Chinese invaded Kham in 1950, they at first treated the Khampas with reasonable restraint, while building roads and consolidating their infrastructure. But previous unpleasant experiences with the Chinese made the people of Batang wary. Then in the autumn of 1954, they imposed new draconian taxes on everything Tibetan – land, cattle and houses. The big estates were redistributed and many landowners summarily executed for no more serious crime than that they could read and owned some land. When the Chinese forbade the practice of religion and sacked the monasteries, Tibetans rebelled. Those refusing to comply with the Chinese were beaten, imprisoned and tortured and had all their possessions confiscated.

As their religion, property and social system came under attack from the Chinese, even the traditionally passive Tibetans rose in open revolt and formed an active guerrilla movement. The Chinese retaliated with tanks and aircraft; they bombed and shelled monasteries known to have a reputation for hostility to the Chinese, such as Batang and Lithang. The ex-monk whom we had met in Chamdo and were giving a lift back to his home in Batang told me stories of the repression of the local people.

Night was falling quickly and the slight breeze was heady with the scent of warm earth and wild flowers. We drove quietly without headlights through the dusk towards the centre of town. All around us, Chinese filled the streets which were lined with small, brightly lit kiosks and in the centre of the town the blare of loud Chinese music shattered the tranquillity of the evening. We drove to the edge of town, walked down a rough track and ducked into the archway of a safe house.

We climbed to the upper floor and found the family had prepared us supper, which was laid out and waiting on the table. Tenzin and Thondup stayed with me to introduce and translate for the group of Tibetans who had patiently been waiting for several days. The other Boys went into town to find accommodation for the night as it was unsafe for all of us to sleep in the same place. It had been so long since I had actually eaten anything much more substantial than noodles and muesli that after a few mouthfuls of *momos* (a typically Tibetan dish of dumplings stuffed with spicy meat) I had difficulty in keeping it down. We talked far into the night and, aching with exhaustion, I decided to film the next morning.

The lady of the house took me to the 'kitchen' corner of the main room, gave me a basin and indicated a pan of hot water on the stove and another one of cold water on the floor. There was of course no bathroom, no drainage, and no privacy. But faced with clean hot water, I threw prudery to the winds, stripped and, oblivious to her clearing up the supper dishes, proceeded to wash off the grime and mud. That night was bliss. I actually slept on a bench-bed and fell asleep looking through the open window at the stars.

The rustle of the wind fluttering the leaves woke me. As I opened my eyes the scent of roses wafted through the window. I climbed onto the ledge and was overwhelmed by the beauty. It was like a perfect Tuscan morning in the hills above Florence as the pale light just after dawn cascaded languorously over the contours of the valley. It had been such a hard night, listening to the painful testimony of Tibetans who had suffered unendurable agony in Chinese jails. Although I had by then listened to many private agonies, it did not get any easier to bear. I felt as though I was drowning. I wondered how Simon Weisenthal coped after nearly forty-five years of documenting Nazi atrocities as horrifying as the stories I had been listening to ever since I had come to Tibet.

But for a little longer, while the house and the valley still slept, I found solace in watching the warm dappled sunlight dance through the trees. In the garden under the window there was a sea of flowers: huge overblown pink roses, enormous sunflowers, tall white gladioli, masses of sapphire-blue delphiniums and lark-spur, all jostling for sun under the canopy of a spreading vine. In a corner, and almost within reach, was a tree heavy with voluptuous yellow peaches.

'You're day-dreaming again!' Thondup laughed as he came up behind me.

I smiled and accepted some coffee. Then we began to discuss the day's shooting.

As the house was surrounded by Chinese homes (Batang is a retirement town for deserving Chinese Communist Party members), it would be impossible to film outside among the flowers. The night before, we had interviewed well over thirty people. All but two were willing to appear on camera. Understandably, the nearer we got to mainland China and the denser the Chinese population surrounding the dwindling number of Tibetans became, the more frightened Tibetans were of speaking openly to me – on and off camera. I also noticed that since we had left Chamdo the numbers of Tibetans wearing Tibetan clothes had declined sharply.

Some former monks of Batang's Chode Gaden Phendeling monastery talked about the destruction of their monastery. Built by the 5th Dalai Lama, Ngawang Losang Gyatso, over 350 years ago, it had housed some particularly beautiful frescos and statues. They told me that during the 1956 *Losar* festivities for the Tibetan New Year, when the monastery was full of pilgrims from the countryside, Chinese planes bombed the monastery to oblivion. Over 2,000 Tibetan monks and pilgrims were killed.

'It was so unexpected,' an old monk who had spent twenty-one years in prison told me. 'All of us, the monks and the people, were performing *choe*. That's all. They gave us no warning and before we could run outside and hide, the roof was falling in and exploding bombs killed nearly everyone. Pieces of bodies flew into the air as more and more bombs fell. They dropped more than eighty bombs that day on the monastery alone. People were screaming, some were lying under big stones that had fallen from the roof. Others were crushed under walls that had collapsed under the bombs. Bits of people were lying everywhere. There was blood everywhere, too. It was like a butcher's shop.'

'But wasn't Batang, like many other areas in Kham, a centre of fierce Khampa resistance in the fifties?' I asked. 'And as it was war with the Chinese, don't you think the Chinese had a valid excuse in attacking a hotbed of Tibetan resistance?'

'Yes, of course there were Khampa fighters around Batang and we could understand if the planes attacked their camps,' the monk said patiently. 'But that day in the monastery there were no fighters, just monks and ordinary Tibetans performing *choe* on what for us is the most important religious ceremony of the year.' (*Losar* is the very rough equivalent – in terms of religious importance – of the Christian Easter, the Jewish Passover or the Muslim Eid el Fatar.)

'There were no armed fighters in the monastery. It is against our religion to use violence. Buddhists would never go with weapons to a monastery or fight within it. Even if the fighters came to pray, they would never bring their arms into the temple. And the very fact that not one shot was fired from the monastery proves the point. It was simply slaughter. Over 2,000 died that day.' Those Tibetans that survived were either imprisoned by the Chinese or sent to labour camps or perished in the catastrophic famine of 1959–62.

The experiences of the ex-monk who had travelled with us from Chamdo echoed, with a few different details, those of the monks from Batang and indeed of monks all over Tibet, who had seen their own monasteries devastated.

'When the Chinese destroyed our monastery,' he said, 'they selected out for special treatment all the incarnate lamas, the teachers with high learning and the administrators. They accused us of all sorts of crimes which were not true. Then began a long period of torture when they tried to get information that we did not have. We were brutally beaten and forced to kneel on broken glass with our bare knees. Some who survived still cannot walk properly today because all the strings [tendons] of the muscles were cut. Then many were thrown on their backs on the ground and eight people, holding arms and legs, pulled the prisoner apart.'

'You mean that the limbs were pulled apart from the body while the prisoner was still living?' I asked incredulously, as I had thought this was a medieval torture that had mercifully disappeared.

'Yes,' the old man said. He had gone white and seemed to have difficulty breathing. I thought he was going to faint. I asked

Thondup to get him some water and tell him not to go on, for it was obvious that the man was under enormous stress at the pain of remembering those events.

'Please,' he said, sipping the water, 'I must tell you. Time is short – and who knows when another stranger will come and take our stories to the outside. The torture also included tearing off the prisoner's ears and nose from his head. The Chinese would also poke their fingers into the eyes of the prisoners and throw dirt into their mouths so that it would choke and suffocate them. And then they would laugh in our faces and say, "Now where is your God? If he exists, call him. You can't practise your religion now! Serve you right!" Then they brought many, many soldiers and workers and staff from China to maintain discipline in the prisons.

'From 1959 until the end of the Cultural Revolution the Chinese opened many prisons in the three provinces of Tibet to accommodate the huge numbers of Tibetan prisoners. All the prisons were so overcrowded that the few remaining temples that were not too badly destroyed were also used as prisons. In the case of our monastery at Chamdo, at one time it held over 5,000 prisoners. Very many of the prisoners had their arms and their legs chained so that people going near the monastery could hear the *cha-ke*, the clanking sound of the chains all the time as though one was in a blacksmith's workshop.

'When you moved to one side there would be a great noise; when you moved to the other there would again be a great noise. It was deafening. Some people went crazy with the noise and all night there was never a moment of peace. Sleep was impossible. Then in the *thumzing* sessions the Chinese soldiers and the prison staff beat us with big sticks and stones. Sometimes the prisoners would take up to one hundred lashes. Sometimes during the meeting the prisoners' bones were broken. Then when they could not stand, the soldiers used to kick them so hard on the ground that some died this way. Then they forced prisoners to beat each other. Whatever means the Chinese found to hurt the human body they did to us Tibetans. And then more died that way, others died of starvation.

'One could see – and I did – that the increase in the deathrate of the prisoners was so rapid: it rose from four or five a day to over twelve or thirteen every day. The Chinese authorities couldn't cope with the disposal of corpses and threw them naked into ravines, like the one I showed you north of our monastery the other morning in Chamdo. There were more than 1,000 corpses there. The other grave was filled up and then a house for Chinese was built on top. We had to fill up both the trenches – full up to the top with bodies – and then cover them up with earth. But when we had to walk over it we saw limbs and heads sticking out.

'Many of us were afraid to walk there and tried not to look, but your eyes were always drawn to the spot. Starving dogs feasted on the human corpses and were turned into man-eaters. For a long time people could not travel in the countryside, as dogs attacked them and there were many cases of Tibetans being eaten by dogs. Never in the history of Tibet have we ever heard or seen such things happening.'

I had to stop filming. I was stunned because I realized that what the ex-monk was speaking about were mass graves, like those of the Polish soldiers shot at Katyn during World War II. Or the mass executions at Babi Yar in Russia. It reminded me of the horror with which I had looked at the pictures of piles of human skulls and skeletons when they were unearthed after Idi Amin's gruesome massacres in Uganda and the gruesome legacy of Pol Pot buried in the Cambodian killing fields. I slowly realized that I was recording the first evidence of mass extermination in Tibet. And although Tibetans in exile had for years talked of mass graves in Tibet, citing the evidence of those few who had managed to survive them and escape into exile in India, it had always been hard to believe.

'This is not exaggeration,' he said in response to my querying. 'These are facts. I have seen them with my own eyes. Ask anyone here, wherever you go in your journey. They will tell you the same thing in different parts of the country.'

The ex-monk got up with difficulty, smiled gently, and shuffled to the door. Already he had been with us longer than had been prudent.

The people of Batang had their own horrors to recount. But when I asked them to show me the ruins of Batang's monastery, they took me to a window and pointed across the valley to a collection of Chinese houses in the distance.

'I don't see it,' I said, looking through the zoom lens of the camera for a clearer view.

'It is no longer there,' one of them said. 'The Chinese took whatever stones or wood were useful for their own buildings, bulldozed the rest and built their houses on top. So that now, not only is there no evidence for anyone to see, but even local people cannot be reminded of what happened.'

It was nearly noon and the Boys still had not come for me. We should have left by ten to reach Lithang by nightfall. Thondup assumed that they were having difficulty finding petrol, as the Chinese issue petrol only in the places in which a vehicle was registered. There was an emergency supply available, he said, but the Chinese asked so many questions that it was not certain that you would get the petrol, even with a hefty bribe.

It was three in the afternoon before we drove out of the beautiful little town and climbed once again into the austere grandeur of the mountains. By eight we had entered a very high valley surrounded by fierce jagged peaks that rose sheer from very near the track into a stormy sky. The long oblong valley looked like a crater of a large volcano but with raw peaks rising from within it as well as on the rim. It was an empty, eerie place without a scrap of vegetation and with not a human being, yak or settlement in sight. It was very spooky and as night fell the skies opened, torrential rain lashed the valley and the black sky was illuminated by forked lightning. Thunder crashed spectacularly about our ears and reverberated alarmingly off the mountains.

It was unbelievably dramatic as lightning crackled all round the van, illuminating the ghostly outlines of the craggy landscape. But there was something very uncomfortable about the valley. The Boys felt it too and were anxious to be out of it. Tenzin took out another sacred incense stick – we had already used up quite a few – and burned it while the rest of the Boys muttered mantras.

The van's electrics started to play up and although there was no one following us – that we could see – I felt that the Boys did not want to stop the van and step into the hostile night. So we relied more on the flashes of lightning than the weak headlights to keep us from tipping into the raging stream that ran inches from the muddy track. Even in the black of the night, the stream glowed distinctly with white-caps.

By eleven it was freezing cold and we had arrived at the outskirts of Lithang. It was a typical Chinese frontier town, with the statutory concrete buildings lit with naked light bulbs, a dusty main street, no pavements and lots of green army three-tonne trucks. Lithang to Dhartsedo was Jigme's sector and he was scheduled to have arranged interviews and safe houses. When we drove into the centre and Sumpa parked outside another Chinese 'hotel' – this one even more brightly lit than the one the Boys had stopped at outside Markham – I was surprised, but even when they jumped out and disappeared I thought that they had gone to book a room and would return to take me to the safe house.

Sumpa had parked the van with the windscreen just under the bright lights and in full view of numerous Chinese passing in front of it. They looked inquisitively at the Markham number plates and peered through the windscreen. On my own again in the van, I slid lower and lower into the seat and prayed to God that Thondup and some of the others would return – soon. My anxiety reached breaking point after several Chinese rattled the van's door-handles trying to get in. After an hour and a half I was becoming desperate and wanting to go to the loo. Then Thondup came up with a plate of hot noodles!

The Boys, it transpired, had taken a room, had eaten and were settling down to several bottles of Chinese beer.

'And what am I supposed to do?' I asked. 'Where has Jigme fixed for me to stay?' After much toing and froing, we managed to prise Jigme from the warmth. Despite his earlier assurances, nothing had been arranged and he told me he would get me a room in the hotel. It was a replay of the previous night outside Markham. But this 'hotel' was alive with Chinese – and they were very much awake and walking around the open corridors under the daylight-bright lights.

'Look, just drive me to the edge of town and I will sleep in the van,' I said, reckoning my chances of not being found were better in the open. Finally, after much grumbling, they got Sumpa out and we drove round the town, only to find that all the roads out of it were barricaded and locked for the night. I had thought of going on foot and bivouacking somewhere, but I did not have a tent, nor a proper ground sheet; the freezing night and my fear of the dark – especially after all the testimony I had heard that day of man-eating dogs – won the day.

'Well, I'll sleep in the van,' I said testily, and suggested that Sumpa drove to somewhere near the hotel and parked in the shadows: they could come back for me early in the morning.

Sumpa parked off the main street in the lee of some small houses, with the van's nose pointing away from the street. He slammed the door and stormed off. I could hardly blame him. He was totally exhausted. Thondup said, 'Well, I will stay with you!' I told him not to be an idiot and that there was no point in both of us freezing to death and being uncomfortable. But he would not hear of it. 'I said I would stick by you and I will,' he said simply and got out his sleeping bag and settled down in the uncomfortable front seat.

I struggled into mine, trying to keep it off the mud on the floor, and spent most of the night slipping off the bench – which in the bumpy ride had tilted to a 45-degree angle towards the floor. When I carefully opened the door to do the necessary outside, all the dogs of the neighbourhood barked into life! Lights went on, passers-by flashed their torches through the windows of the van with strange number plates. The dogs, smelling strangers, howled all night long, making sleep totally impossible.

Dawn was grey, drizzly and cold. Lack of sleep and biting cold are an unfailing recipe for not improving one's tolerance and temper – well not mine, at any rate. There was a lot to see and many people to talk to in Lithang. The town had seen bitter fighting in 1955 between the Khampa guerrillas and the PLA. Its famous monastery, built by the 3rd Dalai Lama in 1580, had been completely razed to the ground, as had Batang's, during the Losar New Year prayer festival in 1956. Over 6,000 people had been gathered in and around the monastery when Chinese planes released their bombs directly overhead; over 4,000 monks, men, women and children were killed. In the aftermath, the survivors were thrown in jail or sent to labour camps.

I was particularly anxious to film the Lithang survivors. I was looking especially for the surviving relatives of the Governor of Lithang, who had been injured in the bombing but was alive enough to be publicly tortured to death in front of the surviving Tibetans. By all accounts, even by the standards of Chinese barbarism in Tibet, the spectacle was particularly gruesome. I was also anxious to find survivors of the families of the refugees and nomads (who were not fighters nor involved with the resistance) who were machine-gunned by the Chinese from the air. The last time I had heard of such killing was in Brazil's Amazon basin when the *rancheros* wanted to clear the virgin Amazonian rain forests of Indians (whose land it was). In order to take it over, they torched the trees, and machine-gunned and dynamited the Indians from the air.

I have an uncanny sixth sense. And that morning as the Boys shuffled up sleepily I smelt trouble. Sumpa drove slowly through some nondescript streets lined with Chinese houses, to the base of a grassy mountain and parked off the road. I was anxious to go and meet whomever had been lined up, but Jigme was distinctly reticent. 'It's too dangerous,' he said. 'Too many spies.' My mind flipped back to the identical excuses of Chuma, our first interpreter, in Lanchow, Chengdu and Lhasa.

I ground my teeth and told him in rather graphic terms that it was his job to have arranged interviews for me despite the dangers. Suspicious, I probed further, and Jigme lost his temper spectacularly and stormed out of the van. He had arranged nothing. No safe houses, no interviews.

'Well,' I said, turning to Thondup, 'I'd better go and have a look.'

'But the lama has gone to Lhasa,' Jigme said, who had returned, a shade too quickly.

'Well, never mind. Let's go anyway and see what we can find,' I said, calling his bluff.

Thondup came with us as we walked up the slope to the ruined monastery past pilgrims who were already circumambulating round a stupa at the base of the monastery. Piles of rubble were still scattered all over the mountainside. Some sort of repair work was going on, and a small modest temple had been rebuilt at the top where the old monastery had been flattened. We climbed into the deserted courtyard and entered the main building at the far end. Jigme was rigid with nerves and kept peering into the shadows of the empty main hall which, like all Tibetan monasteries, had high ceilings. The shafts of light that did penetrate the gloom showed that the *thankas* were bright with new paint.

We followed Jigme along a corridor. He knocked softly on a door. A wizened old man opened it, quickly ushered us in, glanced hastily down the dark corridor, then shut the door with a wooden bolt. The lama had obviously *not* gone to Lhasa. Was Jigme lying, was he petrified or was he just plain lazy? At that moment I did not have time to find out.

Huddled in a dark recess, the three of them talked in tense whispers while all the time looking round the room. Eventually Thondup said to me in an even quieter, barely audible tone: 'It's no use. He is too frightened. He says he will meet you in Lhasa.'

While they were making arrangements where to meet, I walked over to the window and looked into the wide green valley. I made a mental note to take some wide shots from the monastery so that when I interviewed the monk I could put his voice over the scene and hopefully, with some cutaways of the damaged monastery, evoke the scene of the carnage that day of Losar thirty-two years ago.

As we were about to leave, there was a rustling in the shadows in the far corner of the room and a man emerged, rubbing the sleep out of his eyes. Speechless with fear, I pulled Thondup away and we ran down the corridor. I did not want to find out any more. Maybe it was innocent, but all I wanted to do was to put some distance between me and that shadowy room.

By the time we had got to the bottom of the hill I had myself under control and knew that I had to find the courage to return and film exteriors of the monastery. Without a single visual it would be virtually impossible to make a sequence out of the Lithang testimony. I had started to get the tripod and camera out when Tenzin through Thondup told me that it was too dangerous to film and to get back into the van.

For the umpteenth time I explained and argued that I had come to Tibet to film and that I needed the evidence. Maybe they had slept badly, maybe they were hungover or just plain fed up with my incessant filming, but Jigme lost his temper and told me through Thondup that if I insisted on filming they would return to Lhasa without me.

'Go then!' I stormed. 'I am going to do what I came for – film the monastery!' I picked up the tripod, but realizing that if there really were spies about it was probably very dangerous, I must take the risk alone. I suggested to Thondup that he stay with the Boys, as there was no virtue in both of us being arrested.

'When I came on this trip,' Thondup said, 'I promised that I would look after you and go wherever you went. Even to prison. I am not going to break that promise now. So I will come with you.' There was such obvious sincerity in his statement, which at any other time and with anyone else would have been purely histrionic, that I just swallowed and started walking back up to the monastery.

I left Thondup half-way up on a flimsy pretext, went on alone and filmed. When I returned and we walked down the hill to where we had left the van, it had gone! In panic, we looked everywhere on that mountain. Eventually, to see whether they had gone to the eastern exit of the town to wait for us, I pulled my scarf over my hat to hide most of my face and shoved the camera up inside my jacket. Looking once again the picture of fecundity, I deliberately looked down at my filthy shoes, as together we walked as quickly as we dared down the main street of Lithang, which was full of Chinese.

When we got to the other end of town, we walked round the checkpoint talking earnestly. Or rather Thondup talked in Tibetan to the thin air over my head – English might just have been understood by someone and would have instantly drawn attention to us. When we were a quarter of a mile on the other side of the barrier we sat down in the road and had to come to the conclusion that the Boys had kept their word and dumped us. It was only when we thought of making other plans – like trying to see if there was a truck going back to Batang – that I discovered that in my *grande geste* of stalking off I had left behind in the van all the exposed taped interviews, my stills film, my money and my air-tickets. Previously I had kept most of the money in a money-belt next to my skin, but since the flea bites I had hidden it in the bottom of the camera-bag. I had only one fifty-dollar bill and 300 Rmb on me. And I had broken the cardinal rule of television filming – never get separated from your rushes.

That moment, without money, passport, credit cards and, most important of all, my tape and stills rushes, was undoubtedly the worst of my career. I was stuck in the middle of Tibet without a programme at all. In that instant I saw three years' work go down the drain and with it the hopes of all those brave Tibetans who had trusted me enough to tell me their story and have me take it out of Tibet. I had no idea where my rushes were; and even if somehow we managed to get through all the checkpoints (most unlikely) to Lhasa, I had no idea where to find Tenzin and the Boys.

18

Pillage in the Mountains

My despair and self-recrimination were excruciating. Even if I had been able to telephone Channel 4, how could I ever explain that I was stranded without money and passport in the middle of Tibet *and* had lost my rushes? Thondup and I sat despondently by the side of the road and scanned the horizon. There was no sign of life in the wide valley for thirty miles. The immense treeless valley sloped gently away to the rim of mountains on the horizon. And in the centre of the empty valley was Lithang, huddled, grey and small and totally vulnerable as it must have been when the Chinese planes swooped in from the east and bombed it. There was not a tree or bush or even an ant-hill of cover. Nowhere to hide. Nothing moved, only the small river that meandered in lazy curves down the centre of the valley bubbled lethargically. It was a grey freezing day with a low cloud ceiling and the wind had a sharp edge. We sat dejectedly on the cold ground, travellers of no fixed abode, with nowhere to go. Samuel Beckett would have extracted a masterpiece from the dilemma. Numb with cold, all I could think of was that we had to get out of Lithang.

'Well, it's no use sitting here. We'll only die of hypothermia,' I said to Thondup, and got up. 'Let's go and look once more.' The logistics were not encouraging. We were exactly half-way between Chamdo and Chengdu and on the longitude of Laos, hundreds of miles to the south beyond Yunnan. Whichever direction we tried to go there were several hundred miles of rough terrain and we would never get through the first checkpoint without papers.

As we braved the main street again and walked in the direction of the monastery, we decided that the only feasible thing to do was somehow to try and return to Batang where at least we knew our contacts could help us. Here in Lithang we knew nobody and there seemed to be a far heavier concentration of Chinese. The Rmb that I had on me in my money-belt should pay for two standing places in an open lorry going to Batang. The thought of returning to Lhasa in one of those, with all the cold and dust that that entailed – for ten days – was too terrifying even to contemplate . . .

On the outskirts a few little shops opened on to the street selling basic commodities such as bottles of Chinese beer, packets of dry biscuits and plastic sandals. Further into the town we walked past the administrative centre and several two- and three-storeyed utilitarian buildings that looked cold and unwelcome. There was not a spark of colour in the whole drab scene. Even the three small trees in the main street looked grey. We must have made a strange sight. Tall Thondup in green army-surplus clothes with a green Mao cap on his head, a rucksack (containing the tripod) on his back, and a strange small creature in baggy green clothes, wearing a battered hat secured by a scraggy scarf and tightly clutching a plastic-wrapped parcel. The weight of my stupidity in losing my temper crushed me into the ground and it seemed an effort to put one foot in front of the other.

By 1.30 P.M., frozen, hungry and nearly suicidal, I persuaded Thondup to walk back once again to where we had last seen the van. 'Never take no for an answer,' David Plowright had told me when I joined Granada TV's *World in Action* current affairs series as a junior researcher a lifetime ago. 'If you do, you are not worth employing,' he had insisted. The advice has remained with me all my career. I have often stubbornly pursued a story when all the pack has given up and gone home. It is not the easiest, or most comfortable path to follow, and often it is a lonely one, but it has always paid dividends. That bleak afternoon in Lithang I followed it blindly – on autopilot – and went on walking and searching for the infernal van and my precious rushes. In reality I had no other option.

Since there was no pavement or bench, no local café nor even some stones to sit on, we had to keep moving as we were getting suspicious looks and I feared that if we stopped, someone from the PSB would ask what we were doing walking up and down the streets of Lithang. As we dragged ourselves up the steep hill towards the monastery and came round the corner of the white chorten at the foot of the final slope, I looked up from picking a foothold through the rocks and rubble, and shrieked – for there, in exactly the same place that we had left it, was the van! For a moment I was uncertain whether it was a mirage or whether the past five and a half hours had been a waking nightmare. Thondup and I grinned and hugged each other in relief.

It was hardly a time for recriminations. I was just so relieved that I was silent until we had cleared the rim of the encircling mountains an hour later. Tenzin later told me that they had indeed turned back along the road to Lhasa, but when they had cooled down, he had persuaded them to return for us. Perhaps it was superstitious, but I lit an incense stick in thanksgiving and promised St Jude of the Impossible that I would go to Mass every day for a week when I got back. As we drove out of the valley I put my money and papers back into the money-belt, despite the considerable discomfort as the thick wedge constantly rubbed on my flea bites, which were still raw with scratching. I reorganized the smallest bag to contain both tape and stills stock and from then on, wherever I went – even to the loo – the bag went with me.

It was clear that we would not reach Minyak before dark. As we drove down and eastwards from the last range of mountains, it got warmer and from there to Dhartsedo I was overwhelmed by the sheer scale of the deforestation. Somehow when we had earlier driven from Chamdo through Markham to Lithang, and although I knew that once there had been forests in the area, there was then no visual evidence of tree stumps. The Boys told me that the Chinese road gangs in the area (and I presume some of the locals) had removed, over the years, even the remaining fragments of wood from the visible stumps for their own use, so that the area was devoid of any sign of previous forests.

Once below the tree-line, I saw for mile after mile, in fact day after day, whole mountainsides scarred with the stumps of felled trees. Occasionally a few pines had been left standing, which only highlighted the enormity of the devastation. As we passed one small thick clump of dark-green pine trees, the Boys told me that once the whole of eastern Kham had been covered with thick forests. The further east we travelled the more devastating the scale of deforestation became and the greater became the number of trucks fully loaded with large logs. The trucks were all heading east to China and most had Sichuanese number plates.

While the Boys brewed up some tea, I sat on the side of the road surrounded by spectacular wild purple orchids, the sort that you find in inexpensive basketfuls in Malaysia, Singapore and Bangkok – and which in London cost a small fortune for one single spike of velvety flowers.

It was warm and sunny with scarcely a breath of wind in the Tibetan-blue sky. In between the harsh noise of lorry engines straining under the weight of the logs and the steep gradient, came the burble of small mountain streams bubbling up crystal clear from the undergrowth and trickling down the mountainside. Confronted by the scandalous evidence of the destruction of what had been the extensive forests of Tibet, I was graphically reminded of the staggering statistics that had taken me months of research to track down.

The major forest areas of Tibet in Kyriong, Dram, Pema Koe, Kongpo Nyitri, Metok, Po, Zayul and Monyul (in central and southern Tibet) and Chamdo, Drayab, Zogang and Markham (in eastern Tibet) together constitute China's third largest forest reserve. If Derong, Mili, Minyak, Tawu, Drakgo, Nyarong, Lithang, Gyalthang, Karze and Ngapa, which have been annexed or incorporated into the contiguous Chinese provinces of Qinghai, Sichuan and Yunnan are included, the total would constitute the largest forested land-mass in China.

Although the Chinese Government denies the rape of Tibet's natural resources, Tibetan researchers showed me Chinese documents, press reports and transcripts of radio broadcasts proving the extensive acreage of Tibetan forests and their potential worth. For example, a confidential Chinese document called *Xizang xing she he ren wu jiao cai*, which was issued by the Chinese Tibet Military Command on 10 October 1960 for the political education of the cadres, included details of the forests of Powo Tamo, in eastern Tibet and stated that they covered an area of more than 4,200 square kilometres.

The area had three distinct forest belts and each was felled by a separate work force. They were known as the Powo Tamo Timber Belt, Lunang Timber Belt and the People's Liberation Army Lunang Timber Belt. In the vicinity of the forests stood the notorious monastery prison of Powo Tamo that the monk from Chamdo had spoken of earlier. What the reports state, and what the ex-monk confirmed, was that the prison used over 1,000 prisoners in a forced labour programme to fell the trees. It is estimated that in the two decades from 1959 to 1979 two million cubic metres of timber were felled and transported to China from the Powo Tamo Timber Belt and a further three million cubic metres from the Lunang Timber Belt.

The forests that the twenty-eight-year-old report spoke of were now the bleak, completely barren area that we had driven through only a few days before – now the site of the longest airfield in Tibet – and the site of a notorious prison. Looking back, I cannot recall seeing one single tree in the whole area. Researchers calculated that the contents of the area, as felled lumber, lined end to end, would stretch 111,000 million metres.

In a radio broadcast by Radio Lhasa on 25 June 1977, the Chinese claimed that the forests of Ngapa, Kharze and Mili (which were absorbed into the western Chinese province of Sichuan, and which now constitute two-thirds of that province), an area covering more than 500,300 hectares, constituted 70 per cent of the province's forestry reserve. If the area's timber was felled, it would produce well over a billion cubic metres of timber.

Similarly Gyalthang's ancient forests (a hundred miles south of where we were) constituted Yunnan province's largest reserve of timber. In an area covering over 10,000 hectares, the forests, before felling, produced an enormous diversity of sub-tropical trees. These included valuable varieties of firs, pines, Tibetan cypress and dragon spruce. The forests were also a rich source of plants, originally used in Tibet's herbal medicine, but today vital for China's herbal pharmacopoeia.

In a Chinese picture book, *Tung Then Fang Jing* (The Natural Beauty of Gyalthang), published by the Chinese Government, it is stated that between 1958 and 1986, 112 million cubic metres of timber were felled from the Dokhar district of Gyalthang. In 1987 that would have a domestic market value for China of 360 million yuan (US$ 97.56 million).

On 15 July 1983, Radio Lhasa reported that 1,100 tons of *thangchu* (gum) and another 30 tons of a thicker variety of *thangchu* were extracted between 1966 and 1976 from the gum trees in Mili in Kham. It went on to say that a Chinese timber factory in the Mili district claimed to have milled eight million cubic metres of wood, which was valued at 60 million yuan (US$ 16.22 million).

No monetary value had been put on other little-known Tibetan exports to China, such as musk, a highly prized and expensive component in perfume. In the Powo Tamo area alone it was reported that 40 tons of *bemug* and 1,500 tons of *sha-thong-ri* (very rare and costly medicinal herbs) annually went to China. In addition Tibetans report that thousands of kilograms of rare and expensive products, like *yartsa ganbu* (Cordyceps sinesis), *gangla metok* (sassurra involucrata) have been and still are taken to China every year.

On 22 August 1986, a Radio Lhasa broadcast reported that between 1965 and 1985 a total of 18 million cubic metres of timber were transported from Nyitri Gungthang and Drago to China. The same broadcast also said that 130 million square metres of forest at Chamdo provided China with 2.5 million cubic metres of timber between 1960 and 1985 at a value of 75 million yuan (US$ 20.3 million). The broadcast went on to report that 45.7 million trees were felled by a work force of 3,400 between 1955 and 1985 in Ngapa in Tibet's north-eastern province of Amdo. The Chinese put a value on this of 135 million yuan (US$ 36.5 million).

Tibetan researchers from the Research Department of the Tibetan Government-in-exile's Department of Information closely monitor events in Tibet and meticulously debrief all the Tibetan refugees who escape to India. They have collated the statistics and shown me figures to substantiate their claim that in the thirty-year period from 1957 to 1987, Tibetan timber transported to China earned China the equivalent, then, of 54 billion US dollars.

Whenever we stopped or saw a group of Tibetans, we pretended that we had had a breakdown (more often than not it was true!). Thondup would go up and chat to them to find out about their experiences under the Chinese, how they lived, what they earned, their problems, etc., in order to ascertain the quality of their lives – but also to assess the allegations we were investigating. In this way we met Rapten, a woodcutter, who had lived for forty-two years in the mountains near Mynak.

I asked him on camera why so many trees had been cut and who was cutting them.

'The Chinese have cut down all the trees, and it's not only here but all over Kham. Places like Drago, Nyaring, Tawu. They fell sometimes twenty-four hours a day and many people work at it. Now over here there are not so many people cutting because we have no trees left to fell.'

'But what happens to the trees once they are cut?' I asked.

'They put the trees on lorries and take them by road to China. Not only to Chengdu in Sichuan, but some go out via Gansu and Yunnan provinces as well. Sometimes the lorries take them to the rivers, like the Dresho, and they float down to China.'

'But how do you know they go to China?' I asked.

'Because many Tibetans, myself also, work cutting the trees for the Chinese as well, and the trucks that come for the logs have Chinese drivers and we talk to them and they tell us. In fact they complain that the roads are not good between here and Chengdu and that there are many landslides along the way, which delay them. They also tell us that some of the timber goes to places on the river where it is put in the water to float down. It is much cheaper for them to carry the logs that way because petrol is expensive and the mountains are steep and the trucks use much petrol.'

The volume of lorries carrying timber was so great that at one point we counted them. On the morning of Wednesday, 14 September, I noted in my diary that between 8.30 and 10.30 the heavily laden lorries were passing at a rate of one every three minutes. And that night, sleeping in the van on the side of the road, rest was totally impossible – for all of us – because of the noise of the timber trucks that roared past us all night long. They were all carrying mature logs, between twenty and thirty feet long and with a diameter of between two and four feet. When I asked the Boys what wood they were, they gave me Tibetan names for which Thondup could not find a translation. Eventually they pointed out spruce, other pines, oak and other hardwood, broad-leaved deciduous trees.

I was so staggered by the number of lorries that I had a field day filming and started indulging myself in practising shots. Often I started on big close-ups with the logs filling the frame and then panned right or left down to the passing countryside to show the different landscapes, so that the Chinese could not say I had filmed only in one place and that therefore it was not representative. The one factor that linked all the areas I filmed was the acres and acres of tree stumps that dotted whole mountainsides. The mute stumps were a poignant and irrefutable witness of the rape of the country-side.

When we drove through and past Mynak, the Nyakchu river was indeed laden with logs which the locals said were being floated to the saw mills down-river in China. Hidden by the van on the edge of the river embankment, I filmed the logs swirling down the river. I asked Rapten how long the felling had been going on and whether there was any replanting.

'Since 1963 the Chinese have been cutting our trees and trans-porting them to China. For the past twenty years foreigners have not been allowed to come inside Tibet, so the outside world does not know what we have been witnessing all this time. You are the first foreigner to have come here. You can see with your eyes our mountains with no trees and the logs going on lorries to China.'

'But how do I know they are going to China?' I asked once again.

'Because there is only one road – and going that way,' he pointed east, 'you can only go to China. And you ask about replanting? The Chinese do not plant any new trees at all on our mountains. The only ones I have seen are the ones they sometimes plant in the Chinese areas, round their public buildings for every-one to see. All they do is cut down our forests and take them for the benefit of the Chinese; we Tibetans get nothing from them.'

'But the Chinese have certainly built roads and I have seen hospitals and schools in Tibet; surely the money is used for this and ultimately it is for the benefit of the Tibetan people?' I argued.

'That, like everything the Chinese say, is half-truth,' he said angrily. 'Yes, they build roads. But it is for them, so that the soldiers can come to all parts of Tibet more quickly. Where I live there are no Chinese – so there are no roads for Tibetans. And as for hospitals: yes, the Chinese have built hospitals and schools – but for themselves, not for Tibetans. So what do we get out of the theft of our forests? Nothing.'

Knowing the devastating effect deforestation has had on soil erosion and the ecology in the Amazon and other parts of the world, I asked what effect it had had on the Tibetan countryside.

'The Chinese have not planted one single tree,' Rapten repeated.

'But what about other areas?' I asked. I could vouch for the evidence I had seen with my own eyes and recorded on tape, but there were vast areas of Tibet that it would be physically impossible for me to visit on this trip.

He replied: 'I am a petty trader and travel from Lake Kokonor in the north to beyond Gyaltsen in the south and go beyond Chamdo to Lhasa. It is the same. There are no forests. The mountains are bare and the soil now holds nothing. Nothing grows. If you do not believe me, I will take you to these places – or go and see for yourself that I am telling the truth.

'Because the Chinese do not plant other trees to replace the ones they cut down, the soil has degenerated and becomes like this,' and he scooped up a handful of dry powdery earth. Although I did not understand what he was saying at the time, I saw him bend to pick up the dust and fortunately managed to follow his movement with the camera; otherwise he would have disappeared out of frame and I would have lost the poignancy of the earth slipping dramatically, like quicksand, through his fingers.

I could not help but think that while the chopping down and burning of the Amazonian rain forests had exacerbated the greenhouse effect and alerted environmentalists all over the world to the impending catastrophe, here in Tibet, hidden behind impenetrable Chinese barriers, time was running out for Tibet's forests and fragile ecology and also, by extension, for the world.

'Before, when we had forests, the trees would hold the water in the soil and the leaves would fall making nourishment for the soil and then plenty of grass would grow and the wild animals could live on the grass. Now the grass will not grow on this soil, it is sterile and the animals suffer. All the wild animals used to live very close to human settlements before. Now they are nowhere to be seen. Many have died, many have been killed and many have run away.'

Lhasang Tsering, the President of the radical Tibetan Youth Congress-in-exile who has himself travelled clandestinely all over Tibet, recently confirmed the extent of the damage:

'China's unhindered exploitation of Tibet's forestry reserves has threatened Tibet's fragile ecology. Wildlife has disappeared, and eminent naturalists, like George Shallar, have pointed out that wildlife in Tibet is threatened with total extinction. The black-necked crane, one of the rarest species in the world, is scarcely seen now. There were once bears, snow leopards, wolves, wild geese and duck, ospreys, great herds of Tibetan blue sheep, wild yak, deer and gazelles; now they are virtually extinct. And the few panda that remain – apart from those inside zoos and special "reserves" – are rarely found inside Tibet (in the part that is annexed to western Sichuan) because the Chinese have cut down most of their own forests.

'Recently, in the last few years, there has been unprecedented, wide-scale flooding that has affected not only Tibet, but also China, where the rivers that rise in Tibet flow. There has also been terrible flooding in Burma, parts of India and Bangladesh. Ecological and conservation organizations mobilize world attention and concern about the destruction of the Amazon forests. International financiers, the World Bank, all sorts of important people try and work out ways to stop the destruction. They try and offer monetary incentives and write-off schemes to Third World countries with enormous debts, like Brazil, and even offer financial incentives to the multi-nationals involved in the area to change their ways, to stop devastating the forests, to replant and save the globe.

'But what about Tibet? What are they doing for our forests? Remember, most of them have now been destroyed by the Chinese and not only has the world done *nothing* – no sanctions, no proposals – absolutely nothing about it, but most of the world does not even know. Remember all the major rivers of Asia rise in Tibet, so what happens here – whether it is the contamination of our rivers by nuclear dumping, or flooding because the ground has no more trees to hold the soil – what happens to the ecology and rivers of Tibet affects not only 6 million Tibetan lives but the fate of millions and millions of people in the rest of South-East Asia.'

We were running so badly behind schedule that we did not have time to stop and look for one of the most notorious prisons in Kham, at Rama Kha, just outside Mynak. The area had been the scene of heavy fighting against the Chinese in 1956 and in the two years from 1961 to 1962, 1,800 Tibetan prisoners were reported to have died in the prison. We hurried through the colourless little town set on the fast-flowing Nyakchu. It seemed to be entirely peopled with men and women in blue or green Mao suits. We saw no Tibetan-style houses, no people in Tibetan *chubas*, no one with long Tibetan-style hair, no monasteries or shrines, no chortens and not even the flutter of a single prayer-flag.

After driving down through Alpine scenery and taking 'holiday snaps' of the Boys picnicking by tumbling mountain streams, we arrived at Dhartsedo at four in the afternoon.

Historically one of the frontier towns between China and Tibet, Dhartsedo saw many battles, first between the remnants of the Kuomintang forces and the Communist Chinese, and then after February 1950 when it was the entry point for the Chinese 18th army unit of the South-West Military Region, led by General Chang Kuo-hua. Dhartsedo saw fierce fighting between the Tibetans and the Communists. After it was over-run by the Chinese it was quickly incorporated into China's Sichuan province and comes under the Kanze Prefecture.

Dhartsedo is set in a pleasant valley with green mountainsides sweeping down to the small Chinese-looking houses, which are strewn along the valley floor mainly on the west side of the little river. We stopped on the road high above a complex of official-looking three- and four-storeyed buildings arranged round a large courtyard. Through the view-finder I noticed that one of the buildings had three stars on the façade and several flags flying. After I had finished filming it and had panned along the green valley to take in the town strung along the winding river, Jigme told me that it was an army headquarters. I nearly fell off the edge in agitation because I was sure that on the skyline I must have been clearly visible from the buildings.

The largest monastery, Shabten, which had housed over 2,000 monks, had been destroyed in 1955–6 and the monks tortured and imprisoned. Fighting in the region had been intense and Dhartsedo's prisons, Tawu Lungtrang, Miyak Ragha, Rongmi, Drago and Chak-sam-kha, were filled with Tibetans who had resisted the Chinese occupation. Conditions were so bad that the hundreds of prisoners who died were the lucky ones, a Tibetan survivor told me, for many of the rest had to resort to cannibalism.

Tsewang Norbu, abbot at the nearby monastery, was one of the survivors. He was released in 1979. In his testimony he said:

'In the beginning there was an enormous number of prisoners – nearly 20,000. Tibetans in Tawu Lungtrang prison/labour camps complex were mostly used by the Chinese as forced labour for their massive roadbuilding projects and by 1978–9 under 2,000 were left. The way they died was very sad. Some died of torture, but most died of starvation. Every day fifteen to twenty people died in the prison. The corpses were thrown into a truck to be either buried in a mass grave or burnt for fertilizer.'

'What do you mean?' I asked, thinking of the way the bones of Jewish corpses had been made into soap in the Nazi extermination camps.

'They were burnt and then the Chinese put the ashes on the soil to make the crops grow better,' he said simply, unaware of the experiences of the Jews in the Holocaust.

'Some of the prisoners who could not stand the pains of hunger any more used to go up to the corpses and try and eat one when the guards were having tea inside. Sometimes if it was late and they knew that the guards and driver would be inside for a long time, they would try and eat them there and then. Usually they were so weak that their teeth could not cut the flesh, but occasionally they managed to tear off a limb and take it with them to eat later.'

Another man, Pema Rongbok, was also in the prison and confirmed the story.

It was getting late and I knew I would not have the time to look for and find the site of another mass grave at Ramagang, where Ade, a chieftain's daughter who had spent sixteen years in prison, had seen Tibetans 'thrown in head to toe – so as to have more room. They made us prisoners dig the graves, especially freshly arrived prisoners. They had more strength.' She had been to numerous prisons and seen many such graves, for example at Chashen Tha in China proper, where they also took Tibetan prisoners to work as forced labour in the lead mines. She had spent two periods in prison in Dhartsedo, one at the Nga-Choe monastery in 1959 and then again in 1964–6.

She talked with enormous dignity of how she and many other Tibetan women prisoners in Dhartsedo were repeatedly raped all through the summer of 1960. She told me that there were nearly 300 women in the prison at the time and gave me some of the names of those who had been raped: women who had shared her cell – Dolka, Namtso Wnagmo, Yanhchen. She told me that to this day she can still see the face of the man who repeatedly raped her, the Chinese head-jailer – Tang Tutang. She also told me that the Chinese made the women take medicine afterwards. I asked her what and why. She shrugged and said she did not know; they had no choice, but many of the women thought it was to induce abortions should any of them have become pregnant.

Being raped was particularly traumatic for her as when she had gone into prison her two children, a one-year-old and a three-year-old, followed her to the same prison. One day the Chinese guards, for no apparent reason – perhaps they were irritated by the sound of crying – just kicked the baby to death. The elder child became mentally deranged and also died later in prison. It was difficult to listen to her as she continued to tell me about more mass graves at Chashen Tha and so many other locations: the details, all delivered with the flat monotone of someone who has survived a living hell, were overwhelming.

I heard so many blood-chilling stories on that trip to Tibet. I should have filmed all the testimonies for evidence so that one day the perpetrators can be brought to justice, as some of the Nazis were in the Nuremberg trials. But more importantly, they should be recorded as a testimony of man's inhumanity to man. However, time was running out fast and I had to be brutal in my selection so that we could press on. Each day we were delayed brought the possibility that the interviewees in Amdo would leave their locations. It also brought me closer to the expiry date on my visa and diminished my chances of getting the film out safely.

A few miles down the road and out of sight of the army buildings, I was scanning the valley floor through the view-finder for some interesting detail on which to start the shot so that I could zoom out and give the viewer some idea of the scale of the buildings in relation to the whole valley and mountain complex, when I saw a saw mill and some three-tonne trucks unloading huge logs in the yard. When I asked Jigme about the mill and what was the best place to film it from (a top shot can be a bit boring on its own – it is visually more interesting when intercut with some ground-level shots), he told me he had no idea!

We drove down next to the mill and Sumpa reversed. Sitting

on the window-seat, I pulled back the curtains as much as I dared and filmed, again with shaking hands.

The tall iron gate was open and in the background the yard was piled high with a vast amount of cut timber. It certainly could not be said to have come from local trees, for although the valley was green with grass and a few bushy shrubs, there was scarcely a tree in sight. Just as I had fixed on a close-up of planks of timber filling the frame and was about to zoom out to a wide shot of the whole yard, including the gate and the high wall surrounding it, which would have cut beautifully with the top shot I had filmed from the road above, a man in a Chinese blue Mao suit came up to the gates and stared straight into the camera lens (maybe he was short-sighted and did not see me filming!), without seeming to take his eyes off the van.

Through the eye-piece I was totally absorbed in the image I was recording. Part of my mind told me that I was in danger. It reminded me of the cameraman who was shot and killed in El Salvador by one of the gunmen he was filming. Although the cameraman saw his 'executioner' pick up a gun and aim it at him, he went on filming until the bullet slammed home and bled his life into the sand. The Chinese man staring back at me through the lens activated every fibre in my body to run. But another part of my mind was totally mesmerized by every move the man in blue made. It was the cobra syndrome again: instead of running from a dangerous situation, I often find myself transfixed to the spot, not by fear, but by an overwhelming curiosity about the object of my terror. It is only afterwards when I am safe that I begin to shake with retrospective fear and curse myself for being every idiot under the sun. The total absorption of filming a potentially dangerous situation – almost in slow motion – was with me again that evening. The man proceeded to shut the gate and began to shout something to someone at the back.

'For God's sake, stop filming! He's looking! We'll all be arrested!' Thondup yelled, which was most unlike him. Sumpa threw the van – the engine was still running, for we invariably had dramas to start the wretched thing – into gear and roared down the street at such a rate that I nearly catapulted through the windscreen.

When we had left the sawmill behind, the Boys decided they

were hungry and drove into the centre of the town, parked on the main street and disappeared. Remembering that an army fights better on a full stomach, I smiled, made a sick joke about bringing me back a sandwich, and sat back to watch the world go by.

On the other side of the river, which was enclosed by concrete balustrades, I saw some run-down timber houses which, though dilapidated, had great character. They looked entirely different from the uniform concrete monstrosities that deface all of China's cities. They were the last semblance of anything Tibetan I was to see for quite some time. The town was crowded with anonymous-looking people hurrying past in the inevitable Mao suits. I so wanted to get out and explore, to talk to people who had lived through Tibet's recent turbulent history in that town. But the shadows were lengthening in the valley and once out of the sun it began to get cool.

Thondup, thoughtful as ever, came back smiling and offered me some *momos* wrapped in grubby newsprint. I forced myself to accept, quickly rationalizing that it could be no more insanitary than eating fish and chips wrapped in *The Times* back in London. And that, anyway, Chengdu and antibiotics were only a day or so away.

Until dusk we raced the river, as it leapt white with fury over big smooth boulders, along the valley floor and then climbed up over another pass to Luding. As we drove along the top of the ridge almost bumper to bumper with Chinese lorries carrying enormous logs, the sun was dying in a great fireball over the furthest western peaks. I remembered what a Tibetan friend, who came from Dhartsedo, had said to me: 'Through the passes where once the trucks brought the armies of China to invade Tibet, today lorries pass the other way carrying to China our forests and our minerals: our patrimony.'

After spending the night in Luding, the site of one of Mao's epic battles during the Long March, I thought that it would take only another day of hard driving to reach Chengdu. But I had reckoned without the landslides. On the tortuous drive up the last range of high mountains, where the peaks finally tumble steeply down into the plains of Sichuan, we got stuck in a horrendous lorry-jam. There were seventy-two three-tonne trucks, all heavily loaded with huge tree trunks, and we were all braked on one of the steepest parts of the mountain, on a 55-degree slope. We were stuck there without food or water or any distractions – or amenities – for six hours.

By the time the landslip was cleared, and we started moving over the crest, it was gone seven. The eastern face of the mountain was dangerous with slippery mud and parts of the road down had been washed away by streams and more landslides. But it was negotiable, so I suggested we press on and get off the mountain by nightfall. All it needed was for one of the lorries to burn out its brakes and the whole convoy would make the most monumental avant-garde sculpture at the bottom of the ravine. Despite the presence of the roaring lorries, all of whose drivers were equally anxious to get off the mountain, it was in fact a very pleasant drive. The hillsides were thickly wooded, which caused Tenzin, who had by now changed out of his *chuba* and into Chinese clothes, to remark cynically, 'They keep the trees on their side I see!' He did have a point, for the stark difference between the bald mountain on the Tibetan side and the lush vegetation on the Chinese side was quite remarkable.

By midnight we were on the plain and experiencing the unaccustomed luxury of tarmac roads. We were all exhausted, especially Sumpa. At four in the morning of Thursday, 15 September, we drove into the deserted courtyard of the Jinjiang Hotel in Chengdu. I was not sorry to find that it was full, since it was such an awful hotel, and we drove across the road to the newly opened Minshan Hotel, a towering modern block of steel and glass.

It was the most extraordinary sensation to shuffle across the impeccable pale marble floor of the lobby in my dirty Chinese shoes that by now had lost their squeak under weeks of mud. I was dazzled by the bright sparkle of the chandelier (no 40-watt naked bulb here!). In my filthy clothes and dragging even filthier bags across the immaculate floor, I felt that at any moment I would either be thrown out as an insane vagrant, or that I might just break into the 'Skaters' Waltz' and slide around, with giggling abandon, the length and breadth of the enormous and empty hall that stretched the whole length of the façade.

I suggested that Thondup met me for lunch at noon and gave him money for the Boys. The bellhop took me up to a room on the eleventh floor, from where I had a panoramic view of the sleeping city. Outside the plate-glass window it was dark and the sombre pine trees, lit by the elegant round globes of the wrought-iron street-lamps, stood as stiffly to attention as I remembered them.

The room was quiet and as well furnished – with twin beds, crisp white cotton sheets, two upholstered chairs and wall-to-wall carpeting – as any five-star hotel should be. I started to shed my appallingly filthy clothes and ran a bath, but when I turned to the mirror over the vanity unit, I clutched the basin in horror.

19

Dramas in Chengdu and Tashikil

I had heard of other people who had experienced it, but I never thought that it would happen to me. The face in the mirror was deeply etched with grime and fatigue. The brown eyes were bright with fever and sunk into their sockets. They had a disturbing, hunted look and were encircled with dark smudges that ran from the bridge of the nose to the temporal bone. The hair, matted with dust, hung limply to the shoulders. The skin round the jowls and on the body hung in limp folds, as on a famine victim. But what was most disturbing was that all the teeth had gone brown!

Shaking, I sat on the edge of the bath, trying to come to terms with what I now looked like. I simply did not recognize the haggard face that looked at me in the mirror. I had not seen myself in a mirror since I had lost the bag and had no means to prepare myself for the shock. I had (I later found out) lost seventeen pounds in weight and my dentist told me that with the tension I had bitten off all the enamel on my teeth and the underlying dentine had got stained with coffee. It was little wonder that I suffered from such excruciating headaches.

I am not a vain creature. I find it obscene to spend much time and money on expensive unguents to hold back – or erase – the ravages of time. If people cannot accept me with the map of the Orinoco spread on my face that is their problem, not mine. I am always appropriately dressed for the job – from jungle fatigues to long frock and tiara if necessary – but I am most comfortable in jeans, T-shirt and flip-flops. In fact, when acting as my own on-screen reporter, cameramen often have to tell me to go and pull a comb through my hair and put on some lipstick. But what I saw in the mirror was so repulsive that I burst into tears and sat in the bath howling my eyes out.

I slipped the rushes behind a loose panel in the bathroom ceiling and, clean at last after a lot of scrubbing, I slipped between the wonderfully crisp clean sheets, sank my head into the soft pillow and shut my eyes. To my absolute fury I could not sleep. It was impossible to settle down in a comfortable bed. Cursing the perversity of my body, I counted yak, pretended that I was back in that murderously uncomfortable van, tried every known relaxation technique and finally, just after six, drifted off to sleep.

Coffee arrived (room service yet!) at 8.30. I sipped it and looked out across the road to the Jinjiang Hotel, the scene of my abject misery when Chuma, our first interpreter, had done a bunk on us. I knew that I was far from safe and the thought of taking the rushes out to Hong Kong was very tempting indeed. If for nothing more than to feel safe for a few hours.

I could *try* and get a flight out of Chengdu, but the thought of battling with CITS again made me weak with despair. If by some miracle it could all be arranged with my sanity still intact, and if it did not take more than a month to arrange, I could then ship the rushes from Hong Kong to London and return to Chengdu and continue with the Boys. But if the Chinese authorities were on to me, I was a sitting duck at the airport. Remembering also all the visa troubles I had experienced when I went out of Lhasa the last time, I did not want to risk it. I decided that I would go on: I still had the option of walking out of Tibet by the Black Route, which at least gave me a reasonable chance, with the help of the Boys and the network near the border, of evading the Chinese patrols. I also still had all the visuals to get of farming, hospitals, schools and all the mines of Amdo to complete the programme.

The room-service maids must have thought I was totally mad. I sent *everything* to the laundry: sleeping bag, sheet, socks, thermals – the lot. Even the bags themselves. The thought of really clean clothes again was a mirage too devoutly fantasized over to be abandoned with thoughts of cost and budget! My only pair of trousers, now held up with a hotel safety-pin, and T-shirt were still damp from my endeavours a few hours before. It was most odd to have my hair loose after weeks under the ski-mask and I tied it back with my trousers' string. I sat down calmly on a proper chair, indulged in more coffee and planned the day as the swarms of cyclists were flooding Chengdu's streets on their way to work.

The first thing was to get medication for my long-suffering gut. With time running short – I did not have the energy to wade through the bureaucracy at the hospital: I planned to go to the American Consul's office across the way in the Jinjiang Hotel as I felt sure that they would have an up-market first aid kit with everything but the operating table in it! Then I had to let David Lloyd and Channel 4 know I was alive, and somehow tell David that I had got the basis of a good show. Phoning was out of the question. So I decided to telex.

As Channel 4's telex answer back would give away the fact that I was telexing a television company, I decided to telex Chris, the film editor, at home and he would pass it on to David wherever he was. Deciding on a code that was innocent but obfuscating enough for the Chinese, yet was not totally indecipherable for David, was something else. Eventually I decided on a somewhat cryptic message, hopefully in keeping with my tourist cover: 'Had a wonderful holiday! Got delayed, but got super syncpix as was promised by tour operator. Going on with original tour operator's holiday schedule and hope to get more lovely gvpix. Am dying to show you the pix. Feel they will fill up a whole album. Love, Vanya.'

David should have deciphered 'syncpix' to be 'synch' footage of interviewees, as per our original discussion (hence the tour operator to indicate the original proposal) and the gvpix should tell David that I still had all my visuals (gv = general views) to shoot and would proceed as planned. The 'album' reference was to assure David that I had enough material for an edition of *Dispatches*, the series that the film was going into and of which he was the editor, so that he could rest assured that he had a return for his money. David, as ex-editor of BBC TV's *Panorama* and *Newsnight*, was well versed in his reporters and producers sending cryptic messages from places they were not supposed to be in. And at least Channel 4 would know I was alive and had not exactly been sunbathing for the past two and a half weeks!

I felt rather good, almost light-headed. It was exhilarating not to have to wear those awful clothes and above all not to be surrounded twenty-four hours a day with people. To sleep on my own and not hear the Boys snore or grunt (enchanting as they were) was pure bliss. But a niggling voice in my head kept warning me that I still had to travel half-way round Tibet again and get the film out.

It was just too dangerous to leave the film in the hotel. I have never forgotten the experience of a colleague who had been filming surreptitiously in Ethiopia and had left his film hidden in his hotel room while he was out doing more filming. Nothing appeared disturbed when he got back, but when he returned to London and the film was processed, it came out blank. The Ethiopian authorities must have entered his room while he was out, passed a mobile X-ray over all the exposed film and wiped both picture and sound, leaving everything blank. It was so much neater than going to the bother of arresting a foreigner and the ensuing diplomatic row. I never forgot that lesson, nor the one I learnt in Lithang when I left the rushes in the van. The rushes went everywhere with me.

With the telex sent, I went to the US Consulate. It did indeed have some tetracycline. I gave myself a hefty dose, took the rest of the bottle and asked about renewing visas. The news was not good. As the anniversary of the Lhasa riots was approaching on 27 September, the security people in Tibet were not extending or renewing foreigners' visas in Lhasa. The Consulate suggested that I try in Chengdu.

So having bought a fresh T-shirt and some trousers, I found myself outside the PSB bureau in a leafy, sunlit avenue in downtown Chengdu. It was warm and I would much rather have been anywhere else in the world doing anything but quaking in front of the Chinese Internal Security HQ in Chengdu, with my highly seditious rushes on me! It took every last shred of my tattered nerves to walk through the high iron gates, smile angelically at the clerk and ask for my visa to be renewed. Please. I filled in the form and it was taken away with my passport. After half an hour, during which I again sweated pure terror, a PSB officer came in. I feared the worst until he smiled – and asked me in perfect English whether I realized that I was illegally in the country?

I was flabbergasted. 'What do you mean, illegally? I have a visa, and it does not run out until the 27th, a month from when I arrived.'

The officer was unbelievably nice, which made me doubly suspicious. 'But the visa is valid from the date it was issued, not from the date of entry,' he said patiently.

Needless to say no one had told me, and certainly not the

Chinese when issuing it. I assumed that, as in every other country I have ever travelled to, the visa's validity ran from the day of entry. But no, old Tibet hands told me later, China was different. The officer, seeing I was genuinely perplexed, tried to be helpful – and the fact that someone was being so nice to me made me, for some unknown reason – and perhaps in hindsight, fortunately – burst into floods of tears.

The officer was most comforting and suggested that I wrote a confession! The thought of confessions enforced after *thamzings* sent another wave of hysteria through me until the officer gave me pen and paper and suggested the words which were nothing more terrible than the truth which was that I didn't know the visa was valid from the date of issue. I would of course have been prepared to write anything to get myself and my rushes out of that stuffy office in the PSB compound. The officer then disappeared for another agonizing ten minutes during which every disaster scenario possible ran in vivid Technicolor through my head. But he returned smiling and handed me my passport.

'Your visa is valid till 4 October,' he said.

'But isn't it a month's visa?' It was again all in Chinese and therefore indecipherable to me. 'And isn't today the 16th?'

'We can only issue it from the date it expired,' he said, with the inflexible logic that is so infuriatingly Chinese.

'But . . .'

'You have to leave by the 4th,' he said firmly, but politely. 'A tourist visa can only now be extended once. And if you don't leave on the 4th, unfortunately we will regretfully have no option but to arrest you!'

I paid the fee and fled as sedately as I could. Maybe the gods were still on my side after all. How fortunate that I had discovered the visa problem in Chengdu and not at Lhasa airport, where the passport men were not at all as accommodating.

Thondup and Tenzin were waiting for me back at the hotel. Tenzin, a most debonair gentleman, was now in Westernized clothes and was as calm as though he had frequented the lobbies of five-star hotels all his life. So much for the hysteria of the first interpreter when he had said, 'It is too dangerous' to meet publicly and all those histrionic meetings in the park and in dark alleys. What had that been about, I wondered, when Tenzin actually came into the hotel with me, and even had a coffee in my room? Was it, as Seán said, sabotage?

I took Thondup and Tenzin to lunch in the small restaurant across the bridge by the river, where Seán and I had sat and fumed so many meals away. The food, though good, was just too much. My stomach had shrunk and the combination of the heavy dose of antibiotics and the Chengdu smog made me feel decidedly unwell. So I forwent, knowing I would regret it later in the trip, the delicious Sichuanese chicken and cashew-nuts in chilli sauce, bamboo shoots and prawns in hot and sour sauce and the excellent ice-cold beer. I had fantasized about food, delicious food, real food, any food at all, for nearly three agonizing weeks, and now confronted with it, hot and steamy on my plate, I had to push it away.

The bad news was that the van, not surprisingly, was in an appalling condition and needed another thirty-six hours in the garage. Practically everything that could be broken was damaged. There was nothing I could do and so I gave the Boys some more money so that they could do the town. This was their first visit to a big city. Even Lhasa was a small provincial town compared to the bustling metropolis of Chengdu. I was feeling decidedly off-colour and rather than be a misery to anyone but myself, I decided to return to the hotel and go to bed to wait until the antibiotics had begun to take effect. I suggested to Thondup that we met the next day for lunch and we could do whatever food shopping was necessary afterwards.

I returned to the hotel, found the hideously expensive Friendship Store (Foreigners' Shop), paid an exorbitant amount of FEC for a toothbrush, toothpaste and the smallest bottle of cream for my ravaged face. The hotel had also managed to procure some foul-smelling ointment for my flea bites – which mercifully worked. I went to my room, settled down to start the most hateful job in television – doing my expenses – and then promised myself the total indulgence of doing nothing more energetic than reading in bed! I had raided the US Consul's unofficial library of paperbacks – this informal exchange system for book-hungry travellers, like myself, was an absolute godsend in a country where you simply cannot buy foreign-language newspapers, magazines or books. So I stretched out under the covers with James Clavell's

Whirlwind. The ointment began to work and the sheer relief from the torment of scratching sent me into a catatonic sleep.

On Saturday morning, 17 September, I was like a child with a new toy: David Lloyd had telexed me. It was a simple telex, but I was obviously suffering from foreign correspondent's neglect syndrome, for I, quite ridiculously, carried it around with me for the rest of the day and read it with secret glee: 'Dear Vanya, delighted you have had such a good holiday. Understand about the delay, hope the rest of the holiday is excellent and very much look forward to seeing your snaps on your return. Love, Karen and David.'

It was still dark outside on Sunday when Thondup, on schedule to the minute, arrived to collect me at 7 A.M. But the van was still not ready. So for the next six hours I sat waiting outside their hotel, then in the van waiting for petrol as we drove round practically every petrol station in Chengdu trying to cajole a few gallons out of stony-hearted officials.

Finally we were ready to move. I had wanted to film Chengdu's densely crowded streets to show the contrast between the empty landscape of Tibet and the bursting population in the cities of China. It would visually – and dramatically – highlight China's desperate land hunger. But as luck would have it on that Sunday the streets were only thinly peopled with cyclists and traffic.

I filmed anyway and made a reasonable sequence from the central reservation in the main street. I started with a big close-up of the head of the enormous statue of Mao that stands in front of the exhibition hall and looks down, with hand raised in bene-diction, over Chengdu's main avenue of decorative pine trees. I then pulled out to a wide shot showing the statue with its back-ground and the streaming traffic in the foreground. I thought it would also illustrate Mao's dictum to the Chinese to go and multiply and populate Tibet.

While I was filming, a clock somewhere to my right chimed loudly with the solemnity of Big Ben. Suddenly I became acutely depressed by the chiming because it reminded me, in view of both Mao's dictum and Deng Xiaoping's new economic policy which encouraged hundreds of thousands of Chinese to flood into Tibet, that time was running out – fast – for the Tibetans.

The Boys were itchy to be off, so I packed up, said goodbye to

the unlovely city-of-smog for the third time and fervently hoped
I would never see it again. We headed north-west with Tashikil
as our ultimate destination where there was a huge monastic
university – or whatever was left of it – and more important our
contact Dorje, whom I had seen just a few days before I had
re-entered Tibet. The Amdo sector, from Tashikil to Xining, was
his sector, as none of the Boys, who were all Khampas, knew
anything about it.

It was infuriating that the original Amdowan businessman had
not turned up for the rendezvous at the Norbulingka Park in
Lhasa, because without his detailed knowledge of the area I
registered what I saw with my eyes but was unaware of its
significance. Until dusk we drove on good roads through fields
under intensive cultivation and bordered by tall poplar trees. The
road – and it was the main north–south road between Chengdu
and Xining to the north – was dense with lorries and cyclists with
heavily loaded panniers struggling to maintain their balance. As
we got further from Chengdu, the traffic thinned and we began
to see Chinese labouring under bulky loads strapped in bulging
baskets on their backs.

The Chinese peasant is a marvel of industry. There was not one
inch of soil that was not under the plough, and away from the
puffing tractors on the outskirts of Chengdu the dark earth was
furrowed in the time-honoured way with wooden plough and
oxen. Again I noticed that in comparison to any other Third World
country, the Chinese peasants seemed well off. They appeared well
clothed and I noticed many of them were wearing colourful
padded jackets. And the houses, far from the mud hovels of other
parts of the developing world, had electricity feeds from the pylons
marching along the road and were solidly built of rough stone,
with the Chinese traditionally curved, tiled roofs. They seemed
light-years away from the backward Tibetan peasants who mostly
laboured excruciating hours with very little, if any, help from
modern technology and machines and subsisted in small mud
hovels.

With the van making a noise like a cantankerous tank, we
stopped for the night at Winchin, a small Chinese town. We
decided to stay at another Chinese 'hotel'; the entrance was dark
and as we were not too far from Chengdu, I could, if questioned,

just get away with saying that I had got separated from my group and was joining it later. By the standards of Tibet, this Chinese 'hotel' was pure luxury. I actually had a room to myself, a bed, a tin basin. A loo of sorts and a cold-water tap were down a draughty corridor. Taking no chances with any possible 'nocturnal predators', I slept in my newly-clean sleeping bag. By then the Boys, but more especially Tenzin and Thondup, had got down to a fine art the mechanics of smuggling me in and out of Chinese establishments with the minimum exposure. As usual, we were away before light.

The road began to climb north-westwards once again into the mountains of Tibet, but the gentler, occasionally wooded slopes of the east Amdo ranges were not at all as dramatic as the wild peaks and the sensational gorges of Kham. I experienced an unexpected lifting of the spirits and I was eagerly waiting for my first sight of the snows.

We drove for miles alongside a river jammed with floating logs and despite the Boys' tetchiness I got out and filmed. Their impatience with my filming turned to increasingly sour irritation and curt demands why I couldn't just take snaps with the small stills cameras. I tried to explain for the umpteenth time, but they would not listen and infuriatingly talked all the time when I was recording. This made a total nonsense of whatever I had just shot, as their chatter was plastered all over the soundtrack accompanying rural shots without a human being in sight. The more I asked them to be quiet, the worse it got and by the end of the day the atmosphere inside the van was as icy as the first snows of winter lying on the high mountain passes. Perhaps they were tired or projecting their insecurity at being in an area they had no knowledge of and therefore were more worried about the possibility of being picked up by the PSB for not having travel papers. Thondup couldn't help either and told me to be patient until we got to Tashikil where Dorje would be waiting with transport and if necessary we could change 'horses in mid-mountain'.

The perfect winter-wonderland scenery was like every picture-postcard from Aspen to Gstaad, but it was a chilling reminder that winter was approaching and that soon the high passes would be snowed up. I remembered with anxiety that if we delayed further, or had to walk out of Tibet, neither Thondup nor I had the equipment or the clothes to survive the intense cold. Time was not on our side.

Although we had been travelling through the hills and pasture-lands of the rich meat- and dairy-producing Ngapa region of eastern Tibet (now incorporated into Sichuan), I did not see one Tibetan in national dress, nor a Tibetan house, temple or prayer-flag. Whenever we stopped, which was extremely fre-quently as the van developed serious carburettor problems, Sumpa always spoke to the passers-by in Chinese – because, he told me when I asked him, they were all Chinese.

I remembered a report that the second delegation sent by the Dalai Lama to Tibet during a mild thaw between the Chinese and the Tibetan Government-in-exile in 1980 had noted when driving through the same area that all the cans of meat and dried milk produced in the Chinese-run factories in Ngapa were marked 'Made in China' and subsequently found for sale in the markets of Hong Kong, Nepal and many Arab countries. It was particularly significant that none of the Tibetans that the delegation spoke to, nor indeed any of the Tibetans that I came into contact with all over Tibet, had ever bought these products, for the simple reason they were not available for sale in Tibet.

The further north we travelled, the more autumn had begun to burnish whole mountainsides with a final explosion of colour. For a few short weeks the dying summer hung like a defiant memory in the trees before the spectre of winter enveloped the land in a pall of snow. But in the sometimes heavily forested areas of Ngapa, one of the very few areas of woodland that I encountered in Tibet, there was once again absolutely no sign of wildlife. Later, when I asked Tibetans in Tashikil about it, they told me that the panda had once been a flourishing species in the heavily wooded hills of eastern Amdo; but since the deforestation and also as a result of the Chinese hunting panda for export and for zoos so extensively in the region, it is virtually extinct in Tibet, although now an officially 'protected' animal.

As darkness fell the mountains rose more steeply from the narrow valley floors, and the rivers shallowed into streams where white-caps scudded furiously over smooth round rocks. As in Kham, the rivers in Amdo were still flowing down to China, but we were driving up-river, back towards the heartland of Tibet.

When we finally arrived in Zoge at eleven o'clock that night it was freezing cold. Once a trading post for the nomadic region to the north-west, today Zoge is almost an entirely Chinese town. Solid two-storeyed buildings, China's ubiquitous cream-painted concrete house blocks, rose from the edge of the dirt roads running in a dreary grid right through the town. Everything was quiet. Not a light, not a voice, not even a Tibetan dog barked in the absolute stillness – just the gruntling of the van as it spluttered into the sleeping town. All the big iron gates protecting the buildings were locked fast for the night, but eventually the Boys persuaded an irritable Chinese porter to open up and give them a room with four beds for the night.

They tetchily suggested that I also book in. I wearily explained, again, that this was as much a forbidden area for foreigners as the other parts of Tibet that we had been driving through. It was officially closed to foreigners, and we were too far into Tibet for me to risk awkward questions. They were probably cold and tired as well, but muttering loudly, they slammed the doors and without more ado shut me into the van and went into the room! The van was parked right outside their room, on one side of a quadrangle of single-storeyed buildings with rooms for truckers. It was also in the full glare of the lights that lit up the area like daylight.

One in the morning is hardly the time to throw hysterics or ask about going to the loo. I just sat on the uncomfortable seat, unable to lean backwards because the back-rest was at a 45-degree angle caused by the weight of the bags jolting forward on the bumpy road. Thondup came out and, chivalrous as ever, offered to stay the night in the van with me. There was no point in both of us being uncomfortable, so I told him to go back, and tried to unravel my sleeping bag from its sack. It was for me a miserable night.

The van now had even more gaps and holes than the previous ones: custom-made, it seemed, for the merciless wind to penetrate and torture me. It was impossible to sleep on the bags at the back, as before, because the Boys had bought so many presents in Chengdu for their families that the pile of luggage now touched the roof of the van. So for the rest of the night I spent my time sliding off the seat onto the floor and trying to protect my extremities from exposure to the predatory wind that seemed to penetrate even the depths of my Arctic-rated sleeping bag. By two in the morning the outside air temperature had dropped so low that the windscreen had completely frozen over. Unable to sleep, instead of counting sheep or yak, I tried to fathom out how in the arctic night I would amputate my frost-bitten toes!

The next day, Tuesday, 20 September, I was not exactly in my most attractive mood. The lack of sleep, the cold, the excruciating pain in my back activated by crashing onto the floor of the van several times during the night in my sleep and the frustation at not having shot anything productive for two whole days were not guaranteed to make me a bundle of laughs that morning. The Boys, when they emerged sleepily into the cold dark morning at seven, were also in a foul mood. Even stopping for tea in the grottiest hole-in-the-wall I have ever seen did nothing to improve their spirits. The atmosphere in the van was tense, and I was too tired and in too much pain to bother to figure out why. No one's mood was improved by the fact that we were also almost out of petrol and the Chinese were being more bloody-minded than usual about selling it to us. Even the thick wadge of notes I gave the Boys did not seem to do the trick that morning. The thought of remaining even another few hours in that arctic hell congealed me into an even deeper depression.

As the sun weakly attempted to warm the bleak, flat, dung-coloured landscape, without a tree, a bush or even one redeeming feature, the van spluttered from one end of town to the other – all of 200 yards – and back again, in a slow, macabre dance-of-death, like some demented beetle. Everywhere I looked – north, south, east and west – there was just a vast expanse of nothing. Just brown, featureless steppe. As passages of Solzhenitsyn's *One Day in the Life of Ivan Denisovich* kept involuntarily floating up from my subconscious to twitch what little composure I was shakily clinging to, Sumpa finally managed to bribe a Chinese *'Mei you! Mei you!'* (No! No!) merchant into compliance, and we filled our three empty barrels at an exorbitant price of seven times the official cost of petrol.

I had seven days to get back to Lhasa to be in time to film the anniversary of the autumn demonstrations. I was nearly 1,900 miles and at least eight days' hard driving away from Lhasa. For the past five days I had been playing the tourist, taking pretty shots, but I had not shot a foot of constructive sequence – nor had one

interview gone into the can. The frustration was barely contain-
able. The Boys, cantankerous as sin, balked every effort of mine
to film. I cursed them under my breath, and mutely reminded
them that we were both supposed to be on the same side. But the
time for gritty patience (never my strongest suit) was past. I had
no visuals and I stopped being polite – just went ahead and filmed,
irrespective of their fuming. This was not a joy-ride round Tibet,
I huffed angrily to myself, out of earshot; I had a job of work to
do, and I just got on with it.

While the Boys brewed up in the middle of a vast high plain
with mountains so distant that they were barely visible as blue
smudges forty miles away on the horizon, I decamped with the
camera and tripod and began filming a group of nomads who had
pitched their low, black, yak-haired tents nearby. The scene was
straight out of *The Big Country* – a sea of yellowing prairie that
stretched like an undulating mirage to the horizon. Shooting low,
with the tent's securing ropes in the foreground, I followed with
the end of the zoom lens a group of horsemen riding the famous
Singja (Amdowa) horses. Tall men, with dark hats to shield them
from the sun's fierce noon-day heat, they wore their *chubas* tied
round their waists; without stirrups or any of the equestrian
accoutrements of the West, the horsemen sat with the timeless
grace of men born to the saddle.

In the foreground a *drogpa* woman was kneading a tan-coloured
yak skin into suppleness to make clothes for the family. Around
her a gaggle of snotty-nosed barefoot children, dressed in more
holes than patches, came up to the camera with enchanting inquisi-
tiveness and peered straight into the lens. It tempted me to cut
the sequence and concentrate on a series of portraits of the children
à la Cartier-Bresson! But the cuddly urchins were soon bored with
the strange object in the funny clothes and floppy hat bending
over a black box and returned to play with their dog, who,
distrustful of an alien presence, was barking its heart out. Behind
them, a wisp of blue smoke filtered up from the tents into the
Tibetan-blue sky. In the next group of tents more women, in dark
chubas and pink and green blouses, carded and wove wool, chatted
and sang lilting Tibetan folk songs in perfectly pitched voices that
seemed as clear as the mountain air . . . Further, in the middle
distance, a gaggle of older children were minding sheep, while

behind them a group of young boys were practising their prowess at riding bareback and giving an amazingly dextrous display of horsemanship that would not have disgraced the bareback dare-devils of the Moscow State Circus.

It was one of those rare moments in television when, unplanned and unrehearsed, a sequence of fascinating complexity spon-taneously unfolds in intricate detail before the camera. I could have stayed a whole week quietly observing and filming the life of the *drogpa*, but Thondup came up and told me that the Boys were again impatient to leave. With appallingly bad grace I packed up and we drove north.

It was two hours later, after we had cleared the mountains on the horizon and were about to descend into a valley, a patchwork of blue and green that begged to be filmed, that the Boys finally exploded. I was filming on the edge of the road with nothing in sight for thirty miles. I planned to film down from a craggy peak, pan left to the valley and at the same time widen the shot to include the whole panorama. To give the shot perspective and scale I asked Sumpa to drive the van on my cue into the shot just as I was panning down and widening, and then to continue down the slope and disappear out of sight round the next bend to clear the shot for easier editing back home. As luck would have it, the camera jammed just as Sumpa was driving through the shot. I asked Thondup to ask him to drive back the few yards to do it again while I tried to un-jam the entrails of the camera.

Hearing heated voices and slamming doors, I looked up to see the van shoot off down the road, stop, then the Boys get out and sit by the roadside. I smelt problems before Thondup came back. The Boys were fed up with my filming and refused to do anything more to help. They told Thondup that they would take me to Tashikil, dump me there and go back on their own to Lhasa! Well, I thought, at least this time I have passport, money, tickets and all my rushes with me. There followed an undignified slamming of doors, harsh incomprehensible words in both languages and a stony silence as the van drove down the valley, through the rich farming country of Machu Dzong, where peasants in Chinese clothes were harvesting the fields. We came to a modern town that should have been Tsuk but which the Chinese called Karna. It was fairly large and from what I could remember from my research there were iron and coal mines in the area and a 90 per cent Chinese population. We didn't stop.

It was dark when we drove into Tashikil. I had made an arrangement with Dorje to be at the white chorten in front of the monastery, every two hours on the hour, starting from eight o'clock in the morning until eight at night. We agreed that both of us would wait for the other for a week, and already it was the night of the seventh day. It was nearly eight and in the dark it was impossible to find a Tibetan skulking somewhere amid the unlit mud tracks in what seemed a rabbit warren of small mud-brick walled compounds. It was hopeless so I decided to leave it until the morning. The town had recently been opened to foreigners so I knew that I would be comparatively safe and could concoct a story that I was joining my travel group in Xining. I also knew that there would be a hotel for foreigners somewhere. We found it after half an hour of driving over hills and getting stuck down mud gullies that had been deepened to axle-height by the un-seasonable rains.

Thondup decided he would stay with the Boys to try and cool them down. I was too tired to think. Through sign language I checked into a basic but clean room with the unheard-of luxury of an attached shower and a Westernized loo that worked. Of course there was no food, but being more than somewhat upset, I was not hungry. So I showered, climbed into my sleeping bag lying on the bed and prayed that for once the Furies would let me sleep.

It was cold and dark when I woke at 6.30 on Wednesday, 21 September. As there was no electricity, I stumbled around with the aid of my torch and thought that the colder and more miserable the weather, the greater my determination that one day I would find a Pacific island, take a trunk-load of books and read under a palm tree for a year!

As I dressed, I tried to remember what I had read about Labrang Tashikil. I knew it was a famous monastic university built by Kunkhen Jamyang Shapai Nawang Tsondru in 1439. A disciple of Tsong Kapa, the great Buddhist reformer and founder of the Gelupa sect, he was also an extremely erudite man: although born in Amdo, he had studied at Drepung and composed fifteen volumes of teachings that soon became classics in clarity and logic and became part of the monastic curriculum. The new monastery's reputation as an excellent centre for higher learning soon spread throughout Tibet. With Sera, Drepung, Ganden, Kumbum (in Amdo) and Tashi Lumpo monasteries it was one of the top six in the country and attracted students from all over Tibet and abroad. It specialized not only in Gelupa theology but also in Sakyapa (the oldest sect in Tibetan Buddhism) teachings, with degree courses of study in the Perfection of Wisdom (*Prajnaparmaita*), the Middle Path (*Madhyamika*), the canon of monastic discipline (*Vinaya*), Metaphysics (*Abhidharma*), Logic (*Pramana*), Astrology, Kalachakra rituals and doctorate courses (lasting twenty to thirty years) of *Geyche* – doctor of divinity.

A cold grey dawn was smudging the night out of the eastern sky. I wrapped up in all the clothes I had with me, climbed onto the bicycle I had hired from the hotel the night before and set off for the monastery complex at the other end of the valley from the hotel. I wobbled through the maze of mud-brick houses that we had bumped through the night before, and friendly Tibetans pointed to the east when I asked in rudimentary Tibetan for the *gompa* (monastery). It was 7.45, but to find the chorten was something else. There was no sign of Thondup either, who had said he would also meet me there.

Tashikil is not the easiest place to find your way round. The monastery's colleges, temples and administrative buildings were strung out on the north side of the Sangchu river along a narrow valley with 1,500-foot mountains rising steeply from the valley floor. I got back to the main road (which was tarmac and obviously part of the main north–south road), and cycled to the other end of town. On the way back, I saw the spire of something white; I zigzagged down a labyrinth of alleys and found the chorten with pilgrims perambulating around it, reciting their mantras and telling their prayer-beads in pious concentration. But no sign of Thondup or Dorje.

So I cycled back the two miles to the hotel – which was really a two-storeyed, concrete block of rooms along a corridor and another building that held a reception, some sort of a seating area, and a new Chinese pavilion-style inn built round a courtyard. It was very pretty, totally un-Tibetan, hideously expensive and reserved for the ultra-rich foreign tourist.

Thondup, bless him, was waiting outside my room. He too had been to the chorten and not seen Dorje. We returned again to the chorten at 9.45. There was still no show. Now even Thondup was getting nervous. His excursion ticket back to the United States expired on 2 October, we were already in the third week of September and with all our luggage and no transport the prospects of even getting out of Tashikil were bleak.

It was again 'no show' at noon. Thondup and I, the very picture of doom and gloom, shuffled down the main 'road' rutted by unseasonal rains and bordered by small Tibetan stalls displaying a few basic groceries and commodities on bits of blue plastic in the dirt. If Dorje had indeed gone, he had taken with him any hope that we had of completing the film – or of getting back to the capital. The few foreigners in the hotel were all with a tour group and there were no trains or buses to Lhasa.

With Thondup looking into the alleys on the right, I looked for Dorje to the left. After another fruitless hour I suddenly saw Dorje on the other side of the road. I flew across the road, threw my arms round his neck and kissed him on the cheek in relief!

'You mustn't behave like that,' Thondup said, in his best nanny voice. 'People will be looking!' Over lunch in a small Tibetan eatery behind one of those mud walls, Thondup and Dorje talked. Then Thondup turned to me and, in a very quiet voice that made me instantly suspicious, said: 'Now Vanya, hold onto your face. Don't say or show anything.' I wondered what new calamity was about to burst over our heads. It would be so refreshing if one day, just one whole day, it was possible to survive the twenty-four hours without one single drama. But I was in Tibet and Dorje had arranged *no* transport!

There was no point in recriminations. I suggested to Thondup that we send Dorje with some money to see if he could beg, borrow or steal anything on four wheels that could get us out of Tashikil. In the meantime, not daring to ask what else Dorje had not arranged, I asked him to get Dorje to find out where Wangyal Geyche lived, as he should have been waiting for us. I had been given Wangyal's name by the Controller, who had told me that Wangyal, a monk, had been imprisoned for eighteen years in various jails in Amdo; he was the ideal person to lead me to other interviewees and show me the sites of the prisons. The Controller had previously sent word to warn him of my arrival and I hoped that he would still be in Tashikil, and thus I could salvage some of the interviews.

After another back-breaking detour we found Wangyal and Dorje arranged to meet us by the same chorten in three hours' time. I tried to jettison my apprehension about the lack of transport and what it portended and concentrated on the interview.

I asked Wangyal what had happened in May 1958, when the Chinese had destroyed the monastery. He told me that for fifteen days that May, the Chinese had moved troops and equipment up to the tops of mountains overlooking the monastery and then, with artillery poised, all roads into and out of Tashikil were cut. The town and monastery were sealed off.

There were over 3,700 monks in the low mud-brick buildings. All were defenceless and unarmed.

'Remember,' Wangyal told me, 'that no one carrying arms or using arms is allowed within the precincts of a monastery or temple. So when the Chinese say that we were armed and fired at them, it is absolute fabrication! Lies!'

Wangyal went on to tell me that 254 Chinese, army and civilians, entered the monastery and ordered the abbot to assemble each and every monk in the courtyard outside the *Dukhang* (the monastery's main assembly hall which was used for big ceremonies and special functions and which contained a fabulous collection of very old *thankas*). They then divided the monks into nine groups and the commandant of the group proceeded to berate the monks: 'You and the lay people are united in one aim. To rebel against us and the Communist system. If you had not rebelled, we would treat you very nicely. But you have rebelled and so you must be punished!'

I found it difficult to believe the childish language and queried the monk. I also asked him if it was true that the monks were guilty of rebellion and sedition.

'I am not inventing anything,' he told me. 'I was there and was one of the ones singled out for punishment. I was standing in the front row while the officer walked up and down in front of us, screaming at us. For some reason he seemed very angry.'

'Yes, but had you or any of the monks done anything to provoke the Chinese?' I insisted.

'If you call teaching the people that the Buddha preached non-violence a crime, then yes, we were guilty. But their accusations of Tibetans provoking the Chinese by rebellion, or whatever excuse they use – no, it is completely untrue. But you know,' he went on, 'the Chinese have been using these tactics for so many hundreds of years on their own people, or anyone who happens to get in the way of what they want to do at a particular moment in history. We have heard it all before. It is not new. But let the Chinese say what they will, they will say black is white and if there is no one strong enough to challenge them, or in the Tibetan case, if you lock up a whole country from the scrutiny of the world, then who is going to say to the Chinese black isn't white? So to answer your question: no, we were not rebelling or doing anything provocative at the monastery.

'The Chinese had done their preparation. First of all the teachers and incarnate lamas were arrested. I was one of them. We were the worst category, the *shamo nakpo* [black hat] label, the reactionary people – aristocrats, chieftains, landlords, lamas and often just anyone who could read. It was a label that you could not lose for many, many years; and because we were educated, we were meted out especially hard treatment. I was just eighteen at the time and spent the next twenty-two years in prison.'

I asked him about the destruction of the monastery. He told me that shortly after the Chinese arrived, while he was still in the monastery undergoing *thumzing* sessions with beatings and torture because he would not renounce his faith, he saw the Chinese soldiers enter all the halls and colleges of the monastery and strip out all the old statues and valuable *thankas*.

'They started with pulling out a particularly old and valuable statue of the Shakyamuni Buddha. They piled everything in the yard and by August 1958 they had sent twenty-one big trucks of religious objects in gold and silver to China. I remember that each truck had three Chinese soldiers guarding it while it was being loaded. Their guns were trained on us monks and if anyone rushed up to prevent a particular statue or a special *thanka* from being loaded, pleading the great antiquity of the piece, a soldier would hit him with his gun and threaten to shoot. I particularly remember one load of very old *thankas* that were just thrown into the truck without any special covering. They seemed not to care about the antiques or what damage they did to them.'

I asked Wangyal what had happened in 1958 after he and the other monks had been arrested. His story, with minor variations, was identical to that of nearly every Tibetan monk I had met in Tibet. They had all been subjected to the obligatory *thumzing*, beatings and torture. And very many had died. Those that survived had been dispersed to other prisons with more rigorous reputations for breaking prisoners under torture. Some were sent to remote prisons in the desert of Inner Mongolia; but wherever they went, the conditions were harsh: there was little or no food and the enforced labour, building bridges and roads for the Chinese without pay, or clothes, or medical attention, killed most of the Tibetans.

'You must understand,' Wangyal said, coughing consumptively from the TB he contracted during those years, 'for the Chinese, Tibetans are not even sub-human. So why should they expend their precious resources on Tibetans? It was slave labour and the Chinese treated the animals better than they did us.'

Knowing that the Chinese categorically deny any maltreatment of Tibetans, I asked him for the names of the prisons and the prisoners who could corroborate his allegations. He told me that one of the most notorious prisons – and one that he had been sent to – was at Anchi. It had taken two days and one night in the train from Lanchow to Ürümqi, the capital of Inner Mongolia, hundreds of miles to the north-west on the edge of the Gobi Desert. The actual camp was then reached after another train journey to Dunghwa and a further day by truck.

Another labour-camp/prison was at Matsong Shen not far from Anchi. Another was at Yumen and a fourth near Kuichen. There was no escape from these prisons, he told me, as all around them were endless miles of harsh desert. There was no water in the area and he remembered the day every week when military trucks used to come in with water: the prisoners used to wait and rush up and lick the water that had spilt down the sides.

In 1958 he and Gyaltso, another monk from the same monastery, were sent to the coal mines at Maborshen. He told me that conditions there were very hard: 'There was no electricity in the pits. We had to go down a rope into the pit with our baskets on our backs. When we collected the coal we had to haul it to the surface by ropes. In the pit it was dark and cold and the water made your feet white and soft and bits of flesh used to get rotten and fall off. We would have to work non-stop for nine hours a day. Our backs and hands were covered with sores and burns from the ropes; as we had no medicines for them, the sores got bigger and black at the edges. The smell was terrible and many times the holes got so big that you could see the bone at the bottom of the rotting flesh.

'In summer it was a furnace in the desert and in winter it froze. Many prisoners were sent to work on land reclamation in the area, many to build bridges. Sometimes the wind was so strong that it knocked you down and you had to lie flat on the ground: otherwise it would lift you and carry you away like a piece of cotton in a sandstorm. Then when we got back to the prisons, we had more *thumzings*, more beatings and many times I and many other prisoners were put into solitary cells in total darkness with chains round us which were so tight that they would eat into the flesh and cause terrible wounds. Things were so bad that many thousands of Tibetans died. Some who did not, tried to commit suicide. Hundreds regularly tried to jump in the river from the bridge we had built, but the Chinese would fish us out. It was difficult to die.'

'But how many died and what proof do you have?' I forced myself to ask.

'Over 2,000 monks were initially imprisoned from our monastery. Many died. Reincarnate lamas like Detang Rinpoche died of starvation in the late sixties in Lanchow prison. Youngzin Tasng also died in Lanchow in 1959. Gya-tsha Rinpoche died under torture in Tsu prison in 1959. Phari Watsh, who was born in Tsu, also died in Tsu prison in 1960 from torture and starvation. Then Amang Chungwatsah, who was born in Machu Dzong district, also died in Tsu prison in 1960. Then Khonchok Sandub, the tutor to the high lama of the monastery Jamang Shepa, was shot by the Chinese outside the monastery walls. He was accused of organizing a revolt in the area.'

'Was it true?'

'No. He was an old and holy man and only concerned with his books and his spiritual exercises, but the Chinese had to have a scapegoat; and who was going to give him a trial, let alone hear any evidence to the contrary?' Wangyal asked.

'There were many others that the Chinese executed,' he continued. 'Monks like Nargutsang: he was killed at Leushu, thirty kilometres south of Tsu. And Wanlo Tsultim and Jigme Tenzing and Yedem Cholok: all born at Amchok and killed at Amchok in 1960. These I know from personal experience and you can check with other people here, too. But there are so many names.

'And my great friend Gyaltso, who was my cell-mate, also died in prison. You know,' he said slowly, 'when you share great suffering with someone, it forms a deep bond between you. To this day I still miss Gyaltso.

'Then they sent me and other monks who would not renounce our religion to a place we had all heard of and dreaded: Rongwar. It is forty kilometres south of here, not far from Tsuk. It was previously a small monastery. But the Chinese turned all the monks out and made it into a prison that specialized in torture. Between 1959 and 1961, when I was there, there were about 600 monks to start with, but when I left there were fewer than 200.'

'What happened?'

'They died under torture and their bodies were thrown into a shallow valley at the side of the monastery. The grave is full of dead bodies and you can still see their bones today.'

'Can you take me there so that I can film?' I asked.

'Yes,' he said. 'If you dig only a little under the top you will find the bones. The Chinese would not even let us monks perform *choe* for our dead. The Chinese don't believe in anything and their bodies are just put into graves. So even in death they try and reduce us to their level. The Chinese used to say to us: "You should not feel sad that so many Tibetans are dying. They are the enemies of the Chinese and the Communist Party and the State. You should feel happy." They used to say this especially in the morning when very often you would find that the prisoner who had been sleeping near you in the straw, from whose body you had received heat, had died in the night and was lying there stiff in the morning.'

'But why were the monks singled out for this special treatment?' I asked.

'You must understand first of all what part religion – and

therefore the monks, the practitioners and teachers of religion – plays in our society. It is not like in the West where religion is something you do maybe once a week for half an hour. No, for us Tibetans our religion is not simply a matter of faith. It is not simply a matter of whether we believe or disbelieve. The Buddhist religion for Tibetans is part of our language, culture, history; it's part of our everyday life and it has been so for well over 1,000 years since it came to us from India. And in this period we have enlarged and enriched and adapted the religion so that we now cannot separate our religion or our religious beliefs from every part of our daily lives. Our religion is an intimate part of our lives, a connection to our culture, our history and our national identity.

'We have always been an independent people, no matter what the Chinese say and no matter how they rewrite history – they are very good at that and have had centuries and centuries of practice. And for us our religion – and its suppression – is very much part of the Tibetans' struggle.

'Also, it might be difficult for someone who is not a Tibetan and believes in a different faith to understand the great importance our religion holds for us. You see, although there are many forms of Buddhism in the world, and all are good and valid, here in Tibet, because for centuries we were cut off from the outside world, we have been able to preserve our faith in a pure form. So we regard ourselves as uniquely privileged to be the guardians of the entire corpus of our religion; we believe that it is our duty to preserve our religion, enhance it, and enrich our traditions, not selfishly just for ourselves, but for all sentient beings. For all time.

'Monks therefore have a special place in our society and the Tibetans look to us as leaders and guides; and that's why the Chinese believe that by attacking us, by eliminating us by whatever means, the people will be without a rudder and be more easy to manipulate when we are no longer there to stand up for our faith, which for us is inseparable from our identity and the independence of Tibet. Although Tibet was poor and backward by your standards, in the monasteries everyone, irrespective of caste or creed, however poor and humble, had access to education and new ideas, and that's another reason why the monasteries were – and still are – the focus of suppression for the Chinese. Especially today.'

It was getting late and time to meet Dorje. So Wangyal

suggested that we return when we had found transport and he would take us to Rongwar to film the mass grave. He then took us round the monastery and showed me where to film doors and windows that were discreetly barred from the inside. From the outside the monastery looked functioning and well restored, but closer examination did not bear out the fiction.

We came across a marvellous scene of over fifty monks of all ages digging a sewage channel. It was the perfect example of Tibetans rebuilding their own monasteries. I started filming and let the camera pan slowly over the monks, their red robes streaked with mud, digging in unison. I later asked Wangyal why there appeared to be so many young monks when the Chinese forbade entry to anyone under eighteen.

'Our people are very religious, and these youngsters, some as young as eight, are technically illegal here. But these children, born during and after the Cultural Revolution, are the most ardent supporters of our faith. Also, with the education system so bad for Tibetan children, the monasteries are one of the few places where they can not only learn religion, but can also learn to read and write in their mother tongue. Outside in the towns, though the Chinese have built some schools for Tibetans, the standard is so poor that most of our young children cannot even speak Tibetan, let alone read and write in our mother tongue.'

I left him and agreed to return the next day, or at the latest the day after. When we found Dorje, he told us that he could find nothing. I bit my tongue hard and refrained from asking why not, when he had had since last February to arrange it.

'Let's cut our losses and go to Xining,' Thondup counselled. So the following morning, with Astride, a young French girl who had genuinely got separated from her group and who spoke some Chinese, we set out at 4.40 for the bus station. Without any transport, we hired a handcart and trundled the baggage to the bus.

The journey was comfortable and Dorje advised Astride and me to pretend to be asleep when the security inspector checked the bus. Three hours later we decamped in the bus-yard of the next town. Dorje went to arrange transport while Thondup, Astride and I sat on the baggage and took happy snaps of each other as most genuine tourists would do.

By eleven that morning Dorje had returned with a new-looking green jeep. It was only when I heard him talking Chinese to the driver that I realized that the idiot had got us a Chinese vehicle with a Chinese driver! How on earth was I supposed to go and dig up a mass grave, poke my nose around – and film – existing prisons, talk to prisoners . . . with a Chinese driver? Thondup, seeing my face, squeezed my arm. 'Please,' he said. I tried to smile, but my face only cracked and I got into the jeep with a terrible sense of foreboding.

At least, I comforted myself, it was a better vehicle than the last van, which was still under repair in Tashikil. We had gone barely a mile and were just clearing the main market when, on going round a perfectly normal bend in the road, the driver screeched to a halt. In front of the jeep, and only inches from where we had stopped, I could see through the windscreen a large Chinese hand officially and unequivocally telling us to stop.

20

Joyrides in Amdo

'We're being set up to be arrested!' Seán's warning reverberated in my ears and I realized grimly that his prophecy had come true. As we followed the official car in front of us through the crowded streets, I saw it turn towards an iron gate and into a yard with other cars parked in it. My predominant concern was to hide the cameras and the only place I could see to secrete them and the bag of rushes was under the driver's seat. If the Chinese really searched the jeep they would find them in two minutes flat. It was a slender chance – but the only one available. As the driver changed gear I looked at Dorje's face. He was ashen and trembling. There was no need for an explanation. We were foreigners in a forbidden area, the authorities had found out and we were about to face the music.

There was a tense burst of Tibetan between Thondup and Dorje. Thondup told me quickly that, as soon as we stopped, Dorje would try and get out of the back door and slip away. We would meet in Xining the next day, but it was imperative that, as a Tibetan, he should not be seen helping foreigners.

Dorje's hand was on the door-handle. He looked anxiously at the crowded street. I passed him a bundle of Rmb notes and just before we drew level with the gates, he slipped out of the jeep and disappeared into the crowd – another blue-suited back like all the other anonymous Chinese backs. It all happened within the space of thirty seconds and, somewhat shaken that yet another guide had bailed out, I turned to Thondup and asked: 'How is he going to get to Xining? And more important, how are we going to get out of this and get there?' I tried to sound casual, so that the driver would not sense my panic as we slowed down to turn into the gates. There was no point in even thinking of running. It would certainly alert our 'custodians' that something was wrong, that we had something to hide. Anyway, without transport, language, and looking anything but Chinese or Tibetan, I could not exactly melt into the crowd.

'Dorje said that he would meet us in the garden in front of the railway station in Xining at noon tomorrow. He'll get a bus from the town. If he's caught with us he will go to jail. If the Chinese ask about him we are to say that we don't know him and that he was helping us to get a vehicle as he speaks Chinese. Remember we are on our way to Xining to catch up with our groups,' said Thondup in a low voice. All I knew was that I had to get out of the jeep first, before the Chinese had the chance to talk to us inside the vehicle. That way, with luck, they would not see the suspicious mountain of luggage which, as the vehicle had no boot, was piled up behind the back seat. Even before the vehicle had stopped, before the Chinese official could get his hand on the door-handle, I jumped out, smiled and gave the command performance of my life.

The driver of the jeep locked all four doors of the vehicle and gave the key to an official. We were then ushered into a small office overlooking the yard. Astride was a godsend. Her rudimentary Chinese was our only means of communication, since the officials spoke no other language. I told our cover story to Astride in French and told her it was imperative that our things were not examined and that we got out of there as soon as possible. It might have been the urgency in my voice but she frowned questioningly; I said there was more, but that I would explain later.

It soon became obvious that, as I suspected, the officials were very provincial and very junior. And as any problem that is remotely out of the ordinary has to be referred upwards in the cumbersome Chinese bureaucracy, I knew they would soon phone for a senior officer to come down from Xining to sort out the irregularity of foreigners being in a closed area without official guide, permission or papers. Then we undoubtedly would be taken in for serious interrogation, which would result in the certain discovery and seizure of the film – and us. The only chance was to allay the officials' suspicions: to try and somehow talk our way out of it, or see if they were open to bribery.

Then began an interminable wait of six hours. Between pleading with and cajoling the officials, we sat on a bench in the yard. Eventually, unsure of the efficiency of Astride's Chinese, I suggested that the officials try and find someone in the town who spoke English, and said that I had to get to Xining that night to join my group, who were leaving the next day to continue our tour. And, of course, I threw in that our visas were running out. With the possibility of transferring the problem to someone else's shoulders, the officials, who after three hours had become indifferent, smiled and offered us some dried melon seeds and glasses of water.

They came and sat with us, eyeing us curiously, and tried to make conversation. I could not decipher whether the friendliness was a prelude to sexual advances or an overture to their acceptance of a bribe. There is a moment, as I knew only too well from my experiences in the past when I had run foul of authorities abroad and found myself in a confined space with an interrogating officer who has total power over your destiny, when his scrutinizing eyes gradually change from inquisitorial harshness to an unmistakeable sexual arousal . . . It is terrifyingly uncomfortable and invariably made me feel unclean and apprehensive with the primeval fear any woman has, of rape.

It is a fear I have lived with all my career and one that most female journalists and film-makers feel. But it is a taboo subject; and perhaps not to tempt fate by even daring to articulate it, or maybe because of the women's own unpleasant experiences, most keep silent about it. But for me it was not just an academic conundrum. I had often seen that look in soldiers' eyes, particularly in remote areas away from censure or retribution. So far, I had been lucky and managed to escape by the skill of my wits usually with just my nerves in tatters. But when I was making a film about the genocide in South Sudan and was arrested on the Ugandan border, I was lucky to escape with only a badly bruised and beaten body after the soldiers roughed me up.

But the fear of rape, especially now with the complication of the Aids factor, was a constant, if subconscious, concern on difficult assignments. It was one which I went to great lengths to avoid by dressing carefully and unprovocatively, by always being deliberately cool and not over-friendly, and above all by not putting myself anywhere near a situation where such problems might arise. But, as on that morning in the yard with the Chinese, your destiny is not always within your own control.

I knew that although the Chinese play down social crimes like rape, I had read reports that the incidence of rape had increased in China, especially in the rural areas away from Beijing and the larger towns. I also knew that even though Astride and Thondup were around it would not be of any help if it came to the crunch. Astride would suffer the same fate – all white women are prized spoils in most developing countries. And Thondup would have been beaten senseless if he had gone to our defence. So although I smiled politely, I deliberately avoided eye contact and pretended to read my book. But concentration was impossible. The prospect of interrogation and jail, or worse, ricocheted inside my head as I tried to interpret every single move made by every single Chinese sitting on that bench.

Through the gates we could see Chinese with bundles of vegetables in panniers strung from poles across their shoulders or strapped on their backs bustling through the streets shaded with tall leafy trees. The very normality heightened the precariousness of our predicament. Not knowing if and when a senior Chinese official would come through the gates, or whether each time the phone rang it heralded the imminent arrival of the PSB or army intelligence unit, I sat on the small hard bench in the sun in indescribable anguish. All I could think about was the faces of all those very brave Tibetans who had spoken to my camera and who, if the exposed tapes were examined, would land up in jail.

It was 2.30 in the afternoon and I knew that with the approaching night our problems would multiply and our chances of getting ourselves and the film out of the place would diminish dramatically. While Astride and Thondup talked amiably about the inconsequential minutiae of their lives back home – we could not be certain that the Chinese did not, as they affected, speak English, so we kept the conversation to inessential trivia – I extracted a large wadge of Rmb surreptitiously from my money-belt and secreted it into my hand. I walked into the smoke-filled office where the Chinese official sat puffing a foul-smelling cigarette and writing some report. I assumed he was the most senior since he seemed to do all the talking. I made gestures as though I wanted a drink of water, and as he got up to get me one from the flask I quickly tucked the money discreetly but visibly, under the top sheet of paper. I then took the glass and walked outside.

Just as I was wondering whether he would accept the bribe and perhaps do something to release us or charge me with attempting to pervert the course of justice, a small man with a dignified face under a mop of white hair walked into the yard accompanied by one of the officials who had earlier disappeared. Mr Wei was a teacher and spoke English with the halting sentences of one who has not spoken it for a very long time. I was immensely curious to discover what a man with his education (his accent and choice of words were astonishingly refined) was doing miles away from civilization. Was he one of the victims of the Cultural Revolution who had been banished from Beijing or a university, to hard labour in one of the harsh frontier zones as punishment because he could read and write? I held my questions, told him my story, elaborated it with pathetic fabrications – about my sick daughter – my anxious husband – anything that might touch a chord and get us out of confinement before nightfall.

Then followed a laborious bartering session when the officials wanted to send us to Lanchow – where there were more qualified PSB to 'help'! I argued, pleaded or looked sorrowful, depending on their replies, and resisted their arguments. It would not only take for ever to get there, but almost certainly we would be put on a train towards Guangzhou and Hong Kong – both Thondup's 'official' ticket and mine were from Hong Kong to London. And that meant an end to any chance of getting the rest of the filming done or returning to Lhasa for what I was sure would be demonstrations on 27 September and 1 October.

We seemed to be getting nowhere. The Chinese, with not much to do and with a considerable amount of time on their hands in that backwater town, were having fun toying with us. So I took an enormous gamble and told the kindly Mr Wei, in the toughest voice I could summon, to tell the officials that if we were not allowed out within the hour, I insisted on being taken to the nearest telephone and would phone my uncle, the British Ambassador in Beijing (lies), who would take up our detention with the Minister of the Interior. Which would be most uncomfortable for everyone concerned.

There was a flurry of staccato Chinese and the officials started shouting. Then one of them stamped back to the office, returned with a pad with Chinese ideograms on it, wrote out something on one of the sheets, gave it to one of his colleagues, threw him the jeep's keys, turned his back on us and marched back to the office. It was yet another eternity of anxiety (in reality it could not have been more than a minute) before I realized with relief that we were being sent on to Xining, under escort, there and then. So whether it was the bribe, Mr Wei's diligent pleading, or my tantrum and threat I will never know. All I did know was that we were back in our jeep and heading north.

Just before we went through the gates, Mr Wei told us that the officials had issued strict instructions that we were not to get out of the jeep or stop on the road for anything. Nor were we allowed to take any pictures as it was a closed area. He reminded us that the official who was driving us would make certain that we did neither! I thanked him, waved to the other officials and was impatient for the jeep to clear the yard before they could change their minds.

As we drove through the town I saw Chinese men in skull-caps and women in long dresses with scarves draped over their heads and shoulders. They looked vaguely Islamic and I asked Astride to enquire from our driver. They were, she told me, Hui, Chinese Muslims who had originated from north of Xining and had settled in the area between Xining and Tashikil. I then remembered that north-east Tibet and north-west China had been the fiefdom of a Muslim war-lord who held sway over the area for many decades. It was one of the interminable border squabbles that had plagued the region at the turn of the century.

As we drove north through scrubby mountains, the driver, in an effort to be friendly, started pointing out places of interest and indicated a road to the right which went to Kumbum. I burned the lining of my stomach with frustration realizing that we were passing the very turn-off for one of the stops on our schedule. We were due to visit Kumbum and film at the monastery, built by the 3rd Dalai Lama, Sumpa Gyatso, to commemorate the birthplace of Tsangkhapa (1357), the founder of the Gelupa order to which the Dalai Lama and most Tibetan monks belonged. Built in 1588, it was one of Tibet's six greatest monasteries and in its heyday was a sizeable complex of four colleges, a Kalachakra and medical college, with many chapels, tombs and chortens. The monastery was also renowned for its elaborate *thankas* and butter sculptures.

Of course it did not escape the ravages of the Cultural

Revolution, and many monks suffered under the Chinese there. It has been partly restored not only to attract foreign visitors 'doing' the Silk Route tour, but also to serve as a show-piece to illustrate China's tolerance of the Tibetans' religion. But I wanted to see and film it for another reason.

When the 13th Dalai Lama died in 1935 the portents indicated that the child reincarnation would be found in a house with turquoise-coloured tiles; this led the Delegation from Lhasa to a small village near the famous sixteenth-century monastery at Kumbum. For the distinctive green tiles and golden spire of the three-storeyed monastery, as well as the turquoise-coloured tiles on the roof of the house where the child lived, had been seen in a vision in the mysterious still waters of the 17,000-foot Lhamo Lhatso lake 120 miles south-east of Lhasa.

Lhamo Lhatso at Chokhorgyal is the foremost of Tibet's 'visionary lakes'. Visions seen in its mystical glacial waters by the Regent and senior members of the *Kashag* (Cabinet) of Tibet after the death of the 12th Dalai Lama had led directly to the discovery of the 13th Dalai Lama.

Ma Bufeng, the local Muslim war-lord, followed the progress of the Lhasa Delegation with acute interest. And when three-year-old Lhamo Dhondrub, the fifth child of an illiterate peasant family who lived in the house with the turquoise-coloured tiles in the village of Takster, near Kumbum, had passed the rigorous tests proving that he was unequivocally the reincarnation of the 13th Dalai Lama, Ma Bufeng held the family and the Delegation to an exorbitant ransom before he would release the child to be taken to Lhasa for the enthronement.

After the Delegation had raised and paid the preposterous ransom, little Lhamo Dhondrub and his family were taken to Lhasa where he was anointed as Tenzing Gyatso the 14th Dalai Lama of Tibet.

I had also planned to film at Takster, not only to satisfy my intense curiosity, but to see whether, as I was told by Tibetans, the Dalai Lama's original home had been destroyed by the Chinese. I also had another more sinister reason. In the arid desert region around Kumbum and Xining, where the Gobi desert merges into the Teggar desert, were some of the most notorious prisons in Tibet. Thousands of Tibetans had perished there, and the account of the horror was graphically recounted by the Dalai Lama's personal physician, Dr Tenzin Choedrak, in John Avedon's book *In Exile from the Land of the Snows*.

As we drove up into the loess plateau that evening the starkness of the landscape reminded me of Avedon's description of the complex of Chinese prison camps that existed in the desert area, hidden from prying eyes. Hundreds of thousands of prisoners were incarcerated in terrible conditions in the penal colonies strung out in the desert. An article in *Time* magazine in 1979 described the area as a 'black hole from which little information ever reaches the outside world, or even the rest of China'. It was China's Gulag.

There were Tibetans, Chinese and Hui (Muslim) prisoners in a vast complex of 166 camps; but the Tibetans, and especially the Khampas who had rebelled against the Chinese, received the worst treatment. Avedon estimates that in the late fifties and sixties, at one time or another, one-tenth of Tibet's adult population lived as a race apart in Chinese prisons.

I had been told that thousands – some put it at several hundreds of thousands of prisoners – perished from maltreatment, hunger and neglect. Some of the prisons were still in use today – but I could hardly go and film there with a Chinese driver.

Sunset was particularly beautiful that evening. The golden light on the dramatic red earth contrasted with sharp green vegetation in the valley and reminded me of the richness of colour in some of Gauguin's Tahitian paintings. Small picturesque villages of red mud houses begged to be filmed, but my cameras, now ensconced in my lap, had to remain rebelliously silent. But there was again not a sign of anything Tibetan: in dress, domestic architecture, temples – not even a bunch of prayer-flags on a remote mountain pass.

The road was in bad repair in parts, but otherwise had a good surface. In fact, two buses a day plied between Xining and the town where we were arrested. Why then had Chuma, our first interpreter, told me that we could not possibly go on our original schedule from Lanchow to Xining and then south, because the road – the very same one that we were now driving on – had been 'washed away'?

We arrived in Xining at 1.30 in the morning. Warm and at a

much easier altitude, Xining is a large industrialized city. Its streets were well-lit but deserted at that hour. We drove to the only two hotels that foreigners are allowed to stay in. Both were full, so the driver, who had mellowed into a reasonable human being, got us a room in a Chinese hotel which is usually off-limits for foreigners. So by three in the morning, with Astride and I sharing a room, and Thondup and the driver another, we settled in and fell into an exhausted sleep.

Friday, 23 September, and only three days to the anniversary of the demonstrations in Lhasa, dawned bright and sunny in Xining, Tibet's old frontier town on the north-eastern border with China. Today it is absorbed into China's large province of Qinghai which incorporates most of the old Tibetan province of Amdo.

As I opened my eyes – the window had no curtains – I did a double take. For just outside the window and across the street was the enormous green dome of a mosque and a tall slender white minaret. I blinked and wondered if I had wandered into Samarkand or Tehran in a dream. But it was real enough – there is a considerable Muslim population in and around Xining. Before I had returned to Lhasa, I had heard on the BBC World Service that the Muslims 'of north-west China' had held a demonstration. For it to have reached the World Service Bulletin from such a remote area had to mean that it was more serious than a few 'trouble-makers and anti-revolutionaries' and I wondered to what extent the discontent that I had heard had been percolating through the area had spread to the Muslim population of two other of China's vast 'autonomous regions', Inner Mongolia and Xinjiang (Eastern Turkestan).

Astride, a twenty-year-old political science student at the Sorbonne, had been backpacking through China that summer. She was very aware of the political situation in Tibet and was full of enthusiasm to help us. We spent a fruitless morning with CITS trying to find a way to Lhasa. As usual they were completely unhelpful, spoke no English and told us that train tickets *might* be available in one week's time! And as for a bus – 'Completely out of the question!' Foreigners were not allowed on public transport on their own and we could go only with an official group. But what group and how and where were met with a long yawn: the official stripped off his shirt and lay on the iron bed in a corner of his office and told Astride to go away because he was tired!

Thondup and I traipsed to the other end of the town, crossed the bridge over the Hwang Ho (Yellow River), found the station, located the garden in front of it and spent the next three hours admiring the flowers and taking photographs of ourselves. But there was no sign of Dorje. Astride had said she would try and find us better accommodation in the nearby hotel and eventually turned up at just gone three. We wandered disconsolately over the bridge, found a small eatery and spent the rest of the day trying to buy bus and train tickets to Golmud, the town half-way between Xining and Lhasa.

The next morning, having secured a decent room for the night, I suggested that before I became a gibbering idiot with anxiety we set out to film some gvs (general views) in the street. We filmed scenes of the streets full of Chinese, and with Astride and Thondup playing the fool at the edge of the frame I was able surreptitiously to film the few pathetic Tibetans who sat in the dust on the pavement. They were the object of much curiosity for the few foreigners who trained their cameras on them as they huddled in the dust in their dark, dirty *chubas*. They were not begging, but their apathetic eyes and bodies hunched up with resignation reminded me of the fate of the Australian Aborigines, a tourist curiosity in their own land.

We went back to the station garden again at noon, just in case Dorje had missed the bus or had been delayed. The station forecourt and the gardens were bustling with Chinese. The modern station stood stark against the dramatic loess escarpment behind it, and plastered all over the adjacent buildings were billboards and neon signs in Chinese. We waited in the harsh white light that reminded us that we were on the edge of the desert. Behind the gardens, where Lanchowans were promenading, the Hwang Ho was reduced to a sluggish trickle. But again there was no sign of Dorje. By four in the afternoon I was beginning to feel desperate as we made our way again to the bus station. Astride said that she would try and buy us tickets to Lhasa, since she had a student card – in Chinese – which slightly improved her chances of getting tickets, for herself at least. But we hoped that a discreet bundle of Rmb might improve our chances, too . . .

As we approached the station we saw Dorje walking away from it. Thondup grabbed him and we all returned to the recesses of a nearby eatery and tried to make some sense of the situation. If we had not been in public I might have throttled the man, for it appeared he had arranged precisely nothing in Xining. No transport, no interviews, nothing! I simply could not believe what I was hearing.

This was the man that I had personally briefed seven months ago. I had spent hours explaining to him the allegations that we were seeking to check out. I had painstakingly taught him how to check the veracity of interviewees. We had meticulously gone over the route together and what we would film where. It was the same man who only four weeks previously I had met with Seán and the Controller and who had told me that, contrary to what Chuma, our first interpreter, had told us, he had been waiting for us in Xining on time as per the first schedule. He had even shown me photographs of locations right up to Tashikil to prove he had been there. He had shown me photographs of a woman who had been eight months pregnant and who had been subjected to a forced abortion. It was with the same man that we had rescheduled the trip to meet our new timetable. And now he was sitting across a table telling me that he had arranged nothing because he did not know when I would be arriving! On further questioning, it transpired that the 'abortion woman' interviewee was no longer in town.

'What do you mean?' I asked, keeping my temper on a tight rein.

'She had to go and visit a relative,' said Dorje.

'Where? And why can't we go wherever she is?'

He fluffed badly.

'Well, what about someone else?' I insisted.

He hummed and hawed. 'They are all Chinese!'

I was beyond anger. Ice-cold, I realized that the man was lying through his teeth, but why? Was he working for the Chinese? If so, was the display of abject terror when we were held for questioning just a superb performance? If he was working for them, why was he here? Why, against the odds, had we managed to get out of the clutches of the officials? Had he now been sent to Xining to entrap us further? And if he was working for the Chinese, why nad they not arrested me in Xining? Or were they waiting, as Seán had thought, to track all our Lhasa contacts and then pick me up with all the rushes at Gonggar airport?

Or was Dorje just plain incompetent? And if he was, why had the Controller selected him in the first place? Nothing made any sense except I knew in my bones that something was very badly wrong and that if Dorje was indeed working for the Chinese, we were in more danger than we had been throughout the trip.

If we continued with him we could well be walking into another trap. But without him we would be stuck indefinitely in Xining. So I hesitantly took the decision to go on. If I got to Lhasa at least I thought I could just about find my way to two of the safe houses in the Barkhor and there at least was a chance of help in smuggling us out of Tibet. Waiting in Xining would run us out of visa time and ensure our arrest. So I told Dorje to get a car and return the following morning. I also decided that as the probability of running into an ambush in the form of a checkpoint was now a distinct possibility, it was safer not to take Astride with us and expose her to unnecessary risks. I explained this to her and we agreed to meet in Lhasa.

Saturday, 24 September, found us sitting on our luggage in the hotel lobby. Dorje had not turned up at seven o'clock as promised. Astride, Thondup and I sat in silence, having coffee out of our flask. My brain was numb. I could not think of one single way out of our predicament. Every avenue we had tried so far had ended in a brick wall.

Just after ten Dorje appeared in the lobby and Thondup followed him round the corner to a secluded corridor. Since Kumbum monastery was only a couple of hours' drive from Xining, I had suggested that we could go and film the interviews there, as well as film the Tibetans who had protested at Rincon nearby. No one had heard of their protests as, unlike Lhasa, there had been no foreigners or cameras to record the incident. But it was particularly important to include it in the programme, as it highlighted the number of Tibetan protest demonstrations taking place all over Tibet; and it showed that it was not, as the Chinese insisted, only a few unrepresentative 'splittists' from Lhasa protesting. If we drove hard, I reckoned that we could return by late afternoon and then go and film the exterior of the notorious prison camps near Xining; we could drive through the night to Lhasa, to make up the time. We could all take turns at the driving and that way I could just about reach Lhasa in time for the 27th.

Astride helped us to load the jeep that Dorje had hired for us. But when I turned to the driver and smiled the Tibetan greeting of '*Tashi Delek*', he looked puzzled and then said '*Ni hao*' – Chinese for 'Hello'! I froze in my seat and felt sick. Dorje had got another Chinese driver! How could I possibly snoop around a Chinese prison with a Chinese driver?

I then tried, with difficulty, to be positive and asked about Kumbum, Takster and Rincon. Dorje, who had sworn blind to the Controller, in front of Seán and me, that everything had been arranged only five weeks previously, then told me that he did not know anyone in Kumbum at the moment, but that if we went there he might be able to find some monks. But it would take at least three days! And on persistent questioning it transpired that he had not organized anything in Rincon either. In fact he had never been there!

After so many alarms and crises during the trip, after so many times when I thought nothing worse could happen and then it did, after hitting the bottom of my reserves so often and still having to go on, that morning I finally did run out of resolve and if I could have found a way out, I would have abandoned the project.

'Are you all right?' Astride said, with concern. 'You look dreadful.' I just shook my head, gave her a hug and said I'd see her in Lhasa. Then, shaking myself, I suggested that we film the industrial areas and factories of Xining to show how extensively the Chinese were entrenched in what had once been a Tibetan town. But Dorje did not know where the factories were, or anything about the town, not even the altitude or population.

So I filmed some panning gvs from a nearby hill that showed the factories' chimney stacks spewing thick industrial waste into what had once been pure desert air. They were dotted all over the dense urban concentration of Xining, right up to a small Chinese pagoda on a hill.

We then headed west towards the heartland of Tibet. The only positive thing I could say was that the road was excellent. 'It would be,' Tibetan friends later told me. 'It is the main road to bring troops and supplies from Lanchow HQ to Golmud.' Inside the jeep the atmosphere was glacial, especially when I discovered that Dorje did not know where one single checkpoint was.

So we headed west-south-west towards Golmud and what should have been an idyllic odyssey passing through some of the most spectacular scenery in Tibet became another living nightmare. Instead of looking at the filmic potential of the landscape, my eyes scoured the road ahead for checkpoints and each bend in the road became a potential hazard as I had no idea what lay beyond it until we had safely negotiated it – then the process started all over again on the next bend. In the mountains of Tibet there is no shortage of bends.

As we left Xining we drove through neat fields bordered by tall poplar trees whose yellowing leaves heralded the approaching winter. It was like any other rural area of China with peasants in blue labouring in the fields and the roads round the small villages flooded with cyclists. By 1.30 in the afternoon we had reached the empty prairies of northern Tibet. Vast long sweeps of straw-coloured grassland stretched to the horizon on either side of the road without a tree or bush in sight. Not even a pimple of a molehill to hide under. If we ran into a road block then I knew that we had not the remotest chance of escaping. The jeep burned up the miles with the relentlessness of a runaway train gaining momentum with its imprisoned passengers not knowing when it would hit a mountain, only the lethal certainty that it would, sooner or later. I felt completely trapped: there was nothing I could do or think of to extricate myself and my rushes.

There was only one road west. Behind us was Xining and China. To the north, hundreds of miles of Inner Mongolia's steppe and desert. The Gobi somewhere beyond. To the west over a thousand miles of Tibet's vast Empty Quarter and to the south hundreds of miles to the mountains of Kham and then miles of Burma, Thailand and Laos.

In the middle of the afternoon I was jerked out of my gloom by the sight of an expanse of intense blue water on the northern horizon. The fabled Lake Kokonor, Tibet's *Tso Trishor Gyalmo* (the Blue Lake – the Sea of the Queen), the biggest of Tibet's thousands of lakes. Three things have always held immeasurable fascination for me since I was a child. Maps with vast areas of nothing on them but a few topographical squiggles in an ocean of uncharted territory – usually of the earth's most inhospitable regions. Like Saudi Arabia's Rub-Al Khali (the Empty Quarter of burning sands in the south-east), the Gobi desert, now a sea of trackless sand that has drowned the cities of many civilizations beneath its merciless and ever-encroaching sands, and the Chang Thang, Tibet's enormous and enigmatic Empty Quarter towards which we were heading. Another obsession is remote islands dotted in the Pacific with names that spell magic and whose sculpture is quite extraordinary. The third is empty expanses of water like the Caspian and Aral inland seas, Bolivia's Lake Titicaca, Nicaragua's Lago de Nicaragua and Tibet's Kokonor.

I knew Titicaca, had filmed on Lago de Nicaragua and I was at long last approaching Kokonor. Covering 2,400 square miles, it sits like a flattened plaice 10,500 feet up in the prairie of what is now Qinghai province. It is regarded as a sacred lake by Tibetans and legend has it that in the eighth century the spring from which it feeds overflowed and drowned thousands of the nomads in the area. There seemed to be no end to the flood and even more nomads were endangered. Then the Indian sage Padmasambhava, who eventually brought Buddhism to Tibet, heard about it and prayed; magically, because he was then living in India 2,000 miles away, he got to Kokonor, stopped up the spring, saved the nomads and left behind the Blue Lake as a memorial.

The area – the very road we were travelling on – is redolent with history. Both its north shore (where now runs the Xining–Golmud railway) and the southern shore were part of the old caravan routes from Central Asia to China – the southern branch of the Silk Road. And the Sakya 'Pontiff', who in the thirteenth century journeyed from Tibet to Mongolia and converted the Mongol Khan, who in turn bestowed on him the total spiritual and temporal sovereignty of Tibet and thus confirmed and enshrined the independence of Tibet, also preached many sermons round the lake, in the very area we were driving through! In the past centuries the journey that I had hoped to do in two days would take the nomads five months each way.

But more recently, sinister reports have trickled out of Tibet that something is happening round the lake: Tibetans report that children are being born deformed and animals are dying. No one knows why. Some say that the fish in the lake (which the Chinese usually take to Xining to sell for their own consumption) are dying. In 1980–81 there were strong rumours that after China had test-exploded one of its atmospheric atomic bombs at the Lop Nor test-site, to the north-west of Kokonor on the Inner Mongolia border, the winds had unexpectedly blown east and carried radioactive fall-out across the shores of Kokonor and eventually to Japan and the United States. Despite profitable trade negotiations in progress with China, both protested so strongly to the Chinese Government that China then decided to abandon atmospheric nuclear testing and has since exploded nuclear devices underground.

It was reported that considerable numbers of nomads were suddenly evacuated from the area around Kokonor and taken for treatment to China. China denies any nuclear accident, but even it cannot deny the nuclear testing which the Stockholm International Peace Research Institute has monitored and documented and the records of which are to be found in every International Institute of Strategic Studies in the Western world. But while I was in Tibet, I also heard reports that a branch line from the main east–west Golmud–Xining railway turns left towards the lake and no one knows where it goes to. The only thing that they do know is that, like the whole region, it is officially forbidden to Tibetans and foreigners. Nomads who have strayed into the area report that the grass round there is burnt and dead for several miles. With my visa running out, I was unable to check these allegations. Nor could I hope to locate the alleged underground nuclear installation reputed to be sited between Thensong and Gangtsa on the northern shore of the lake, or the one at Tonyela, which was, frustratingly, not far from our road.

We drove for three hours along the southern shore of the lake, which has an intensity of blue that I had not seen even in Tibet. Mile after mile after mile of blue water merging into blue sky. There was not a tree, a shrub or even any lakeside rushes and on the lake no sign of life. No boats, no fishermen, no one swimming or playing. I was itching to go up, paddle, taste the water to find out whether it was icy, or warm from a hot spring, or salty like the Dead Sea. But of course the driver refused permission, so I did not. Nor could we deviate to look for the small Dunganor

Lake, which is near Kokonor. It was there in 1706 that the 6th Dalai Lama, Tsang-Yang Gyatso, one of Tibet's most celebrated lyrical poets, was murdered, by the Chinese in circumstances shrouded in as much mystery as any murder in the Borgias' Rome.

About 5.30 that evening I saw the first Tibetan thing in days – the black yak-haired tents of the Tibetan *drogpa*. I persuaded the driver to stop, and as he could see that I was interested in filming an obviously 'tourist' attraction, he agreed. I got out of the car with the camera and fell lucky. A nomad had just married and a lama had come to bless the couple. The bride, bedecked in her bridal finery of a deep coral necklace and new *pangden*, the striped apron conferring her marital status, was offering *choe* with the family and there on a makeshift altar under the opening in the tent to allow the firesmoke out was a picture of the Dalai Lama. It was a lovely sequence and needed more care and time, but it was nearly seven and we had a very long way to go.

The driver stopped at a small excellent Muslim roadside restaurant where Thondup, Dorje and the driver enjoyed huge slabs of freshly killed halal meat. After seeing the poor animal's head casually placed on a chair and dripping blood all over the floor two feet from our table, I suddenly lost my appetite. Later we pulled into a truckers' hotel near the salt marshes of Dulian and from the window of my concrete 'box' of a bedroom I looked onto another magical Tibetan landscape. It was a cold clear night, and the mist was rising slowly from the brackish waters of the salt marshes. Beyond a clump of reeds a pale full moon diffused the mist with an ethereal silver light. It seemed to hang like spun gossamer between the shimmer of water and the immensity of sky. It was absolutely breathtaking to watch the mist curl in sensuous, languorous tendrils, like the mist rising smokily from Venice's winter lagoons in Joe Losey's hauntingly beautiful film *Eva*.

We were away before light. As the dawn suffused the sky with a cold grey wash I saw that the landscape had changed. In the flat bleakness of the scrub and sand I could feel the emptiness of the vast desert nearby. As the grass became more sparse and the sand drifted across the road, camels began disdainfully to lurch slowly out of the horizon in groups of twenty or more. I felt that the formidable Gobi desert was not far away. As we drove west towards the Chang Thang I grew increasingly excited. In this empty expanse of hundreds of miles of drying marsh, sparse scrub and stony desert where little lived other than a few hardy nomads and their flocks, the deep silence was broken only by the harsh wind. It was largely unexplored and stretched west to the border with Pakistan 1,900 miles away.

It was an area I had wanted to see all my life. The very name, Chang Thang, musical and mysterious, conjured all the romance and enigma of immense empty spaces – but it also held the special lure of virgin territory in a mystical land that only a few exceptional explorers had ever managed to penetrate and traverse. Extraordinary men like the Jesuits Antonio Andrada in the sixteenth century and Ipolito Desideri and P. Freyre in the eighteenth century; also, the Swede, Sven Hedin, in the nineteenth century had laboured across its empty wastes and documented the life of the few nomads and recounted tales of magnificent temples, now either swallowed by the encroaching desert or standing in majestic and lonely ruin. But today a solitary Chinese road, servicing their military outposts on the western borders, bisects the otherwise virgin area. Since we were turning left and south hoping to reach Golmud by nightfall, there was no hope of experiencing the real solitude of the depths of the Chang Thang. Another time, I promised myself.

On Monday, 26 September, Thondup and I sat outside the hotel in Golmud in yet another freezing grey dawn, waiting for Dorje and the driver. We had precisely twenty-four hours to get to Lhasa, if – as the backpackers in the hotel had intimated – the roads into the capital were not blocked by Chinese military turning back all foreigners approaching Lhasa, as they had after a previous demonstration. By eight Dorje and the driver had arrived. There was a lot to film, for Golmud was an important army base, the terminus for the railway from Xining and China and an important oil-pipe terminal. I also knew that there was an airport nearby because when driving in flat stony desert on the way there we had seen a number of wooden structures with blinking red lights on the top – aircraft beacons.

It was a vital link in China's new and highly organized Rapid Deployment Force: troops and supplies could be rushed by air, road and rail from China to Golmud in the middle of Tibet to provide a back-up supply base from which to service Lhasa and the sensitive posts on the Indian border. Although Dorje was supposed to know the town well, and had been there four times to my certain knowledge, he said that he didn't know where anything was.

Previously a stopping point on the north–south caravan routes, today Golmud is a sprawling town of well-constructed, low, two- and three-storeyed buildings neatly painted in white. The streets were lined with newly planted poplar trees which were too regimented to be attractive, but certainly and most effectively obscured the numerous official-looking buildings. There was nothing Tibetan about the town and no one wore Tibetan *chubas*. There were no street signs or landmarks, just neat buildings laid on an endless grid in a featureless plain that stretched to the horizon. Maybe it was my imagination, but it seemed as though it had been deliberately made anonymous, in the same way the British removed all signposts during World War II so that if the Germans landed they would be lost. It was that same feeling.

The railway station looked like a piece of scenery, like a 'flat' from a movie set. Large and imposing, it was set down in the middle of nowhere. We were driving around in circles trying to find the army base, the oil terminals, the airfield, all of which I knew were there but which Dorje, Kafkaesquely, denied any knowledge of. It was just too hopeless: I had enough information to know that the place was bristling with military and if a jeep with unusual number plates kept driving around, it would only be a matter of time before we were picked up. So I asked the driver to put his foot down for Nagchukha.

On the mountains the Mongol-influenced square nest of prayer-flags, with their distinctively Mongol sun and moon printed amid the prayers, had given way to the traditionally Tibetan inverted conical shape of twigs, and I felt we were now approaching the heartland of Tibet. Yak and *drogpa* were scattered round the mountains and in the occasional stretch of desert, camels, yak and sheep drank in photogenically reflective oasis pools surrounded by low sand-coloured mountains. If you blinked you could almost hear the noises and smells of the caravanserai of Kublai Khan and his hordes, as they watered their animals on their rampaging escapades through Tibet and on to China. Today Chinese-made tractors drawing small flat trailers full of Tibetans phut-phut down a road where once must have resounded the mighty Khan's blood-curdling cries.

By two the next morning the driver was swerving all over the road in exhaustion. It was obvious that if we drove through the night, we would end up dead, rather than get into Lhasa later that day, so we pulled into a filthy 'hotel' at Yangshi. I was so tired that I barely noticed the mud floor, soiled bedclothes and the stench of urine, and it must have been below zero for the water in the metal basin had frozen solid. By 5.30 the same morning – Tuesday, 27 September – we had left the revolting hotel, although I knew we would not get to Lhasa that day. By eight we were driving over the spectacular Tangola Pass and by eleven we were at Amdo town, where I knew there was a tricky checkpoint at the entrance to the Tibetan Autonomous Region. There was no Tenzin to hide me this time, but I thought I could just about get away with it, if we were stopped, by bluffing with the story of my rapidly expiring visa. Time was evaporating like ether.

By luck, a very heavy army convoy was passing through, so we slipped into the rear of it and got through the checkpoint. After driving at breakneck speed through some more ravishing mountains, we arrived on the outskirts of Nagchukha at four in the afternoon.

As we drove slowly down the main street that afternoon, unlike the first time I arrived in the town, there was not a soldier in sight. But when we stopped to ask where the petrol station was, people said that it had been full of soldiers the night before. I was still carrying the incriminating Nagchukha interview tape on me, so I was anxious to get across and out of the place as soon as possible.

We had the usual hassle over the petrol, but with the driver being Chinese it was much easier. We still had a two-hour wait – the official on the pump told the driver that there was a shortage of fuel because there had been heavy army convoys to and from Lhasa and Golmud for the past two days. Indeed I had remarked on – and filmed – immensely long convoys of three-tonne army trucks coming from Nagchukha towards Golmud. The convoys drove all day long until I lost count of the number. And even at night the convoys continued to drive, lighting the valleys with their headlights. Something was certainly afoot to warrant the extraordinary number of trucks, but what were they transporting? Some appeared empty but most had tarpaulins tightly covering their loads. They were quite spectacular and usually ran to thirty-three trucks per convoy. In the middle of the day, with a slight heat haze, they shimmered towards the jeep and drove straight into my telephoto lens. It was one of the most striking images of the film – and one of the most frightening to record as often in the view-finder I would find the soldier in the driving cab looking straight down at me through the lens.

All day as we raced towards Lhasa I was in a ferment to know what was actually happening in the capital. When we finally reached Lhasa it was 1.30 A.M. on Wednesday, 28 September. The town was dark and silent and as I did not know if there was a curfew – there had been several heavily armed checkpoints on the road – I decided to go straight to the hotel. A lone vehicle driving around at night would have attracted immediate army attention. Dorje for once did something – he talked us through the check-points without them discovering me or turning the jeep inside out 'looking for weapons', as the soldiers said when Dorje asked them why they were armed. 'Subversives!'

It was nearly two when I checked into the Lhasa Holiday Inn. We agreed that since Lhasa was likely to be in ferment, it was safer for Thondup and me not to appear to be connected. So we agreed to meet at 10.30 later that morning in a side chapel at the Jokhang.

I was worried to find that Seán had not left me a note at the hotel to say that he had got the rushes I had sent down with the interviewees from Nagchukha. Nor was there a telex waiting for me telling me that he had got out in one piece. For all I knew he might have been caught at the airport and still be under arrest somewhere in Lhasa or Beijing.

I got to my room and placed a long-distance call to David Lloyd at his home. But not surprisingly the operator told me that there was 'trouble on the line' and an indefinite delay on all international calls. With total predictability, the Chinese were behaving as they had previously when they anticipated trouble, by cutting the phone and telex lines to the outside world, and preventing foreigners from entering or leaving Lhasa so that no news would get out. They had failed miserably in the past, but at two in the morning I had no way of knowing what, if anything, had happened in Lhasa that day.

After luxuriating in my first bath in two weeks, I set my alarm on the hour, every hour, and badgered the poor hotel operator until 7 A.M. when I finally got through to London. David Lloyd is an immensely cool man; at the BBC he was well-known for his sang-froid in the middle of the blazing crises that often erupt around senior editors of current affairs television programmes. But that morning – it was 11 P.M. by London time – I thought I detected a hint of relief in David's voice!

We babbled on about my 'holiday' and, hopefully keeping the anxiety out of my voice, I asked him whether Seán was back safely from his travels and whether he had had his 'holiday snaps' processed. When David said all was well, I thought my own sigh of relief would blow the communications satellite transmitting the call right out of the sky! But what was worrying was that David seemed to have no knowledge of my two-hander – television slang for the two-handed (two interviewees) interview in Nagchukha – which should have been delivered to Seán the night before he left for London. I explained in a voice now squeaky with anxiety that I had given it to a friend to give to Seán. David promised that he would check with Chris, the film editor, and get hold of Seán, and call me back as soon as possible – lines to Beijing permitting. 'And by the way, do hurry home, we all miss you back here,' David said, which translated meant: please get out of there – soon!

As I put the phone down, I knew that although I might have a show 'in the can', getting it – and Thondup and me – out in one piece was quite something else. During the fractured night I had thought a lot about Thondup's safety. The next demonstration was scheduled for 1 October, and I knew that I would have somehow to find a way – and a place to hide – to film the army and the demonstrators. The probability of being caught was horrendously high. If I was caught with all the film on me I had not a snowball's chance in hell of talking my way out of it. And as the army has totally arbitrary powers, they would ransack my room and the whole hotel until they found my rushes. But if they found Thondup . . . I decided to over-ride the protests that he would loyally make about leaving me on my own and book him out on the first flight on Saturday, 1 October to Katmandu. That way, by the time any demonstration had occurred in Lhasa, he would be safely airborne.

I spoke to the hotel's charming Hong Kong Chinese manager and asked him to validate only Thondup's ticket, explaining that it would be my last opportunity to go with some friends to Ganden (lies!). (It would have taken a week to arrange this with CITS.) I collected the bag I had left at the hotel at the beginning of the trip with my few tourist clothes, sent everything else to the laundry, changed and walked down to the coffee shop for breakfast at 7.30. It felt most peculiar to be wearing my own jeans, T-shirt and track shoes again, and to feel my hair hanging free of the ski-mask was decidedly strange. I kept touching it as though I could not believe it too had survived the journey – so far. And it was pure, unadulterated bliss to feel the soft silk of a new set of undies!

I remember that wonderful, courageous war photographer Tim Page, who was medi-vacked out of Vietnam with half his head blown away, telling me that after a difficult assignment you should give yourself a few days to 'come down' and adjust to the obscenities of the 'real' world. It was a luxury I could ill-afford. My priorities were to hide the rushes where the hotel staff, innocently or otherwise, would not find them, and then to go into town to try, somehow, to find Tenzin and discover what happened to my Nagchukha tapes – and if possible arrange some way of driving out of Tibet.

My anxiety levels shot through the roof when a group of tourists in the lobby told me that Lhasa was crawling with military, and that martial law and a curfew were about to be clamped on the city!

21

Lhasa: A State of Siege

My rushes hidden, I caught the hotel shuttle bus downtown and got off at the Jokhang. Lhasa was unchanged except for the distinct chill in the air and the yellowing of the poplar trees lining the roads of the Chinese quarter. Approaching the tree-lined avenue leading from the People's Park to the square in front of the Jokhang, I noticed several green army trucks parked under the trees in the side lanes, which were usually reserved for cyclists, and a fair number of soldiers in uniform sitting around. They had that unmistakeable alertness that all armies have when 'relaxing' on active duty – and waiting.

Once in the square, I walked casually towards the Jokhang among a light sprinkling of pilgrims and tourists and surreptitiously looked up to the roofs of the white PSB buildings on both the right and left immediately facing the temple. There, lining the roofs, were PSB men in civvies and a couple of soldiers in uniform. They were all intently scrutinizing the crowds in the square below with binoculars, focusing their attention on the inside of the Jokhang's upper courtyard and roofs which, from the superior height of the PSB buildings, were entirely open to view.

I found Thondup in the upstairs chapel and we perambulated round the courtyards as we tried to make sense of our predicament. The first thing was to try and find Tenzin and the rest of the Boys who should by now have returned to Lhasa. It was imperative that I found that tape of the Nagchukha interview, as I could not leave Tibet without it.

I suggested that Thondup went to find our original contact in Lhasa, as he might be able to lead us to Tenzin. Meanwhile I would try to locate Marie-Chantal, a Belgian academic from Louvain University and at that time working undercover in Lhasa for an international human rights organization. She was collecting information on the violations of human rights and recording eye-witness reports of what actually happened during the 1987 disturbances and those earlier in the spring of 1988. Marie-Chantal spoke fluent Tibetan and had extensive contacts all over Lhasa. I hoped to get her to agree to be interviewed on camera. Her excellent research and knowledge of the Tibetan scene, and her considerable academic and medical qualifications would give great weight to her evidence. I also wanted to check with the backpackers – undoubtedly the best bush underground around – what was happening in Lhasa and where the checkpoints, if any, were.

I thought I would just walk round the Barkhor, talking to Marie-Chantal or one of the backpackers, as though we were sightseeing and buying tourist souvenirs, in the remote hope that I might see Tenzin or one of the other Boys, or even one of the earlier contacts, so that I could set up more interviews with Tibetans and complete my schedule. I wanted to discover what had happened the day before on the anniversary of the September 1987 demonstrations, what the mood of Tibetans was now and, more important, their prognosis for the future. Thondup and I agreed to meet on the hour every two hours in the same chapel so that we could liaise.

Marie-Chantal, a tall blonde striking woman in her mid-forties, was staying at the small Tibetan-run Kirey Hotel. As we sat in the Barkhor square or walked round pretending to examine the tourist merchandise on the stalls, always extremely careful of who was in earshot, I asked her what had happened the previous day and why at this time we were hearing about demonstrations in Lhasa. A serious researcher with a formidable academic record, she explained to me: 'You must understand that what you are seeing today is not just a spontaneous outburst, it is the culmination of the grievances of the Tibetans against the Chinese that go right back to the Chinese invasion in 1949. I don't have to tell you that since then, and especially during the Cultural Revolution, the Tibetan people have suffered horrendously. And because the Chinese installed an informer system inside Tibetan society, Tibetans have pent up inside themselves – for decades – bitterness and frustration.

'Previously, Tibetans could clearly define and identify the "enemy". They were the Chinese administrators, the military, the police who were oppressing them, putting them in jail. But recently, with the new "liberalization" policies in China, vast

numbers of Chinese, who are not officials of the State, have
flooded into Tibet, attracted by the economic opportunities here,
and have taken the jobs and lands of the Tibetans. They are the
less easily targeted enemy, if you will. These are not the people
who oppress you, who put you in jail, but in the long run Tibet
will be inundated with them. For instance, all the jobs in Lhasa
go to the Chinese – look at the big construction works going
on – all the workers are Chinese and the Tibetans see all the
opportunities going to them. And this has exacerbated the acute
frustration Tibetans have felt for decades; and with no recourse
to redress the situation, it has channelled a lot of the Tibetans'
feelings into the demonstrations.'

'But surely they have some redress?' I suggested. 'After all, they
have a Tibetan, Dorje Tsering, in a top job in the government of
the Tibetan Autonomous Region.'

'To begin with, Tibetans regard him as a quisling,' Marie-
Chantal said. 'He only does what Beijing tells him to do, and the
others are as bad.'

This is the man, Tibetan colleagues had pointed out, who, in a
recent BBC interview, had said, 'The disturbances [in Lhasa]
didn't happen because of the lack of unity between the two nations.
Of course, a few splittists hang out the two banners of nationalism
and religion to hoodwink the people. But the Tibetan people
know what's what. It's possible that a small number of splittists
may deceive a small number of people, but it's a day-dream to
deceive all Tibetans and talk about independence.'

Afterwards he went on to say, 'An independent Tibet is impossible. A semi-independent Tibet is impossible. But even though
it is impossible, some Tibetans will struggle for it. No matter how
they struggle, independence will be unrealistic. The PLA was here
in the past, is here now and will always be here. For as long as
the People's Republic [of China] remains as an independent
country, the PLA will never leave Tibet.'

'But the real issue here,' Marie-Chantal continued, 'which no
one in the West, in the mad scramble to get into the honey-pots
of China's opening markets, is willing to look at, is a classic case
of colonial exploitation of the Tibetans by the Chinese.'

'Come on!' I protested.

'There is no difference between what China is doing here to the

Tibetans, in taking their jobs and land and resources, and what the Belgians did in the Congo. Or the British did in their colonies all over the world. Who's going to censure them? Who censured the British for what they did to the Aborigines? Or, for that matter, what the Queensland Government did to them not even a decade ago?

'The Chinese colonial attitude and behaviour here has resulted in many demonstrations all over the country for many years. The only difference is that as Tibet was officially closed to foreigners no one saw them. But when a few years ago Tibet was opened up to foreigners, they came in and saw for themselves the reality of the situation, talked to Tibetans and discovered that it differed greatly from the propaganda put out by the Chinese – which until now is all that has officially come out of Tibet.

'Also, don't forget, Tibetans now have more contact with the outside world. They are more aware of what is going on outside. More conscious of human rights, of individual freedom. And they now recognize the value of demonstrating peacefully when there are foreigners around. But don't forget there have been demonstrations all over the country that go unreported only because those areas are closed to foreigners.'

On 27 September 1987, 200 Tibetans led by thirty monks from Drepung monastery marched round the Jokhang, carrying home-made Tibetan flags (a criminal offence). They demonstrated by chanting peacefully for religious freedom and the release of some monks who had been previously arrested for demanding the same thing. Twenty-one monks and forty lay Tibetans were promptly arrested. The demonstration and arrest were witnessed by several Westerners in Lhasa at the time.

'Actually,' Marie-Chantal said, 'that demonstration last September had a rather curious genesis. Shortly before, the Chinese had coerced nearly 14,000 Tibetans into watching the public executions in Lhasa of two Tibetans popularly believed to be on trial for their nationalistic beliefs. Then, when the Dalai Lama was in Washington, also in September, speaking to Congress about his Five-Point Peace Plan and making Tibet a Zone of Peace, the Chinese, worried about the impact of American pressure, began a "smear" campaign through a local radio broadcast, accusing America of "interfering in the internal affairs of China".

'Then, as far as I can ascertain, some of the Drepung monks met near the Barkhor, and decided that they should show solidarity with the Dalai Lama and their countrymen and make some kind of a peaceful demonstration. Nothing more than just walking round the Jokhang and shouting their support for the Dalai Lama and speaking out for human rights and independence for Tibet. That evening, as I understand it, in front of Paldan Lhamo, the patron protector-deity of Tibet, they swore an oath that they would carry out a protest, and the following day they tried to demonstrate. And you know the rest – they were arrested, thrown into jail for five months and thirteen were released last January. But one of their group is still in jail.

'The demonstration might have gone unnoticed but for two things – the police who beat the Tibetans with alarming brutality and then arrested them, and the foreign tourists who witnessed it and carried reports of it to the outside world.'

On 1 October, China's National Day, a public holiday to celebrate the anniversary of the Chinese Revolution and therefore a day of particular sensitivity to Tibetans, thirty-four monks (twenty-three from Sera monastery, three from Nechung and eight from the Jokhang) led a peaceful demonstration of lay Tibetans round the Jokhang. I asked Marie-Chantal (and later the Tibetans) what had happened.

They told me that the monks were peacefully asking for the release of their colleagues who had been arrested and had since disappeared into Chinese police stations and prisons, since when nothing had been heard of them. At that point they were joined by between thirty and sixty lay Tibetans. Then the Chinese PSB and army started videoing the demonstrators, just as they were doing that morning from the roof-tops, and also from street-level. The Tibetans, realizing that this would lead to further arrests and imprisonments, tried to wrench the cameras from the Chinese, a tussle ensued, the Chinese opened fire and the unarmed Tibetans retaliated by throwing stones at the cameras. By then the crowd had swelled to over 3,000 Tibetans.

The Chinese charged into the crowd of monks and arrested other Tibetans, dragging them into the police station at the side of the Jokhang. Other Tibetans then tried to storm the police station to secure their release. Eye-witnesses reported that the arrested monks then started to pray inside the inner courtyard of the police station; suddenly, from a first-floor window, four shots were fired into the praying monks and one monk from Nechung was shot in the back of the head. The crowd outside heard the shots and tried to storm the police station to save them. In the ensuing fracas many Tibetans were killed and scores injured.

The Chinese maintained that the Tibetans attacked them with weapons and that they opened fire only in self-defence. The facts, as given to me by many Western eye-witnesses who were there at the time (there were about fifty in the crowd), are different. They told me that when the unarmed Tibetans tried to storm the police station to obtain the release of those inside, the Chinese opened fire. Then a foreigner, who was in the front of the Jokhang, reported that he saw a Tibetan snatch a gun, dropped by a soldier who had fled the wrath of the crowd, and smash it on the pavement. All the foreigners and Tibetans, who have independently given eye-witness reports to various human rights organizations in Switzerland, Britain and the United States, maintain that, contrary to Chinese allegations, at no time did they ever see any of the Tibetans with any weapons whatsoever.

And two Americans, Dr Blake Kerr and a lawyer, John Ackerley, who were on holiday in Lhasa, informed Amnesty International that they saw the Chinese open fire at point-blank range on the crowd, and some of the Tibetans, lacking other means, threw stones in self-defence. But when most of the Tibetans just ran away from the gunfire, they were shot – in the back – by the Chinese.

Robert Barnett, a British eye-witness, who later gave evidence to the United Nations Sub-Commission on Human Rights, reported:

'I saw a group of up to a dozen policemen standing on the roof of the police building and shooting their rifles from there . . . one police officer stepped forward from the group; he took careful aim with his pistol; he did this repeatedly and without haste. I was able to see from where I was standing about thirty yards away that he was firing low and deliberately into the crowd.'

The Chinese authorities have issued a statement denying that Chinese soldiers or police shot into the crowd. However, Western eye-witnesses reported that they saw nine Tibetans (names with-held by the Tibetan Government-in-exile, but available to human rights organizations) killed, including a seven-year-old boy shot in the back, but the Tibetans list a further twenty-three fatalities and Westerners describe giving first aid to another nine Tibetans with gunshot wounds and hearing of detailed descriptions of seventeen others. The real number is in all probability higher, as again Tibetans were afraid of being picked up by the authorities and refused to be taken to Chinese hospitals for treatment.

The Tibetans, incensed at the carnage, attacked the police station to try and obtain the release of the monks. In the confusion that ensued, the Tibetans set fire to the building, a much-hated symbol of Chinese surveillance on their holy of holies, the Jokhang. When fire first broke out at the gate of the police station, some Tibetans rushed in, trying to release their colleagues, and one monk received severe head and arm injuries. The fire damaged only the front and ground floor of the building. The fire brigade were denied quick access to the building and the fire soon spread. Army and armed police reinforcements were rushed to the scene. The Chinese complained that they had been trapped inside the police station, but in fact most were seen escaping over the adjacent roofs to safety in nearby buildings, and others ran through the alley at the side of the police station.

The Chinese and Tibetan versions differ considerably as to the number of Tibetans injured and killed. The Tibetans maintain one Chinese and thirty-two Tibetans died. The Chinese give a different version of events: their figures state that only six Tibetans were killed and nineteen Chinese security officials were injured.

Accurate numbers are hard to assess as the September and October 1987 and March 1988 demonstrations were massive, with many people from all over Tibet participating. Most of those from outside Lhasa did not register, as Chinese law requires them to, with the Lhasa City Police Registration Office, as they had trav-elled to the capital without official permission; they therefore did not go to the Chinese-run hospitals for treatment, as their details would be registered on admission and it would have led to their certain arrest.

On 6 October 1987 eighty monks from Drepung monastery and sixteen from Nechung demonstrated peacefully in Lhasa for the release of their colleagues and for the independence of Tibet. They were promptly arrested by the Chinese.

Within hours of the October 1987 disturbances, the Chinese began mass arrests of Tibetans, foreigners were expelled, and the authorities drafted into Lhasa and the surrounding area a detachment of 6,000 Wujing (specially trained commando-type armed police, who are sent in to quell riots all over China); they were air-lifted in from Chengdu.

But after the October demonstrations took place, tourist groups were suspended, the borders were sealed and the country was again cut off from the outside world. A night curfew was imposed on Lhasa and Amnesty International reported the wide-scale arbitrary arrests of Tibetans. The Chinese authorities also organized 're-education' sessions in the monasteries, schools and work units, which Tibetans told me were reminiscent of the oppressive indoctrination and *thumzing* sessions during the Cultural Revolution. Despite the ban on demonstrations, many took place, even in Lhasa itself; although they went unreported to the outside world, statistics were collated by the Office of Information and International Affairs of the Tibetan Government-in-exile in India. The following are some recent examples:

17 October 1987: at Lhasa No.1 Middle School an argument broke out between Tibetan and Chinese students when a Tibetan challenged the assertions of the Propaganda Committee: a student was arrested and taken into custody. Subsequently over forty students disappeared and are still missing.

14 November 1987: eighty monks at Ganden monastery demonstrated against the police presence in their monastery. Some were arrested; the event was also reported by a correspondent for AFP (Agence France-Presse) in Beijing.

20 November 1987: Tibetan students demonstrated for human rights and against forced abortions at Rekong in Amdo.

25 November 1987: for one week Tibetan students boycotted classes in Ngapa in Amdo, demanding better conditions.

1 February 1988: over 200 students and ten teachers of the Nationalities Institute and about 100 monks demonstrated in Rekong, Amdo. Ten teachers and nineteen monks were arrested.

On 5 March 1988 the Monlam Prayer Festival came round again and Lhasa was tense. The Chinese had ordered all the monks to attend the Great Prayer Festival. It was a propaganda opportunity for the Chinese, as they had invited the world's press, including BBC TV cameras, to film the event. In itself the ceremonies were spectacular enough, but this occasion was specifically chosen to prove the point, via the world's camera crews, that the Chinese allowed religion to be practised freely in Tibet. The monks from the big monasteries in and around Lhasa – Sera, Drepung, Ganden and Nechung – decided to boycott the charade, but the Chinese brought such enormous pressure to bear, including heavily armed troops, that the monks were forced to attend and were duly filmed by foreign television cameras carrying out their *choe* – devotions.

The monks bitterly resented the fact that they and their Monlam Prayer Festival, an ancient ceremony instituted in 1409 by Tsong-khapa, the founder of the Gelupa sect to which most of the monks belonged, had been so crassly manipulated. Their resentment boiled. A large contingent of soldiers was again drafted to the Jokhang, and after the statue of the Maitreya (future) Buddha had been circumambulated round the Jokhang, in keeping with traditional Buddhist ritual, monks from the three great monasteries, Ganden, Sera and Drepung, began to chant for the release of a very senior and revered clergyman, the Tulku Yulu Dawa Tsering, a fifty-three-year-old monk from Ganden monastery. He had been detained for questioning on 26 December 1987 and had not been seen or heard of since. The demonstration was peaceful, but the monks began to shout their demands to some Tibetans working for the Chinese Government in Lhasa (plain-clothes operatives and Tibetans from the TAR Religious Bureau), who had been watching the festival from a raised dais, with the rest of the officials, at the Sunchoera, at the side of the Jokhang.

One of the officials' bodyguards became over-anxious and without provocation fired and killed one of the Khampas in the demonstration. The crowd erupted angrily and started abusing the Chinese. The officials fled as the army opened fire at point-blank range on the crowd, and others chased many of the monks into the Jokhang and clubbed thirty of them to death. A police video shot by the Chinese was ingeniously purloined by the Tibetans and smuggled to the West, where it was shown widely on television. The monks could be seen being chased like animals by the Chinese soldiers and policemen, and when they were caught, five or six Chinese laid into each monk with such ferocity that the sight of their thick batons crashing down on the skulls of the monks reminded me, when I saw the video, of the bloody culling of seals. It was exceptionally nauseating.

Tibetans claim that they have proof that the dead comprised twelve monks, including a thirteen-year-old novice, who were beaten to death by the police. Eighteen Khampas were also killed in the Jokhang. Another two monks were strangled by the Chinese and eight other Khampas were killed. A further 144 monks went missing.

The world saw on that video how many unfortunate monks were literally battered to the ground. In the fracas one Chinese policeman was killed by the Tibetans after the rampage started in the Jokhang and the other Tibetans saw what was being done to the monks. The Chinese authorities completely and categorically denied any brutality on the part of their soldiers and police and maintained that they acted only in self-defence. But when the video was transmitted on television in Britain and around the world, there was a resounding silence from the Chinese.

Although the Chinese tightened security, the demonstrations did not stop:

16 March 1988: hundreds of Tibetans demonstrated in Xining, Amdo. Eighteen were killed, fifty-seven seriously injured and 195 received minor injuries.

23 March 1988: monks of Rekong monastery demonstrated in Rekong for human rights.

17 April 1988: twelve nuns of Chubtsang nunnery demonstrated in Lhasa.

24 April 1988: six nuns of the Shungseb nunnery demonstrated in Lhasa. All were arrested.

25 April 1988: eighteen nuns from two nunneries, Chubtsang and Phaphungkha, which are west of Sera monastery, demonstrated in the Barkhor. Plain-clothes police agents were sent in after them and all were arrested just as they were completing the first round of the Jokhang.

17 May 1988: about thirty nuns from the Ghari nunnery demonstrated in Lhasa. All nuns and several lay onlookers were arrested.

30 May 1988: six monks from Ganden monastery demonstrated

outside the Jokhang. The army sent in over 600 soldiers. All the monks were arrested.

24–25 June 1988: eleven monks of the Ba Choedhey Gon monastery demonstrated in Ba, Kham.

We had walked round the Barkhor and I suggested that we go up to the Barkhor café on a balcony on the south-east corner of the square with a panoramic view of the Jokhang, the Potala and the surrounding mountains. It was the only place in Lhasa where you could have a snack in the sun and was always crowded with backpackers.

As we walked up, we found the entrance locked and barred. The owner was apologetic and said, '*Gyami!*' (Chinese). He smiled, unable to say more as there were two soldiers sitting at a table behind him. It was obvious that the Chinese did not want any tourists up there with a perfect view to film or photograph any demonstration in the square below. So we returned to walking round the Jokhang. For the next two days both Thondup and I hunted for Tenzin and the rest of the Boys; Marie-Chantal also took me clandestinely to meet many Tibetans, monks and laymen who corroborated what had happened.

Marie-Chantal decided that walking around the Jokhang was becoming a bit obvious so we decided to go on our bikes for a sightseeing tour as many tourists, especially the backpackers, do. We made our way north-east towards Sera monastery through the northern suburbs of Lhasa to where it is set against the stark mountains that rise sheer from the valley. It was rather bizarre to be cycling slowly and apparently enjoying the superb scenery and weather while actually discussing the minutiae of prison conditions and torture. I asked Marie-Chantal, who had clandestinely interviewed hundreds of ex-prisoners, what happened to Tibetans when they were put into jail. What she told me was confirmed later by Tibetans, particularly monks, who showed me scars on their heads, their backs, and all over their bodies, from the torture.

'Before talking about torture,' said Marie-Chantal, 'I should explain something about what happens to Tibetans when they are arrested for the kind of political activities that have been going on here for the past year. These activities include not just demonstrating in the streets, but also the writing of letters, talking to foreigners, putting up posters. These are all activities that you get thrown in jail for. And that,' she said, indicating an innocuous-looking gateway with willow trees tumbling over the high wall and looking like the entrance perhaps to a nobleman's estate or some educational institution, 'is Drapchi. Before 1959 it was the headquarters of the Tibetan Military Regiment, but after the Chinese occupation it was converted into a prison and today is one of Lhasa's four most notorious prisons.' It was only when we cycled round the bend in the road and came level with the gates that I saw the two soldiers with AK 47s standing just out of sight inside the gates and very much to attention.

'When Tibetans are arrested,' Marie-Chantal continued, 'they are not formally charged. They are in a kind of judicial limbo. They are often taken off in the middle of the night to prison. Relatives are not informed about the arrest. They are not informed of the location of the prisoners and they may be held there for months or years at a time, or be transferred to prisons or work camps in the country and nobody knows where they are.'

'Like *Los Desaparecidos* of Argentina and Chile? Those who were arrested by the death squads at night and vanished during the Terror?' I asked.

'Worse, because in South America where you have vast American interests the US can still exert some pressure, but Tibet?' She shook her head.

'Everything here is totally arbitrary and once you are in a Chinese jail, officially you cease to exist. You become a non-person for the prison authorities to do what they will with you. It is like what we read of in Stalin's prison camps in Siberia in the thirties. You simply disappear.

'The only way to find out anything about these prisoners is through their cell-mates and fellow prisoners who, if and when they are released, talk with great reluctance to a very few members of their close family about conditions in the prisons and who still remains inside. So word leaks out to the Tibetan community and the relatives of the prisoners eventually – but they do not always manage to find their loved ones. If they are lucky and do, no contact is allowed with the prisoners and food and clothing are denied. If the family try and bring food and clothing it is most often refused. And then if the prisoners – and remember that, despite the fact that the Chinese automatically label them common criminals, these Tibetans are not criminals but political prisoners – are released, sometimes after years of incarceration, they are released as though nothing has happened! It's rather like the case I told you about yesterday of the man who had suffered horribly for many years in Gurtsa prison – to the north of Lhasa – and then one day without warning he was just suddenly released and told he hadn't done anything! Now how can one adjust to a normal life after that? There are no medical niceties like psychiatric rehabilitation therapists in Tibet, you know. There aren't even enough doctors to cure their bodies, let alone any to heal their minds.

'Following the October 1987 riots a number of monks and lay people were arrested. According to the monks I talked to, prison conditions are obviously not good, but torture was not the main concern – though some were tortured, especially the lay people. But after the March 1988 demonstration and violence, stories of serious torture begin to emerge. A whole range of torture is taking place in prison, apart from the usual vicious beatings by the police which, more often than not, result in broken bones, damaged kidneys, genitals . . . But in prison it includes having their hands tied behind their backs and being strung up to a beam that pulls the arms out of their sockets. There are numerous incidents of Tibetans, and especially nuns, like those of the Shungseb nunnery, being beaten, then stripped naked and dogs being set on them to bite and savage them terribly! But the most frequent torture at the moment seems to be with electric cattle prods, about three and a half feet long, which Tibetans call *lok-gug*.'

'Like the *picana electrica* that they use on torture victims in Paraguay?'

'Yes. Some of the most horrendous stories of torture come from very young nuns who have taken part in the demonstrations and admitted that they did not do anything more than throw stones when the police opened fire. At other times they were just peacefully chanting for the return of the Dalai Lama and for Tibetan independence – which here is a treasonable crime. These girls, and the youngest I spoke to was fourteen, are beaten and dragged off to prison. Some of the things that happen to them are just too horrible to describe.

'Invariably the nuns are stripped naked, which for Tibetans, being terribly conservative, is a traumatic experience in itself, but for young nuns . . . After they are naked, the Chinese guards strike their bodies all over with these electric cattle prods – on their eyes, their noses, their nipples, into their ears, up their vaginas – and remember these nuns are virgins,' she said.

'The pattern is,' Marie-Chantal went on, 'that while one soldier administers the electric prod, another one interrogates the prisoner for names of other people who have been involved in the demonstrations and if the girl, who has often just spontaneously gone on the demonstration to show solidarity, genuinely has no knowledge, the prodding goes on for hour after hour until she collapses. And it goes on day after day, month after month. The nuns are kept in isolation, and then after months sometimes they are just released without any explanation, without anyone to collect them. Nothing. Sometimes they are in such a shocking state that they collapse on the road outside the prison and a passing stranger takes them to hospital, or to friends, where they spend weeks recovering.

'The difficulty is,' Marie-Chantal said, 'to get this sort of information out. No journalists are allowed in. None of the human rights organizations such as Amnesty International are officially allowed in to investigate for themselves, to find out what is going on. And any attempt by Tibetans themselves to communicate the situation to foreigners is severely punished by prison and torture again.'

What Marie-Chantal said corroborated my own filmed interview with the four nuns over a month earlier. The four girls, barely out of their teens, had told me, on camera and unmasked, that after the main demonstrations in March that year, five of them had decided, quite on their own and not put up to it by anyone, to walk round the Jokhang demonstrating for freedom of religion.

'Each one of us was caught hold of by three Chinese and our hands were twisted and pulled behind our backs and we were thrown into the truck. And when we tried to raise our hands they hit us with electric rods on our hands and when we reached there the six of us were taken to a room and kept standing against the wall with our hands spreadeagled against it and then each one was held down and beaten by six police . . .'

'We were taken to the police station and handcuffed. I was

thrown on the floor, they stamped on my face,' the next nun said, trying to control her tears. 'They repeatedly prodded us all over with electric rods and they kicked me so hard in my chest that I found it difficult to breathe . . .' She was incoherent with sobs as she relived such painful memories.

I asked the third nun sitting near her what had happened in prison: 'The public security people took us to prison and our bodies were searched . . . We were stripped naked and beaten very badly and knocked down; we were kicked so much that I could not breathe. Even then I tried to get up and four or five people beat me . . . and then we were poked countless times by seven or eight people and told that we were opposing the communist system. And they beat us so badly, and they beat us with a chair so much that now none of us is in good health and we are still undergoing treatment.'

I asked them whether the Chinese had known that they were nuns when they were arrested and especially when they stripped off their clothes and left them naked.

'Yes,' one said. 'They could recognize us from our robes. The colour of our robes is different from the clothes ordinary Tibetans wear. They could easily distinguish us.'

I asked them if the Chinese tried to rip off their clothes.

'Yes,' the third one said. 'They had no pity on us and they started beating us with sticks and the *lok-gug* [electric rods].'

'What did you feel while this was happening to you?' I asked.

The third girl answered the most audibly: 'It was terrible. But I do not care whatever punishment they give us. Even if they kill us. There is no freedom . . .'

The nun in the middle continued: 'It is the same situation in the monasteries . . . Our monastery is in ruins; many of our monks and nuns are in prison.' They were simple girls, farmers' daughters from the provinces, born during the Cultural Revolution; they had never known a life of freedom under the Chinese, had never seen the Dalai Lama; and they could barely read and write. These girls were not political agitators, as the Chinese like to label anyone who disagrees with their policies. That those girls, and so many others, had undergone torture and pain for their beliefs was irrefutable evidence of the failure of the Chinese to extinguish a faith that even today flourishes despite decades of persecution.

It was nearly six and the evening was drawing in when we returned to Lhasa. We found Thondup and began to walk round the Barkhor once again in our search for Tenzin and the Boys. While we pretended to be looking at the trinkets on a stall, Thondup told me that he had found Tenzin: Tenzin had the Nagchukha tapes and would arrange the other interviews. I could have kissed the whole world in relief! Thondup told me that he had arranged a meeting at seven when it was darker and suggested that we meet at the corner of the Kirey Hotel.

'Be careful,' Marie-Chantal said. 'Although there is no official military curfew, the Chinese have put up notices in all the smaller hotels warning foreigners that they must be in their hotels by 11 P.M. at the latest. All hotels will close their doors at that time and afterwards no foreigner will be permitted in. The town is very jumpy. The Chinese have been sending special squads around warning people to be wary of foreigners. For heaven's sake don't carry anything incriminating on you. There was a rumour the other day that even foreigners are being stopped and searched; it hasn't happened to anyone I know personally yet, but I do know of five foreigners who have had their rooms ransacked and searched by the police.'

'Where?' I asked, immediately worried about my hidden rushes.

'You should be OK in the Holiday Inn. The Chinese don't want to alarm the rich tourists,' she laughed. 'It is the small Tibetan-run hotels that the backpackers go to, like the Kirey, the Banakshol and the Yak that they are after because it is the backpackers, the students, who talk to the Tibetans – who try and find out what is happening. They are the people the Chinese want to intimidate.'

Thondup melted into the thinning crowd and Marie-Chantal and I agreed to meet early the following morning to go and talk to more Tibetans.

I got back to the hotel and checked that the rushes were safe. Then I put the camera, batteries and tripod into the rucksack, hired a bicycle from the hotel – rickshaws disappear off the streets after dusk – and wobbled back to the Kirey Hotel. I thought it would be safer to transport the equipment at dusk rather than risk being seen wandering through the Tibetan quarter during the day. I locked the bike in the forecourt of the Kirey Hotel, then gritted my teeth as again I hesitated on the edge of the darkened labyrinth of alleys, before feeling my way along a wall. Soon, I heard Thondup softly call my name. Mercifully this time there were not too many mud puddles to sink into, for with the coming of autumn the ground had dried.

The Tibetan quarter seemed quieter than usual; there was no laughter, no children's voices, and I could feel a tension even in the darkness. The unnatural stillness reminded me of Wlady, an old Pole I had once interviewed about what happened the night before the Nazis attacked the Warsaw Ghetto. It was as though the whole area was waiting for something to happen. Maybe I was tired, but in addition to my habitual fear of the dark, I distinctly felt the hair stand up on the back of my neck. After a few minutes we ducked into a familiar doorway, through an open door and were quickly shepherded into a dark room lit by a candle. Tenzin, resplendent in his *chuba*, was full of smiles. We both apologized, laughed and hugged each other. I told him how I had missed him and the rest of the Boys! Fatigue and tension – and on the trip we certainly had our share of both – play havoc with the temper and equilibrium, we both agreed. Tenzin said that in another life I must have been a Khampa!

Tenzin then gave me *two* Nagchukha tapes. He said that they had not got to Seán before he left Lhasa . . . There are times in life when you just do not ask questions! That night was one. And for some reason all I could think of was to check them to see that in the intervening four weeks they had not been 'wiped'. I also felt it was imperative to get them out of that room and into my secret hiding place with the rest of the rushes. I played them through the camera's eye-piece and felt enormously relieved that, thank God, I still had a picture without any apparent damage or break-up.

It was now after eight and Tenzin suggested that I had better return to the hotel. I tucked the tapes into my money-belt and agreed to meet Tenzin the next evening so that we could film the rest of the interviews we had agreed on, and also so he could smuggle me into a hiding place from which I would be able to film surreptitiously the front of the Jokhang on 1 October – if the rumoured demonstration did materialize. It was important to get into position the evening before, in case the army shut off the square, or forbade all foreigners to leave their hotels, as they had before. I left the Sony camera and all the paraphernalia at the safe house, as the next day, the eve of the anniversary of the October demonstration, the Chinese might tighten procedures at the checkpoints and confiscate the camera.

As we walked through the dark alleys to the edge of the Tibetan quarter I felt distinctly uneasy. Then I left Thondup at his hotel, collected my bike and cycled westwards through completely empty streets towards the Potala. An eerie silence muffled the darkened town and was only accentuated by the barking of dogs. The Potala, a dark brooding presence against the even darker mass of mountains behind, seemed to have fewer lights burning in the high windows. In the Chinese quarter beyond the Potala, even the small Chinese restaurants, which were usually noisy with PLA, Chinese customers and tinkly music, were silent and barred. There were no overt signs of military or of any checkpoints on that main road. There was nothing but the uncomfortable dark and the swish of the cycle's rubber tyres on the tarmac.

Back at the hotel there was a hilarious telex from Chris: 'Have hunted for your two-handed sofa everywhere. Unable to find. Rest of consignment OK and being attended to. Love Chris.' Decoded, that meant that he had been unable to trace my 'two-handed' Nagchukha interview and that the rest of the tapes were being processed and got ready for editing on my return. I spent another sleepless night trying to get through to London. When I finally got through to Chris at five in the morning – Lhasa time – I told him through our code that everything was OK and that my 'lover' (Thondup) would phone him or David when he got to his next destination within thirty hours. Chris, like David, is very cool, and having received similar messages from me over the past fifteen years knew exactly that I was saying that I would evacuate the rushes with Thondup.

Saturday, 30 September, was a perfect autumn day. Clear and sunny, it was a picture-postcard morning with regulation clouds playing tag across an impeccable sapphire-blue sky. It was the time for picnics, for lying in the long grass and smelling the mown hay, for picking bunches of poppies and celebrating the last of the summer. But at the Holiday Inn the shuttle service was cancelled and the hotel staff advised guests not to go down to the centre.

Jumping on my bike, I waved and rode off down the main street which had very little traffic on it.

I met Thondup in the Jokhang as arranged; as there was not much for him to do, I suggested that he take some money and buy his wife a present. I then met Marie-Chantal, as pre-arranged, by a carpet vendor who sold beautiful old Tibetan carpets of muted blues and beiges with the traditional Tibetan designs. Marie-Chantal told me that she had arranged several more interviews for me in Drepung monastery, but we would have to be even more careful as the Chinese had stationed more troops round the monastery in preparation for the anniversary tomorrow. We both wondered how much more violence and bloodshed the next day would bring. The Chinese persistently accused the Dalai Lama of instigating the violence inside Tibet, but I knew from my long years of meeting with the Dalai Lama that violence is completely and utterly anathema to him. In India, when I had put the Chinese accusation that the Dalai Lama was behind the violence in Tibet to H. E. Kalon (Cabinet Minister) Tashi Wangdi, a minister for the Tibetan Government-in-exile and chief negotiator with the Chinese, he replied: 'No, that is completely untrue. It is also untrue when the Chinese say the problems are solely confined to Lhasa. Nor is it true, as the Chinese allege, that it is also being instigated from outside or by foreigners. Now if you look at the Chinese explanation of the events of September and October last year [1987], they keep changing their own position.' He went on to explain: 'First they said that it was the Dalai Lama who had instigated the trouble, then they said it was the foreigners. Later they said it was a few elements inside Tibet. Then they denied that their soldiers or police did any shooting. Then they later admitted that things had happened because of their own erroneous policy in Tibet, and then they made a volte-face again and blamed it all on the leftist influences in Tibet. The Chinese do have the most extraordinary ability to rewrite events and history at a moment's notice and whenever it suits them. Facts do not seem to hold great relevance for them.'

Marie-Chantal and I cycled westwards past the Holiday Inn, past some enchanting groves of fluffy willows by the banks of the Kyichu river and towards Drepung. I asked Marie-Chantal (as I had every Tibetan I had met on the trip) about the Chinese allegation that the demonstrations and violence were instigated by the Dalai Lama and his 'clique'. She – as well as every Tibetan I had asked – unequivocally denied the charge.

After a tortuous route through back doors and over roofs to escape detection by the Chinese openly stationed in uniform inside and outside the Drepung monastery complex as well as the planted informers whom I could not distinguish from the other monks, we met several monks and discussed the current events and their analysis of the situation. I also asked them all about what had happened on the anniversary of the 27 September disturbances. They told me that because of the enormous military presence and because they knew that they would get the same treatment and torture as their colleagues had experienced, they had decided to send only a token seven monks to demonstrate. 'Why should we have our heads broken unnecessarily?' one monk argued. 'We will wait until they are not prepared.'

In one of the several lulls while waiting for another group of monks to arrive at our rendezvous high in one of the rooms of a deserted and ruined building, I asked Marie-Chantal and a senior abbot why the monks had taken such a prominent role in the demonstrations and why they had been singled out for such punishment by the Chinese.

Marie-Chantal explained: 'In the absence of their own legitimate government – and by that they all mean the Dalai Lama and the *Kashag* (Cabinet) and Assembly – Tibetans look to the clergy as their natural leaders. You have to understand how very difficult it is to plan any kind of political activity: there's a good deal of daily surveillance in the work units and within the neighbourhoods and it makes it very difficult for the lay people to get together and plan any action at all. So Tibetans look to the nuns and the monks to be the first to go out and demonstrate on the street and make some kind of statement. And then what ensues really involves everyone in Lhasa.'

'I understand,' I said. 'But why are we only now in the last two years seeing Lhasa up in the headlines? Why not in the past forty years of the Chinese occupation?'

'These demonstrations are a new phase in the expression of political and national consciousness among Tibetans. But this hasn't happened out of the blue. Even before the uprising of 1959, there has always been an underground resistance in Tibet. They put up posters (an indictable offence), write letters, just simply disobey Chinese or Communist Party officials, sabotage in small – and sometimes silly and humorous – ways the whims of the government . . . And then of course there was the well-known Khampas' rebellion in Kham and the epic struggle in the Mustang campaign. There are also the little-known traditional resistance groups like the *Tagdruk Tsogpa* (the Tiger-Dragon Organization) and the *Shonnu Tsogpa* (the Youth Association, the precursor of the militant Tibetan Youth Congress-in-exile), various *thanglang tsogpa* (the voluntary organizations that provide support) to the groups in Kham, and the *Cholsum Tsogpa*, who sent people to Lhasa to demonstrate. But one thing I must say about the demonstration,' Marie-Chantal insisted, and she called on the monks to corroborate, 'all the demonstrations over the past two years that I have witnessed – those that resulted in violence and those that did not – they all, in their inception, were non-violent.'

After interviewing the monks at Drepung, we cycled back to Lhasa and agreed to meet the following morning at 6.30. I returned to my own hotel and found Thondup sitting in the lobby. It was most unusual for him to break cover, so I collected my key from the desk and walked round the corner. Thondup followed. We rode the lift up and down for fifteen minutes while we talked. The news was the last thing I expected.

Tenzin had sent a message that it was too dangerous for me to film any interviews that evening. And as there was a very strong rumour that Lhasa was going to be sealed off tomorrow, and all road and air links were to be cut, he could not drive me to the border on the 2nd. Maybe the next day, or the day after – the 4th – the day my visa ran out! And from Lhasa to the border was at least two days of very hard driving: more realistically, three days. And if events turned out as Tenzin predicted, the roads south would be crawling with PLA; there would be strict checkpoints; I would be out of visa time, illegal and with all my rushes still on me!

22

Alone in the Forbidden Kingdom

The lift bell pinged at the fourth floor, the doors opened and a gaggle of burly tourists dragging heavy mountaineering equipment got in. An insane idea began to germinate. In the corridor I asked Thondup to return downtown and get the camera from Tenzin, and then try and buy some cassettes of Chinese music with sleeves that had Chinese writing and pictures on them.

It was a quarter to seven when Thondup walked out of the front door. I immediately followed the group of mountaineers as they made their way towards the coffee shop for supper. With some trepidation, I tapped a 6ft 6in giant of a man on the shoulder and heard myself saying: 'I wonder if I could talk to you, please?' He smiled and I suggested that we walk round the garden.

'Look,' I said to him, 'I am not a tourist. I am a film-maker and journalist and I have just shot a film about the genocide in Tibet. The people who were going to drive me out are now too frightened, and as I plan to film the demonstration outside the Jokhang tomorrow, in all probability I will be arrested. If that happens, the PSB will go through my things and find the film. The Tibetans who have taken terrible risks speaking on camera will be imprisoned – and all for nothing. Nobody outside will know what has been and is happening in Tibet.'

The man looked very surprised, and before he could reply, I hurried on: 'I heard you and your friends say that you are flying out to Katmandu tomorrow. Please, can you smuggle out the tapes for me with you tomorrow? I know you don't know me, but you are the only chance I have.'

He must have thought I was totally certifiable, approaching a complete stranger with such a preposterous proposition in a country which was in a highly unstable and inflammable condition, with a heavy military presence, where collaborating in such an insane undertaking ensured certain imprisonment if he was caught. But I was right out of ideas and options and there were only seven hours until the airport bus left the hotel.

It seemed a very long silence, during which the fate of the programme again dangled by a thread. I knew he was weighing up the possibilities of being caught. Finally he agreed and told me that he was a teacher from Grenoble; he was there on a mountaineering trip; he had heard the accusations of genocide and yes, he would be glad to help. I suggested that he did not put the tapes in his luggage as I had heard that the X-ray machines at the airport were very powerful and the image and sound could be wiped off – the same thing applied to hand luggage. He agreed and said that as the expedition had obviously filmed, it would be quite understandable for him to be concerned about the safety of the tapes of what was, for him, a once-in-a-lifetime journey. I fervently hoped that the customs men at the airport would think twice about arguing with the formidable bulk of the giant from Grenoble.

I told Pierre that I had asked Thondup to go and buy Chinese pop-song tapes and would slip the Chinese sleeve inside my own tapes to disguise and further safeguard them should the Customs want to inspect what he was carrying. I also gave him the name of two friends in Katmandu with whom to leave the tapes and asked him to send me a telex saying 'Happy Birthday, Love —' The name at the end of the telex would tell me where the tapes were.

I also asked him to keep an eye on Thondup, who would be travelling on the same aircraft. Should there be any suspicion and Thondup was picked up, Pierre was to immediately contact the American Embassy in Katmandu. We agreed to meet later in my room and not say much, just in case the rooms were bugged. We entered the lobby separately, he then went to the coffee shop and I went to my room to scribble out a shot list for Chris so that he could start assembling the rushes for editing on my return to London.

At eight that evening Thondup came up to my room, gave me the camera and Chinese tapes and together we went to work on substituting the Chinese music sleeves for the Video 8 ones. I taped the package securely and Thondup and I walked round the corridors talking about last-minute details. I gave him David Lloyd's phone number in London and asked him to get David to phone me the next night. If I was not in my room, it would mean only one thing: I had been arrested. Then perhaps David could get on to the British Ambassador in Beijing . . . I tried to thank him, but how do you find words to thank someone who has risked his own life for you not once, but so many times during that awful trip? I just gave him a hug and wished him Godspeed.

The Frenchman came for the package at nine, and actually handing it over was a most strange sensation. Ridiculously it was like handing over part of myself . . . Later, feeling bereft, I wandered down to the bar and ordered a large and terribly expensive Armagnac. I tried to think about all the unknown problems that were ahead of me tomorrow. I was unusually restless when I returned to my room, and decided to take a stroll round the gardens to clear my head. The hotel gates were locked and the streets outside were completely deserted. But a few minutes later I heard the rumble of heavy vehicles approaching. I walked in the direction of the sound and looking through the railings of the side entrance into the darkened street I saw a convoy of thirty-four three-tonne army trucks full of soldiers heading towards the Potala and the Jokhang.

I slept fitfully and was up at four in the morning of Saturday, 1 October. I dressed warmly, loaded my rucksack with the Sony, the lithium battery, lens and spare tapes and went down for breakfast. The coffee shop was unbearably cheerful with a babel of voices talking about 'home'. Bruce Chatwin once said that the ability to feel at home in a place depended on being able to leave it. Right at that moment I felt distinctly uncomfortable and would not have put any bets on my sleeping in my own bed at home by the end of the week. I saw that both Thondup and the teacher were also eating at separate tables. In the lobby, full of passengers checking their belongings, I managed surreptitiously to point Thondup out to the Frenchman.

As the airport bus drew out of the gates and gained speed on the dark main road, I felt a spasm of the most awful anguish, wondering if I had done the right thing and whether I would ever see my rushes again . . . And without the comforting presence of Thondup I realized that I was now completely and utterly on my own and cut off from anyone that could help. It was a feeling I never want to experience again.

As I pedalled off on my bike in the direction of the Potala and the Jokhang, I tried not to dwell on uncomfortable possibilities. I rationalized that if things went wrong at the airport I would be picked up by noon at the latest and that there was absolutely nothing I could do. It was not paranoia. Foreigners had recently been arrested and hauled in for some very unpleasant questioning. Anyway, there was nowhere to hide and nowhere to run. The PLA had effectively sealed off the town. So I tried to concentrate on the more urgent problem of finding somewhere to hide and film unobserved.

The Chinese quarter was like a ghost town. Nothing moved and everything was shut. It grew lighter as I cycled east towards the Tibetan quarter but even there the roads were deserted. I parked the bike, collected Marie-Chantal and we casually strolled towards the Jokhang through the back streets to the Barkhor. Emerging on the north-east side we looked at the square and at the bottom we could see the trucks of soldiers parked under the trees, in a direct line of fire to the front of the Jokhang.

In the pale light a few pilgrims were circling round the Jokhang; they exuded a curious intensity in the way they hurriedly shuffled past, telling their prayer-beads more quickly than ever. More significantly, and very un-Tibetan, they neither looked right nor left – not even to the Jokhang – but just kept looking straight ahead, almost as though they were afraid of eye contact, or what they might see. From the two large incense burners in front of the Jokhang the pilgrims burned a few branches and sent a thin plume of white offertory smoke into the grey-blue sky where the pale moon still hovered, uncertain of what the day would bring.

It was the time of day that normally captivated me, but that morning instead of appreciating the birth of the new day, my eyes were immediately drawn to the number of green shiny helmets that lined the roofs of the PSB building on the corner and the other one a few doors down on the opposite side. Something, maybe a movement, made me look up to the roof of the Jokhang. There, too, silhouetted against the brightening sky, were the unmistakeable shapes of uniformed hats. Many of the watchers had trained their binoculars onto the crowd. The Chinese were in position and waiting.

The air was electric with tension as we walked round the Barkhor. All the shops were shuttered and the stall-holders had put up their metal tables with the legs facing defensively outwards. Tibetans in small anxious groups appeared briefly in the alleyways and then disappeared rapidly, their faces taut with tension. Several backpackers who had also defied the Chinese proclamation putting the Barkhor off-limits to foreigners came up to us and we exchanged bits of gossip and the latest sightings of military positions, and as we walked round we tentatively staked out which alleys we would run down if we were chased by the Chinese – as many of the backpackers had been on the anniversary a few days earlier. There was a wonderful warmth of camaraderie between us.

At 7.30 we heard what appeared to be a martial cry and the tramp of army boots coming towards us. We turned and there – marching deliberately anti-clockwise in a manner guaranteed to give maximum offence to the devout Tibetans, who traditionally walk clockwise round the Jokhang – was a company of soldiers. With bayonets drawn, they also carried AK 47s in an exaggerated show of force, considering the small straggle of Tibetans in the street. They were the dreaded Wujing, the crack special force of the armed police who were specially trained in anti-terrorist tactics and suppressing rebellion. Trained in the suburbs outside Beijing, they were the SAS of the Chinese forces. Intimidating they certainly were, and one of the young girl backpackers ran off into the shadows of a dirt alley. I was reminded of President Kennedy's warning: 'Those who make peaceful revolution impossible make violent revolution inevitable.'

'They've started,' said Steve, a tall, bearded Californian, a political science student from UCLA. He had been in Lhasa the previous year and told us that the soldiers marched round at about ten- or five-minute intervals, depending on the tension.

The light was getting stronger so I suggested to Marie-Chantal that we get off the street and find somewhere to film. The only place I could think of was a new building going up where the Chinese had knocked down one of the lovely old Tibetan houses at the northern corner of the Barkhor, opposite the Jokhang and directly in sight of the PSB building. It was covered with scaffolding and as we had been walking round I had looked up and seen that some of its windows overlooked the square and the alleys to the side of the Jokhang, so that if there was trouble and people started to run, I could follow them with the lens round the corner.

Waiting for a lull in the flow of people, we darted through the scaffolding at the entrance and found ourselves in a large courtyard full of builders' paraphernalia. We climbed up a bamboo scaffold to the unfinished top floor and found the room with the windows I had seen from ground-level. It did indeed provide a grandstand view of the Jokhang, the square and the side street. It also provided a perfect view of the two of us if the PSB happened to train their binoculars in our direction from the roof of either the Jokhang or the PSB building. So apart from the one wall which was blocked to their sights because of the angle, we ducked everywhere. I got out the camera, set up and waited.

If the monks come out now, I thought, as I flattened myself against the wall and filmed as much as I dared, with the troops waiting like coiled springs ready to pounce into action, it's a perfect recipe for a riot.

There is a growing impatience among Tibetan refugees in exile to hit back at the Chinese. And even inside Tibet I had detected some rumblings. I had discussed it with the Dalai Lama because I knew that violence was anathema to him, both personally and as the head of Tibetan Buddhism, and was not a path he advocated. He had told me: 'Yes, there has been such discussion for some time now inside Tibet – and outside too – an attitude among certain people that is causing me great anxiety. If Tibetans follow the path of violence then it will result in more suppression, more killing, more torture. I have warned Tibetans that if we follow that path the Chinese will have an excuse, and find it much easier to crush us. But if we follow the Ghandian method of non-violence, and with reason and patience we try to change the Chinese mind – and of course we will suffer in the short term – then ultimately I believe that will be our strength. Non-violence, I feel, is our only hope.'

Because of the alarming growth in the number of Chinese swamping the Tibetan population, the Dalai Lama, who was awarded the Nobel Peace Prize in 1989, feels time is running out: 'If this situation continues, within a short period of time the Tibetan people will be a minority in their own land,' he told me. He has now begun to speak out in public: on Capitol Hill to the

Senate and House of Representatives on 21 September 1987, to the European Parliament in Strasbourg in June 1988 when he put forward a Five-Point Peace Plan, and to the Human Rights Commission in Bonn in July 1988.

Although he accepts that his people are in a desperate plight, because of his fundamental belief in non-violence he still wants to try and negotiate with the Chinese, and in his Five Point Peace Plan he offered a temporary compromise. He wants the control of Tibet's internal affairs and economy to be in the hands of a democratically elected Tibetan administration which would ensure the promotion of Tibetan civilization, culture and religion, while at the same time opening up the country to modern technological progress. While demanding the removal of all nuclear weapons and nuclear testing sites from Tibet, and thereby declaring Tibet to be a Zone of Peace once again, he was prepared to concede responsibility for defence and foreign affairs to the Chinese.

The plan evoked severe criticism from the Tibetan community in exile and some Tibetans accused him of surrendering their claim to independence. But the Dalai Lama says that practical autonomy must come first, otherwise their very survival is threatened.

'The question of independence now is simply not relevant,' he told me. 'There has been so much destruction of the Tibetan people and culture already that faced with this great flood of Chinese settlers the threat is now to be assimilated or eliminated. And if death occurs, and we are swamped or eliminated, there will be nothing left. So we have to compromise. There is no time for anything else.'

For the Dalai Lama the preservation of a unique civilization is all-important. Political control of frontiers is, perforce, secondary. But that is not good enough for many militant Tibetans in exile who want action now. Lhasang Tsering, President of the radical Tibetan Youth Congress-in-exile (which also has strong links with Tibetans inside Tibet) told me: 'We do not immediately plan or foresee a guerrilla movement as we had in the past' – the high-profile resistance operation, the Mustang campaign, backed by the CIA in the seventies. 'What we plan is sabotage tactics. Things which I obviously cannot discuss at the moment. But we have many options in preparation. Ultimately I believe our future will depend on . . . our ability to control the situation inside Tibet.

What we want to do, and plan to do, is to keep it destabilized. We are not going to beg for help any more. We are going to force people to be involved inside Tibet . . .'

But I put it to him that perhaps he was being unrealistic to talk of a guerrilla war with his limited resources pitted against the Chinese, who have more than a quarter of a million men under arms in Tibet.

'I don't plan to smash China,' he said coldly. 'I won't commit a murder where the body is totally unrecognizable. I will blind the eye, prick the heart . . . I will operate pin-point attacks at strategic positions where it will hurt most.' He spoke with a determination that made me believe then, and in subsequent conversations, that this was no idle rhetoric. However, I still felt I had to ask whether it was not all just a pipe-dream.

His reply echoed the feelings of so many Tibetans inside Tibet; a highly educated and deeply motivated man, he put it eloquently: 'I fight not because I have any guarantee for success. I have no guarantees for success, no insurances against failure. I fight because I must. It is my birthright. Second, I fight because what is going on inside Tibet is wrong. And ultimately we have been brought up to uphold certain values; one of them being that it is better to die on one's feet than to live on one's knees.'

Brave words indeed, in the face of the massive Chinese army presence in Tibet. But they are sentiments that the Dalai Lama does not support. As I filmed the Chinese army patrolling in intimidating strength round the Jokhang and clearly determined to suppress any trouble, I felt the widening polarity of the two peoples. In the square below, the Tibetans were calm even though the Chinese had shut and locked the Jokhang and barred them any access to their own temple. The few that had ventured into the streets and patiently prostrated themselves before the Jokhang were following their path of non-violence and stoic patience which are the central tenets of their faith. But for how much longer could a people who had suffered so much, for so long, continue to suffer? So many young Tibetans, despite being good Buddhists, had told me that it was not by pacifist tactics that the PLO (Palestine Liberation Organization) had finally gained acceptance on the world stage . . .

It had gone eleven and the sun flooded the forecourt of the

Jokhang. I prayed that Thondup, the Frenchman and my rushes were all safely airborne by now. I had no way of knowing until I got that telex. We had been up in the building for longer than was wise to stay hidden in one unsafe place and I had exhausted the number of shots I could use in the cut film from that top angle. I needed some ground-level shots of the Chinese coming straight at me – and sequences of Tibetans and whatever else I could manage to grab. I realized that this was not the day to plan and set up elegant shots with moody lighting and lots of retakes.

Marie-Chantal left to check out the monasteries, to see if anything was happening there. We arranged to rendezvous in front of the Jokhang, or at the Kirey if the square was blocked off, every hour on the hour until the other turned up. I saw Steve and some of the backpackers, tagged along and looked around for something to shelter behind while I filmed the street. I heard the soldiers coming round again, found a low wall, got behind it and asked the students to give me cover.

'Hey, what are you doing?' Steve asked, concerned, as the others covered me, but turned their backs so as not to appear too obvious. 'You'll not only get arrested, you'll get your head bashed in if they see the camera,' he said, as I pulled the Sony from the small bag and started to switch it on.

'Look,' I said, 'I'm not a tourist. I'm making a film for Channel 4 television in London about the Tibetan problem.'

'Great!' they replied, almost with one voice, and I had an instant support team. I switched on, asked them to separate slightly so that I could set a focus, then keeping the camera steady, I stood up as though I was watching a victory parade, which in a macabre way I was. I covered all but the lens with a sweater, told the lads to move·back and pressed the record button. I hoped the shot I had seen in the eye-piece of the soldiers coming head-on towards camera at the tight end of the zoom lens would work.

Then to check whether it had recorded, I asked them to cover me again as I played the footage back through the eye-piece. It was adequate, the horizon was at a bit of an angle, but I was not too worried because I knew that back in the editing suite I could electronically rectify it. Until two in the afternoon the lads carefully shepherded me around the Barkhor under the noses of the Chinese. If the stakes had not been so high it might have been amusing.

The backpackers, all young, enthusiastic and outraged at the plight of the Tibetans, were only too willing to do anything to help. I was touched by their enthusiastic generosity, for they well knew the penalties of getting caught. They were all students, from Britain, the United States, Australia, France and Germany, and I wished I had more time to explore and enjoy their friendship. In sticky situations you strike up intense relationships with the people with whom you share the danger, whether they are interviewees or sympathizers, and then sadly you rarely see them again.

I wanted to take a shot from a window looking down a dark alley to show the soldiers crossing the entrance. So Steve and I sneaked up an alley and knocked on the door of one of the houses; amazingly we were let in, and in the most conspiratorial way – words were not necessary – somehow the Tibetans knew that we were there to help and they let us onto the roof. With one leg over the parapet and Steve holding onto the other, I leaned out high over the alley, waiting for Bob, our look-out, to whistle from the road to tell me that the soldiers were coming. It was the best shot of the film, as row upon row of soldiers moved in and out of the frame.

After quietly filming the faces of the Tibetans – I did not dare do any vox pop (man-in-the-street) interviews – I then gave one of the lads the exposed tape to hide, in case I was caught shooting the next sequence; we then all moved in front of the Jokhang and sat on a bench right under the noses of the Chinese at both the PSB observation points. I needed a low-angle shot of the soldiers coming right into the camera . . .

It was one of the most frightening things I had done. More people were walking round the Jokhang and the soldiers must have changed shift. The new ones looked a much tougher bunch and their squad leaders all had walkie-talkies. They were also marching round at less than five-minute intervals and I decided that I had better start shooting, as the lads warned me that plain-clothes PSB in leather jackets with giveaway bulges under their armpits were snooping around the crowds and moving people on. I saw a couple come towards us and tensed. I had no doubt that they would use their guns at the least provocation.

The scene was quite surreal. Tom, a big Australian, in order to cover me from the overhead prying eyes had to lean over and practically envelop me while I set up the eye-piece at an angle and tried to keep the camera body on an even keel; his running commentary had us all in absolute fits of laughter. Some of the lads were goofing around in front allowing me an opening, on cue, to let me line up the wide-angle lens, when suddenly from the right-hand corner of the Jokhang a column of soldiers marched straight at us.

'My God,' Steve shouted loudly, forgetting that I had asked them to be quiet when I was turning over. 'They're coming straight at us! Oh my God, Vanya, for Christ's sake hurry up!' Just at that moment a group of Tibetans, mesmerized by the oncoming troops, quite innocently wandered straight into my line of vision and blocked the troops. Steve was demented. 'Joe, get those f . . . . . . out the way,' he screamed and leaped to yank the startled Tibetans out of shot. I just sat there, unable to move a muscle, with my finger on the record button, and my floppy straw hat covering, I hoped, the rest of the camera. I prayed to all the firmament that this once-in-a-lifetime shot was recording.

Marie-Chantal found us in the square. She told me that the monks of Drepung and Sera could not come out of their monasteries as they were ringed by PLA with heavy weapons. The word was that the troops would stay in position for the next three days to ensure that they were on hand to squash the first murmur of trouble. We all wandered down to the end of the square, past the troops who were sitting around waiting, and found a stall selling some Sichuan-style snacks. While eating, I tried to film from under my arm with the telephoto lens trained, hopefully, on them.

We returned to the front of the Jokhang and sat chatting, each of us casually scanning the horizon for trouble. By four in the afternoon Marie-Chantal said that although it was obvious nothing was going to happen, the tension was still so high with the Chinese aggressively marching round the Jokhang that it would only have taken a small incident of rough treatment of a Tibetan by one soldier to have ignited a riot . . .

There were two full days before the next scheduled flight. If it was true that nothing was happening in Lhasa, it would be wise to get out of town, just in case the rumoured clamp-down on foreigners took place. I suggested to Marie-Chantal that I hire a Chinese car and we drive to Gyantse and Shigatse, Tibet's second largest town, and check what was happening there. It would take us out of the spotlight as well as give me my last opportunity to film some badly-needed visuals to illustrate the interviews in the film. I also wanted to film the interview with Marie-Chantal, and in Lhasa it was now out of the question. So while I wandered round the rapidly emptying Barkhor, she arranged transport and said we would meet at 6.30 in the morning. I returned to the hotel to see if there was any news from Thondup or about the rushes.

As everything was shut indefinitely, it was impossible to get a CAAC ticket or make a reservation. It was now two days to the expiry of my visa, so I settled down to a long sleepless night trying to get hold of friends in Nepal to arrange a reservation on the Royal Air Nepal/CAAC flight out to Katmandu on the 4th. Fortunately I had taken the precaution of getting open tickets with practically every airline to every major town near Tibet, and one was to Katmandu.

In the hotel garden a cocktail party was in progress given by the local administration in celebration of China's National Day. Looking down, I saw the American Embassy's political councillor, who had obviously flown across from Beijing. For a party? It did not make sense. Something was afoot, I felt, to warrant one of the Embassy's most senior councillors – and a Tibet specialist – suddenly appearing in town. Was I doing the right thing leaving town in the morning, I wondered?

They should have been two idyllic days. Visually, it was a filmic dream but the over-riding anxiety of not knowing whether Thondup and the rushes had got out safely, whether there would be a clamp-down on foreigners and whether I was booked on the flight on the 4th was a nerve-racking knife-edge. But I dutifully filmed farming scenes in the fertile Tsangpo valley – the bread-basket of Tibet – which because of the fertility and proximity to Lhasa and the Nepalese border was decidedly more prosperous than most areas I had seen so far outside Markham. It was another area redolent with history which we did not have time to explore. We followed the craggy narrow valley with dramatic peaks rising from the valley floor that the British Younghusband expedition had marched through in 1904 when, staking Britain's claim to ward off the advances of the Russian bear, they had attempted to intimidate the Tibetans into Britain's colonial sphere.

We drove through Gyantse, with its picturesque old fort set on a dramatic hill and its defensive walls snaking over the adjacent mountainside which all basked in the afternoon light. And after a night in a truckers' stop in Shigatse, the historic seat of Tibet's second highest cleric, the controversial Panchen Lama who spent most of his time in Beijing, I filmed an excellent interview with Marie-Chantal. I set her against the ruins of Shigatse's ancient fort, its craggy ruins rising sheer into the impeccably blue sky. And still visible on what was left of the ramparts of the fort after the rampaging of the Red Guards was the bank of loudspeakers through which the Chinese played hours of incessant propaganda during the Cultural Revolution and which, even now, was occasionally used for political indoctrination or martial music.

We headed back to Lhasa through fields of harvested barley where peasants with yaks prepared the land for the next season's crops. We raced on a good road – it was the main road to the Nepalese border – through avenues of yellowing trees and the dramatic brown mountains that rose to peaks already covered with the first snow of winter. We reached the exquisite Yamdrok Yumtso – Tibet's fabled 15,000-foot-high Turquoise Lake – which meanders for miles through some of the most beautiful mountains in Tibet.

It was gone ten at night when we approached the outskirts of Lhasa and the checkpoints manned with brusque and nervous soldiers toting AK 47s. The Chinese driver spent twenty minutes talking to them and finally we were allowed to go on. Again, the hotel gates were locked and the roads as deserted as when we left. Marie-Chantal said she would phone me from the Kirey where the backpackers would undoubtedly have the latest news.

I checked in to the Holiday Inn for what remained of the night and collected two telexes. I could have wept in relief. There was a Birthday Greetings telex telling me that my rushes were safely waiting for me in Nepal; the other confirmed that I had a seat on the flight. But I still had a lot of what the Chinese would interpret as inflammatory footage of soldiers, the PLA, the Wujing and the police, all of which were considered to be in contravention of the Chinese Penal Code – the wide-ranging prohibition which could indict both Tibetans and foreigners under the all-embracing 'counter-revolutionary' label, which carried stiff sentences and sometimes even the death penalty. And I had yet to check whether the airline authorities would accept the telex as confirmation of a seat.

The next morning Lhasa was dark and silent as the airport bus pulled away from the hotel. I turned to have one last glimpse of the city that has seen so much bloodshed and pain. In the dark the Potala brooded under a moonless sky. Behind in the east, dawn was once again etching a faint, exquisite line of silver on the outline of the surrounding mountains. It was that magical time of day when the earth hangs suspended between day and night, before, as one old monk told me, the day has time to stain the world with cares. In the Potala a few dim lights flickered. In another time before the Chinese, the monks would have been chanting their morning mantras to the guardian deities of Tibet. But that morning, in the still mountain air, the Potala was silent. The dawn was a parting gift. As we sped along, the fast-flowing Tsangpo almost within touching distance of the road, sky and water merged in a luminous diffusion of nacreous rose amethyst. I fell asleep with nervous exhaustion and woke with a start when the bus drew up before the low airport departure building.

As the bus was unlocked, I checked the bandage on my arm. Having a healthy respect for the thoroughness of the PSB and knowing that I was at my most vulnerable at the airport, I had folded a barely decipherable shot list (due to fatigue, my memory was now unreliable) and taped it to my arm, for if they went through my baggage they would also examine any piece of paper with writing on it. It was only after we had checked in at the counter, seen our baggage disappear through a hatch, and then moved into another room, the door of which was locked after us, that I began to perspire uncomfortably.

It was full of uniformed men and women who were examining baggage and passports. I noticed the door at the other end was also locked when one of the passengers, probably looking for the loo, tried the handle. The officials opened everything and seemed to spend an unconscionably long time examining the Sony. I made a point of showing them my incoming customs declaration form which had registered all the electrical items that I was temporarily importing into the country. When they took the Sony away, I sat on a bench and repeated to myself that it was probably only because, as a new model, they had not seen a machine so small with so many buttons on it . . . I took out a book and tried to distract myself, but again every disaster scenario ran through my head.

Half an hour later, during which time I must have shed kilos, he returned, handed back the camera and passport and went on to the next person . . . At 10.20 precisely, the guards unlocked the last remaining door and let us out into the cool air to walk to the CAAC aircraft waiting on the runway. Apart from the soldiers, several MiG fighters further down the runway and a specially adapted high-altitude Sikorsky helicopter not far from the aircraft, the airfield was deserted. Just the wide green valley flanked by the mute mountains . . .

As we took off and climbed above the meandering river by now silver with the harsher light of day, I still could not relax. We were still in Chinese airspace and in a Chinese aircraft. And it was not unknown in the annals of Communist history to recall aircraft to base.

As we soared to 35,000 feet and the peaks of the Himalayas appeared on the horizon, I looked at Everest approaching, *Chomolungma*, the Goddess Mother of the Earth, as Tibetans call her, and inevitably I looked back on the most extraordinary journey in my life.

As I left Tibet with Lhasa under tight military control, it was impossible to check every allegation that was made to me by the Tibetans I met. The visual evidence of deforestation was there to see, and however much the Chinese might try and refute it, the blighted mountainsides spoke more eloquently than a thousand denials from the Chinese Embassy. I was not able to fully document all the deprivations and hardships of the ordinary Tibetan farmers and nomads in the high mountains, nor fully explore the discrimination that burdens the lives of the Tibetans living in ghettos in the towns, who have not benefited from the prosperity that the Chinese claim they have brought to Tibet. I was unable personally to exhume the mass graves, unable to witness the painful forced abortions, the traumatic sterilizations. I did not have time to track down the deformed babies and the dead animals that Tibetans claim are the results of nuclear radiation, nor verify the existence of alleged nuclear bases, nor investigate reports of clandestine dumping of nuclear waste. And I was unable to go into the prisons to interview the monks and nuns and ordinary Tibetans, whom it is alleged are still being tortured and imprisoned by the Chinese. But I did see the Chinese army in intimidating strength everywhere in Tibet, and in Lhasa particularly, holding a nation in a state of siege, in what the Dalai Lama calls 'the worst crisis in our 2,100-year history'. But there seemed to me to be more than enough evidence in what the Tibetans said to justify the sending of a United Nations fact-finding mission to Tibet, as a matter of the utmost urgency, and appointing a special Rapporteur for Tibet, as they have for Afghanistan and Iraq, to investigate the mounting evidence of the continuing genocide of the Tibetan people.

But perhaps the most convincing testimony is the courage of the people who talked to me. Each of them risked, and still risks, arrest, imprisonment and possibly death. But they put their country first, wanting the world to know what is happening to their beleaguered and afflicted people.

'If it is going to do some good for the people of Tibet, then I have no regrets for what I have done here and for what I have said to you,' said Kelsang, one of the men I interviewed near the alleged nuclear base at Nagchukha. 'I don't fear the consequences, even if it means death.'

The doctor who had spoken so openly about forced abortions and sterilizations said: 'The whole Tibetan people are being suppressed by the Chinese. They have no real power. No educational skills. So if the world does not help, there is very little hope.'

Each and every one of the young nuns whom I interviewed, and who had been severely tortured by the Chinese, told me: 'We do not care whatever punishment they give us – even if they kill us. If it helps the Tibetan cause, so be it.'

And Lobsang, the old monk, who had spent twenty-two years in prison, who had suffered torture and the degradation of cannibalism, said:

'If I die in prison it is for Tibet.
If I survive in prison it is for Tibet.
I have no regrets if I die on the way to Tibetan independence.'

Time is running out for Tibet – a nation that has refused to hold the world to ransom by hijacking planes, kidnapping, perpetrating senseless violence on innocent victims – a nation that for 1,200 years has lived in peace and wants no more than to be free and to continue to live in peace.

Epilogue

The film *Tibet: A Case to Answer* was transmitted by Channel 4 television nationwide in Britain on 9 November 1988 amid considerable controversy. The Chinese Ambassador in London raised strenuous objections to the film being screened, but Channel 4 proceeded with transmission.

However, they gave the Ambassador the opportunity to reply to the allegations raised in the film by appearing on Channel 4's *Right to Reply*. This programme gives any member of the audience who objects to the content of a programme the opportunity to meet the programme-maker face to face in the studio to discuss their objections. I was ready to meet the Ambassador, but he refused to meet me.

Instead he went into a 'video box' facility and read a prepared statement which, predictably, disputed the film's statistics. For example, he said that the programme was totally wrong in stating the area of Tibet as 2.5 million square kilometres when it was in reality only 1.5 million. The Ambassador was of course using the figures for the Autonomous Region of Tibet as established by China, not the state of Tibet that existed before the invasion. This device is used frequently by the Chinese authorities to confuse most people who are not completely familiar with the details of the history and present conditions of the country. And very few people are.

The film met with considerable critical and public acclaim and was, unprecedented for British television, repeated again soon after at prime time on 21 December, and then again on 17 July 1989. After the first transmission, Channel 4 wrote officially to the Chinese Ambassador asking for an assurance from his Government that no reprisals would be taken against any of those who had appeared in the film. To date there has been a resounding silence from the Embassy and no assurances have been given whatsoever. They have not even replied to Channel 4's letter.

The film has subsequently been screened in seventeen countries including the US, Australia, Canada and the Scandinavian countries. In some countries, like Canada, it has been screened on three different networks. In most of the countries the Chinese Embassy has tried to stop the film being transmitted. In the ensuing press row when the film has been attacked by the Chinese Embassy after transmission, all the television stations have refused to take the film off the air, but the Chinese authorities were given the opportunity to debate their case with me in studio. In Sweden, where the Chinese Embassy raised strong objections, the Ambassador refused to meet me in the studio but nominated a distinguished Swedish film-maker, who had gone to Tibet under Chinese sponsorship and supervision to make a film around Lhasa, to reply. His objections were predictably similar to the Chinese.

In Australia, the Chinese Ambassador declined at the last moment and although the film was screened twice, the studio discussion between us was cancelled.

Before the original transmission of the film I gave the names and details of all participants to Amnesty International. And the UN Rapporteur for Human Rights took the evidence in the film, particularly that of the nuns, to put it before the UN Sub-Commission on Human Rights.

The film has also been screened for members of both Houses of the British Parliament and for select members of the US Congress, and for members of the European Parliament.

Meanwhile in Tibet the situation has worsened. A foreigner who speaks fluent Tibetan and who came out of Tibet in January 1989, reported that in Drepung monastery twenty-one monks were arrested following the peaceful demonstration on 27 September 1988 (the one I missed); nine of the original number were released but a further two were arrested in January 1989. In Sera monastery thirteen monks had been arrested and not heard of since. Twelve monks had tried to escape to India, but only two made it; the others were caught and severely beaten and imprisoned by the Chinese.

On 4 October 1988, the day I left, monks of the Rato monastery near Lhasa were arrested for speaking in support of the Dalai Lama's leadership in front of the Chinese security forces stationed within the monastery. No information on their whereabouts is so far available.

On 10 December 1988 demonstrations in Lhasa to mark the fortieth anniversary of Human Rights Day resulted in nineteen deaths, over 150 seriously wounded and hundreds of arrests. One foreigner, Christa Meindersma, a Dutch national standing in the crowd, was shot at close range, but not killed. Subsequently many foreigners were arrested and held for questioning, and later released.

On 30 December 1988 over 300 students and teachers from Tibet University demonstrated in Lhasa. No casualties or arrests were reported at the time.

On 20 January 1989 four monks from the Shekar monastery were arrested for hoisting the Tibetan national flag on top of a nearby hill. Their whereabouts are at present unknown.

On 7 February 1989, for the first time since the Dalai Lama fled Tibet in March 1959, the Tibetan national flag was hoisted on top of the Jokhang in Lhasa. The Chinese tore it down. No arrests have been reported to date.

On 13 February 1989 Tibetans again demonstrated in Lhasa for human rights.

On 20 February 1989 nine monks and three nuns demonstrated in Lhasa.

On 5 March 1989 thousands of Tibetans demonstrated in Lhasa during the Monlam Prayer Festival, the first anniversary of the 1988 Monlam confrontation. The monks, nuns and lay Tibetans began demonstrating peacefully until, according to nine eye-witness accounts, the police on the roof of the police building, who were video-taping the Tibetans, threw a beer bottle into the crowd. A Tibetan responded by throwing a rock at the wall of the building and the police opened fire on the crowd below, from the top of the police station. Violence spread throughout the Tibetan quarter during the 6th and 7th. Chinese troops, who were waiting on the edge of the Chinese quarter, moved in, shooting deliberately into the Tibetan crowd. According to several eye-witness reports, they also entered Tibetan homes and a Tibetan restaurant, on the pretext of searching for demonstrators, and several Tibetan occupants were shot and killed. The Tibetans retaliated by smashing and burning Chinese shops. To date – and reports are still being cross-checked – ten Tibetans were killed when the Chinese opened fire, and hundreds seriously wounded, although informed

Tibetans believe that the fatality and casualty list is much longer.

After three days of pro-independence demonstrations and violent military confrontations, China imposed martial law in Lhasa at midnight on 7 March 1989. It is still in force at the time of writing.

On 21 March over 40,000 non-resident Tibetans were expelled from Lhasa. Since then, there has been very little information available from Tibet. But Tibetan refugees who have managed to escape bring alarming accounts of imprisonment, torture and intimidation. They claim that in the aftermath of the declaration of martial law there were widespread arrests, detention without trial, and torture of Tibetan prisoners. There have also been reports from foreign tourists and people working in Tibet that they too have been subjected to harsh interrogation, and they verify and corroborate the Tibetans' evidence.

Tibet's borders were subsequently sealed again and all travel for ordinary Tibetans to India (on pilgrimage) was forbidden. Those few escapees that did manage to penetrate the PLA patrols were shot on the border, as was reported in *The Statesman*, the highly respected Indian newspaper, on 27 June 1989. The paper reported that seven Tibetans had been shot by the Chinese on the Ladakh–India border. Other refugees who manage to evade the Chinese patrols, and they are really only a handful, are now detained in severe conditions in Indian and Nepalese prisons, in an effort to maintain good relations with China whereas before martial law the refugees were allowed to cross freely and were granted asylum. An Indian press report revealed that at least five refugees who had escaped to Sikkim were returned to the Chinese by the Indian authorities. Once again a curtain of silence has cut Tibet off from the outside world.

In March and April 1989 I travelled to India and Nepal to talk to the refugees to hear first-hand accounts of what was happening inside Tibet. What they told me and what I have heard subsequently speaks of a deepening repression inside Tibet; tougher measures are being taken by the Chinese authorities who have drafted in hard-line military and civilian personnel to crush any remnant of Tibetan protest.

After the declaration of martial law on 7 March 1989, the Jokhang was ringed by Chinese troops. They are still reported to be camped in front of it. The three great monasteries of Sera, Drepung and Ganden are similarly surrounded by Chinese troops and machine-guns and cannon are trained on the monasteries. This is in addition to the Chinese security personnel stationed inside, as they are in all monasteries in Tibet.

All the roads into the Tibetan quarter of Lhasa now have armed Chinese checkpoints and the freedom of movement of Tibetans is even more severely curtailed. For example, if a Tibetan wants to travel to a village outside the city, or sometimes even to the other side of Lhasa to visit a relative, they have to have written permission from their work unit, from the work unit of the person they are going to visit and from the Chinese army. There are now at least seven checkpoints between the Holiday Inn and the Jokhang, though when the few tourist buses pass (Tibet has recently been opened once again to very limited and highly controlled tourist travel in Lhasa and a few nearby towns), the soldiers move out of sight into a side road. There are also eye-witness reports of tanks patrolling the area near the Jokhang and of American-bought Sikorsky helicopters being used for surveillance work in Tibet.

Some foreign tourists were arrested and maltreated during the March 1989 demonstrations and made to sign confessions. Other foreigners, especially those who have been in Tibet for some time, such as teachers, were interrogated by the police wanting the names of any Tibetan contacts. In one case an Austrian student had to remain under house arrest in his hotel for three weeks. He was repeatedly interrogated and denied any access to his Embassy – or any foreign official during that time. It was only when the Austrian Embassy did eventually hear of his arrest that pressure was brought on the authorities and he was released and expelled. It was the same for an Italian woman tourist: eventually she was released. Then all foreign tourists were expelled.

Because the Chinese economy badly needs the foreign exchange brought in by tourists, on 20 June 1989 Lhasa was opened up for a limited period to select groups of tourists. But severe restrictions have been imposed. Tourists can travel only in groups tightly supervised by the Chinese. They are allowed to sightsee only in Lhasa with the group and in a Chinese bus. They are not allowed to talk freely to Tibetans. They are not allowed to eat in Tibetan-run hotels and restaurants, but only in the Chinese-run Holiday Inn. Chinese guides are with them every minute of their tour and the photographs that they take are strictly supervised, as is any contact with Tibetans, for example when they are walking around the Jokhang. Reports have also emerged that tourists' film and tapes are being examined as they leave the country and luggage is meticulously searched by the security forces for any letters or documentation relating to Tibetan protest.

In September 1989 the Tibetan Government-in-exile claimed to have proof that about 800 Tibetans have been killed in Tibet since the disturbances of 1987. The Bureau of His Holiness the Dalai Lama in Switzerland placed a petition with the United Nations Sub-Commission on Human Rights. And although the Chinese claim that they wish to continue to hold discussions with the Dalai Lama, they have laid down impossible conditions. In October 1989, Reuters reported that Gong Liefu, spokesman for Tibet's regional government, said that the Dalai Lama must unequivocally renounce any claim to independence or semi-independence. And Ngapo Ngwang Jigme, Vice President of the Standing Committee of the National People's Congress and the highest-ranking Tibetan official in China, said that China would never recognize the Tibetan Government-in-exile and would refuse to negotiate with anyone who was connected with it. The Chinese insist that the Dalai Lama and the *Kashag*, the cabinet of the Tibetan Government-in-exile, cease to call themselves by those names. At the moment, and especially after events in Tiananmen Square, talks about the future of Tibet with the Chinese are dead-locked.

Meanwhile, arrest of Tibetans continue, as a result of the Chinese analyses of police videos and still photographs of Tibetans taken during demonstrations. The arrests usually occur at night when, according to many eye-witnesses, the Chinese surround the area with armed troops, cut it off from the scrutiny of Tibetan observers, and then conduct a house-to-house search till they find the names and faces that correspond to the video and still photographs. It is reliably reported that up to 2,000 Tibetans were arrested in the aftermath of the March 1989 disturbances. And some Lhasa residents allege that more than 300 Tibetans have been executed, or killed in Tibetan prisons, since the imposition of martial law.

On 20 October 1989, Reuters carried an interview with Colonel Feng Lanqun, secretary-general of the martial law command in Lhasa: 'For the time being we cannot withdraw. Factors contributing to unrest still exist. But generally the situation is normal and peaceful. In the last seven months there have been no riots or unrest. Social order has been guaranteed.' Yet in the same dispatch, Reuters reported that that very week there had been a demonstration of nuns round the Jokhang, calling for Tibetan independence. They were all arrested.

Later in the dispatch the Reuters correspondent, Guy Dinmore, reported: 'Residents [of Lhasa], however, say that the situation is very unpredictable. "It is like a lid on a kettle," said a foreigner, predicting that troops would stay in place for two years or more. "As soon as they leave, there could be trouble again."'

Colonel Feng went on to tell the Reuters correspondent: 'The vast majority of Tibetans welcomed the military presence. Martial law meets people's hopes. Life has improved and returned to normal. Lhasa is stable.'

Tibetans I spoke to insist that the reality of life in Lhasa and Tibet is very different to the Chinese version.

But daily life for Tibetans is even further restricted. Many measures that were enforced during the Cultural Revolution, and then relaxed, are now back in force. The system of control by local committees in all areas and in the workplace has tightened. Political control has intensified and indoctrination (in the form of propaganda speeches made by loudspeakers and the obligatory attendance at almost daily re-education sessions, reminiscent of the *thumzings* of the Cultural Revolution), is back in operation in Tibet.

There is once again a restriction on the practice of religion. For example, when the Dalai Lama ordered that prayers be said for the deceased Panchen Lama, they were forbidden by the Chinese, who also decreed that no further admissions of new monks to any monastery in Tibet would be permitted. Nor are the monks allowed to receive any alms whatsoever.

Since August 1989 the Chinese authorities have embarked on a draconian policy of sentencing Tibetans, often for minor offences.

For example, in September 1989 fifty-seven-year-old Tsering Ngodrup received a twelve-year jail sentence for having taken part in demonstrations and inciting young people to sing 'reactionary Tibet Independence songs'. And even children are being sentenced to hard labour for putting up protest posters.

With the enormous increase in arbitrary arrests in Tibet, new prisons are being built to accommodate the numbers. The five notorious prisons in Lhasa – Gurtsa, Sangyib, Drapchi, Wutri-Tui and Lhasa Chun Chue – are full. And a new one has been established at Dechen Dzong in Toelung, west of Drepung monastery and twelve miles from the heart of Lhasa. Despite the fact that China signed and ratified the UN Convention Against the Use of Torture in 1986, reports still trickle out of torture as excruciating as any I had taken evidence of, especially at the military prison situated under Chakpori Hill in the shadow of the Potala, where, apart from severe beatings, the Tibetan prisoners, particularly nuns, are still being stripped naked, immersed in freezing water, beaten with electric cattle prods, hung upside down by their feet for hours and then thrown to dogs that the Chinese have deliberately kept starved for days.

Some people in the West have expressed doubts about the validity of the statements of Tibetans about the barbarism of the Chinese. But on 3 and 4 June 1989, when the Chinese leadership ordered the PLA to massacre their own people in Tiananmen Square, the world, as well as many Chinese themselves, began to believe the atrocities that had been perpetrated on the Tibetan people for the past forty years.

The Chinese authorities still deny their violation of human rights in Tibet today. In the same way, they have denied the brutality of the Chinese army in Tiananmen Square. The facility and speed with which the Chinese authorities rewrote the history of the events of Tiananmen Square appalled the world; but the Chinese have done exactly the same in Tibet for forty years, and who has raised a protest? Which country has imposed sanctions on China? Which country has taken China to the Security Council for violating human rights in Tibet? There is a deafening silence.

But as the Dalai Lama said: 'The winds of change are blowing through the Communist world.' Who, ten years ago, would have thought that the Soviet Union would have a Gorbachev as President? Who would have believed that perestroika was possible? That Communist regimes in East Germany, Czechoslovakia and Romania would be toppled? That a non-Communist would become Prime Minister of Poland or President of Czechoslovakia? That the Berlin Wall would be breached? But while we applaud the changes and offer massive IMF (International Monetary Fund) loans and credit facilities to shore up the fragile, nascent democracies of Eastern Europe, are we really content to sit by and send trade delegations to a country that has butchered one-sixth of Tibet's population and is still perpetrating a bloody policy in Tibet as gruesome as that of the Nazis' extermination of the Jews, or as horrific as Pol Pot's slaughter of hundreds of thousands of Cambodians? How much longer can we ignore the continuing genocide in Tibet? Are we, the supposedly civilized world, more concerned with economic gain from the Chinese markets, than bringing effective pressure to bear on China to stop the carnage in the Tibetan killing fields?

Appendix: Casualty Statistics

In 1984 the Dalai Lama's Bureau of Information issued the following breakdown of casualty statistics, province by province. The figures include deaths up to 1983. The Bureau claims to have ready for international verification a list of cross-checked names of the Tibetan dead.

HOW KILLED	Ü-TSANG PROVINCE	KHAM PROVINCE	AMDO PROVINCE	TOTAL
Prison & Labour Camp	93,477	64,877	14,784	173,138
Executed	28,267	32,266	96,225	156,758
Battles	143,255	240,410	49,042	432,707
Starvation	131,253	89,916	121,982	343,151
Torture	27,951	48,840	15,940	92,731
Suicide	3,375	3,952	1,675	9,002
Total	427,578	480,261	299,648	1,207,487

Undoubtedly the Tibetan Government-in-exile have additional names and figures, but they punctiliously refuse to release them till the exhaustive verification process is complete.

Suggested Reading List

Andrugtsang, G.T., *Four Rivers, Six Ranges: A True Account of Khampa Resistance to Chinese in Tibet*, Information Office of H.H. the Dalai Lama, Dharamsala, 1973

Atisha, T.P., *A Survey of Tibetan History*, Information Office, Central Secretariat, Ganchen Kyshiong, Dharamsala, 1984

Avedon, J.F., *In Exile from the Land of the Snows*, Michael Joseph, London, 1984

Batchelor, S., *The Jewel in the Lotus*, Wisdom Publications, London, 1987

—— *Tibet Guide*, Wisdom Publications, London, 1987

Bell, Sir C., *The People of Tibet*, Oxford University Press, Oxford, 1924

—— *Tibet, Past and Present*, Oxford University Press, Oxford, 1968

Bonavia, D. & Bartlett, M., *Tibet*, Harrap, London, 1988

Bushell, S.W., 'Early History of Tibet from Chinese Sources', *Journal of the Royal Asiatic Society*, London, 1880

Butterfield, F., *China: Alive in a Bitter Sea*, Times Books, New York, 1982

'China's Minority Nationalities', *Modern China Series No.3*, Red Sun Publishers, Beijing, 1977

Choedon, D., *Life in the Red Flag People's Commune*, Information Office of H.H. the Dalai Lama, Dharamsala, 1978

Chopel, N., *Folk Culture of Tibet*, Library of Tibetan Works and Archives, Dharamsala, 1984

—— *Folk Tales of Tibet*, Library of Tibetan Works and Archives, Dharamsala, 1984

Dalai Lama and India, Institute of International Affairs, New Delhi, 1959

Das, S.C., *Journey to Lhasa and Central Tibet*, Manjusri Publishing House, New Delhi, 1885 (reprint, 1970)

David-Neel, L.A.E.M., *The Superhuman Life of Gesar of Ling*, Shambala Publications, New York, 1988

Dowman, K., *Power Places of Central Tibet*, Routledge, London, 1988

Ford, R., *Captured in Tibet*, Harrap Ltd, London, 1957

Furen, W. & Wenquing, S., *Highlights of Tibetan History*, New World Press, Beijing, 1984

Gashi, T.D., *New Tibet*, Information Office of H.H. the Dalai Lama, Dharamsala, 1980

Geological Evolution of Tibet, Royal Society microfiches, London

Ginsburg, G. & Ginsburg, M.M., *Communist China and Tibet*, Martinus Nijhoff, The Hague, 1964

Goodman, M.H., *The Last Dalai Lama*, Sidgwick & Jackson, London, 1986

Harrer, H., *Seven Years in Tibet*, Paladin, London, 1988
—— *Return to Tibet*, Penguin, London, 1983

Hedin, S., *Adventures in Tibet*, Manas Publishers, New Delhi, 1904 (reprint, 1985)

H.H. the Dalai Lama, *The Opening of the Wisdom Eye*, Theosophical Publishing House, London, 1972
—— *My Land and My People*, Potala Publications, New York, 1983

Hicks, R., *Hidden Tibet*, Element Books, Shaftesbury, 1988

Hopkins, J., *Buddhism of Tibet*, Snow Lion, New York, 1988

Humphries, C., *Buddhism*, Penguin, London, 1974
—— *Exploring Buddhism*, George Allen & Unwin, London, 1974

International Commission of Jurists, *The Question of Tibet and the Rule of Law*, Geneva, 1959

International Commission of Jurists, *Tibet and the Chinese People's Republic*, Geneva, 1960

Kemp, R., *The Potala of Tibet*, Stacey International, 1987

Lamb, A., 'Tibet in Anglo-Chinese Relations', *Journal of the Royal Central Asian Society*, 1957/8

Malik, I., *Dalai Lamas of Tibet*, New United Process, New Delhi, 1984

Migot, A., *Tibetan Marches*, Rupert Hart Davis, London, 1955

Mitter, J.P., *Betrayal of Tibet*, Allied Publishers, Bombay, 1964

Moraes, F., *The Revolt of Tibet*, Sterling Publishers, New Delhi, 1966

Murphy, D., *Tibetan Foothold*, John Murray, London, 1966

Norbu, D., *Red Star Over Tibet*, Envoy Press, New York, 1987

Norbu, J., *Warriors of Tibet*, Wisdom Publications, London, 1987

—— *Horsemen in the Snow*, Information Office of H.H. the Dalai Lama, Dharamsala, 1979

Norbu, J. & Turnbull, C., *Tibet: Its History, Religion and People*, Pelican, London, 1972

Norbu, T. & Harrer, H., *Tibet is My Country*, Wisdom Publications, London, 1987

Normanton, S., *Tibet: The Lost Civilization*, Hamish Hamilton, London, 1988

Olshchak, B. & Wangyal, G.T., *Mystic Art of Tibet*, Shambala Publications, New York, 1988

Patterson, G.N., *Tragic Destiny*, Faber & Faber, London, 1959

Peissel, M., *Cavaliers of Kham*, Heinemann, London, 1972

Petech, L., *China and Tibet in the Early XVIII Century*, Leyden, 1950

Powell, A., *Living Buddhism*, British Museum Publications, London, 1989

Rahul, R., *The Government and Politics of Tibet*, Vikas Publishers, Delhi, 1969

Richardson, H., *Tibet and Its History*, Shambala Publications, New York, 1984

Rinpoche, T.T., *Buddhist Civilization in Tibet*, Routledge, London, 1987

Roerich, G., *The Blue Annals*, Vol.1, Calcutta, 1949

Shakabpa, T.W.D., *A Guide to the Jokhang*, Baptist Mission Press, Calcutta, 1976

—— *Tibet: A Political History*, Potala Publications, New York, 1984

Snellgrove, D. & Richardson, H., *A Cultural History of Tibet*, Shambala Publications, New York, 1986

Snelling, J., *The Sacred Mountain*, East-West Publications, 1983

Tada, T., *The Thirteenth Dalai Lama*, The Centre for East Asian Cultural Studies, Tokyo, 1965

Taring, R.D., *Daughter of Tibet*, John Murray, London, 1970

Teichman, E., *Travels of a Consular Officer in Eastern Tibet*, Cambridge University Press, Cambridge, 1922

Thungpa, C., *Born in Tibet*, George Allen & Unwin, London, 1987

Thurlow, C., *Stories Beyond the Clouds*, Library of Tibetan Works and Archives, Dharamsala, 1981

Tibet, No Longer Medieval, Foreign Languages Press, Beijing, 1981

Tibet: The Sacred Realm, Philadelphia Museum of Art, Aperture Inc., 1983

Tibetans in Exile 1959–1969, Information Office of H.H. the Dalai Lama, Dharamsala, 1961

Tucci, G., *Religions of Tibet*, Penguin, London, 1988

—— *Tibet, Land of the Snows*, Paul Elek, London, 1973

—— *To Lhasa and Beyond*, Istituto Poligrafico dello Stato, Libreria dello Stato, Rome, 1956

Tucci, R., *The Tombs of the Tibetan Kings*, Serie Orientale, Rome, 1956

van Walt van Praag, M., *Status of Tibet: History, Rights and Prospects in International Law*, Wisdom Publications, London, 1987

Wangdu, S., *The Discovery of the Fourteenth Dalai Lama*, Khett Thai Publications, Bangkok, 1975

Yu Dawchuyuan, *Love Songs of the Sixth Dalai Lama*, Academia Sinica Monograph, Series A, No.5, Beijing, 1930

Journals
Beijing Review
Far Eastern Economic Review
National Geographic
Tibetan News Review

Reports from the Information Office of H.H. the Dalai Lama, Dharamsala